Capital Acts:
Washington DC Performing Arts

Stephen Moore

with

Johnny Holliday, Stephen Lorenz,
and Charles David Young

BookLocker
Trenton, Georgia

Copyright © 2024 Stephen Moore

PRINT ISBN: 978-1-958892-06-0
EBOOK ISBN: 979-8-88531-679-8

All rights reserved. No part of this publication may be reproduced, stored in a retrieval system, or transmitted in any form or by any means, electronic, mechanical, recording or otherwise, without the prior written permission of the author.

Published by BookLocker.com, Inc., Trenton, Georgia.

Performing Arts – United States
Performing Arts – Biography
Performing Arts – Interviews

BookLocker.com, Inc.
2024

First Edition

Love Her Madly Duke Ellington

Dedication

To the late journalist, **John Segraves**, for inspiring and encouraging his "After Dark" newspaper column readers to appreciate and support live performances in the city. And we thank his son, **Mark Segraves**, for carrying on this tradition of insightful entertainment reviews, and for creating the charitable **After Dark Fund**, a non-profit group dedicated to supporting local musicians in the DC, MD, and VA area.

© Guitar Player

Foreword by Buzz McClain
Who on Earth Writes a Book About the History of Washington Entertainment? This Guy Does.

This has to start with a confession.

When my longtime friend and colleague Steve Moore told me what the subject of his next book was going to be, I shook my head. He had just come off the success of publishing an expansive history of the long-running Birchmere night club, which struck me as daunting enough, but a history of entertainment in the nation's capital? Like, all of it, from 1790?

I told him forget it. "Nobody wants to read that," I recall saying.

It sounds harsh, but truly, I didn't mean it that way.

What I really was trying to do was save my friend a lot of agony at the Library of Congress and at local libraries' history rooms, digging through archival material; I wanted to spare him countless hours on the telephone with performers and untold days upon days on the internet researching, verifying, and writing information that most likely had never been compiled into one tome. In other words, this was going to be hard work! Months and months of grinding exertion! I wanted to convince him to take on something a little less challenging, whatever that might be. Enjoy your retirement, Steve, you deserve it. Go play guitar.

Happily, Steve didn't listen.

Instead, he devoted a considerable amount of time and effort to create the collection of historical research and contemporary interviews you now have in your hands. Several of the narratives will be familiar—who doesn't know about the Muppets? — but some of it, very likely most of it, will be new to you. Or, if the name is familiar, you might not be aware about the local origins of seminal acts that got their starts in the Washington area, the world-famous Ringling Brothers circus and entertainment pioneer Al Jolson being examples.

You will also learn about some of the talented artists DC claims as its own but never made it into the show business mainstream despite undeniable and astonishing talent. Danny Gatton, for instance. And John Fahey. And Eva Cassidy. The list goes on.

Steve has been writing about Washington's entertainment and entertainers for decades, and he does it for the love, not the money. I know this firsthand: I was the entertainment editor at the Journal Newspaper in Washington's suburbs in the 1980s when Steve's 10,000-word biography-with-interview about a local radio personality came over the transom. It was a delightful read, but man, I couldn't trim it to a useable length to squeeze it in my little weekly section without destroying the value.

So, I spiked it, and broke the news to my new stringer Steve, who understandably might never have worked for me again, except he's a kind gentleman. He understood the situation, smiled that smile, and followed up for many years with more manageable sized personality features about regional performers and entertainment history. Some of those remain vivid in my memory as some of my favorite stories since they invariably echoed my own recollections as a child growing up in the area. He got to meet Pick Temple and Ranger Hal. How cool is that? If you watched television as a kid in DC in the early '60s, those were your afternoon go-to. Steve's "where are they now" stories were delightful nostalgic trips down memory lane.

Of course, Steve was paid for those Journal stories, but it was...minimal to say the least. (He reminds me now and then I never paid him a kill fee for that first unwieldy story. The check's in the mail, Steve.) Despite the token pay, the stories he wrote individually, and with his writing partner Donn Murphy, were brightly composed with clarity and purpose, an authoritative tone, and an underlying, undeniable sense of joy regarding the subject. I'm happy to report that tradition continues in this book.

To sum up: It's a good thing Steve doesn't ask for my opinion very often, or we wouldn't have this volume of entertaining and informative material. On the other hand, he can offer pretty good advice when asked: When I faced one of the most difficult decisions of my life, he gave me his opinion—and convinced me to marry my wife. I took his advice.

P.S. Steve asked me for a recollection of my all-time favorite Washington, DC, performances. Here they are:

For homegrown talent, just about any night the Wanktones and the Slickee Boys shared a bill, a very good time was had by all. A lot of laughs and a lot of rockabilly and power pop rock. Friendships were forged and a true self-sustaining, stimulating, and supportive music scene existed among like-minded bands and their fans.

For national talent, David Johansen came to the vaunted Wax Museum in Southwest Washington 1982 just as his new and extraordinary "Live It Up" live album was constantly on my turntable; the band did the album flawlessly, with all the songs in order (!), and during the blistering finale of the New York Dolls classic "Personality Crisis," Johansen offered himself for spontaneous crowd surfing. He sweated on me as he went overhead.

By the way, to top it off, Tommy Keene opened that show. You'll read more about him in these pages. Enjoy the ride.

Buzz McClain

David Chappell and
Linwood Taylor
www.guitardavechappell.com
www.facebookcom/linwoodtaylor
© DC.LT

Bill Starks @ DC Legends show
http://billstarksmusic.com/
© SM

Jon Steinman
w/Pinetop Perkins
www.facebook.com/theliftersmd
© JS

Table of Contents

Foreword by Buzz McClain v
Chapter 1 – The Learned Pig 1
Chapter 2 – Who's That Theater? 13
Chapter 3 – Sousa the Thundered 31
Chapter 4 – You Ain't Heard Nothin' Yet 37
Chapter 5 – Henson & Associates 47
Chapter 7 – DC Met the Beatles 57
Chapter 9 – The Joy Boys 75
Chapter 10 – Mark Russell: Playing for Laughs 85
Chapter 11 – Tenderly, Felix Grant 93
Chapter 12 – Mentor, Donn B. Murphy 101
Chapter 13 – Brooke Johns, Vaudevillian 109
Chapter 14 – Sir Duke 115
Intermission – Native Cast 125
Chapter 15 – Dinner with Mr. B. 139
Chapter 16 – Come Gather Round People 145
Chapter 17 – The Big Three First 153
Chapter 18 – DC's Comic Beat Goes On 159
Chapter 19 – Everyday Holliday (Stage One) 167
Chapter 20 – Roberta's First Take 175
Chapter 21 – Lady Helen Hayes 187
Chapter 22 – Byrd's Nests 199
Chapter 23 – Bob Berberich's Beats 207
Chapter 24 – Slickees, Nighthawks & Razz 217
Chapter 25 – Connie B. Gay's Country Club 233
And Now..... Chapter 26 – Best in Show 243
Chapter 27 – Chapin, John J. & Joan 257
Chapter 28 – Songwriters' Delight 267
Chapter 29 – Daryl Davis: Roots & Blues 277
Chapter 30 – Bo Diddley and Disciples 283
Chapter 31 – Fahey's Sonic Frets 291

Chapter 32 – Kids in TV Wonderland 301
Chapter 33 – Rumblers 311
Chapter 34 – Danny G, the Telemaster 321
Chapter 35 – Chuck Levin, The Music Man 327
Chapter 36 – Eva: Purity of Voice 333
Chapter 37 – Chuck 2 Go-Go 343
Chapter 38 – Groovin with Root 347
Chapter 39 – Cathy Ponton King: Irish Fire 355
Chapter 40 – Crazy for Ken Ludwig 359
Chapter 41 – Patty Reese: Showbiz Phenom 363
Chapter 42 – The Stoneman Family 367
Chapter 43 – Back to Bluegrass 371
Chapter 44 – Lepson & Crews 377
Chapter 45 – Select Radio Signals (AM) 383
Chapter 46 – Select Radio Signals (FM) 389
Chapter 47 – Johnny Holliday (Side Two) 403
Chapter 48 – House of Musical Traditions 415
Chapter 49 – Ron Holloway & Horn 421
Chapter 50 – Dr. Cleve from the Heart 429
Chapter 51 – How DC's Early Punk and New Wave
    Scene Changed the World (Just Kidding) 433
Chapter 52 – Pat (WPAS) and Mike (WAMA) 441
Chapter 53 – Clubs, Committees, and Cool 467
Chapter 54 – Stephen Wade Banjo Luminary 479
Encore - Keeping the Beat for Local Music
    Perspective by John Kelly. 8/22/2017 485
Appendix 1: Thank you Gary Oelze 489
Appendix 2: Bookshelf of Inspiration 493
Authors Bios 495
Acknowledgments 499
Index 501

Capital Acts: Washington DC Performing Arts

Emmylou Harris, John Starling, and Linda Ronstadt in 1986 at the Birchmere. © Connie B. Smith

Celine Celeste, early favorite star of Washington stages

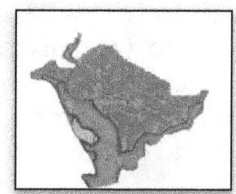

Chapter 1 – The Learned Pig

The District of Columbia got off to a rough start, both physically and culturally, when created on July 16, 1790. Few countries in history had ever had the opportunity to plan its capital in advance, but it was still under construction ten years later when the branches of the US government outlined in the Constitution finally moved from the temporary capital, Philadelphia, to the official capital of the United States.

Indigenous peoples have inhabited America since 10,000 BC, with the Nacotchtank Indians thriving on the tidal Potomac riverbank for four thousand years. Captain John Smith had explored this area in 1608, traveling up the "Eastern Branch"—later the Anacostia River. He reported that the Nacostine villages in this area had spirited trade centers visited by other Native Americans, such as the Iroquois inhabiting the northeastern regions and the Algonquin more widespread across North America's eastern and central lands. With abundant game, fish, and other natural resources, their name originated from the Algonquin word "anaquashtank," meaning "a town of traders." Consequently, "Potomac" is thought to mean "something brought."

Nacotchtank (today the Southeast community of Anacostia) was the most significant community living in wigwams and longhouses. Two smaller villages were located on the narrow bluff between MacArthur Boulevard and the C&O Canal, above where Georgetown is today.

Their dances, hero legends, creation myths, rituals, ceremonies, and folktales would be the first "performances" shared with other Indigenous tribes before devastating contact with Europeans. Their music was ancestral drum, flute, and vocal ceremonial and spiritual songs. In a letter to a merchant in London, the founder of Maryland, Leonard Calvert, also described "Anacostan" as one of the best places for trading with natives.

As a Washingtonian growing up in Anacostia, with southeast neighbors like Danny Gatton and Lafayette Parker "Pick" Temple, I first became aware of this native history mainly through local names like Potomac River, Takoma Park, Chesapeake River, and the Wigwam Restaurant on Route 301 in southern Maryland.

Driving through Piscataway with my parents to Waldorf's many slot machine bars is where I remember seeing "Native American" faces. I would later learn of the forced displacement and total loss of the Nacotchtank's ancestral territory through a combination of treaties, coercion, and military actions that prefaced the establishment of our Capital.

In the year 1800, Pennsylvania Avenue was still a muddy trail between tall trees and grass. A disdainful New Yorker surveying the fledgling village of swamps, thickets, and rude buildings proclaimed grandly: "We only need here houses, cellars, kitchens, scholarly men, amiable women, and a few other such trifles to possess a perfect city." Added Treasury Secretary Oliver Wolcott, "The people are poor, and as far as I can see, they live like fishes, by eating each other."

The "Mall" was a cow pasture. Stagecoaches, horses, river boats, and walking were the only way to travel. Early records paint comical tales, including several congressmen losing their way after a dinner party and "wandering until daybreak in their carriage weaving through bogs and gullies in search of Capital Hill, only a mile away."

By Jefferson's own account, it took him four days and three nights to travel westward from Washington through Loudon County to his Monticello home in southern Virginia. Washington was indeed primitive compared to the previous capitals of the new republic: Philadelphia, Princeton, Annapolis, Trenton, and New York City, But George Washington and Thomas Jefferson chose the fledgling village over such contenders as Kingston, NY and Williamsburg, VA and persuaded Congress to create the District of Columbia as the permanent capital of the United States.

The recorded experiences of the capital's early residents, visitors and elected officials are almost totally negative. Indeed, a disillusioned Congress came within nine votes of abandoning this capital permanently after its few public buildings were torched by the British in 1814.

Meanwhile, the world was turning. Napoleon Bonaparte became the leader of the French Empire, and the expenses of his conquests ensured the 1804 Louisiana Purchase by the US, doubling the size of America. King George III survived two assassination attempts, and Beethoven performed his first symphony. Beethoven's biographers say that "certain listeners thought his work 'strange, overly extravagant, and even risqué." A year later Beethoven confided to friends that he thought he was going deaf.

In Philadelphia, George Washington had heard a musician a few years earlier named Alexander Reinagle. Born in England, Reinagle was a good friend of Johann Sebastian Bach's son, Carl. He performed concerts, composed bountifully, and managed concert programs. He wrote the song "Welcome Mighty Chief," sung at President Washington's inauguration, and dedicated it to First Lady, Martha. In addition, the President hired Reinagle to give piano lessons to his five-year-old daughter, Nelly.

President Washington couldn't play music, but he loved it mightily. There was usually music and dancing wherever our first President slept. Numerous taverns, clubs, and assembly rooms began to serve Washington DC's earliest citizens. In addition to offering food and drink, they supplied commerce and trading opportunities—including slaves—while featuring musicians, magicians, and other acts for fun.

Alexander Reangle partnered with Thomas Wignell, an English actor and singer, to build a theater in Philadelphia called The Chestnut. It joined the Old Theater as the first two venues in Philly. Reinagle and Wignell brought their Chestnut Company to the Blodgett hotel at 8th and E streets NW—then the largest privately-owned building in the city—in June of 1800 for what is considered DC's first theatrical performance.

Samuel Blodgett Jr., a Revolutionary War officer, built Blogett's hotel as a prize for a lottery to promote his real-estate investments.

Purchased by the government in 1910, Blodgett's hotel served as headquarters of the US Postal Service and later the Patent office until it eventually succumbed to fire in 1836 like so many other DC structures of the time. 9000 drawings and 7000 models of inventions were destroyed.

The premiere Washington DC theater show almost didn't go on. As the group arrived, a summer thunderstorm and flood wrecked the troupe's scenery. Waiting for their costumes to dry, the performers set up their patched scenery flats in the public meeting hall of Blodgett's.

Wignell and Reinagle's show on opening night was Otway's *Venice Preserved*, ironically titled because the cast, including Mr. Wignell as Jaffier, Mr. Cooper as Prime, and Mrs. Merry as Belvidira, received a pre-show drenching on the way to town. This popular tragedy was first produced in England in 1682. The three lead characters are assassinated, commit suicide, and go insane in that order. This drama was a hot theatrical ticket. Another play, *The Secret*, was also shown during the company's debut run.

Actor John Wilkes Booth, born in Bel Air, MD, in 1838 merely 57 miles from the DC line, once told a friend that he was "done with the stage and that *Venice Preserved* was the only play he would consider in returning to performing." His statement was later assumed to be a veiled hint of his plot to assassinate President Lincoln.

The city's first newspaper, *The National Intelligencer*, took no notice of this first theater production or other tavern presentations until 1801 when a hotel assembly room "about two hundred paces" from the Capitol on New Jersey Avenue announced the remarkable Learned Pig would appear.

It was claimed the incredible porker knew the days of the  week, could read, spell, and tell time by consulting the watches of audience members, among other marvelous tricks. DC's patrons could witness this fantastic animal for a pricey fifty cents.

The pig moved on to appear at the Spread Eagle Tavern in nearby Alexandria, Virginia for a suburban twenty-five cents.

An ad in the *Alexandria Gazette* proclaimed that the pig could also perform mentalism, revealing which card a patron had picked and concealed from the deck.

"Intelligent" animal acts like Morocco, the Thinking Horse and Munito, the Talking Dog were popular a century before the Learned Pig. Trained by a Scotsman, the original Learned Pig toured Europe and died in 1798. The pig that appeared in DC was owned by a William Pinchbeck who claimed President John Adams witnessed this Learned Pig in a performance "met with universal applause." Of course, these animals were trained to respond to verbal clues and whistles to appear intelligent. And there is no truth to the rumor that one was elected to Congress and engaged in pork barrel legislation.

In 1802 a group of citizens gathered, hoping for entertainment more substantial than tavern singers and prestidigitating pigs. They elected Congressman John P. Van Ness, who later became mayor of the city, as the new chairman of a group formed to build a proper theatre in the nation's capital. Work began the following year, and the first building erected specifically for the performing arts was cleverly dubbed The Washington Theater.

A colorful procession formed at the corner of Pennsylvania and 12th Street on the day of the cornerstone laying, marching down to the building site at 11th and C Streets. Leading the parade was a band of the city's earliest professional musicians, "dressed in knee breeches with their buckled slippers flashing in the sunlight."

On November 16, 1804, the theatre was ready with its premiere performance. This was a "Grand Medley Entertainment" by the celebrated Mr. Maginnis from London, who had performed in many European capital cities before coming to America. His show offered songs, magic, and "spectacular effects." The new theatre was an immediate hit and operated with some success—and intermittent dark periods—for the next eighteen years. A few classics were played, including Richard Brinsley Sheridan's School for Scandal in 1805. Playgoers enjoyed other long-forgotten shows like *Ways and Means* or *A Trip to Dover* and *Wives as They Were and Maids As They Are*. Other titles offered by DC's first theatre included *The School for Reform*, *How to Rule a Husband*, *Day After the Wedding*, *The Wives' First Lesson*, and *Three Weeks After Marriage*, or *What We All Must Come To*.

Six years later at The Washington Theatre, James Fennell with the Philadelphia and Baltimore Actors Group, played lead in *Othello*, *Richard III*, *MacBeth*, and *King Lear*, apparently the first Shakespeare performances in the city. Tragedy struck in 1820 when the theatre caught fire at seven in the morning. Luckily, a snowstorm the previous evening protected the roofs of the adjoining buildings, but DC's first theatre was caput. While the final opinion was that the fire was accidental, theatres of the period were prone to combustion. Fires also destroyed the Philadelphia, New York, and Montreal theatres within six months.

In more auspicious performance spaces, Washingtonians were also entertained by the President's own Marine Band, which played at the chief executive's request for entertainments and ceremonies at the Capitol Building and the White House. Saturday concerts became popular on the White House lawns from May to November. President Thomas Jefferson himself decided that the band needed extra oomph and requested the addition of two clarinets, a bassoon, two French horns, and a bass drum to enhance the band.

Eighteen seasoned Italian musicians were imported to bolster the band, arriving at the US Navy Yard in 1805. Resentment from the proud Marine players caused all but a few of the Italians to resign. Fortunately, Giatano Carusi, his wife, and three sons from Catania, Sicily, stayed on. Carusi became a Washingtonian musician of great popularity, as was the Italian march style that Carusi helped introduce to the Marine band. It was Carusi who purchased the charred remains of the Washington Theater and restored it to distinction. Reopened in 1823 as Carusi's Theatre, it became DC's fashionable venue for concerts, entertainments, and especially balls. Presidents John Quincy Adams, Polk, Jackson, Van Buren, and Taylor held their Inaugural Balls there.

Carusi brought European cosmopolitan culture to DC's new high society. As a music hall, early performances included Borska, then known as the greatest harpist in the world; Talburg, pianist; Viex Temps, violinist; Anna Bishop prima donna, and many other nineteenth century favorites. "The greatest furor created within its walls," declared *The Evening Star*, "was when (opera soprano) Adalina Patti, a mere child, sang two songs in concert – all that her manager would allow her to sing."

Another pair of Philadelphia actors, William Warren and W.B. Wood arrived in Washington in 1821 and proposed building a second theatre. They sold sixty shares at $150 each to such distinguished gentlemen as John Quincy Adams, (not yet President) John C. Calhoun of South Carolina, and Commodore John Rodgers, who had commanded the frigate, "President" during the War of 1812. This raised enough money to build the New American Theater, located only a few blocks from the capitol building at Louisiana Avenue and 4th Street, holding 700 people. With this venture they broke the Washington Theater's monopoly on entertainment. The choice was now the American Theater or the New American Theater. Very catchy names. Sensibly, smoking was fiercely prohibited.

Plays popular in New York and London attracted DC audiences too. The premiere presentations were *She Stoops to Conquer* and *The Spoiled Child*. Soon well-known actors Edwin Booth and Edwin Forrest appeared in shows. Another actor, John Howard Payne, wrote and starred in Clari or The Maid of Milan starring an actress, "Mrs. Warring" who sang for the first time Payne's extremely popular song, "Home, Sweet Home," a favorite of both Confederate and Union soldiers during the Civil War.

The DC theatrical seasons ran for only five weeks during the winter with performers often returning to their homes away from Washington. One who stayed was Joseph Jefferson, a comedian whose stage personas "Paul Pry" and "Billy Lacaday" were popular. Another DC stalwart actor, "Old Joe" Jefferson and his performing family lived inside the New American Theater Audiences loved Old Joe's songs like the parody of "Nobody Coming to Marry Me" as "Nobody Coming to Bury Me." His son, Joe Jefferson Jr., eventually became an actor, as well as the scene painter and manager at the theatre.

As DC's population grew, so did the demand for entertainment. In 1831 the New American Theater was enlarged to fit a thousand patrons. However, during the 1830's, Washington remained a work in progress. Washington incurred its first debt of $1.75 million dollars by 1837. That would be near $56 million today adjusted for inflation. With few incentives to build factories or any other inventions of the Industrial Revolution, the government town suffered economic ups and downs. By mid-century the New American Theater had gone downhill, reduced to a bath house, a bowling alley, and a pistol-shooting gallery in that order, until its reincarnation as "Canterbury Hall," a variety theater during the Civil War. One of the more popular performance venues in DC, it featured plays, burlesques, comedy routines, circus acts, and melodrama. An observer described its atmosphere as consisting of "soldiers and roughs, screeching, catcalling, smoking, and spitting" with "scantily clad ladies."

Records show that much of the popular entertainment of the Civil War era was indecent. DC's early capital acts ran from the highbrow to the gutter.

Lust murders were sentimentalized in ballads like "The Jealous Lover." Abortion was sensationalized in "Tam Lin" and "Mary Hamilton." Occasionally separate performances suitable for families or for "men only" were held. Some of the most popular bawdy songs included dreadfully indecent lyrics like "Up start the crab fish and catch her by the c*nt. Which made him have a mighty mind to clip, kiss, and f*ck."

In 1872, Carusi's Theater was elegantly revamped as the Washington Theater Comique and later became Kernan's Lyceum in 1891, named for James L. Kernan, a theater manager and philanthropist based in Baltimore. But like many of DC's entertainment venues, even this stately theater degenerated into "cheap variety" and "crude buffoonery." It eventually became "Strictly a man's house." An urban pattern emerged as DC's folk music and jazz clubs of the next century sometimes turned into strip joints.

Both the New American and the Washington Theater perished by fire in the late 1800s. The hurly-burly DC theater life of these two-of-a-kind early American playhouses, patronized by Senators, society ladies, soldiers, and strumpets came to an end. It would take two men with higher aspirations and a rivalry forged in the fire of the Civil War to set the stage ablaze in Washington once more (metaphorically of course).

* * *

"Get down you fool!" said Col. Wendall Holmes as President Abraham Lincoln ducked whistling bullets from Rebel muskets fired from Virginia at Fort Stevens, four miles north of the city in Maryland. Part of DC's temporary defenses, these fortifications were often manned by clerks and convalescent troops.

Washington was under attack by Confederate troops in July of 1864 and the Civil War raged on. Bluecoats and civilian workers streamed into the city, swiftly transforming it into a colossal base camp for the Union army. The saloons thrived, the jails jammed with drunken soldiers, and the ladies of the night were kept busy. Restaurants sprung up. Reportedly, it took twenty men to shuck oysters for the hungry patrons of

Harvey's restaurant. For many the winds of war blew prosperously. Music hall managers catered to troops and camp-followers. Even under attack, wartime Washington was open for entertainment.

Patriotism swelled with public displays for DC's citizens. Large public spectacles on Pennsylvania Avenue with military parades and grand reviews of the "Army of the Potomac" attracted hundreds of sightseers to the city. It was said that the "sheen of the brass and the flash of the bayonets mesmerized the crowds," while the blare of bands and cannon fire was breathtaking.

An enormous military display took place near Bailey's Crossroads in November 1861 with 50,000 troops assembled to march off to war. Mrs. Julia Ward Howe, a visiting Bostonian, was so inspired she returned to her Washington hotel room at the Willard and wrote new lyrics for the popular abolitionist song, "John Brown's Body," and the "Battle Hymn of the Republic" was born.

Patriotic songs were popular at The Varieties Theater located on 9th Street near Pennsylvania Avenue—a barn-like building with bare rafters and shoddily plastered walls—a few blocks from the White house. Blustering with flags of the stars and bars, the popular venue provided a medley of nationalist songs each evening in a musical finale.

The question on the minds of two young men from Baltimore was, how they too, could join in on the heady prosperity to be found in wartime Washington.

by Elizabeth Raum (2004)

Chapter 2 – Who's That Theater?

Grover and his playhouse © National Theatre Archives

The National Theatre is the second oldest operating theater in the USA (and follows the Walnut Street Theater founded 1808 in Philadelphia). The debut presentation at the National, "Man of the World," opened on December 7, 1835. The "Man" (and stage manager) was Thomas Ward, an Englishman born in Liverpool in 1799.

The National was built in 1835, a few blocks from the White House by William Wilson Corcoran, heading a group of wealthy philanthropic investors. Born to a successful merchant family in 1878, Corcoran would become the co-founder of the "right on the money" Riggs bank and a renowned art collector. He studied mathematics and the classics at Georgetown College for a year before dropping out. Still, he gets extra credit for creating the Corcoran Art Museum after running out of space at his home in Lafayette Square for his collection of statues. Other theaters in the capital city came and went but the National survived.

Attracted to the new federal capital, the arrival of two notable production managers, Leonard Grover and John T. Ford, marks a turning point for theatrical history in DC. Both ran theaters for DC's sophisticated classes; the National Theater, briefly known as **Grover's Theater** stands as a tribute to the new American culture.

A popular comedic playwright and actor, Leonard Grover was born on December 9, 1833, in Baltimore and lived until March 7, 1926. His best-known plays are *Davy Crockett* and *Our Boarding House,* (believed to be the origin of the phase "make no mistake.") He took management of the National Theater in 1862 and settled it to stability.

On a Saturday night in September 1837, the National Theater management invited Indian leaders of the Sioux, Sacs, and Foxes from beyond the Great Lakes to attend a "Grand Melo-Dramatic Spectacle" called *The Mountain Nymph.* They sat in the front rows of Washington's only theater and were in town to make treaties with the new government that was advancing ruthlessly into their lands. Scattered in the audience were other Indians wearing U.S. military jackets – gifts given them that day by the "Great White Father," President Martin Van Buren.

According to the National Intelligencer newspaper of the day, the Indians cheered and clapped when the agile and fairy figure of the Mountain Sylph (a spirit) entered stage right from a high (theater) mountain top. A young chief of the Yankton Sioux leapt from his seat and flung his eagle feather war bonnet onto the stage, praising the dancer. It was a head dress, which he had often worn in bloody conflict with the enemies of his people. Miss Annette Nelson, the star, accepted it with smiles and added it to her costume.

Future British Prime Minister Winston Churchill appeared on stage at the National in 1900 to give a lecture "The War As I Saw It," on his exploits during the South African Boer War.

The many vibrant years of the National Theatre's existence as the premier playhouse of Washington, DC, offers a detailed look at the history of the American theater. The National Theatre survived through a series of six buildings in the same location and stands today. As a result, almost every major touring star and attraction of the middle and late nineteenth century and twentieth century played here. The roster of performers surprises with its variety: Laurence Olivier, Mae West, John Barrymore, John Travolta, Rex Harrison, Jennifer Jones, Henry Fonda, Ethel Merman, Tallulah Bankhead, John Gielgud, and Leontyne Price.

Celine Celeste, a French dancer and pantomimist was the hit star of the first National's opening season. She returned over the years in melodramatic roles

The National Theatre was visited by many twentieth century breakout stars of the stage and screen. Actor and director Warren Beatty was a stagehand, doorkeeper, and rat catcher at the National in his junior year at Washington Lee High School in Arlington, Virginia, claiming he was inspired by the theatre success of his older sister, Shirley MacLaine. Beatty was also a star football player in his senior year, with an interest in bluegrass music. By the age of thirty-five he was producer and the star of *Bonnie and Clyde*, a landmark film of the New Hollywood era. This film brought bluegrass music to an international audience.

A young Robert Redford was also on stage at the National Theatre the night an irate high school teacher led her student group of 200 out of the theater, shocked by the saucy language of Neil Simon's 1963 romantic comedy, *Barefoot in the Park*.

While the National Theatre carries an illustrious history, it was also a site of contention. Theaters in the nation's capital before the Civil Rights movement were racially segregated. Black actors could appear on stage, but Black audience members had to sit in the balcony or designated sections.

Todd Duncan was a young man of thirty-two when he made his debut in *Porgy and Bess* opening on October 10, 1935, and it was immediately clear that a major new talent had been given to the music world. He had already had his first brush with fame when he appeared in an "All-Negro" Opera in New York's Mecca Temple. Duncan's friend and performer Happy Mitchell told George Gershwin, "You better hear this young negro."

Gershwin had already auditioned one hundred Negro baritones for Porgy and Bess. But he called Duncan—who was then teaching music at Howard University—to ask him to come to New York that Sunday to sing for him. Duncan considered Gershwin too "Tin Pan Alley" and refused. The truth was Duncan was scheduled to sing at his Plymouth Congress Church, and that gig was more important to him than singing "Ole Man River" for George Gershwin.

Todd went the following Monday. He sang "Ole Man River" and Gershwin asked him, "Could you look straight at me and sing that?" Duncan repeated a few lines and Gershwin said, "Ah, will you be my Porgy?"

Duncan responded to the most popular composer of Broadway, "I don't know if I want to be your Porgy or not. I need to hear the music first."

I spoke with Todd Duncan by phone in 1984. Born in Danville, VA, he described Porgy as a "wonderful guy. He's a Negro in South Carolina without legs. He moves about in a goat cart. Selling pencils or anything else from the goat house. He's a leader in Catfish Row. He had a great mind and a very lofty spirit. He found his soul, and that's the way I played the role."

But Duncan protested the National's segregation. He said he "would never play a theatre which barred him from purchasing tickets to certain seats because of his race." Later, Helen Hayes joined with her friends, Father Gilbert Hartke, founder of Catholic University's Department of Speech and Drama, DC, theatre impresario Patrick Hayes, and *Washington Post* theatre critic Richard L. Coe, to try and permanently desegregate the National Theatre. Their initial efforts failed, but they did convince members of the Actors Equity performers union to refuse to play the theatre.

In retaliation for their attempt to desegregate audiences, the then New York management of the National Theatre shut down live performances in 1948.

One outstanding event during the "shutdown" was the DC premier of the British film about a ballerina, *The Red Shoes*. Based on a Hans Christen Andersen fairy tale, the film's reviews were mixed before it made its way to America. The National's showing of the movie helped its reception and eventual critical acclaim. Walt Disney's *Fantasia* ran for seven weeks at the theater before it went completely dark. It did not reopen for live performances until 1952, this time as an integrated theater.

The many vibrant years of the National Theatre's existence as the premier playhouse of Washington, DC, offers a detailed look at the history of American theater. Famed Senator and orator, Daniel Webster once sang on stage with the Swedish Nightingale, Jenny Lind.

Washington native and "First Lady of the American Theater" actress Helen Hayes (McArthur) came back to the city for the 150th anniversary of the National and was named the honorary chairman of the celebration. She described her endearing first visit to the theater at five years old, "I was brought by my mother, and we sat in the balcony. When the play ended, I clung to my seat, thinking that if I stayed there the actors would return to the stage."

Indeed, almost every major touring star and attraction of the middle and late nineteenth century and twentieth century played the National. The roster of performers surprises with its variety: Laurence Olivier, Mae West, John Barrymore, John Travolta, Rex Harrison, Tim Curry, Katherine Hepburn, Henry Fonda, Ethel Merman, Tallulah Bankhead, Sir John Gielgud, Leontyne Price, and thousands of others. A selected list of National players:

Congo Melodists
India Rubber Man
Adams, Edie
Adams, Maude
Bailey, Pearl
Bankhead, Tallulah
Barrymore, Ethel
Barrymore, John
Beatty, Warren
Bennet, Constance
Berle, Milton

Bernhardt, Sarah
Bloom, Claire
Booth, Edwin
Booth, John Wilkes
Bryce, Fanny
Burke, Billie
Burke, Tom
Burton, William
Calloway, Cab
Channing, Carol
Clift, Montgomery
Cline, Her *
Coburn, Charles

Cohan, George M.
Colbert, Claudette
Cook, Donald
Cornell, Catherine
Covert, Earle
Crabtree, Charlotte
Cronyn, Hume
Cushman, Charlotte
Dean, Julia
Donaldson, Norma
Douglas, Kirk

Duncan, Todd
Evans, Maurice
Everhart, Rex
Ferguson, Craig
Fields, W. C.
Fiske, Minnie
Fontaine, Lynn
Forrest, Edwin
Furness, Betty
G.W. Custis *
Garner, Peggy
Gilbert Billy
Gish, Lillian
Gordon, Ruth
Gray, Alexander
Tracy, Spencer
Henning, Violet
Grisi, Gialitto
Guillaume, Robert
Hackett, James,
Harper, Valerie
Harris, Julie
Harrison, Rex
Hepburn, Audrey
Hervio, Nano
Holtz, Lou
Huston, Walter
Ives, Burl
Jefferson, Joseph
Johns, Brooke
Jones, Allan
Jone, Jennifer
Jones, James Earle
Keene, Laura

Kemble, Fanny
Kiley, Richard
Kitt, Eartha
La Gallienne, Eva
la Verne, Lucille
Lawrence, Carol
Leigh, Vivian
Lester, Jerry
Lewis, Jerry
Lind, Jenny *
Lugosi, Bella
Lunt, Alfred
Marshall, E.G.
Martin, Mary
Martinez, Tony
Mayo, Frank
Maywood, R.C.
McCann, Dudley
McKellen, Ian
Menken, Adah
Menzel, Idina
Merman, Ethel
Mitchell, Thomas
Modjeska, Helena
Moreno, Rita
Morgan, Helen
Mostel, Zero
O'Donnell, Rosie
O'Neil, James
Oakley, Annie
Osterwald, Bibi
Paige, Geraldine
Palmer, Peter
Paul, Monsieur

Penn & Teller
Pennington, Ann
Preston, Robert
Price, Vincent
Redford, Robert
Reeves, Steve
Reilly, Charles N.
Reynolds, Debbie
Rice, T.D.
Richardson, Ralph
Rivera, Chita
Rogers, Will
Russell, Rosalind
Scott, George C
Seymour, Jane
Shaloub, Tony
Spacey, Kevin
Stephens, Major
Sting
Struthers, Sally
Tandy, Jessica
Terris, Norma
Thomas, Marlowe
Tomlin, Lily
Tone, Franchot
Torn, Rip
Tree, Ellen
Ullman, Liv
Wallack, James *
Wheatley, Emma*
Wynn, Ed

* First Season

In 1865, President Abraham Lincoln first saw John Wilkes Booth playing Romeo opposite Miss Avania Jones's Juliet for Booth's debut performance at Grover's National Theater. Soon after, on that fateful April 14, Lincoln agreed to see *Our American Cousin* at Ford's Theatre while his son Tadd was a few blocks away at Grover's watching *Aladdin and the Wonderful Lamp* on the night of his father's assassination. For the record, *Our American Cousin* was a pretty good play and was popular until Booth just had to make a killer entrance.

The National has one spooky legend. Irish-born American actor John McCullough was reportedly murdered backstage at this theater in 1885 and buried by his fellow actors in the dirt under the stage rather than in a pauper's grave. A night watchman claimed to see McCullough's restless but hospitable ghost roaming backstage on the eve of a new attraction, inspecting the scenery to be sure that all is ready for the opening night audience. Live horses were also used in early productions.

Although still turning a profit, by 1869, Grover's National Theatre was in questionable shape. DC citizens warned the city council about various fire hazards like flammable scenery next to lit footlights, and their fears proved to be well-founded when one of its fires destroyed the theatre in 1873.

A commonplace occurrence in early theatre, another fire in February 1885 at the National was answered with yet another restoration, which yielded an impressive five-story beauty built in Italianate style, remaining relatively unaltered until 1922. Significant improvements included comfortable seats, better carpeting, and, most importantly, electric lighting, briskly replacing gaslight systems across the country. With these, the National Theatre was ready to enter its modern era. Shakespearean classics, opera, circuses, melodramas, and equestrian plays with real horses have all been performed at this venerable 13th and 14th street block on Pennsylvania Avenue, the ceremonial boulevard of the nation's capital.

By 1885, American theatre had become big business in the United States, and the National in DC was a major attraction for touring New York productions. This coincided with a growing affluent middle-class in federal Washington who could afford to spend more on evening entertainment.

Despite competition from other establishments looking to benefit from that new wealth, the National Theatre successfully continued hosting many significant performances in its early days: in 1904, the Metropolitan Opera brought celebrated productions of *Faust*, *The Barber of Seville*, and *Carmen*. Washington's John Philip Sousa appeared with his band in

April of that same year; and two massive productions of the sword-and-sandals epic *Ben-Hur* wowed audiences.

The famous Ziegfeld Follies, a music, dance, and comedy review in New York, was also popular in Washington, despite, or perhaps because of their risqué content. During this time, the National began a reputation as a premier pre-Broadway tryout site for productions looking to make it on the Great White Way.

Of the many National show premiers over the years, one charms for a local reason: The 1957 pre-Broadway debut of *West Side Story* co-starred **Chita Rivera** as Anita. Born Dolores Conchita Figueroa del Rivero in Washington, DC, on January 23, 1933, Chita Rivera was the daughter of Katherine (née Anderson), a government clerk, and Pedro Julio Figueroa del Rivero, a clarinetist and saxophonist for the U.S. Navy Band. The first *West Side Story* run in Washington, DC, was a critical and commercial success.

The following shows proclaim the National Theatre's significance as a venue for hosting runs and tryouts for productions that went on to achieve success on Broadway.

- ***Hello, Dolly!*** - starring Carol Channing in 1964.
- ***1776*** - The Tony Award-winner about signing of the Declaration of Independence in 1969.
- ***Annie*** premiered in 1976 with debut on Broadway later that year.
- ***Rent*** - Groundbreaking musical by Jonathan Larson in 1996
- ***Once on This Island*** - Lynn Ahrens/Stephen Flaherty musical in 1996.
- ***Hairspray*** - based on John Waters film in 2002
- ***Avenue Q*** - Tony Award-winning musical in 2003
- ***Thoroughly Modern Millie*** – 2002 musical
- ***The Color Purple*** - 2005 musical n of Alice Walker's novel
- ***The 25th Annual Putnam County Spelling Bee*** - musical comedy 2005
- ***In the Heights*** - Lin-Manuel Miranda's musical in 2007

- ***Dear Evan Hansen*** - in 2015.
- ***Matilda the Musical*** - Roald Dahl's book adaptation in 2013
- ***Spring Awakening*** - Rock musical in 2002

President Kennedy and First Lady Jackie at the National. © D.B. Murphy.

The National Theatre in 2024 © S. Moore.

J. T. Ford and his namesake theater. © Ford's Theater

Ford's Theatre always reminds us of a national tragedy. Born in Baltimore on April 16, 1829, **John Thompson Ford** was the son of early settlers, with some of his Maryland ancestors fighting in the American Revolution. He studied in public school for a few years before becoming a clerk on his uncle's tobacco farm in Richmond. Not caring for this work, he turned to becoming a bookseller and budding playwright. A relatively successful farce about contemporary life, his first satirical play, *Richmond As It Is*, went on the road with a minstrel group called the Nightingale Serenaders. The aspiring dramatist Ford traveled with the group through America and Canada as their business manager.

Adept at his chosen career, Ford returned to Baltimore in 1854, becoming the manager of the Holiday Street Theater for the next twenty-five years and building the city's famed Grand Opera House in 1871. On the city council, he was briefly acting Mayor for two years. During this time, Ford created theaters in Washington. Opening as Ford's Athenium, the first was on Tenth Street in 1861, previously the First Baptist Church. Dire prognostications followed this desecration of a sacred space. They quickly proved true when the fire destroyed the building the following year. He rebuilt it on the same site and called it his place.

Fatefully, Ford was good friends with John Wilkes Booth, then a promising Shakespearean actor aligned with what he hoped would be the Confederate States of America. Booth's older brother was Edwin, considered by many historians as America's most excellent actor. J.W. Booth was a familiar face, having performed at Ford's theater several times, including once with Lincoln in attendance in 1863.

After Lincoln was assassinated, John Ford and his brother were briefly incarcerated for questioning. The theater was seized by the government, and Ford was given $88,000 for it by Congress. Even though cleared of conspiracy, Ford remained bitter toward the U.S. government for decades.

Today, behind the original façade lies a totally re-created interior (the original auditorium was torn out and replaced with government offices and then a museum). It's all fabulously fake—except Booth's real assassin's gun on display—but meticulously crafted and historically accurate to the last possible detail.

Native Washington DC journalist, **Roger Mudd**, born February 9, 1928, was "collaterally related" to Dr. Samuel Mudd, imprisoned for setting Booth's broken leg following the assassination. I interviewed Roger by phone in 1985. He told

 me "There were three Mudd brothers who settled in Charles and Saint Mary's County. Doctor Mudd descended from one brother, and I from another. The third branch went to the West Coast. We are six generations removed so I'm related to Dr. Samuel Mudd is the best way to describe it."

Roger also confirmed the phrase "your name is Mudd" came from his famous disgraced relative. Mudd graduated from Wilson High School, joined the army in 1945, became a WTOP radio reporter in 1956, and was the news anchor for NBC News living in McLean, VA, when I talked with him.

I asked him at what point he decided that broadcasting was what he wanted to do in life.

"I'm still not sure," he answered, adding "I was quire late, really. After college, after graduate school. I had very little prescience about that or any early feelings that's what I wanted to do."

Among Mudd's assignments in the 1960s was the presidential nomination campaign of Senator Robert F. Kennedy in the 1968 Democratic primaries. He was at the Ambassador Hotel in Los Angeles when Kennedy was assassinated in a kitchen passageway of the hotel in June 1968. As Ethel Kennedy, the Senator's widow, later reminisced, "It was because of Roger who led me through the crowd, that Bobby and I got to say goodbye to each other."

Roger Mudd died on March 9, 2021, at age ninety-three of complications from kidney failure. He was widely respected for his integrity and professionalism at NBC and CBS.

* * *

Folger Theatre

In 1879, Henry Clay Folger, then a student at Amherst College, discovered the works of William Shakespeare. Soon after, he began collecting Shakespeare, Yana, and other Elizabethan books and manuscripts. One of his earliest rare books that Henry purchased was a William Shakespeare 1685 Fourth Folio, acquired in 1889 from Bangs and Company for $107.50 It's there today.

He began work as a clerk for John D. Rockefeller at Standard Oil and retired as the chairman of the board. The cornerstone was laid for Folger's great legacy, the Folger Shakespeare Library.

Sadly, he died two weeks later, but his great vision carried forward, and the building he planned included an indoor adaptation of an outdoor Playhouse. The official name is the Elizabethan Theater in honor of Queen Elizabeth the Virgin Queen, whose reign ushered in England's significant era of dramatic writing. However, the theater is inevitably, if inaccurately, known popularly as the Folger Theatre.

The Aldridge Theater
On the Howard University campus, it honors the first great Black tragedian of the English-speaking stage, Ira Aldridge. Born in 1807 and confronted with minimal opportunity in the American theater, he left the United States at age seventeen, never to return. Billed as a "Tragedian of Color" and "The African Roscius" (Roscius was a famous actor in ancient Rome), Aldridge was a great success, first in London and then throughout Europe. He was lionized and decorated by many countries during his lifetime, yet never honored in his native land. He is buried in Poland and his grave is tended today by the Society of Polish Artists of Film and Theater.

The Coolidge Auditorium.
Elizabeth Sprague Coolidge began playing the piano at age eleven. Professional performer and later patroness, she gave $94,000 to the Library of Congress in 1924 for an auditorium "planned for and dedicated to the performance of chamber music." She commissioned works by Britain, Hindemith, Ravel, Stravinsky, and others, earning herself code-name "the Lady Bountiful of Music."

The Hartke Theater

In 1937, a former child movie actor and ex-football player became the well-known and widely loved Father Gilbert V. Hartke, OBP [Order of Preachers]. I visited Father Hartke in 1983 and he helped me with this *Capital Acts* project.

The Catholic University priest established the first and foremost speech and drama department in a Catholic institution of higher learning As chair of the Drama Department, he trained many young actors and theater professionals including **Ed McMahon**, **Susan Sarandon**, **Jane Henson**, **Laurence Luckenbill**, **Jason Miller**, and **Jon Voight**.

He commandeered an obsolete U.S. Army Motion Picture Playhouse and moved it to campus becoming their first theater. He raised funds to build the permanent theatre that today stands in his memory.

The dashing, silver-haired, Basso Profundo Dominican was as dramatic as any character in the plays which swept across his stages. He was once the kindly, visionary, celebrity, and irrepressible public relations priest of Washington and in the entertainment centers of both coasts. He also had great hair. Father Hartke died in 1986. His biography is a wonderful account of his life: *Father Hartke: His Life and Legacy to the American Theater* by Mary Jo Santro Pietro.

Lisner Auditorium, on the George Washington University Campus (capacity 1495 seats), has been used both for college functions and for presentations of theater, dance, and music. Little Feat's Lowell George's final song, "Spanish Moon" was performed there.

German born Abraham Lisner, financier and philanthropist left $750,000 in his will for the construction of the auditorium. This venue has become his most prominent legacy. (The Lisner appears in subsequent chapters).

The Warner Theater (capacity 2000 seats) at 13th and E Street NW, opened its doors on December 27, 1924, as The Earl

Theater named for a similar Earl Theater in Philadelphia. For the next twenty-three years, the Grand Movie Palace on 13th Street was an owner's gold mine. It was said at the time that the theater was christened The Earl because Cosmopolitan, a name preferred by some, was too unwieldy for a marquee. The basement of the theatre featured the Neptune Room restaurant.

Vaudeville flourished during the Earl's early days. The grand staircase, enlivened by shimmering tapestries, welcomed patrons to the mezzanine and balcony. A crystal chandelier long since gone crowned the oval ceiling dome and theater goers' cheers reverberated off the walls of the Ozark marble. This Earl was a Pearl.

In the early 1930s, a business merger landed the Earl Theater in the corporate lap of Hollywood's Warner Brothers, Harry and Jack. Harry, strolling through the Earl's lobby in 1947, asked who Earl was. Informed that he was a former Pennsylvania governor., Warner shot back. "I own that theater. Put my name up there." And what Harry wanted; Harry got.

R. Taylor
© S. Moore

Last of the extravagant presentation houses for film and vaudeville in downtown Washington, the Warner's majestic lobby and lavish plaster ornamentation narrowly escaped destruction when its owners attempted to gut the space and plug in modern offices. Saved by public fiat, The DC Historic Preservation Review Board agreed in 1985 to designate the Warner Theater and Office Building as a historic landmark.

In the 1970s, the emphasis was on rock and jazz concerts, with touring musical productions spaced occasionally between one-nighters.

Richard Taylor, a native Washingtonian DC musician into roots rock since he was ten years old, first played in the band Zehn Archar, and later as Richard Taylor and the Ravers. In 1978, he heard that The Rolling Stones were launching a tour to promote their *Some Girls* album.

He explains: "I had a friend who worked at a Glen Burnie record store who told me the Stones were doing a show at the Fox theater in Atlanta. I thought maybe they'd come to DC, and she confirmed they'd be playing the Warner. We decided to go into DC every morning to the Warner to see if that was true. And the very first morning we got there we saw The Rolling Stones on the marquee. My friends and I parked our car and ran there. They were allowing two tickets per person. Each of us got two tickets. There was no line. A third person joined us, and we started grabbing people off the street—folks just going to work—and gave them money to buy us tickets. The only show notice given was on the building's marquee the morning before the show, all seats were quickly sold out. The show on June 15, 1978, the next day was Mick and Keith with Bill Wyman, Charlie Watts, and Ronnie Wood. Ronnie was doing most of the solos, just like on the record."

When asked if the crowd behaved any different in a small venue than in other Stone's shows in the stadiums Richard had seen, he answered, "I don't think the words 'behave' and 'The Rolling Stones' go together. They played as renegades, outcasts. They were the Stones. It was incredible although I don't think Mick was feeling well. He didn't do an encore. It sounded great because it was the Stones who had some of the best sound people in the world."

Ronnie, Charlie, Mick, Keith, and Bill. © YouTube

Raucous, booming, and wildly popular music wasn't new to 1978. DC weekly concerts—free to the public, rousing and invigorating—began some ninety years earlier in nearby

Lafayette Square about 2,100 feet from the Warner Theater. "Start them up" could have been a unifying cry when the President's Own band raised their instruments.

The Knickerbocker

Amidst the greatest snowstorm in Washington's history, on January 28, 1922, several hundred people bravely attended a show at the Knickerbocker Theater, the city's largest and most modern moving picture theater of its time.

Built in 1917 by businessman Henry Crandall, who owned the chain of eighteen theaters in the Delmarva region, the Knickerbocker Theater could accommodate 1700 guests. Besides being a movie theater, it was also a concert hall with a ballroom, cafes, parlors, and lounges.

Outside and inside.

Tragically, during the intermission of the twenty-eighth show, the flat roof of the Knickerbocker Theater, heavily burdened by the snow, collapsed onto the crowd. The roof collapse led to the destruction of the theater balcony and parts of the surrounding brick walls, resulting in the deaths of ninety-eight individuals and injuries to 133 others. The worst theater disaster with the accompanying snowstorm marking the city's single greatest snowfall on record.

In 1923, Thomas Lamb constructed a new theater within the original structure of the Knickerbocker, preserving its facade. It became the Ambassador Theater showing live shows and films.

By the 1950s, The Ambassador was facing challenges and experiencing dwindling attendance. In 1967 Joe Mednick, Anthony Finestra, and Court Rogers, all in their early 20s, we're selling fire extinguishers on college campuses nationwide. But they ventured to explore the scene on 8th Street in San Francisco and next arrived in DC with a psychedelic gleam in their eyes. They rented the Ambassador and with the help of **Mike Schreibman** made DC history. (See Chapter 52)

Poster from early show implies, "Are you Experienced?"

FORD'S NEW THEATRE.
Tenth Street, near E.

JOHN T. FORD - - - - - - Proprietor and Manager
(Also of Holliday street Theatre, Baltimore.)

MONDAY EVENING, NOVEMBER 9, 1863.
Last Week of
MR. J. WILKES BOOTH,
And Messrs. CHAS. WHEATLEIGH,
HARRY PEARSON,
G. F. DE VERE,
AND THE GRAND COMBINATION COMPANY

THE MARBLE HEART.

Phidias..
Duchalet } .... Mr. J. Wilkes Booth.
Diogenes
Volage } .... Mr. Chas. Wheatleigh.
Georgias
Chateau Margeau } .... Mr. Harry Pearson.

ON TUESDAY—HAMLET.

ADMISSION:
Dress Circle........50 cents | Orchestra Chairs....75 cents
Family Circle.......25 cents | Private Boxes....$10 and

☞ Box Sheet now open, where seats can be secured without extra charge.   nov 4—

Chapter 3 - Sousa the Thundered

Music became a vital part of the nation's capital, especially during the Civil War. Since 1801 the Marine Band—America's oldest continuously active professional musical organization—held concerts at the White House and regularly on weekends near the barracks on 8th Street in Southeast Washington, flanking the Anacostia River.

During marches down DC streets, they were frequently accompanied by visiting brass bands, with impromptu parades of residents joining in. The brass attack of "Yankee Doodle" and "Columbia, The Gem of the Ocean" resounded brashly up and down Pennsylvania Avenue, providing musical bravado and counterpoint to the encroaching horrors of the Civil War.

The young son of a talented trombonist took advantage of his father's position in the Marine Band to pursue his own career in music. In 1861 seven-year-old John Philip Sousa, born in a house at 636 G Street SE, "Phillip S.," as his family called him, enrolled in John Esputa's Conservatory of Music located at 511 8th Street a few blocks from the Marine barracks. The cosmopolitan musical conservatory provided advanced courses in voice, violin, piano, and various horns for the sixty pupils enrolled. Phillip energetically studied everything the school offered, in addition to trombone lessons in his father's home at a "sophisticated" instrument popularized after Beethoven used it in his "Symphony No. 5."

By the age of eleven young Phillip began accompanying his father to Marine Band rehearsals, often allowed to play symbols and horn with the troops. Reportedly, his foremost dream was to lead the orchestra of a traveling circus, but his father quashed this yearning by enlisting him in the Marine Band as a boy apprentice. His stint in the service lasted seven years; and during this time, he began studying privately with a pianist named George Felix Benkert, a local orchestra conductor.

Unlike Esputa, Benkert recognized and encouraged young Phillip's nascent gift for composing and offered the young talent some very unorthodox advice. To create something truly profound and original, he suggested Phillip avoid composing on the piano because his fingers might fall in familiar places. Benkert, whom young Sousa idolized, died at an early age, but his pupil followed his advice and fulfilled the confidence placed in him.

As Sousa continued his musical education in Washington, his instructors realized that young Phillip possessed perfect pitch, the ability to identify by ear and sing specific notes, combined with an outstanding ability to sight read. At twelve he had extraordinary musical gifts for the "food of life," as Shakespeare called it in *Twelfth Night*. Despite his later fame with "The Star-Spangled Banner," when Philip presented his first musical composition, "An Album Leaf" to the Conservatory's headmaster, Esputa tossed it out, dismissing it as "bread and cheese" and lost forever was the first original music written by the man who became America's March King, John Phillip Sousa.

By age twenty Sousa was playing the violin in Benkert's small Symphony Orchestra in the Ford's Theatre orchestra. A busy musician across Washington, at the same time he worked as a conductor and the first violin chair for the pit orchestra for vaudevillian shows at the Washington Theatre Comique, a position he held for several seasons. This experience with up-beat, fast-paced variety theatre of the nation's capital, and his childhood memories of the military band, fueled his lifelong passion and talent for exciting marching band music. The silly sounds of Washington's early theatre can be heard in the theme to Monty Python's Flying Circus, also known as Sousa's "Liberty Bell March."

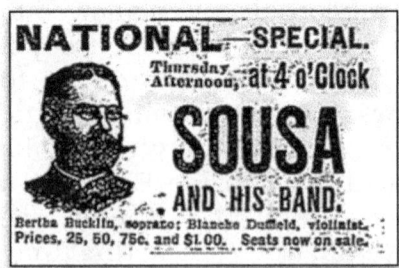

Located at 11th and C Streets and established in

1872, the site of the Washington Theatre Comiques had seen iterations of a "Washington Theatre" since 1804. It was razed in 1931 to make way for Federal office buildings. Because the landscape of DC has altered so much in becoming a global capital, it's a challenge to locate where the musical history really happened.

The famous Sousa was asked how he managed to achieve rhythm so successfully, and he responded thoughtfully:

> "Oh, that's a part of the question why one musical enterprise gets ahead, and another does not. Why does one band give gooseflesh while another fails to stir you in the least. I'm sure I don't know. The thing has never been explained. Rhythm of course you must have in music. Our hearts beat rhythmically.
>
> "Our daily existence is motion. And then take what we call nature. I suppose the trees would amount to nothing if they had no gales to blow them. Waters become stagnant that have no breezes sweeping across them. Plants don't thrive in places where the wind never reaches them.
>
> "Yes, indeed, rhythm I would call one of the most important things in the world. We have sound waves, and we know that when different sound waves are not conflicting the effect is grateful and that when they produce those that are conflicting, we have noise. Regularity of vibrations constitute music, I think some philosopher says, which is about the same as identifying music with rhythm."

Photo: Sousa's house at 636 G Street SE   © S. Moore

John Phillip Sousa was a household name, and his music was part of our lives when I was growing up. My father, GySgt Paul D. Young, was a career Marine. He recovered from a severe wound in the Korean War during the horrific 1950 Battle of Chosin and was stationed at the Marine Corp Barracks at 8th and I Streets—"The Oldest Post of the Corps." There he proudly served on the United States Marine Corps Color Guard Platoon at the end of the Truman administration.

In 1952, twenty years after the composer and bandleader's death, 20th Century Fox released the film, *Stars and Stripes Forever*, based on his autobiography, *Marching Along*, and praised actor Clifton Webb for "regally playing" Sousa. A young Robert Wagner stands out as Private Willie Little in Sousa's Marine Band although he is erroneously portrayed inventing the Sousaphone. A discordant error.

In the end, the film shows a real Marine battalion marching along to the title tune, and there's my father in a scene filmed on the parade grounds at headquarters. I saw the movie many times on TV as a child, and later bought a VHS copy for my parents to enjoy. I made a solo pilgrimage to Sousa's impressive grave at

Congressional Cemetery in DC a few years ago, hearing "Stars and Stripes Forever" in my head and imagining the final scene of the movie as I stood silent. I've also enjoyed the extensive Sousa exhibit at the National Museum of the Marine Corps.

In 1987, "Stars and Stripes Forever" was declared the National March of the United States. His music marches onward, leaving us his legacy as one of the most significant native son composers from the nation's capital.

He is buried in the Congressional Cemetery.

Charles. D. Young

Capital Acts: Washington DC Performing Arts

1952 movie *Stars and Stripes Forever*.

Chapter 4 - You Ain't Heard Nothin' Yet

My admiration for Al Jolson began when I was ten, watching The *Jolson Story* on afternoon TV. Al's "up" personality and passion for expressive, emotional music ("Sonny Boy" and "April Showers") won me over.

In 1921, at age thirty-five, New York's Broadway star caused a sensation when he opened his musical *Bombo* at the newly renamed Jolson's Fifty-Ninth Street Theatre. The owner of the briefly titled "Imperial Theatre," Lee Shubert, changed its name to appease Al Jolson, the "master of minstrelsy" who balked at moving his show uptown from the Winter Garden, where he had hit performances for years. Known then by his nickname "Jolie," he was the youngest man in American history to have a theatre named for him, and he received an overwhelming response on opening night, called back for thirty-seven curtain calls. With two dozen ragtime and "plantation" pieces to highlight his singing and dancing, Jolson played "Gus" in *Bombo*, an Italian in blackface transported back in time and brought along as an enslaved person with Christopher Columbus on his voyage to the New World. The show ran for 219 consecutive performances and launched Jolson on a national tour.

Jolson's shows and hit recordings entertained and shaped American culture. His talent and charisma caught the attention of Hollywood, and in 1927, with his starring role in *The Jazz Singer* he became the highest-paid star of the decade. As one of the first openly Jewish actors, (with others like Burt Lahr, Fanny Brice, and Eddie Cantor) Jolson played a singular role in bringing Black American music to the masses, a significant cultural shift. In doing so, he also helped Jewish immigrants assimilate into the "melting pot" of mainstream American culture, a testament to his influence and impact. In multiple ways, Jolson's early life parallels the immigrant and generational conflict story of *The Jazz Singer*, adding depth and resonance to his personal journey.

Born Asa Yoelson in 1885 (no records of his exact birthdate exist) in Seredzius, a small Lithuanian village still part of the Czarist Russian Empire, he came with his parents and four elder siblings to New York in 1891 with the many other immigrant East European Jewish families seeking escape from poverty and persecution. His father, Moses Yoelson, was a rabbi and cantor, and in 1894 found work at Talmud Torah Congregation in southwest Washington, DC, near the waterfront. Their first house was in a small alley at 208 4 1/2 Street SW, and later nearby at 482 School Street Both Yoelson homes were demolished to make way for the Southwest Freeway (Interstate 395) in the late 1950s.

At the age of ten, Asa lost his beloved mother, Nechema, who had taught him to sing and play violin. Deeply affected, the young boy was in a state of withdrawal for several months. Even though Asa sang at the synagogue, his father's attempt to instill Jewish traditions fell short when he and his brother Hirsch became newsboys. They soon discovered the vaudeville acts and ragtime music in the neighborhood saloons.

In 1895, the brothers' path took a new turn when they were introduced to DC's early burlesque scene by a then renowned minstrel comedian and banjoist, Al Reeves who encouraged the young Jolson's. The stage life of turn-of-the-century Washington soon fascinated them, and by 1897, they were performing under their Anglified names, "Al" and "Harry."

During the 1898 Spanish-American War, the Jolson boys entertained the troops encamped around the city, becoming friendly mascots. They used some of their street earnings to buy tickets to the National Theatre, further fueling their passion for the stage. The rapscallion "Jolson" brothers had chosen show business for their future, frequently running away from home for theatrical escapades. Al briefly fulfilled his boyhood dream of joining a circus, owned by Walter L. Main, the largest travelling circus at that time.

At age twelve, however, he boldly bolted to New York City to follow Harry. But after visiting a relative in Yonkers, he was soon sent back to Washington on the train. Instead, Al got off in Baltimore but was subsequently picked up by a Catholic morality squad and, for several weeks, lived at Saint Mary's Industrial School for Boys, a then "progressive" reformatory and orphanage in Baltimore.

Despite these struggles, in 1899, near the age of his bar mitzvah, Al Jolson made his first professional stage appearance in Washington at thirteen. His role was so small that his name didn't appear in ads or reviews. There is some poetic justice for the future star playing an anonymous street urchin, a silent figure in a milling mob scene in *Children of the Ghetto*, a scandalously revealing play about Jewish marriage by the "Jewish Dickens" playwright Israel Zangwill. But Al was conflicted with his cantor father, Moses, who wanted his son to follow a religious life. After only three performances, his father learned what was happening and pulled him out of the show. A substitute waif finished that week on stage.

At age fifteen, "Al Jolson" left Washington for New York. Still often working with his bother Harry as part of the song and comedy duo the Jolson Brothers, he entertained as a member of Victoria Burlesques until 1902. In 1904, the brothers joined with comedian Joe Palmer in doing a joke and song medley in blackface called "A Little Bit of Everything."

By 1906, Jolie regularly did blackface minstrelsy comedy, where non-Black performers used burnt cork or makeup to portray a caricature of Black people on stage—the "happy-go-lucky darky." By the middle of the 19th century, blackface had become a distinctive American artform. Jolson's music then was Civil War-era songs and ragtime tunes on New York's vaudeville stages, while developing his signature singing style.

In 1909, Al joined Lew Dockstader's Minstrels troupe and made his initial Broadway debut in 1911's *La Belle Paree* at the newly built Winter Garden. This was the first of several large theatre productions that launched Jolson to fame.

Jolson's stage popularity led to his becoming one of the nascent recording industries' first breakout stars. Taking a lead role in Vera Violetta in 1911, Jolson caught the attention of the Victor Talking Machine Company and soon released his song "That Haunting Melody" by George Cohan from the play, which quickly became a hit. Jolson followed that up in 1912 with his first million-seller, "Ragging the Baby to Sleep". Now Jolson could demand The Imperial change its name for the celebrity headliner.

With a run of successful Broadway and touring shows, Jolson became a star on the American stage. Simultaneously, he was a familiar voice from his hit recordings of reprised theatre songs, made special using a brilliant bird-like whistling technique. Jolson had a second million-selling disc in May 1913 with "The Spaniard That Blighted My Life" from a Winter Garden production. Jolson scored yet another massive hit that year with "You Made Me Love You," starting a decade-long stint with Columbia Records. Self-penned songs like "Sonny Boy," "California, Here I Come," "April Showers," and the endearing "Avalon," became signature Jolson hits, along with his classic rendition of George Gershwin's "Swannee."

Unsurprisingly, Sam Warner chose Jolson to star in *The Jazz Singer*. Jolson had already appeared in a short film musical short, *A Plantation Act*, demonstrating the new Vitaphone sound-film process. Initially, Warner Brothers had George Jessel who originated the role in the stage production of *The Jazz Singer*, but Warner brothers balked at Jessel's fee and was replaced with Jolson. "Blackface" wasn't the issue because Jessel did that often on the stage. Producer Sam Warner died of an infected tooth abscess the night before the movie's 1927 debut.

Backed by many film scholars, Al Jolson gets credit with starring in the first true "talkie" motion picture. Yet there was only two minutes of dialogue in the movie. The thrills came from the sound of eleven musical numbers. And music was used before in Warner Brothers's 1926 *Lights of New York*, featuring a brief recording by the New York Philharmonic.

Nonetheless, *The Jazz Singer* was the first film to bring all the pioneering technologies of a modern sound film together, with a musical score interweaving scenes, conversations continuing from one room to another, and Jolson's grand song numbers like "My Mammy," "Toot Toot Tootsie," and "Blue Skies." Advertisements billed the film as a "talkie," and reviews promoted the impact of the new Vitaphone sound system.

In terms of filmographic history, it's easy to compare the astounding moment for audiences when Al Jolson loudly ad-libs his trademark slogan, "You ain't heard nothing yet!" to the stunning scene when Dorothy opens her eyes in the first film with the groundbreaking use of Technicolor, *The Wizard of Oz*. Jolson's first "talkie" transformed the industry in the same way. In January 1928, only 157 of the estimated 200,000 movie theatres in America were wired for sound. But by the end of 1929, 8,741 theaters had been updated for sound movies, coinciding with Al Jolson's even bigger hit film, *The Singing Fool*, the first recorded sound motion picture. The silent movie era was over, and Hollywood never looked back.

Al's childhood southwest home at 1787 Irving Steet, SW; and with Frank Morgan, in the 1933 film, *Hallelujah, I'm a Bum*. © KSPD

As modern society and the civil rights movement have come to terms with past racist stereotypes, Al Jolson is now the unfortunate poster boy for blackface. By the time the Jolson movie came out changing attitudes about race and racism was effectively ending blackface.

However, Jolson's African American contemporaries praised him for fighting discrimination against Black performers on Broadway, and he was well-reviewed in black publications. The newspaper of Harlem, the *Amsterdam News*, praised *The Jazz Singer* as "one of the greatest pictures ever produced...Every colored performer is proud of Jolson."

Ironically, this first sound movie musical opened the door for Black actors and singers to appear on the silver screen because the authenticity of voice and sound exposed the falseness of whites performing in blackface. In this way, formerly prohibited jazz and city blues stars like Hattie Smith became welcomed on screen.

In sum, blackface is a painful part of American cultural history. Black minstrel acts were driven from vaudeville theatre stages in the North by racial restrictions on performing on stage and screen; white performers used blackface for popular plantation songs, dances, and spirituals. Racial restrictions against Black musical groups performing in the North also brought Jewish influence on the American "industrialized folk music" known as jazz, introducing new urban sounds and European syncopation by Jewish music masters like George Gershwin and Irving Berlin.

The compelling story of generational conflict and Americanization through jazz also underscores *The Jazz Singer* as a way for Jews to neutralize post-World War I antisemitism. The rising nativism pushed Black people and Jews together, both culturally and physically, into the melting pot of New York City so immigrant Jews (like the Jolson family) often saw themselves as allies of Black Americans, sharing similar ostracization and discrimination.

Aware of these cultural politics, Al Jolson helped pave the way for many jazz legends, including Louis Armstrong, Ethel Waters, Duke Ellington, and Cab Calloway. Jolson attempted to have an all-black dance team featured in a Broadway show at a time when Black people were banned from Broadway productions. Jolson was instrumental in promoting the work of Black playwright Garland Anderson, resulting in *Appearances*, the first Broadway production with an all-Black cast.

Familiar with discrimination, Cab Calloway commented about their movie together, *The Singing Kid* (1936). "Talk about integration, when the band and I got out to Hollywood, we were treated like pure royalty. Jolson and I lived in adjacent penthouses in a plush hotel. We were costars in the film, so we received equal treatment, no question about it."

"Al Jolson was no racist," states Washington's own Daryl Davis, longtime pianist for Chuck Berry, and author of *A Black*

Man's Odyssey in the Klu Klux Clan. In his book, Davis shares his experiences and insights into his encounters with members of the Ku Klux Klan and his efforts to engage them in dialogue and promote understanding and change. His work has been recognized for its unique approach to combating racism and prejudice.

Al Jolson became the scapegoat star who killed the silent movie but is today remembered for "promoting blackface." By 1939 Jolson was still using his "Mammy" blackface style, but the pressures of the Depression, the nascent Labor movement, and Civil Rights activism in 1960s helped moved the country toward racial solidarity and his popularity waned. Jolson gained more attention in the Hollywood gossip columns concerning the marriage and rapid divorce from his third wife, former chorus girl Ruby Keeler. Shortly after the end of World War II, fanfare for Jolson's career was revived.

According to film historian Krin Gabbard, *The Jolson Story* "goes further than any of the earlier films in exploring the significance of blackface and the relationships that whites have developed with blacks in music...the film seems to imply an inclination of white performers, like Jolson, who are possessed with 'the joy of life' and enough sensitivity to appreciate the musical accomplishments of blacks." Jolie played a singular role in bringing Black American musical advancements such as jazz, ragtime, and the blues to white listeners, independently helping all American people understand our richly amalgamated music. Jolson remained a role model for many Black performers like Sammy Davis Jr., who impersonated him early as a child.

A lifelong Republican, Jolson was also the first performer to entertain U.S. troops overseas after the attack on Pearl Harbor, and his subsequent tours for G.I.s became his trademark. A call back to when Al entertained troops as a kid in Washington getting ready for the Spanish-American War, Jolson became the first entertainer to perform for service members in the Korean War.

He delivered an outstanding forty-two shows in sixteen days. Still, he passed away on October 23, 1950, shortly after

returning to the United States, partly due to the physical exhaustion of his demanding schedule.

Jolson performing with a Black actor in *The Singing Fool* (1928). While this actor was uncredited and only played a minor role, the fact that he was included at all, with speaking lines was controversial at the time.

More DC Area Technical Innovation

The Bliss Electrical School was founded on October 15, 1893, in Takoma Park, Maryland (where Montgomery College is today). Two Washington DC Bliss students would change the world.

Charles Francis Jenkins became an engineer who contributed to the invention of television. He developed an electrical transmission device that sent pieces of a picture along telephone wires to be reassembled to another device. Jenkins became America's most successful early television pioneer. The Federal Radio Commission granted Jenkins the first American television license in 1928. Operating from Washington, DC, its call letters were W3XK.

Jenkins later teamed up with another DC student at Bliss, **Thomas Armat,** and together, they built the first practical motion picture projector. They received a joint patent in 1897. They called it the Phantascope, and it was first exhibited in NYC. Thomas Edison bought the patent rights, added some of his own tweaks, and marketed it as the Vitascope. Armat won a special Oscar in 1947 for his contribution.   *Steve M*

Jim Henson Idea Man is a 2024 American documentary film about puppeteer Jim Henson. Directed by Ron Howard, it opened the 77th Cannes Film Festival in the Cannes Classics section on May 18, 2024. It premiered on Disney+ worldwide on May 31, 2024. © Walt Disney Co.

The Jim Henson Memorial Statue and Garden was dedicated on September 24, 2003 at the University of Maryland. The 450-pound statue was created by artist **Jay Hall** and funded by the classes of '94, '98, and '99.

Chapter 5 – Henson & Associates

Jim Henson with Fritz Roland, co-owner of Rodel Studio.
© Del Ankers

One of the privileges of being a journalist is having special access to individuals, locations, and extraordinary experiences. During the autumn of 1984, I had the opportunity to meet and interview Jane Henson, the wife of Jim Henson, at the Muppet headquarters on E. 69th Street in New York City. At that time, their Henson Associates company was releasing their fourth feature film, *The Muppets Take Manhattan* (by trying to launch a Broadway show in New York City) so I was aware that Jim and Jane were actively engaged in publicity. I contacted Jane regarding this Capital Acts project, and she was interested in the idea.

Our arrangement was to meet and have a discussion on the book-in-progress, and if that went well, Jim Henson would personally contact me. This encounter was incredibly thrilling, and I successfully passed the audition. After we met I heard her tell a producer that I was a "gentle" interviewer.

From the outside, the Muppet headquarters was an average, three-story townhouse on East 69th Street, across the street from Hunter College, where a polished oak door led me into a chandeliered vestibule. There was no outdoor sign announcing the nature of the Muppet business inside, but I did spot a tiny image of a generic Muppet on a small ground-level window.

Inside were framed posters on the wall anchored by Jim Henson standing with Kermit on his hand with other promotional pictures.

The receptionist welcomed me, asking if I wanted something while I waited for Jane. "We have coffee, tea, and ice cream," she offered.

"Nice," I thought.

An open stairway extended to the top of the building, with an impressive mobile of multicolored circus balloons. The room behind the receptionist was a vast, open two and a half story workshop with a skylight in the ceiling. It extended below and beyond the original wall of the house and into a closed back courtyard ringed with wooden benches. Muppet makers abounded, working on various projects on drafting tables. On shelves throughout the room were cans of epoxy, tools, drawings, paints, rolls of cloth, a pile of animal heads, and bits and pieces of strange and familiar creatures, including a row of Miss Piggy wigs. Protective of their puppetry trade secrets, I tried to take a picture of a beautiful mobile of colorful balloons but was politely told, "no photos."

Soon Jane Henson came out and we had a great afternoon conversation. Jim Henson phoned me a week later. I submitted my story to Buzz McClain, at the *Journal Newspapers*, and this was my first published work for the Journal newspapers: "Muppet maker: Former Hyattsville resident Jim Henson looks back on 30 years of puppet magic." I wrote:

"It's been a very nice career," says Muppet creator Jim Henson, "because it feels that one thing has led to another, and very slowly, we worked our way up to the point where we could handle big movies."

Thirty years ago, when he fashioned his first puppet, James Maury Henson was a Northwestern High School Senior from Hyattsville, MD. Henson was doing scenery for the high school puppet club, but his ambition was to work in live television.

The origin of the Muppets explained to me by Jim, Jane, and Del Ankers who co-owned Rodel Studios where they first filmed their commercials goes like this: Local TV host Roy Meacham was searching for young puppeteers to do a children's version of the CBS Morning Show, with hosts Walter Cronkite that featured the puppets of Bill and Cora Baird.

Meacham's producers visited the La Petite Players puppet club at Jim's high school to recruit talent. Jim saw this as an opportunity to enter the television industry and, at the age of seventeen, went to the library to learn about puppet making. He created some puppets in his bedroom, auditioned with his classmate Russell Wall, and successfully landed the job. The "Junior Morning Show" began airing in June 1954.

"We did a pantomime to the song, "Sh'boom," and they put us on the air," Henson remembers, "but the "Junior Morning Show" folded in three weeks." Jim said. They hired Henson for another show, "Barn Party", which also featured a young Willard Scott. On NBC staff, Willard also performed for live audiences then at the Sheraton Park hotel on Saturday mornings.

Scott says of this time, "We became friends immediately. I remember Jimmy sitting on the steps of WRC, amazed that the station had offered him a contract. I said, 'Jim, just be sure that you don't sign the rights to the puppets over to the station.'" He made sure.

In Willard's 1982 autobiography, The Joy of Living, he tells of his early days in "Barn Party," interacting with "Jim's innovative bunch of puppets: "I worked with a bald-headed Muppet with a big nose, named Sam, sort of the way Fran Allison worked on 'Kukla, Fran and Ollie.' I'd do a commercial for peanut butter by Schindler's. Sam would open his mouth,

I'd give him a big spoonful, and he'd go 'ahh,' And then there was the frog named Kermit."

In his "Farmer Willard" character, he also performed before live audiences at Sheraton Park hotel on Saturday mornings. It was next off to Bozo School even though Willard never liked clowns, and thought they were stupid and grotesque. In 1983 Willard told me that "in the last three or four weeks of the Bozo show, I was putting my makeup on and drawing on my clown lips, I began to cry. I was on the verge of the nervous breakdown."

Shortly afterward, Henson enrolled in the University of Maryland. There he met fellow theatre arts major and future wife, Jane Nebel. "Although he was very shy as a man," recalls Jane, "he was very sure of himself as an artist and clearly steps above everyone else."

Sam, Jim, Kermit, Monster, and Jane © Del Ankers (by permission).

However, the puppets had not gone unnoticed. Jim and Jane began collaborating on making and performing with them. In February of 1955, they were hired to do puppet pantomimes for Inga Runvold's afternoon TV show, *Inga's Angle*.

"There was nothing serious about the puppetry. We were working our way through college. It was kind of a lark," said Jane.

(Several of their school and TV colleagues were hoping that a serious affectionate relationship might emerge.)

The puppets evoked great audience response, and WRC soon gave them a spot of their own. The five-minute show, *Sam and Friends*, ran locally at on WRC-TV from May 9, 1955 to December 15, 1961.

The program was highly innovative and somewhat bizarre. Jane says, "The program was bizarre, but because television was so new, it could take bizarre things easier." One of the early characters was the lizard-like creature named Kermit who Henson had made from an old, green coat his mother had discarded. Kermit made his debut doing commercials for Eskay Meats, a sponsor of *Sam and Friends*.

"It was a most wonderful time," says Jane. "WRC let us do whatever we wanted." Two other creatures from this period were "Wilkins" (the nice "Kermit"-looking one) and "Wontkins, (the short grouch who would get blown up or some other insult) used for ten-second commercials for Wilkins Coffee. They made 179 of these—a fabulous success—and used them as templates for other regional coffee makers. Jim, by the way didn't like coffee. All commercials were filmed at the Rodel Studios in Georgetown.

Jane Henson told me that L. Ron Hubbard, the founder of Scientology, was recording at Rodel at this time also, and Jim was "fascinated" by him. Hubbard was a dropout from nearby George Washington University.

Upon graduation from Maryland where Henson had driven in an old Rolls Royce and after four years with *Sam and Friends*, Henson began contemplating a move away from puppetry. "At that point, I was breaking up with a girlfriend, and I wanted to go off for a year and paint," he told me. "I went to Europe where I met other puppeteers. They changed my feelings toward puppetry. I saw it as a valid art form. I came back to Washington because I was enthusiastic about getting back to work. I also came back to Jane."

Jane Henson in Jim's office. She gave me a book and signed it "Thanks for keeping alive a special time in my life."

Their first exposure came in a 1957 clip on the Steve Allen Tonight Show. Kermit the frog, singing "I've Grown Accustomed to Your Face" to a purple monster operated by Jane. © S. Moore

Henson's previous ambiguity towards puppetry as a career had been an impediment to their relationship up to this point. "Unconsciously," Henson explains, "that was splitting us up – and Jane was engaged to another guy. We slowly got together," The "getting together" was followed by marriage and five children.

Jane Henson requested Johnny Holliday to narrate the University of Maryland film tribute to Jim (class of 60). © J. Holliday

Chapter 6 – Circus Boogie Feld Brothers

Spectacular entertainment in the early 1800s was found in the tents of the circuses. England created the modern circus in the 1770s and George Washington, then the Commander-in-Chief of the Continental Army, saw an American circus in Philadelphia. It included a trick rider, clown, acrobat, ropewalker, and a boy equestrian. These shows became especially important for rural communities to come together and witness exceptional feats of skills and exotic animals they'd otherwise never see. The entertainment's eventual three-ring "bigness" factor also helped influence future USA projects like amusement parks, department stores, and shopping malls.

Hachaliah Bailey, born in 1774, worked in his family's lumber business in New York. He bought an elephant—one of the first two in the US—named "Old Bet" in 1808 from a sea captain and began exhibiting it at fairs and markets. He launched the Bailey Circus, one of America's earliest big tops, by adding a trained dog, several pigs, a horse, and four wagons. Bailey purchased land near the intersection of Northern Virginia's Leesburg Pike and Columbia Pike and moved to what is now Bailey's Crossroads, where his animals enjoyed their winter vacations.

Bailey was the role model for a young P.T. Barnum, who wrote about meeting him. Barnum had a complex personality with a mix of traits. He was ambitious, entrepreneurial, and sometimes deceptive but also a philanthropist. In 1871, Barnum would eventually join Bailey's adopted nephew, James Anthony Bailey, to form Barnum and Bailey's Greatest Show on Earth. P.T.'s most famous phrase might be "There's a sucker born every minute," but my favorite is "The noblest art is that of making others happy," which shows a more compassionate side to his character.

A year after Bailey died in 1906, the Ringling Brothers operated two shows separately until 1919, when they merged to form *Ringling Brothers and Barnum and Bailey Circus*. In the following years, the *Greatest Show on Earth* and big circus tents became prominent in America. These shows became the big show, especially for rural citizens of the country. This entertainment's eventual three-ring "bigness" factor also helped influence future USA projects like amusement parks, department stores, and shopping malls.

The Feld Brothers: Irvin and Israel

Washington plays a significant role in developing our American circus, driven by an unlikely focus on music recording and deft promotion. In the 1930s, two Hagerstown, Maryland, brothers Irvin (May 9, 1918 – September 6, 1984) and Israel Feld (Sept 21, 1910 – Dec. 15, 1972), sons of Russian Immigrants, were teenagers when the Great Depression decimated their father's clothing store. Irvin started selling "snake oil," all-purpose medicines, door-to-door to help his family survive.

A widespread occupation in America was known then as "snake oil" salesmen. The actual snake oil was brought to America by Chinese railroad workers—the oil of the Chinese water snake, rich in omega-3 acids. They used it to treat arthritis and rub it on their aching joints after working on the railroad.

By high school graduation, Irvin Feld was an expert on all-purpose medicines and a music fanatic. He and his brother came to DC in 1938 with about $700 saved up from selling their medicines. They set up a discount pharmacy in the then African American neighborhood of 7th and Blank Street. The NAACP assisted the brothers in navigating the challenges they faced due to then discriminatory practices and policies.

Irvin's passion for music was a driving force in his life. He would later own two recording labels—Super Disc, a jazz and blues label, and Quartet, featuring gospel.

The Feld Brothers hooked up loudspeakers outside the store to attract customers and began selling records in the store. Irvin also installed a small recording "studio" and began recording numerous local musicians and singers. One young musician, Arthur Smith, was stationed in DC with the Navy when Irvin Feld captured an instrumental tune he had written in 1945. He called it "Guitar Boogie." This would powerfully change the world.

Arthur Smith was born in 1921 in Clinton, S.C., and grew up in Kershaw, S.C., where his textile mill-working father taught music and fronted a local jazz band. At age eleven, Son Arthur joined his Dad's band first on trumpet and later on guitar. By age fourteen, Arthur was playing on the local radio with his first band, The Crackerjacks.

Smith played "Guitar Boogie" for Irvin Feld on an acoustic guitar, with Don Reno on rhythm guitar and Roy Lear on bass. Irvin Feld released it on his regional and independent Super Disk label credited to The Rambler Trio. It is a modified twelve-bar boogie-woogie based on earlier popular piano pieces of the 1920s. Since Smith was inspired by his jazz-influenced Dad, he admitted that he was influenced by Tommy Dorsey's big band song "Boogie Woogie" growing up. He liked the big band. The song did very well for both Smith and The Feld Brothers. Smith promoted it on the popular Carolina Hayride radio program on Charlotte, North Carolina, radio station WBT. It was covered by Les Paul, Lawrence Welk, Bill Haley and the Comets, and Bo Diddley and became known as one of the pioneer of a new genre—rock and roll.

Ten Years After

The 1957 song "Guitar Boogie" also played a role in the lives of a couple of young aspiring musicians living across the Atlantic Ocean. A novice guitar-playing teenager was hoping to impress an older art student guitarist with his chops on two instrumental songs, "Twenty Flight Rock" and "Guitar Boogie," hoping to impress his older friend John and members of the fledgling band on their first public appearance at a garden party. Paul, the younger lad, has recalled this incident in many subsequent interviews:

"I could play (these songs) in rehearsal, so they elected that I should do it as my solo," McCartney remembers. "Things were going fine, but when the moment came in the performance, I got sticky fingers; I thought, 'What am I doing here?' I was too frightened; it was too big a moment with everyone looking at me, the guitar player. I couldn't do it. So that's why we brought my friend George Harrison in."

The Quarrymen later renamed themselves **The Beatles.**

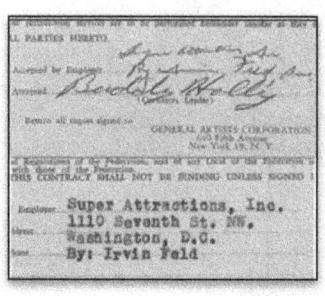

And speaking of the Beatles Irvin Feld noticed Billboard's the 1957 "That'll Be the Day" chart entry by a group called the Crickets. Feld booked this new band for a R&B tour, starting in Baltimore, going to the Howard Theater, and on to NYC. Below is a picture of **Buddy Holly's** contract signature.

When gospel music star and first guitar heroine of rock and roll, Sister Rosetta Tharpe, took the stage in her $800 wedding dress at DC's Griffith Stadium on the evening of July 3, 1951, she drew a bigger paying audience than the ballpark's main attraction, the Washington Senators baseball team, did that afternoon. An estimated 20,000 Tharpe fans enjoyed the event, advertised as "the most elaborate wedding ever celebrated."

This is one highlight of the musical *Shout, Sister, Shout*, by a Helen Hayes award-winning playwright, Cheryl Hayes, based on George Washington University professor Gayle Wald's outstanding biography. The Washington Post and others praised the performance. DC Theater Arts newspaper proclaimed it "A touching biographical tribute to a lesser-known musical pioneer."

Segregation remained prevalent in Washington, DC in 1951, leading to the unfortunate omission of coverage of her wedding by the three main newspapers, namely *The Washington Post Evening Star* and *Daily News*. However, the Washington Afro-American paper showcased her wedding on the front page and *Ebony* magazine dedicated three pages to what they describe as the best wedding witnessed in the nation's capital.

One odd twist to this story is that the ballpark wedding was planned before Rosetta lined up a groom. Twice divorced by 1951, Tharpe met with DC's preeminent concert promoter Irvin Feld who made an offer she liked: "Find a husband; we'll promote the wedding." Tharpe soon met Russell Morrison, a roadie for the Ink Spots, and knew she'd found her groom. The Ink Spots, the predecessors of doo-wop music, also became Rock & Roll Hall of Famers, and were so popular that many all-white venues integrated to include them in their lineup, a rare occurrence in those forties and fifties.

Decca Records was at Griffith stadium to record Sister Rosetta's wedding and the concert that followed, quickly issuing an EP complete with liner notes by musicologist Alan Lomax.

Biographer Gayle Wald says, "It is fitting that the show is the best-remembered achievement of her career because the essence of her gift and her art lay in her ability to communicate with an audience."

Inducted in the Rock & Roll Hall of Fame in 2018 as early rock influencers, one of her lesser-known titles is the "Godmother of Rock and Roll."

© *Charles D. Young*

One of Irvin Feld's great contributions to DC performing arts was his talent and strategies for presenting music concerts in large public arenas like the Carter Barron Amphitheater, a 4,200-seat outdoor venue in Rock Creek Park at 4850 Colorado Avenue, NW, Washington, DC 20011.

Feld (and later Cellar Door Productions) promoted popular entertainers (Frank Sinatra), musicals (*Carousel* with John Raitt), and classical music (National Symphony Orchestra). The Feld Brothers also produced all three of The Beatles' DC-area concerts: Washington Coliseum (February 1964), Baltimore Civic Center (September 1964), and D.C. Stadium (August 1966).

Some of the artists who played Carter Barron are:

Armatrading, Joan
Armstrong, Louis

Atlanta Rhythm Section

Axton, Hoyt
Ayers, Roy
Band, The
Belafonte, Harry
Betts, Dickie,
Black Ivory
Bland, Bobby "Blue"
Borge, Victor
Brick Express
Bromberg, David
Brown, Chuck
Brown, James
Bryson, Peabo
Buffett, Jimmy
Butler, Jerry
Carter, Eddie
Charles, Ray
Charlie Byrd Trio
Citizen Cope
Clayton, Jan
Cole, Nat King
Con Funk Shun
Corea, Chick
David Brass Construction
Bromberg, David
Davis, Daryl
DC Black Repertory
DC Blues Festival
Earth, Wind, Fire

Ferguson, Maynard
Fitzgerald, Ella
Four Tops
Goodman, Benny
Green. Al
Guess Who, The
Highlights, The
Howard, Mickey
Impressions, The
Jackson, Freddie
Jackson, Millie,
Joe Cocker
Kennedy, Pete
King, B.B.
Kingston Jazz Crusaders
Kool and the Gang
Kristofferson, Kris
Labelle
Legendary Orioles,
Lewis, Ramsey
Liston, Lonnie
Makeba, Miriam
Mancini, Henry
Mann, Herbie

Marcus Johnson Project

Mathis, Johnny
Maze
Merman, Ethel
Miller, Marcus
Mint Condition
Moore, Melba
National Symphony Orchestra

Nero, Peter
Odetta
Ohio Players,
Ojays, The
Oscar Peterson Trio
Outlaws, The
Palmeri, Eddie,
Patterson, Rahsaan
Payne, Freda
Peter, Paul, & Mary
Petteway, Al
Preston, Billy
Proctor and Bergman,
Pryor, Richard
Raitt, John
Rankin, Kenny

Ray, Goodman, & Brown

Righteous Brothers
Robinson, Smokey

Ross, Diana & Supremes

Roundtree, Richard

Roy Eldridge Quartet

Sanchez, Pancho
Sapphire, Uppity Blues Women
Scott-Herron, Gill

58

Capital Acts: Washington DC Performing Arts

Selwyn Birchwood Band

Sergio Mendes & Brazil '66

Shakespeare Festival

Shakura
Shaver, Mary
Simon, Joe

Sonny Terry and Brown McGee

Springsteen, Bruce
Stylistics, The
Sweat, Keith
The Jewels
The Nighthawks
The O'Jays
The Outlaws
Travers, Mar
Tucker, Teeny
Turner, Eddie

Tyner, McCoy
Uggams, Leslie
Vera
Warwick, Dionne
Weird Al Yankovic
Weston, Kim
Whatley, Jody
Whispers, The
Williams, Denise
Wonder, Stevie

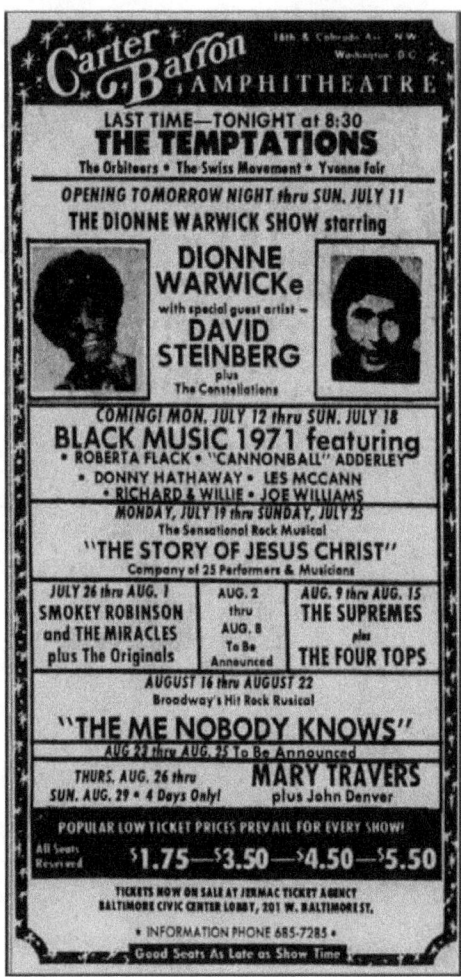

Chapter 7 – DC Met the Beatles

The Beatles arrive in Washington DC. © Dennis Brack

When the Fab Four brought Beatlemania to American soil in the winter of 1964, the Director of the FBI, native Washingtonian J. Edgar Hoover, was concerned that their public appearances might provoke race riots. Christian evangelist Billy Graham broke a lifetime rule by watching TV on the Sabbath to catch the "lads from Liverpool" on *The Ed Sullivan Show.* Newly sworn in President Lyndon Johnson joked that they were the advanced guards for former UK Prime Minister Sir Alec Douglas-Home adding, "they need haircuts." *Life* magazine later listed their US arrival as number ninety-six in the hundred most important historical events that shaped America.

They were the Beatles and in 1964 they were number one. In 1983 for this book project, I was trying to remember details about the Beatles coming to Washington, DC, the phenomenal group that changed my life and our world.

I thought a disc jockey had played their first single, "I Want to Hold Your Hand," on a Washington radio station, but I couldn't remember his name. I called radio stations around town and finally "Young" Dave Brown, a DJ with DC 101, confirmed "It was Carroll James. But he's not in the radio business anymore." I found him in the phone book, and he picked up when I called.

"Are you the first DJ to play the Beatles in America?" I asked. He replied "Guilty." I quickly left work and in about an hour was at the door of his Silver Spring, Maryland, home. As he escorted me to his home office, he handed me an old cassette tape and said, "Take this with you when you leave; you might like it." More on this audio artifact later.

I immediately loved Carroll as he talked about his WWDC afternoon radio show. He would do "old school" comical voices—fun and corny. Born in Frederick, Maryland, raised in nearby Hagerstown and a Princeton graduate, he had served in the Coast Guard. His early broadcasting experience was a morning radio program on WJEJ while in high school. He graduated to stations WRC and WMAL in DC and WBAL in Baltimore.

With my tape recorder running, Carroll humbly explained his story: "I received a letter from a Sligo, Maryland, Junior High School fifteen-year-old student named Marsha Albert requesting that I play a record by an English group called the Beatles."

"She saw them in a brief clip on the Jack Paar TV show in the fall of '63. Paar had seen them in London and showed a minute of them singing "She Loves You" with girls in the audience screaming. His comical comment was "It's nice to know that England has finally reached our cultural level."

Carroll thought: "Sure, that sounds like fun—anything for our listeners. So, I went to one of our WWDC staff members, Jo Wilson, and asked her how we could obtain an English recording. She suggested that Tony Linley, a representative for British Overseas Airways, could probably have someone fly it over real fast." The Beatle's single, "I Want to Hold Your Hand" was released in the UK on November 29 with one million advance orders for the single. "We got a copy of it the next day."

"It arrived that afternoon, so Fred Fiske (another popular WWDC broadcaster) and I listened to it. I thought it was an exciting record, but my experience had been that European recording artists couldn't get arrested here in the USA, so I was skeptical. Fred didn't like it at all."

"I called up Marsha Albert to come into the studio as fast as possible because I wanted her to introduce this record. She was scared to death. It's funny, but I don't remember this being around Christmas time, but it was." (Carroll may have forgotten Christmas because it had only been a month since President John F Kennedy's assassination. The country was still in shock.)

He continued, "I wrote out an introduction for Marsha, and she said, 'Ladies and Gentlemen, for the first time in America, the Beatles singing "I Want to Hold Your Hand,' and we played the record at 5:15 p.m. The switchboard lit up like the proverbial Christmas tree. Listeners just went wild. It was a crazy thing because we didn't build it up or hype it. We just played it, and the reaction for an unknown group was phenomenal. It was spontaneous combustion. So then, I continued to play it every day. I would fade it in the middle and say, 'this is a WWDC exclusive' so the other stations couldn't steal it."

Meanwhile, in New York City, a lawyer named Walter Hoffer got a call from Capitol Records They wanted to know who controlled the publishing rights for the song. Hoffer was the American representative for NEMS Enterprises, the British company founded by Brian Epstein who managed the Beatles Capitol Records was preparing to release 200,000 copies of the single into the usually sluggish post-Christmas market. When they heard about the reaction in Washington they called Hoffer, requesting publishing clearance to ship some advance copies into the DC area. The Capitol executives who one week earlier had been hesitant to press 200,000 copies of the forty-five now put three Capitol production plants to work through the Christmas break to produce one million copies. The release date was moved up one month to January 1964, all because of the reaction of Washingtonians. This was confirmed in the 1981 Beatles biography, *Shout: The Beatles in Their Generation*, by Phillip Norman.

Around this time, Olive "Johnny" Johnson joined the WWDC staff. She had been friends with McCartney since Paul was eight. Previously, she worked as a personal assistant to

Brian Epstein. In a transatlantic phone call with Brian, they made arrangements for Carroll to emcee this first concert.

When the Beatles landed at New York's Kennedy Airport on February 7, they were stunned, greeted by thousands of screaming fans. Their scheduled performance on *The Ed Sullivan Show* two days later had already received 50,000 requests for the seven hundred available seats for their debut on American television. By contrast, only 7,000 had requested tickets for Elvis Presley's Sullivan debut in 1957.

But when they met backstage a bellicose Sullivan greeted Carroll with the following, "You're the guy who's been saying you discovered the Beatles. You can forget that crap because I've booked them since October." The dour Sullivan had scouted the Beatles in Europe in the summer of 1963 and signed them for his show. Playing at the nearby Birdland down the street from the studio, famed jazz musician Dizzy Gillespie also happened to be backstage that night for the Beatles performance, he "just stopped by to get a look at them."

Seventy-three million people watched the Beatles performing on *The Ed Sullivan Show* that night. Reportedly, the crime rate for that Sunday evening was the lowest in half a century. However, the American press were not so enthralled with the lads from Liverpool. *Washington Post's* reporter Richard L. Watts called the Beatles "asexual and homely" while *Newsweek* wrote, "Visually, they are a nightmare. Musically they are a near disaster, with guitars and drums slamming out their merciless beat. It does away with secondary rhythms, harmony, and melody. Their lyrics, punctuated by nutty shouts of 'yeah yeah yeah,' are a catastrophe."

As a counterpoint, the Post's music critic, Richard Harrington, wrote a beautiful piece called "The Birth of Beatlemania" in 1989 about the lasting cultural impact of that singular television broadcast. After the assassination of John Kennedy, the arrival of the Beatles "provided an emotional revival." He included overlooked facts about the famous broadcast. Also appearing on the show were comedians Mitzi McCall and Charlie Brill, impressionist Frank Gorshin, a tumbling act called the Four Fays, and thirty-seven members of the cast from the Broadway musical *Oliver!* (including Artful

Dodger Davy Jones, who a few years later would surface in the "prefab four" Monkees).

Next stop after the Sullivan Show appearance was their first American concert at DC's Washington Coliseum. On the morning of February 11, it began snowing heavily in the nation's capital.

John Lennon said, "We're not going to fly in a 'fookin' blizzard." So, a special train was secured for the ride down from New York. John nicknamed it the "Beatle-more and Ohio" express. When they finally arrived at Union Station, hundreds of screaming fans were on hand to greet them. The Beatles killed some time before the show at the Coliseum, goofing around out on the snow-covered mall in front of the Smithsonian.

The Tape

Carroll met the Beatles in a remote studio outside the already packed venue to record an interview on the historic winter night in the nation's capital.

This interview was on the tape that Carroll handed me when we first met in 1983. I called Carroll immediately after I listened and asked if anyone had heard it. He replied, "Yes, we played snippets of it on my radio show." I replied ambitiously, "Listen, if I get our article published, let's put this out on a record and sell it." He agreed but was skeptical about the commercial value of his early experiences and nobody—including friends and family—thought I was going to get anything published.

I wrote up my visit with Carroll James as best I could and sent it to John Sansing, the editor of DC's Washingtonian Magazine. Many friends advised me, "Be prepared for rejection!" and told me stories of people beginning their journalism careers with failure. I said, "Thanks for the warning," but as a Beatles fan, I secretly thought, "Are they kidding? This article is a scoop. And it's about the Beatles." I was certain it was going to fly.

Sure enough, I received a letter signed by Sansing: "We would like to run your material as an anniversary piece. We pay twenty cents a word." That was about $86, and I shared this exciting news with my wife, Margaret. "OK! Now I am a writer," I said with a wide grin.

I called Carroll with the good news. "This is going to change your life," He was not convinced. At work I got two calls at my job the day the December issue of Washingtonian magazine with my article came out. The first call was from Susan Stamberg, the host of *All Things Considered* on National Public Radio (and the first female host of a national news broadcast) asking for Carroll's number. The second was from the *Good Morning America* TV show wanting to invite Carroll to fly to New York to be on their show. They got my phone number from the Washingtonian staff. The media attention helped put James back in the broadcasting business and it was soon after that we started seeing and hearing him doing TV and radio commercials.

Photo shows "Young Dave" Brown and James getting a special Capital records award.
© C. James

The Record

We made the record and sold it via ads in *Rolling Stone* magazine, which also bought reprint rights to the Washingtonian article for their 20th anniversary Beatles issue in February 1984. That gave me a *Rolling Stone* writing credit. One of our first mail order buyers was a "Stevie Moore" from Ohio.

Side One of the seven-inch (EP) 33 1/3 rpm with a picture sleeve was Carroll's nine-minute interview with the Beatles, recorded just before their first American public concert at the DC Coliseum. Side Two contained young Marsha Albert's spirited introduction of the first American broadcast of "I Want to Hold Your Hand" on James's radio show. We also included snippets from the Beatles first Washington DC press conference and one later in September at the Baltimore Civic Center that I was lucky to attend.

Capital Acts: Washington DC Performing Arts

> Carroll James was always a class act and a very nice man. The day I arrived from KYA in San Francisco to work at WWDC in Washington I received a telegram from Carroll wishing me success here in the city. Carroll had previously hosted *CJ and Company* in afternoon drive time before he was let go. I remember thinking what a classy gesture this was especially since I was one of his replacements.
>
> He and his wife Betty were invited by Sullivan to see that first Beatles show. Betty sat with John Lennon's first wife, Cynthia, and remembers her as completely overwhelmed by the unprecedented fanfare for her husband's band. Capitol Records gave Carroll a special gold record award.
>
> *Johnny Holliday*

Carroll James Interview Excerpts

CJ: Excluding America and England what is your favorite foreign country you've visited?
John: Excluding America and England, what's left?
Paul: Our favorite foreign country is England.
CJ: Does anyone in the group know a foreign language?
John: We all speak fluent 'shoe.'
CJ: What are some of your biggest musical influences?
Paul: Sophie Tucker is a big musical influence. A. Very big influence. She's our favorite American group.
John: Big Death Arthur, who plays with Small Blind Johnny were big influences on me.
CJ: George, you're the only Beatle who visited America before to visit your sister who lives here. At that time, did anyone in the US know the Beatles?
George: I was here in September, and I visited record stores in New York and no one had heard of us.
CJ: If you boys hadn't succeeded in the music business, what would you have done or been?
Paul: I fancied being a schoolteacher.
George: I was going to be a baggy sweeper. That's someone who baggy sweeps up and down the line in the airports.
Ringo: I'd like to open some women's hair shops.
John: I couldn't say honestly what I'd be doing.

The First DC Show

They took the stage at 8:31 p.m. and performed 12 songs. On the bill were The Chiffons and Tommy Roe. The Chiffons were unable to make it due to the previous day's snowstorm. Instead, the opening acts were Jay & The Americans, The Righteous Brothers, and Tommy Roe. At 8000 fans, it was a crowd four times larger than any previous show they had played.

Carroll James died in 1997 at the age of sixty from cancer. Honored in his New York Times obituary, James was "a Washington disc jockey whose promotion of the Beatles on his radio program helped make the group famous in the United States in the weeks before its first appearance on the *Ed Sullivan Show* in 1964. The Washington Post was more direct, referring notably to James as the DJ "who in 1964 was the first to play a Beatles record on the radio in the United States."

Although Carrol won a special Capitol Records Gold Record radio researchers have found playlists and Top 40 charts that came before his WWDC broadcast. D. L. MacLaughlan, a UCLA researcher reported that Chicago WLS radio station played the Beatles "Please, Please Me" on Vee Jay records released ten months earlier in February 1963. Nevertheless, the Beatles and Capitol records considered James's promotion of their label's first American single important and historic.

Carroll James at Georgetown Univ.
© S. Moore

Carroll and I remained good friends. He did voice-over work for us at Georgetown and invited me to join him when he took his teen-age daughter and friend to DC concerts. My favorite shows were Michael Jackson with the Jackson Five's Victory Tour and Paul McCartney at RFK stadium on July 4, 2000. Carroll attended Paul's pre-show press conference, and when he joined me in our seats, he was excited that Paul remembered him affectionately and signed a picture sleeve of an interview disc that Carrol brought.

One month later, on March 14, 1964, a ninety-minute closed-circuit broadcast of the DC concert sold 500,000 tickets to about one hundred theaters and **the Washington DC Coliseum**. The company that handled the transmission of the show—National General Corporation—made 4 million dollars.

This was the first time closed circuit was used for a concert. Previously, it had only been used for boxing matches. So, Washington DC can claim "the first pay-per-view concert in America" award.

The Beatles returned on September 13, 1964, to play the Baltimore Civic Center, and again on August 15, 1966, to DC Stadium. I saw both shows. I saw both those shows.

After the 1966 concert, my friend, Skip Cookman, drove us to the Shoreham Hotel where the Beatles were staying. We saw

Brian Epstein in the lobby and managed to get on their 5th floor before a guard turned us away. Skip asked the guard to give George a guitar pick he'd brought.

On August 29, 1966, Johnny Holliday emceed the final show in Candlestick Park of their three US touring concerts. The last public performance by the Beatles as a group was January 30, 1969, on the rooftop of the Saville Row building of Apple Corps, nearby Abbey Road.

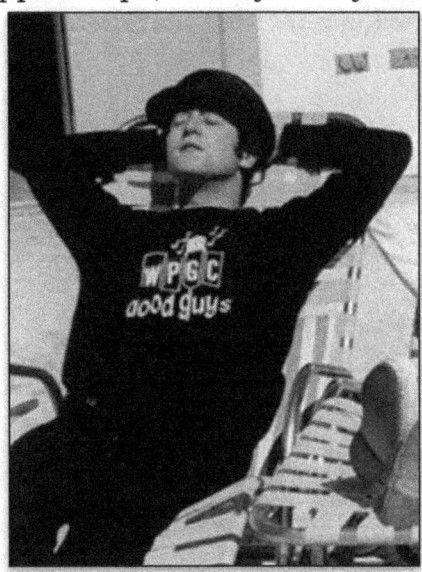

After DC show and snow the Beatles relaxed in Miami. John wearing his WPGC Good Guys shirt. © The Daily Mail.

The Uline Timeline by Valerie Paschall

1941: Miguel Uline opens the coliseum, as **Uline Arena**, naturally. The original purpose of the building was as a hockey rink for the Washington Lions.

1950: The arena now houses basketball team The Washington Capitals. Their first African American player, Earl Lloyd made his debut in the stadium in October. The Georgetown Hoyas also use this as their home stadium.

1953: President Dwight D. Eisenhower hosts one of his two Inaugural Balls at the arena.

1956: Boxing champion Joe Louis makes his professional wrestling debut.

1959: The arena is sold for $1 million and renamed the Washington Coliseum. The sports team of the time to call the arena home? It's another hockey team, the Washington Presidents.

February 11, 1964: Ladies and gentlemen, **THE BEATLES**! Two days after their appearance on the Ed Sullivan show, the Fab Four played their first

American concert for over 8,000 people. To give a sense of perspective, that's over twice the capacity of DAR Constitution Hall.
1965: Bob Dylan plays at the Coliseum. A photo from the show later graces the cover of Bob Dylan's Greatest Hits.
1967: Concerts are banned from the venue because a riot happens outside a show by, get ready for it, The Temptations.
1969: The final professional sports franchise to call the stadium home, the Washington Caps (then a basketball team) spends its one and only season in the arena.
1971: Washington Coliseum is used as a temporary prison for 1200 protestors of the Vietnam War.
1994: The Coliseum takes on another unsavory new life as a trash transfer station.
2003: The battle begins to preserve this site. Waste Management applies to get the place demolished and the DC Preservation League adds it to its Most Endangered Places list for that year.
2007: The Washington Coliseum joins the National Register of Historic Places.
2013: Douglas Development announces its intent to turn the arena into an office space.

Paul, John, and George inside the mobile studio before the 1964 show. With Carroll is Murray the K. Carroll gave me this previously unpublished photo.

© S. Moore

Chapter 8 – The Kennedys

At the Creative Cauldron in 2024 © S. Moore

Maura and Pete Kennedy—beloved recording artists The Kennedys—met in Austin, TX, in 1992 when Pete was playing in Nanci Griffith's band. Pete and Maura drove 500 miles to meet at Buddy Holly's grave in Lubbock, TX for their first date. Maura was born and raised in Syracuse, NY, lived in Austin briefly and moved to DC. "I was not expecting the Washington area to be such a great music scene, but it was," she says.

Pete grew up in the Barcroft apartments across Four Mile Run drive from the first Birchmere. He was an early regular player at Bethesda's Red Fox. "When the Seldom Scene switched to the Birchmere, I began to walk across the street and go there. My dad really liked Jethro Burns, so he'd come in and see him." Maura adds: "His dad's name is also Pete Kennedy, so my husband would announce him from the stage, 'Ladies and gentlemen, the original Pete Kennedy.' His dad would stand up and wave to the crowd."

Pete Kennedy took his first guitar lesson at Arlington Music, where the basement repairman was ex-Country Gentleman John Duffey. Soon after that the Beatles changed the world. I first met Pete in 1985 when my *Journal Newspaper* editor, Buzz McClain, who was invited but couldn't attend, sent me to the Birchmere to be a judge for the Marlboro Country Music talent contest and battle of the bands for local musicians. Pete Kennedy, Jon Carroll, Peter Bonta (all on guitars), Jim Robeson (on bass and lead vocals), and Robbie Magruder (on drums) came together and named their band Silverlake to compete for the contest, which included a potential recording contract. They were the superior group, but my fellow judges told them to turn down when they started. Not a great beginning.

Pete remembers, "The band that did win sabotaged us by turning our amps up after we did our soundcheck—and after they played before us. The judges had to tell us to turn down."

Some patrons disagreed with the contest results, which led to something of a shoving match. For the record, Judge Steve voted Silverlake.

Pete Kennedy, Robbie Magruder, and Jon Carroll.
© Oelze

> "I've known Pete forever. He used to sit in with the Rosslyn Mountain Boys all the time. I played President Clinton's Inaugural Ball with him and Maura at the Air and Space Museum. I did gigs with him and Danny Gatton at Moose Lodges. Once Pete was playing Ford's Theater in a tuxedo and walked across the alley and took off his jacket and played the 9:30 club with us in his tee shirt. He's the one guy you can't stump."
>
> *Bob Berberich*

In his 2018 ***Tone, Twang, and Taste: A Guitar Memoir*** (Highpoint Life), Pete details his stellar career: "Like many of us who became avid collectors of all things Liverpudlian. The real goal was to get every Beatles record that came out. And they came out in a flurry, consuming most of our allowance." said Pete on his first music obsession.

I loved this book, as did critics, readers, and musicians, including the late Nanci Griffith who proclaimed, "Pete Kennedy is a wonderful player who is like a professor of music, prowling about on stage in the guise of a folk guitarist." Here Pete describes an early music strategy that helped secure his career:

"In order to do freelance work at venues with union stagehands, I had to belong to the Musician's Union. This would also give me health insurance and a pension plan, so I went down to the union hall, a small house on Wisconsin Avenue in DC. There I met with Sam Jack Hoffman, the president of the local He was an entertainer from the vaudeville era, and before we got down to business, he pulled out his scrapbook and regaled me with stories about the great old days. Finally, it was time to audition.

"I got my guitar and figuring that standard songs were the meat and potatoes of the union, I start playing 'The Girl from Ipanema.' Sam Jack waved for me to stop. 'That's great,' he said. 'But can you play any rock music?' I quickly tried to imagine a vaudeville musician's idea of rock music, and I played the intro to 'Proud Mary.'

"Jack nearly jumped out of his chair. 'That's great! You're exactly what we need!' I signed on various dotted lines and then it was time for my initiation. I was instructed to go into the basement and take a seat on the couch. There, a slide show would play, describing the benefits of union membership. I went down and took a seat on the couch, next to the only other initiate that day. It was Emmylou Harris. We watched the slideshow.

"Afterwards, the union people seemed to have all gone to lunch, so we made our way out the front door. On the stoop, she told me she was heading down to Austin to play Armadillo

World Headquarters, a legendary music venue. Then she would continue to Los Angeles, where, as she put it, she had her fingers crossed, because it looked like she might have a record deal. That certainly worked out well, and it was a source of pride for the Red Fox family musicians that she became the once and future Queen of Country Music.

"Now that I had a union card, it was time to do some work, and I started getting calls right away. They were usually prefaced with. 'Chip Cliff gave me your number and he says you can play 'Figaro.'" Whatever they said, I could play. I simply agreed and then figured out how to play it. My motto became, 'It's great to be the worst person in the group because you are learning from everybody else, even as you annoy the heck out of them.' Quote. I had never, for example, played in certain configurations before, including any kind of orchestra. That was all about the change.

"The phone rang. 'Pete, this is Dave Bragonier.'

"'Hi, Dave.' I didn't actually know him.

"'Pete, I'm the contractor for the National Symphony Orchestra. We've got a major concert coming up at the Kennedy Center. Aaron Copeland will conduct his Third Symphony, and his protégé, David Del Tredici, is going to conduct the world premiere of his new piece, the 'Lobster Quadrille' from his 'Final Alice.' I'm looking for a player who is expert on the mandolin, can follow a conductor, and can cite-read an orchestra part.'

"Since I was woefully deficient at the entire skill set he had just outlined, I answered without hesitation, 'I'm your man.'

"'Excellent!' He gave me the rehearsal dates and times. I hung up and surveyed the situation. This was either a great break or a potential public flogging. Either way, it was the essence of freelancing; accept a gig you're not really qualified for, then work your tail off to a be qualified by the time the downbeat rolls around."

Capital Acts: Washington DC Performing Arts

In the early 1980s Pete Kennedy took part in several all-night after-hours jam sessions with a youthful Keith Whitley. Here, he sits in with Keith and his band just as Keith's Nashville career was about to take off, while Birchmere founder/owner Gary Oelze makes a very rare appearance onstage.   © Connie Brandt Smith

Circa 1974 ads

Kenny Kramer, the real inspiration for the Seinfeld TV character had a spotty career doing stand-up and quit the biz in 1981. But here's proof he played DC clubs.

Chapter 9 – The Joy Boys

Ed and Willard (1965) © Courtesy of E. Walker
My visit with Ed Walker in his home © N. Walker

From childhood on, I immensely enjoyed Ed Walker's radio and TV broadcasts. He and Willard Scott began their Joy Boys on WRC radio in 1955. I phoned Ed early in the Capital Acts project, and he took an interest and offered, "Anything I can do to help."

We talked often as I updated him on the book's progress and became friends. Edward Heston Walker was born blind on April 23, 1932, in Fairbury, IL. His family moved to Washington when he was four. Ed's story begins:

"My childhood on Euclid Street NW was very nice. The bus and streetcar lines were close. I first remember sitting on the porch with my dad, listening to ball games and sipping iced tea. A family friend, Ted Belote, an engineer at Mutual Broadcasting, would take me to the radio station and remote broadcasts of the Army Band. "I was just hanging around, but it greatly influenced me."

"I was in a special school—the Maryland School for the Blind in Baltimore—from Kindergarten through High School, competing with other blind kids. It's all different now. They don't send blind kids to a special school. The children are mainstreamed now, with training, in the public schools."

Ed would listen to the other students' voices on the bus to and from school, and his expert abilities as a mimic grew from these trips: "I was certainly more interested in how they sounded than how they looked," he laughed. "I couldn't look at the scenery, so I used to listen to people talk and pick up their accents. For example, in Baltimore, they'll use the word 'payment,' and that means 'street'; they'll say 'zink' for sink.

"I had many memorable teachers who gave more than nine to five. We had competitions and sports like wrestling, which is great for blind people because it's a contact sport. We used to do plays, which is more difficult than in regular school because you need the stage set up long before the show. We'd have to memorize the stage and learn our lines. One young music teacher would take us to the symphony and try to develop a little class in us gawky teenagers. I wouldn't have gotten as much attention in a public school."

"When I was eight years old, I asked for a 'wireless phonograph' for Christmas." Ed continued: "They were little oscillators or small transmitters. I got a turntable and connected an antenna to it. This was very illegal, but I had a little radio station in my basement. My broadcasts could be heard a couple of houses away. I would pretend I was doing radio shows."

Coincidently, across town in Alexandria, VA, a kid named Willard Scott and friend, Roger Gordon, were also "broadcasting" from a likewise illegal basement station. Willard and Roger, however, hooked up a phono oscillator with a broadcasting range of five miles. Unfortunately, the FCC soon came down on them as their "broadcasting" interfered with airline communications at National Airport.

Walker collected records beginning at age six and, in high school, began running the sound system and playing those records at the dances. "I would do little intros, and then gradually it became a show. The school administration wasn't enthusiastic about me pursuing a radio career. The school counselor wanted me to become a social worker or a piano tuner. My mother wanted me to be a minister."

In the fall of 1950, Ed enrolled at American University the first blind student to attend. AU had previously had a radio station, but it burned down. Ed, with his new friend Roger Gordon—yes, the same Roger who, along with Willard Scott, almost sabotaged air flights at National Airport—helped start a new radio station, WAMU.

"One of our first shows was *Ed's Waxworks* playing my big band records. Someone else might bring me Gregorian chants. You never knew. Roger read the news and sports from the *Evening Star* newspaper." This new radio station slowly gained the respect and support of the university's administration. It ran on what was called "'carrier current;' Instead of using an antenna, we fed the signal into the power lines."

Ed recalls, "The first remote transmission we did was a talent show at the girl's gymnasium. I knew that the girl's dormitory had a switchboard, so we patched our station microphone to a mic at the gym, and with miles of telephone wire, it worked. I was a big hero because I had figured out how to do it."

Later, Ed and Roger Gordon would cover the AU basketball games. Roger and his friend Ronnie Webber would do the play-by-play color with Ed serving as the engineer.

During an *Ed's Waxworks* show, one of Roger Gordon's friends slipped in next to Eddy. The intruder started making some ad-lib kidding remarks which might have upset a less unflappable character, but Ed handled the situation with aplomb. From this unlikely beginning, a great partnership was to develop. Student Willard Scott was the intruder who recalled, "If it took Eddie by surprise, he never showed it because he never missed a beat. From the moment he parried a response, I knew we were on to something. We were like one mind, one thought. We had an uncanny ability to second-guess each other to read each other's thoughts. We were a natural team."

Ed and Willard soon became best friends and decided they were ready for their own radio show. They approached several local commercial stations for an audition, and station WOL hired them. Their first show, Going AWOL, premiered in May 1952 on Sunday evenings and soon expanded to Saturdays. It was a hit.

In describing that show, Ed says, "We wrote comedy sketches and did fake commercials. In those days, we would sit down and write the material. We did routines on the political conventions imitating President Eisenhower, 'let's go to the secret caucuses,' and you'd hear cards shuffling. And a take-off on the radio show, *Strike It Rich* (where people in need of money for medical reasons competed for cash), and we called it *Strike It Poor*. There was a popular French movie then called *Scaramouche*; We changed it to *Scratch a Pooch*. It was all satire. We lampooned Arthur Godfrey as our character 'Arthur Clodfrey.'

"When they expanded our show to two nights, we learned we couldn't write all the material, so we began to rely on our ability to work off each other, which we developed over the years as *The Joy Boys*."

Willard on Ed

"Behind the scenes, Eddie was in control of the minute-to-minute broadcasts. There's an old saying, 'There are those who like to work, and those who like to watch.' When we did a radio show, Eddie did all the work—in braille. He would cue the engineer for the commercials and give the time from a braille clock. He's a perfectionist—one of the most orderly, organized people I've ever known, and a fanatic about details. He wanted to be in control, so I stepped back willingly and enjoyed my role as his sidekick." Ed did oversee the logistics and order that made *The Joy Boys* a smooth-running show for seventeen years.

Willard Scott once squeezed my nose. Hard! Part of Willard's 1960's afternoon *Bozo the Clown* TV schtick let kids in his audience pinch his red bulb nose as he discreetly pressed a hidden noisemaker in his pants. Scott served as Bozo on WRC-TV for three years, followed by doing the first three commercial spots as Ronald MacDonald, the show's sponsor.

However, this nose-squeeze wasn't from my childhood. Putnam Publishing, my then employer, published Scott's 1983 memoir, *The Joy of Living*. At a dinner of sales and marketing people, Willard spoke about the book a few months before its publication. He revealed. "If you were to look at my resume, you'd see I'm bald, overweight, don't make all the smooth moves, and dress like a slob. I take tremendous pride in the fact that I beat the system".

I was excited about the book and the only one at this sales conference who'd been a Willard Scott fan since his Bozo days. I sat at Willard's table, and we got to know each other over dinner. As we got up to leave the event, Willard surprised me with my own nose squeeze. I was instantly transformed into an eight-year-old kid sitting in front of a vintage Westinghouse TV set, loving Bozo. Years later, I was in a bookstore in Middleburg, Virginia, when a limousine pulled up in front of the store. Willard popped out to pick up a book he'd ordered. He was still in his TV makeup, on his way to his nearby home from one of his occasional *Today Show* remotes from the DC NBC-4 studio. As always, he lit up the room, said hello to all, and made everyone smile.

Charles D. Young

Willard invited me to his office at 30 Rock when he was doing *The Today Show*. Willard's spirited autobiography *The Joy of Living* was just published, and he was promoting his book. He was the first Ronald McDonald and I enjoyed his story about the time he was driving back from an appearance at a McDonalds near Gaithersburg, MD, when his car broke down. A farmer picked him up in a truck. "I was in my full clown suit and make up and we drove in silence. He never asked me why I was in the clown suit. He just let me out where I could get a taxi."

The Willard-Walker team broke up in 1954 after Ed graduated from American University. Their WOL radio station was sold. Ed took a job with radio station WPGC, and WRC hired Willard was as a page and staff announcer. The job at WPGC was Ed's first solo stint, and there were difficulties.

Visiting Willard at 30 Rock in his Today Show office. © S. Moore

Ed recalls, "I had to work Sunday afternoons and do the news on the hour. It wasn't easy [for me] to get the news, so I began listening to station WPIK on my headphones because they used the same news service WPGC used. WPIK would read it right off the wire, so I figured nobody would know the difference. I would patch a pair of headphones into a receiver, listen to WPIK, and repeat what I heard. It worked, and I got proficient at repeating what their newsman said. This continued until I got ready to do the news one day, and WPIK had the religious *Old Time Religion* program on. I rustled some papers and said, 'Due to technical difficulties, the news will not be aired.' Later, the station owner called me to ask what had happened in the news. I told him, and that ended my news career."

The Joy Boys were reunited on the air on WRC in 1958, where their new program replaced *The Lone Ranger* and the *Longines Symphonette*. *The Joy Boys* popularity steadily increased, and within a year, they were shifted to the highly desirable "drive time" slot from four to six in the afternoon. By 1963, the program had become so successful that WRC gave them a full four-hour evening slot from seven to eleven.

When NBC management (owners of WRC) decided that WRC should convert to a top forty format, *The Joy Boys* was canceled. Willard moved to WRC-TV as a staff announcer. Ed was fired.

"This was a low point in my life. I was very scared. My wife, Nancy, and I decided to rent a beach cottage, and I went there to figure out what I would do. I got a call from Charlie Stopak, who used to be a director at Channel 4. He said ABC was starting a show called *AM America*, and we want you to audition for a follow-up local show called *AM Washington*.

"I said, 'Gee, I don't know.' I had never done much television, and everything I did was videotaped so they could re-shoot it [if necessary].

"Charlie Stopak said, 'Well, you don't have to do much—sit there and talk to people. You can do that,' he said. They let me use an earplug, and the director would give me directions. They had it all worked out. I thought, sure, if they have that much faith in me, so we did it."

Ed was the co-host on the new morning television show with Ruth Hudgins, an African American woman who had begun her career as a secretary at the station and graduated to a public affairs show covering the Black Community. Together, they were an affable good team. Ed worked from notes in braille on a clipboard in his lap. This worked very well, as he could read the notes without looking down at them. The show lasted five years, which is an excellent run for TV.

Because *AM Washington* was a low-budget show, many of the guests were authors who were glad to appear to plug their latest book. (Note: In 1991, Donn Murphy and yours truly appeared on Ed's show promoting our *Helen Hayes: A Bio-Bibliography* book.)

It became a particular challenge for Ed when the show was expanded from thirty minutes to an hour, as this meant interviewing two authors, and their books were invariably too new to be available in braille or on records. Always resourceful, Ed enlisted the aid of an old friend, a former schoolteacher, who volunteered to read the books for him. He'd send her the books by courier; she would read them and then call Ed's answering machine and record a book summary of her analysis of the work and several sample chapters in their entirety. Ed would sit in his office at night, often until one a.m. doing his "homework." This might have daunted a lesser person, but Ed found it all mentally stimulating.

"It was wonderful because I had been a disc jockey, and it doesn't take much intelligence to do that. I started reading everything. I did *AM Washington* five times a week and began doing my present radio show at WMAL on the weekends."

Ed Walker actively supported many community events. His work with the Mayor's Advisory Council on the Handicapped earned him the "Public Citizen of the Year" award in 1977 from the Metropolitan Washington chapter of the National Association of Social Workers. He served on the Columbia Lighthouse Board of Directors for the Blind. He was the first recipient of the prestigious Touchdown Club's annual award to an accomplished handicapped person.

Always modest, Ed shunned publicity for the public service side of his life. He was proud, however, of the Ed Walker

Chapter, Inc., of the Big Band Society, which then had 1,500 metro area members. The Society had dances once a month and was responsible for regularly bringing such well-known groups as the Les Brown, Bob Crosby, and Glen Miller orchestras to Washington.

Ed seemed happiest talking about the many celebrities he met and interviewed. He scored quite a coup in getting an interview with the notoriously press-shy Frank Sinatra during his Kennedy Center engagement. He also interviewed Bing Crosby, Jack Benny, Arthur Godfrey, Mel Blanc, Bob Hope, and hundreds of other performers. "I can't be blasé when I meet with these people I admire,'" he said, "I get excited, and I'm like a little kid."

In 2009, Ed Walker was elected to the National Radio Hall of Fame in the category "Local or Regional – Pioneer." *The Big Broadcast* radio show where Ed presented his favorite old-time radio shows with commentary on WAMU radio lasted three decades, and a tribute to Walker was featured on National Public Radio in 2014.

Walker was diagnosed with cancer and retired from *The Big Broadcast* in 2015 to address his health and spend more time with his wife and two daughters. His last radio show, recorded from his Sibley Memorial hospital bed a week before, was aired on Oct 25, 2015. He died three hours after the broadcast.

And despite Ed's great success, I always detected the feeling of sadness on his part that Willard never became a partner in his professional life after they split up. He told me, "I'd like to get back together with Willard in some fashion before it's all over. Willard has always been the groundbreaker of this team. A lot of what I've done is because of my association with Willard. People were not willing to take a chance on me but because I was linked with him, they would. He was the eyes of the team."

* * *

WTOP radio newscaster **Neil Augenstein** posted a moving tribute broadcast on October 26, 2015, for Ed. It is still online at: https://wtop.com/local/2015/10/radio-legend-ed-walker-dies-at-83-three-hours-after-final-broadcast

An excerpt from Neil's broadcast: "Walker 'died quietly in his sleep at 2 a.m.' says Ken Mellgren, Walker's longtime friend and former boss at WWRC.

Last week, after making his diagnosis public, Walker invited WTOP's Bruce Alan for an informal interview at his assisted living facility. Alan said his friend's condition worsened quickly in the past week.

'When we talked about his career a week ago, he was clearly enjoying the memories and the experiences, and telling stories of fun times,' says Alan."

When **Johnny Holliday** first came to Washington in November of 1969 to do the morning radio show at WWDC, his bosses, Bill Sanders and Pat Whitley picked him up at the airport. "On the drive into the station," Johnny remembers, "they had the car radio on. I had taken an all-night flight from San Francisco. Bill told me, "This is your competition." At that moment, Jackson Weaver was announcing a lost cat. After that they played a march song. They played a march song every morning at 7:25 a.m.

"My reaction was 'Are you kidding me!' Bill and Pat both insisted these guys own the morning radio market. "I figured it would take me six weeks to knock them out of their number one morning ratings spot. And in a few months, Johnny with his funny characters and pop music managed to reach the number two spot—and stay there. "I could never best those guys. I gave them a good run for their money, but always number two."

The WMAL morning team **Frank Harden** and **Jackson Weaver,** team ruled radio for thirty-two years. Gary Lloyd wrote in the *Georgetown Dish* that "they onetime represented 28 percent of the market share, that's one in every four listeners, unheard of in this day and age. The show ended in 1992, when Jackson Weaver died of kidney failure. Frank continued on for several years after Jack's death with Andy Parks and Tim Brant, but it was never the same."

Chapter 10 – Mark Russell: Playing for Laughs

Mark Russell © Oelze

"1988 was a year dominated by two events, and two events only: the presidential campaign and Oprah Winfrey's losing of sixty-seven pounds. That's it. Television seemed to cover little else in 1988. George Bush won forty states—and Elvis was sighted in every one of them."

Mark Russell, New Year's Eve

I first heard the name Mark Russell in a family tale about Mark firing my mother, Pat, from the Carroll Arms Hotel bar on Capitol Hill, one of her first waitress jobs. Mark, then the restaurant manager, reluctantly did it at the owner, Mr. Heslop's request. Mom got fired a lot, primarily for hanging around the bar drinking after her shifts.

An early-morning call to the politico punster's home to set up a time for this meeting activated his personal answering machine: "You have reached the Ramada Inn," beamed the familiar voice. "If you wish to speak to the Mayor, leave your name, phone number, and how much you care to spend at the sound of the tone."

The next moment, a gracious Russell is on the phone with a well-crafted monologue about then-Washington Mayor Marion Barry's latest imbroglio. An interview with Russell was as fresh as the morning news and often dissolved into laughter on both sides. Seeming relaxed and modest behind his black-framed glasses, he could not resist the funny line, and an easy conversation soon turned into a barrage of wry jests.

With Taffy Danoff and Mark. © S. Moore

Joseph Marcus Ruslander (b. August 23, 1932, Buffalo, NY)
In the 1950s, he moved to the Washington, DC, area with his family and was accepted but didn't go to George Washington University. He often joked "as a young man I dodged the draft. I did this by joining the Marines. And after the nuns in Catholic School, Marine Corp boot camp was a piece of cake."

He said he was wounded during the Korean war but the injury was minor. When discharged, he gradually began playing piano around town, developing his political humor act. He is best known for his thirty-two years of first performing at the Shoreham Hotel's Marquee Lounge, Specials TV appearances, and later his PBS specials. "Just the other day a man stopped me on the street to tell me how much he enjoyed my program on PMS."

Russell always said that most of his jokes and songs are topical and have "a shelf life shorter than cottage cheese."

Nonetheless, a January 5, 2013, show at the Birchmere included parodies of Vice President Biden and Senators Rand Paul and Mitch McConnell. He asked the crowd to shout, "Darwin was wrong," when he mentioned their names while spoofing them.

He also referenced then-President Obama's vow not to negotiate the debt ceiling crisis with the Republicans. He said, "I wonder if he's going to negotiate with the Chinese when they cancel our credit and turn off our utilities." And to the tune of Auld Lang Syne: "For old acquaintance be forgot, let's shake hands and just be friends, till we meet again in two more months, and screw the people once again."

Taffy Danoff of the Starland Vocal Band and Mark. Taffy's smoking during this interview inspired Mark to suggest we sell the photo to a cigarette company.
© S. Moore

Mark was an American original with the homespun and haywire nuances of Will Rogers, Tom Lehrer, and Steve Allen (with whom he resembled). With Art Buchwald, he shared the mantle of Unofficial Court Jester and US Government Gadfly. But while Buchwald was a columnist, Russell was a musician and monologist who thrived in front of an audience, delivering his droll blend of topical satire and snappy song parodies.

"The thing I do best is perform live," he stressed. And Russell's best was just fine.

"I've always had great respect for Japan–I really have. At the turn of the century, they gave us Japanese cherry trees with all the beautiful cherry blossoms. Why did they do that? Because they knew that we would want to take pictures of them."

Mark Joseph Ruslander first saw those cherry blossoms in 1951, when his parents, with younger brother Danny, moved here from Buffalo. Both Ruslander boys played the piano. His younger brother played the piano at the Washington Mayflower Hotel. Their father was an upbeat gas station attendant who encouraged his boys to enjoy music and show business.

Mark continued: "I went into the Marines in '53 and didn't do any professional playing until I got out three years later. My first job in the DC area was at Captain Guy's across from the old Trailways Bus Terminal," Russell recalled with contagious amusement. "It seated twenty people, tops. It was a real toilet. The show featured a Hawaiian dancer, a trumpet player, and me on the piano. That whole block is now the Convention Center. I went and took pictures of it before they tore it down."

Russell soon moved from the strip joints to the respectable Carroll Arms Hotel on Capitol Hill. "The crowd was wheeling and dealing, talking politics. Senator John Kennedy in one corner, Hubert Humphrey in another. I'm just a non-entity.

I couldn't say, 'Hey everybody, listen to these jokes.' It was just me playing piano against the wall in a little dining room. Then, gradually, I started writing song parodies about what was happening on the Hill and doing them for whoever would be sitting closest to the piano.

"On Fridays, there was a party in almost every office in the Senate. There was no security in those days, no metal detectors. Nothing like that. The press would go to those parties and wouldn't care who was with whom or where the booze and the crab claws came from. The National Medical Association? Boeing?

"So, I put together a little band with Sammy Ferro, a local musician. He'd play his trombone—a really funny guy—and I'd play washboard or cowbells. In the late afternoon, we'd march down the halls of the Senate Office Building looking for the parties with the idea of calling attention to ourselves. When the parties broke up, the people would follow us back to the Carroll Arms to drink."

When happy hour passed, remnants of the Hill crowd remained to hear Russell's fledgling act. Word spread and Russell's future as a political satirist was soon confirmed by a popular majority of those early audiences.

In 1961, Russell moved across town to the Shoreham Hotel's Marquee Lounge for $300 a week. When he finally left, a neat twenty years later, it was reported that he could command $8000 per concert appearance. Mark said, "The Shoreham was really it in those days, the undisputed best hotel in town. The Beatles slept there following their 1966 show at DC Stadium. When I first started there, Senator Russell Long came into the lounge while I was doing some bit–I don't recall what it was about—but the Senator from Louisiana jumped up out of his seat and yelled, "That's not funny."

"I was so inexperienced then that his remarks stopped me in my tracks, and I couldn't recover." The following week, *Variety*, the show-business newspaper, carried the headline, "Russell vs. Russell," creating sudden high-profile publicity for the comedian and giving his career a good push forward. However, the assassination of President Kennedy two years later cooled Russell's career.

"I was wiped out," he recalls. "New York recovered quickly but DC mourned for months, and it was some time before political humor was welcomed back."

In 1971, Russell hit his lowest emotional point. A divorce and self-described "nervous breakdown" left him doubting whether he could continue in humor. Then came the flood of salvation: Watergate.

"Oh yes. Watergate. It was wonderful. The material kept coming. My adrenaline really started flowing. The Saturday Night Massacre—when Nixon fired Special Prosecutor Archibald Cox then heading the Watergate investigation was the single busiest night I had during my years at the Shoreham," Mark noted.

As our 1989 interview winded down, I let the cat out of the bag by reminding Mark that he had fired my Mom. He jumped up from the couch, raised his arms nervously, and shouted, "Heslop made me do it. Heslop made me do it. I liked Pat, but Heslop made me do it." It was an instant rewind to the young, inexperienced Mark Russell. I replied, "That's OK. She's not mad about it." Mark relaxed, and we laughed. He phoned Mom and their renewed relationship became an even funnier family story. A week later a signed photo arrived in Mom's mail inscribed "To Pat. Please tell me I look the same"

Mark's final performance was at the Carolina Theatre of Greensboro, NC, on October 30, 2016. It was a week before the Clinton-Trump election. He opened his bi-partisan show with this introduction:

> "I live in Washington, DC, for the same reason a coal miner lives near the shaft. We are a city in perpetual gridlock, especially the Congress where last spring they wanted to commemorate the holiday, Cinco de Mayo, but they couldn't decide on a date."

Mark died from prostate cancer at the age of ninety. A legendary political satirist—long before Stephen Colbert and Jon Stewart—and always on top of his game.

For thirty years on his PBS comedy specials, his observations left viewers laughing and reflecting. When asked if he had a large writing staff, he'd say "Oh, yes. One hundred in the Senate and 435 in the House of Representatives."

Chapter 11 - Tenderly, Felix Grant

Sitting in with Felix Grant at WMAL. © S. Moore

Johnny Holliday recalls radio legend Felix Grant: "When Felix Grant started his first job at $37.50 a week for WWDC in the 1940s, everything was live. Tape didn't exist, and only the music was recorded. All the commercials were scripted. For sports, there were no recordings to go to. No other sounds but the announcer's dominant voice. This is one of the reasons for the need for different kinds of voices early on.

"Felix was the complete professional. I almost wanted to call him 'Mr. Grant' as I was so awed in his presence. His smooth, distinctive voice was heard on DC airwaves for over forty-five years. Thirty of them were on his *Album Sound* jazz show on WMAL. He drove a red Thunderbird convertible and was always dapper, dressed in a suit and tie. Someone at the station once joked that Felix was so suave that he farted Old Spice.

"He was also meticulous with his impressive personal collection of jazz records. Now housed at the University of the District of Columbia. He's been credited for introducing bossa nova and reggae music to American audiences. He'd wheel the records he selected for airplay into the studio. In a small grocery cart. Sometimes, I'd find records in my box at the station that he thought I'd like.

"The engineers were constantly getting lectured on the proper way to handle his prized discs. One engineer got fed up with the nagging, took one of his more valuable records, and secretly replaced it with an old public service announcement disc. When Felix introduced the song. The engineer accidentally dropped it on the floor and rolled his chair over it. Felix nearly had a hemorrhage.

"Anyone who knew Felix well will tell you he was a loner. He had an apartment with his wife at the Watergate. Some tenants thought the floor might cave in from the weight of his record collection. Felix came and went each night with his little grocery cart and rarely socialized with the radio crew.

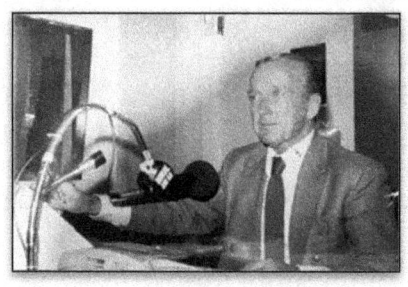

"On October 25, 1983, my co-author Steve Moore sat in with Felix during his show and taped the following candid conversation. The single interview questions were: how did you get started, and what is Felix Grant all about?

It's the most personal account."

Felix Grant: "I first saw Washington, DC, during World War Two. I was in naval boot camp in Baltimore and got a 17-hour pass. I hopped a train on a Sunday morning and walked the concourse out of Union Station. There was the capital. I couldn't believe it. There was no television in those days, so you didn't see the pictures of Washington the people are used to today. I walked the Mall, took in the Washington Monument, the Lincoln Memorial, and ended up in a little beer joint called Brownlee's.

"The second visit was in 1944, but by that time, I had spent a few years at sea in a couple of hair-raising war ventures, including getting sunk by a torpedo in the Pacific. The Navy had chosen me to give speeches for the war-planned tour as they considered me one of their war heroes. Many of the folks working in the plants were getting bored in what looked like dead end jobs. Many were drinking and losing faith that their work was meaningful. Collectively, they were slowing down the war effort. So, I went out with other war survivors to give some evidence, some incentive, that they shouldn't quit. It was effective.

"My commander was Jack Egan. Jack had been a road manager for the Tommy Dorsey Band, a former editor for Downbeat Magazine, and had lots of public relations experience. He befriended me and helped me do a minuscule amount of radio work for a Coast Guard service program on WWDC.

"Then, the war abruptly ended. We heard about the ADEM bomb. That's how I thought it was spelled A-D-E-M. But I couldn't conceive of what they were talking about. I had all the points I needed to get out of the service, and with the cheek in the door of the radio, I tried to try for a job and made the rounds of six stations in DC. I got an offer at the old WINX part time for nineteen dollars a week. Here was a job I wanted more than anything else in the world, but I had to turn it down. It was physically impossible to live in Washington on nineteen dollars a week. It really hurt me to give that one up.

"My mother had a big apartment in New York City. So, I had a place to go and to sleep. It wouldn't cost me anything, so I packed my things in my rooming house on a Friday morning, getting ready to head to New York City when the phone started ringing. In rooming houses in those days, the phone always seemed to be on another floor from where your room was. It kept ringing, so I thought I might as well go downstairs and answer it, although it wouldn't be for me.

"But it was WWDC asking me if I was still looking for a job. I got palpitations as the guy wanted to know when I could start. Come on over in the morning on Saturday, and we'll assign you something. I couldn't believe it. That phone call really changed my life and, I guess, the lives of a lot of other people who have listened to the music on my radio show over the years.

"I worked at WWDC until 1953, and then I came over to WMAL primarily because they also had a new TV studio. It seemed to me that they had more potential than the other stations. It took a salary cut—from $120 to $60 a week—to make the switch. I was sure I'd make out better in the long run, and it was the smartest move I ever made.

"The Evening Star newspaper owned WMAL, and it took me a while to figure out that the Star management was very paternalistic, and I don't mean that negatively. They felt that an employee was an integral part of the organization's whole structure and didn't put any super pressures on me. If I wanted to do something different then they'd give me enough rope to disappear over the horizon before they would ever cut it. And even then they'd have reservations, like maybe he's 'out of sight.'

"When I started doing my jazz program in 1955, I would play Ray Charles, Dinah Washington, and many acts that had never been played on Washington radio. There were some serious questions raised. I got more crap from rednecks calling me on the phone and complaining before my show. WMAL listeners had not been in the habit of hearing Billie Holiday and Louis Armstrong. Many didn't want those voices in their homes, but I never mentioned any of this on the air. I didn't share the criticisms with my listeners. I ran a one-man show and have continued for so long, but I just felt I'm responsible for what I play, and so be it.

"Playing jazz on the radio is not the easiest thing in the world. You're always looked on as the oddball. Also, the thing that has confused a lot of people is that I always spoke English. I always hated the flip-finger-snapping kind of radio jargon. Like, hey man, what's happening? One of the guys here at the station tells a story about me that never happened. He said, Yeah, I heard Felix introduce the song 'It does not mean a thing if it does not have that swing.' When I heard that story, it made me sound like a prig or ass in some respects. I didn't like the comment.

"A woman once wrote to me that she wasn't really very fond of the music I played, but she loved listening to my show. I thought, Gee, imagine listening to something you don't particularly like every night. That was kind of interesting.

"I have to be very careful so that the radio management doesn't misunderstand me or that it looks like they have no control over what I say or play. It's their radio station, and they allow me to be on the air. They tried to fire me four years ago, but it backfired on them. They thought they could withstand the flack. But the outcry at the time was so strong that they gave in. The public relations and the media made it look sensational, but if they really wanted me off, they would do it. Everybody can be replaced. "They did replace Felix Grant with John Lyon and Eddie Walker one year later. Eddie recalled. "I wouldn't have done it unless Felix was permanently fired. They were grooming John and me for the morning team. Because we thought Harden and Weaver were going to retire. But the station was sold, and station manager Andy Ockenhousen went instead. So, it never happened."

Felix Grant is credited with hosting the first radio station in the US to regularly feature Brazilian music when bossa nova began. In 1974, he traveled to Jamaica to record shows by Bob Marley and Jimmy Cliff and later played the new reggae tapes on his show.

He died of liver cancer October 12, 1993, at his home in Washington. He was seventy-four. His radio show theme song, "Tenderly," launched the start of great jazz for students, cab drivers, and his fans every evening for three decades. He had dozens of versions of "Tenderly."

Johnny Holliday

"To Tell the Truth"

"My name is Willis Conover. I'm a familiar name and a familiar voice to radio listeners around the world. From Sweden to Ceylon for an hour and a half a day, six days a week, fifty-two weeks a year, I broadcast a radio program, which can be heard in every country in the world. My audience is the largest of any international broadcast and has been estimated at some 30 million people.

"The program is called *Music, USA* and appeals mainly to the universal appetite for good jazz. Most of the music I play comes from my own personal collection of some 60,000 records. People in this country can hear the show only if they have a short-wave radio. Since the program is beamed overseas by the US Information Agency's famous **Voice of America**."

Signed, Willis Conover

Willis Clark Conover, Jr. was born in Buffalo, NY on December 18, 1920, and died in Alexandria, VA, on May 17, 1996. He was a jazz producer and broadcaster on VOA for over forty years. He produced jazz concerts at the Newport Jazz Festival and the White House and for radio and TV. People of all colors were welcomed at his shows which helped desegregate DC nightclubs.

He attended Maryland State Teacher's College in Salisbury, Maryland and first became a radio announcer for radio station WTBO in Cumberland, MD.

Conover later moved to Washington, DC, and focused on jazz in his programming, especially the *Duke Ellington Hour* on Saturday nights. He spoke slowly so people in the European countries might better understand him. As for politics he once said, "I am not trying to overthrow governments. I am just sending out something wonderfully creative and human. If it makes people living under repressive regimes stand up a little straighter, so be it."

Our thanks to **Steven Cerra** for this tribute to Willis Conover.

https://jazzprofiles.blogspot.com/2014/05/willis-conover-1920-1996-jazzs-voice-to.html

Capital Acts: Washington DC Performing Arts

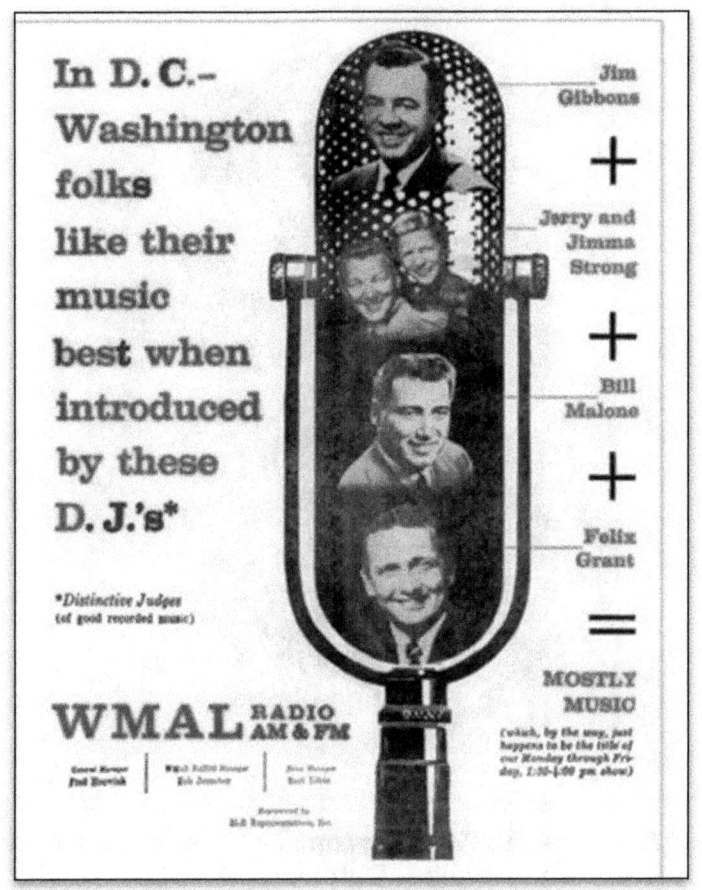

***Movie Theaters of Washington, DC* (Images of America)**
Paperback – October 15, 2018
By Robert Headley and Pat Padua

From the publisher: "This book charts the history of motion picture exhibition in the Nation's Capital. In 1894, entertainment venues were repurposed to show newfangled moving images and continued to do so through the downtown heyday of such 1920s Baroque movie palaces like the 3400 seat Fox. In the late 20th century, shoebox theaters dotted the nearby suburbs. Theaters like the Warner survived the dark days of downtown's commercial decline to be repurposed as thriving stage venues…"

This book is a reminder of the movie theaters many readers will remember. Thanks Robert and Pat !!

Chapter 12 - Mentor, Donn B. Murphy

Young Warren Beatty with Donn in 1958. © D. B. Murphy

I first met Donn B. Murphy, Professor of Theatre in the Fine Arts Department at Georgetown University, in 1983. I then worked across campus as a research assistant for the Department of Physiology at GU's Medical Center. Father Gilbert Hartke had suggested I meet Donn to discuss my Capital Acts book idea.

Already a founding member of the non-profit National Theatre Corporation established in 1974, the stage was always at the center of Dr. Murphy's life. With a PhD in Theatre and Psychology earned on a Ford Foundation Fellowship at the University of Wisconsin-Madison, Donn began his story about his early time in the city.

"I came to Washington in 1954 to study at Catholic University with Father Hartke. The Shubert Theatre (located at 10th and F Street) was open then, and Arena Stage operated at its original location. Catholic University was going full speed and being reviewed regularly as one of the major theatres in the city. I worked as an usher and later weekend ticket taker at the Shubert Theatre. But I used to scout around all the equivalent of 'Off-Broadway' theaters. I was in every church basement that had a theater in DC.

"*The Amen Corner* by James Baldwin was first performed in a hot upper-floor room at Howard University, with black cloth tacked over the windows. An audience of no more than a hundred people seeing this emotional, complex Black play. The world premiere of *The Amen Corner*. The play about the church's role in Afro-American family life was Baldwin's first work for the stage following the success of his novel *Go Tell It On the Mountain*. Actor Marlon Brando helped Baldwin financially to write this play, and Murphy assessed there was no sense then that government money should be used to support the arts in DC, or anywhere else at that time.

"After I began teaching at Georgetown, I took over the Mask & Bauble Dramatic Society, one of the country's oldest [student] acting groups at more than 150 years. I arrived just after Eileen Brennan had appeared. It was a student organization that I directed for twenty years. We turned out several people who went on to Broadway from Georgetown. One of them is John Guare, who won the Tony Award for his play The House of Blue Leaves. The other was Jack Hofsiss, the youngest person to win a Tony Award for directing *The Elephant Man*. He first directed Stage One in our little black box theater in Georgetown. It's like a theater lobby, one hundred seats maximum, stuck in the basement of a temporary building beside the boiler room. The students like John and Jack could have free reign with their imaginations to do whatever they wanted."

Dr. Murphy was quick to applaud the many successes of actors he met there. "The same place where two young men, Gerome Ragni, and James Rado, from New York, came down, went to school here in the 1950s and returned to make a name for themselves on Broadway." The pair went on to write the production and thirteen song lyrics for a show about hippie counterculture and the Vietnam War, handing the material to Canadian composer Galt MacDermott, who set the lyrics to music in just three weeks. Their collective work became the Broadway hit, *Hair: The American Tribal Love-Rock Musical*.

Murphy continued, "Other people from Georgetown include William Blatty, author of the 1971 novel *The Exorcist*, who received his bachelor's degree in English from Georgetown in 1950. His book was set in the Georgetown environment. This gave the students quite a thrill during that filming year, 1973.

They looked out their dorm windows every night and saw the smoke pots making fog around the bedeviled house. Actors of the caliber of Max Von Sydow are practicing their lines, and Ellen Burstyn is roaming the campus in makeup. It was a pretty hectic fall. I was in a mob scene. I think all of us probably worked one scene or another. And we all watched the stunts, the fellow jumping out the windows and crashing down the steps."

The Exorcist "stairs" still make for a cult attraction in Georgetown. Donn also did notable work outside DC, combining his performing arts and psychology background. From 1960-1979 at the Chestnut Lodge Psychoanalytic Hospital in Rockville, MD, Dr. Murphy conducted a theater workshop for patients where he produced and directed plays including *A View from the Bridge*, *The Glass Menagerie*, *John Brown's Body*, and *The Importance of Being Ernest*. In the 1970s, with Kathleen Barry at Work Trap National Park for the Performing Arts, he wrote, directed, produced, designed, and appeared in five interactive children's programs.

As my long talk with Donn the first time we met was ending—I had to get back to work—he shared some surprising news.

"I'll be President of the National Theatre this April first," he announced. I congratulated him and returned to my lab across campus. As I walked in, the phone rang at my desk. It was Donn.

"Steve," he said, "You seemed so nervous talking to me. Do you need some help with this history project?"

I rapidly responded, "Yes," in total disbelief.

Donn enthusiastically agreed to help my biographical exploration of talented but overlooked local performers, and we soon became best friends and a successful writing team.

Birth of the Kennedy Center

Before she became The First Lady of Camelot, Jacqueline Kennedy was a regular neighbor in Georgetown. The young newlywed and her Senator husband lived in a comfortable three-story townhouse at 3321 Dent Street near the University, where she took continuing education classes in American history. A regular sight in the upscale part of Washington, in 1957, the growing Kennedy family moved nearby to a large house at 3307 N Street, where Jack later announced his run for the Presidency.

Professor Murphy recalled his fateful encounter with Mrs. Kennedy: "One day in the late 1950s, I was in the hall when the college students, especially a few young women, said, 'Oh look out the window, there he comes, there he comes. And that's Jackie.' I had no idea who they were talking about. I was so immersed in theatre directing at Georgetown and teaching that I was not up on politics. They said I'd have to look. And it was Senator John Kennedy walking along the sidewalk inside the GU gates. I can see him now with a coat collar turned up. The dark Navy, probably cashmere coat with his hands thrust in the pockets. And then, some paces behind him, this lovely woman pushing a little child. It would have been Caroline in the stroller. The students said we had to talk to him.

"We all went out to greet them and say hello. Senator Kennedy asked what sort of work we did, and we told him. 'Why are you all here on a Sunday?' he asked. 'We are working on a play.' He was very interested in that, and apparently, Mrs. Kennedy as well, who tucked that in the back of her mind because after he was elected President, I got a call from the White House saying that Mrs. Kennedy wanted to do theater performances in the East Room of the White House and would like some technical assistance. Could I lend a hand? She asked.

"Of course, I was happy to do so, and we talked about how we could make a stage arrangement and have it properly lighted for performances. The Park Service developed a subtle but attractive stage with dark, maroon plush wings. The stage surface was black canvas, and the whole thing was dignified and beautiful. It was difficult for the performers because there was such little wing space and because the ballet dancers used to hit their heads on the chandelier. They didn't remove the giant crystal at the bottom. The students came along to help with the lighting in the White House, and of course, that was a tremendous treat for them because they would all be hiding backstage during the performances."

Mrs. Kennedy wrote a letter to Georgetown in 1961 to personally thank Donn Murphy and the Mask and Bauble Society, "for the tremendous effort you put into the production of The Magic Flute. As always, you did a wonderful job." Mask and Bauble became the official lighting and production crew for theatre, ballet, and opera in the White House until the end of the Johnson administration, the lucky students setting up sets for Shakespeare dramas and later in black tie, mingling with DC's political elite in the Chief Executive Mansion.

"When the performances ended and the guests were served champagne, the Kennedys always ensured that a butler brought the students a tray of champagne. Afterward, they would be invited to stay for the party, and some of the young ladies got to dance with President Kennedy, which was a great thrill. So those were beautiful times, and we saw and met many celebrities.

"My pride was to be able to drive my black Mustang convertible up 1600 Pennsylvania Avenue, and they would know I was coming, and there would be a little wave. The gates would open, and I could park right in that front circle before the White House. It was only on certain afternoons when we prepared for the performance, but that was quite a thrill.

"One evening, we helped with the performance of the Jerome Robbins Ballet. Once all the stage lights were up, the students and I were backstage. Little gilt chairs were set up for the dinner guests. But the students and I didn't presume to take chairs. We stood in the back and hoped we wouldn't be distracting or too noticed. We thought we'd stay in the back in the window wells and watch the show. Suddenly, Tish Baldridge, the White House social secretary, a very tall and commanding woman, swept into the room, looked at us, and said, 'Oh, all you people come with me.' And she ushered us all into the adjoining Red Room and closed the sliding door.

"So, we were sequestered in trying to make light, small talk. But furious that we had been moved out of the East Room. We were going to miss the performance. We couldn't admit we were quite disappointed. We could hear the guests coming out to dinner. Then suddenly, Tish appeared at the other sliding doors, which opened not into the East Room but into the Great Hall.

"We found that we had become the receiving line for the guests that included the Shah of Iran. I spoke to him as he and the President moved through. The Shah was moving on to the next person when a light lit in President Kennedy's mind. He remembered who I was. The butler was telling him the names of the people, but he hadn't connected me. Once Kennedy realized this, he reached across the Shah and said, 'Oh, and by the way, we want to thank you so much for all the work you have done to make the theatricals possible.'

"I still admire the man because most of us, if we remembered the name and had moved on down the receiving line, would have thought, well, an opportunity missed. However, President Kennedy was a man who simply didn't miss an opportunity. And I thought how bright and brilliant of him, under the stress of that night, with the Shah of Iran as his guest, to care enough about my contribution.

"Then came the wife of the Shah of Iran, wearing in her hair a diadem of emeralds, which were as big as small eggs. We read about this in the story books when they said she wore a jewelry crown.

"Jackie was next in line in a gorgeous white dress with her hair in one of those enormous beehives she made famous. And she had only one piece of jewelry in her hair above her forehead. It was a sunburst of tiny diamonds. And that one thing somehow balanced the emeralds. That's a memory of an evening in Washington that I will never forget."

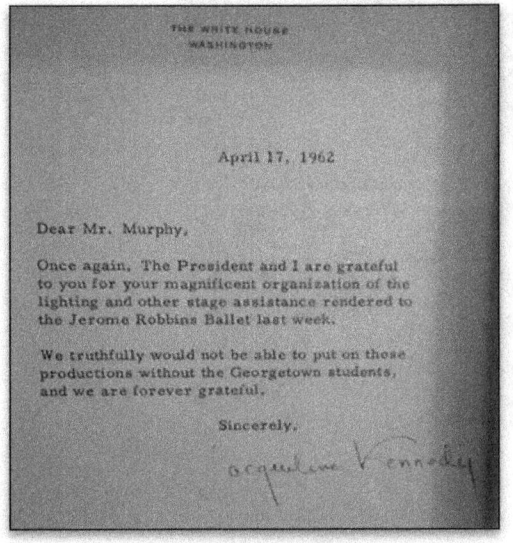

Photo: A thank you from the First Lady:
© D.B. Murphy

> Dear Mr. Murphy,
>
> Once again, The President and I are grateful to you and your magnificent organization of the lighting and other stage assistance rendered to the Jerome Robbins Ballet last week.
>
> We truthfully would not be able to put on these productions without the Georgetown students and we are forever grateful.
>
> Sincerely, Jacqueline Kennedy

With Margaret and Donn at the
Helen Hayes Tribute in 1991.
© Emma Schwarz

Chapter 13 - Brooke Johns, Vaudevillian.

When I first met Brooke Johns in 1986, there were boxes of yellowing press clippings, old photos, and vaudeville memorabilia crowding his stately house on the grounds of his Brooke Manor Country Club "eighteen miles from the White House" he would say.

Brooke's Maryland domain was 207 acres surrounding his seventeen-room mansion, with an eighteen-hole golf course and cool clubhouse a few yards away. He lunched each noon in the expansive dining hall of his club.

He was our local world-renowned vaudevillian who retired in 1930 to what was then the countryside of Olney, Maryland. On my first visit I noted several old cars in various stages of renewal, hundreds of crowing chickens, at least a hundred neatly organized neckties (he showed me in his bedroom), and a framed banjo head autographed by President Calvin Coolidge and "Edward P," the Prince of Wales, later King Edward VIII (Brooke's "music buddy," he would say). The Prince who abdicated the throne in 1936 enjoyed playing drums with Brooke strumming the banjo in the roaring Twenties.

He was discovered in Miami Beach when a New York Times photographer captured him playing banjo for some bathing beauties. The picture was published up north promoting Miami for tourists. It wasn't long before he was playing in the *Ziegfeld Follies*.

And Brooke Johns was one Washington, DC, entertainer who refused to fade into the past. Governor Harry Hughes named the Rockville, Maryland, resident Goodwill Ambassador for the state of Maryland, an honorary degree recognizing achievement in the arts. Hughes commented that Johns had done a "remarkable job of spreading joy and good feelings."

The former *Ziegfeld Follies* star and banjo player had celebrated his 91st birthday on Christmas Eve with the release of a record *Return to the Roaring Twenties* on the local WEBCO label.

Johns spoke at length about his friendships with Al Jolson, Will Rogers, and Eddie Cantor. He went on tour during the next few years, taking the American Vaudeville stages "by strum." His RCA-Victor recordings of his hits as "Hard-hearted Hannah" and "Tessie, Stop Teasin' Me." It was Eddie Cantor who heard Brooke decline a showgirl's teasing that suggested he write a song about it.

Brooke's vivid memory recreated the excitement of a recording session in the medium's earliest days. "Six men would be running around the studio with microphones trying to capture the orchestra properly, and the manager would stop us with a loud whistle if things weren't going right."

Brooke with Eddie Cantor in the 1920's and a
1925 program for B. F. Keith's Theater for Christmas

However, the old banjo man was quite at home in the laid-back ambiance of a modern recording studio. "It's a very relaxing and pleasurable place for a historic old duck like me," he said.

I was there when Johns recorded this album with backup from accordionist Carmelo Pino, banjoist George Johnson, and vocal harmony by Taffy Danoff. The WEBCO studio was owned and operated by Wayne Busbice, brother of "Buzz" Busby, the Washington, DC, pioneering mandolinist.

Although a damaged nerve in his hand kept Johns from strumming his own banjo in his later years, it remained his most prized possession.. A lifelong Republican, Brooke told me that he was planning to get his old friends Richard Nixon, Gerald Ford, and Ronald Reagan to sign it, too. However, he boasted it was still "the most valuable banjo in the world, but with these politicians' signatures on it, I doubt if you could ever tune it properly again."

George, Wayne, Brooke, Taffy, John Taylor, Steve, Carmello © S. Moore

Hearing these plans repeatedly to get the banjo head signed during subsequent visits to his club—he gave my wife and I memberships to his club—I finally asked him, "Well, how are you going to do that?" He didn't know. So, I wrote letters to each of them on Georgetown University letterhead. It took me two months, but I was able to get Reagan, Ford, and Nixon to sign the banjo head. President Reagan was the most enthusiastic because he not only remembered Johns from his youth, he was a big fan.

I called the *Washington Post* and shared this tale to columnist John Kelly when President Reagan died. John used my story for his column, and we began our friendship then. The URL for the story is:
https://www.washingtonpost.com/archive/lifestyle/2004/06/15/the-presidents-and-the-banjo/70646d2e-3e3a-417d-bbb7-25be3672a258/

In 1924, Brooke Johns with screen star Gloria Swanson starred in a ground-breaking silent film called Manhandled, a serious story about the New York City life of a "shop girl" whose life changes when invited to a high society party. The movie is remarkably fresh for a 1924 relic, with a party scene a highlight—offering some fun as Brooke John strums his banjo while partner, Ann Pennington offers lively dancing in their cameo appearance.

The American Film Institute chose *Manhandled* starring Gloria Swanson for their silent film series held at the Kennedy Center and invited Brooke as their special guest to the screening. Before the film began, Brooke was introduced to the crowd and received a standing ovation. It was a wonderful moment. Another big ovation from the crowd erupted when Brooke and Ann's scene ended.

I knew Brook Johns and had visited him at his home with a friend. We accompanied Brooke to the screening. Brooke was so busy in his vaudeville heyday with Pennington that he'd never seen the film. In the car on the way back, he grinned, "Ann and I were pretty good!" The audience at the Kennedy Center agree.

Charles D. Young

Brooke and Ann Pennington © Courtesy Hazel johns

Brooke with the framed banjo head signed by The Prince of Wales, and Presidents Coolidge, Nixon, Ford, and Reagan.
© S. Moore

Christmas *B.F. Keith's Theater News*.
Hazel Johns and Margaret Moore the day the banjo
and banjo head were all signed.

Chapter 14 - Sir Duke

Edward Kennedy Ellington was born in Washington, DC, on April 29, 1899. His parents instilled in him the belief that he had the power to accomplish anything. Therefore, Ellington disregarded limitations and transcended genres to become one of America's most eminent composers.

His parents were part of DC's burgeoning Black middle class. Mother, Daisy, the daughter of former slaves, occasionally worked as a maid for Washington's socialites. James, his father, was a butler for the wealthy Cuthbert family and, for a brief time, worked to make blueprints for the US Navy. With parental insistence on proper formal education, church attendance, and respectable dress and manner, Ellington was exposed early to the world-class sophistication and cosmopolitan life of the nation's capital.

His father once catered at the White House. Elegant meals and fine performances were expected at home; both parents played piano, and when having one in the home itself was a marker of class, the Ellington's had two. With his parents' firm upbringing in manners and appearance, the well-dressed youngster eventually got his nickname "Duke" from a childhood friend for his consistently dapper style.

At age fourteen, Ellington discovered Frank Holiday's Billiards, next door to the Howard Theatre. He quickly became familiar with dozens of talented pianists at the pool parlor, including Henry Grant, Doc Perry, Gertie Wells, and Eubie Blake. Soon bored with the music he easily replicated and inspired by his job as a soda jerk at the Dog Café on 7th street, he wrote his first composition, the rollicking "Soda Fountain Rag."

In his memoir *Music is My Mistress*, he said, "I'd play it as a one-step, two-step, waltz, tango, and fox trot. My listeners never knew it was the same piece."

 Ellington worked after school in 1915. Thirty-four years later, he's on the cover of *Time* magazine.

Like most city youth, Ellington quickly became caught up in the World War I dance craze, steps epitomized by the Foxtrot or frenetic Charleston. Instead of pursuing training in design, Ellington gave up his art scholarship at Armstrong High School to start playing piano for dancing at clubs, dances, and parties. Ellington later confessed to skipping more music lessons than he attended. The prodigy perhaps felt that the piano was not his most remarkable talent. In many ways, he was proved right. Ellington's true genius was manifest in producing over two thousand astounding musical compositions, simultaneously organizing, and playing in his eponymous orchestras on multiple world tours to universal acclaim.

Despite his parents' lessons in social elegances, near his home on Ward Place (now 22nd Street NW) Duke quickly became familiar with dozens of talented pianists at the pool parlor, including Henry Grant, Doc Perry, Gertie Wells, and Eubie Blake. Soon bored with the music, he easily replicated it.

From his early days performing in Washington, Ellington was already reaching for a new level of complexity, artistry, and sophistication that redefined the popular associations of "degradant" jazz music. Though a talented pianist, rather than just a performing musician, Ellington thought of himself foremost as a composer, like another DC "capital act" that made jazz the quintessential American creation, Jelly Roll Morton.

By his early 20s, Ellington had established his four-piece combo, Duke's Serenaders. The band featured greats, including Otto Hardwick (bass/sax), Arthur Whetsel (trumpet), Sonny Greer (drums), and Elmer Snowden (banjo). Their first performance was at the True Reformers Hall, an African American fraternal organization only a few blocks from

Ellington's home. The spacious, well-appointed venue on the corner of 7th and T Street, where Ellington, Snowden, and other DC musicians often congregated, was designed by Washington's first African American registered architect, John Anderson Lankford.

The Serenaders played gigs around the capital city, including pre-performance supper shows at the Howard Theatre, where Sonny Greer had been in the pit band. By 1918, as the nation's capital danced its way into the Jazz Age, Duke's Serenaders was a fixture in the lively nightclubs on U Street and played dance parties almost nightly in Southwest DC near the waterfront. With bootleggers and brawls at these dances, interruptions where frequent, and once in 1921 playing at Georgetown's Odd Fellows Hall, a large fight broke out and Ellington's band had to make a quick exit. Undaunted, Ellington refined his musical skills in "battle of the bands" held at the Lincoln Colonnade. But in 1922, when Ellington got an offer from Wilbur Sweatman to play with him in New York City, he rapidly headed up to where he knew the "real" jazz scene was happening, eventually settling in Harlem.

Unfortunately, the first trip to the Big Apple was not successful, with few booked engagements, so Ellington briefly returned to DC, gathered up a few of the Serenaders, and returned to New York in 1923, now playing as the group Elder Snowden's Washington Black Socks Orchestra. But it only took a few months before banjoist Snowden was forced out over financial disagreements, and Ellington was selected as the band's new front man.

Briefly redubbed as The Washingtonians, they usually played at the Hollywood Club in Manhattan, later changed to The Kentucky Club. In turn, the band renamed itself Duke Ellington and his Kentucky Club Orchestra, with the fantastic trumpeter Bubber Miley adding his unique muted style.

It began as the Atlantic Building at 9th and V Street, N.W in 1888, the largest commercial structure in the city and one of the first with a passenger elevator. The National Zoo idea was born at a meeting in this building. A "grand opening" ad of the Music Hall ran on January 12, 1948, featuring Louis Armstrong. It was briefly owned by Duke Ellington before. It became the home to WUST 1120 AM Radio in the fifties, and then the 9:30 Club in the 1980s. Today it is the Atlantis.

As the Roaring Twenties took hold, Duke Ellington made New York his primary location for recording and performing in large venues like The Cotton Club and The Apollo. It is vital to point out that Ellington became a major musical force during the Harlem Renaissance, a new Black consciousness of cultural, social, and political power after the Great War. Ellington's trombonist, Joe "Tricky Sam" Nanton, was a noted advocate of Marcus Garvey, a Black activist leader of the Pan-African movement that attracted many middle-class African Americans. Ellington's jazz compositions reflected the creative surge of new Black art music and poetry from Harlem.

By nurturing his hometown connections in Washington, Ellington brought the fruits of the Harlem Renaissance back to the capital city. Returning often to see family and perform, many people turned out to see Duke playing at Murray Casino, a lively nightspot on U Street, The Lincoln Colonnade, or his familiar place, the Howard Theater. Many African American youth in DC began to copy Ellington's manners and dress style, impressed by his elegance and confident stage presence, along with his orchestras' consistently sharp formal attire. Ellington brought a new, modern kind of sophistication back to Washington, intertwining classical European elements of Debussy and Revel learned from his mentor, jazz pianist Henry

Grant, with the contemporary urban complexities of orchestrated jazz, instilling new sensibilities to American music.

For his native city of Washington, Ellington's compositions had a unique appeal to the cosmopolitan, social, and cultural aspirations of DC audiences. The Duke Ellington Society of Washington, a scholarly international fan club, was founded in 1959. A PBS documentary *Duke Ellington's Washington* was released in 2000.
https://www.pbs.org/ellingtonsdc/theDocumentary.htm

Duke Ellington's genius brought his music learned from the barrelhouses and socialites' estates of DC to the world. Ellington died on May 24, 1974, from lung cancer shortly after his 75th birthday. Twelve thousand people attended his funeral at the Cathedral of Saint John the Divine in New York, and he was buried in the Bronx next to his parents.

Will Marion Cook

Born in 1869, he was the son of John Harwell Cook, the Dean of Howard University Law School.

Both parents were Oberlin graduates. At age fifteen, he began violin studies and composition at Oberlin Conservatory.

With the support of abolitionist, orator, and statesman Frederick Douglass and members of the First Congressional Church, money was raised for Cook to attend the School of Music Hanns Eisler Berlin in September 1890.

An early African American newspaper noted the formation of a new Washington, DC, orchestra with Frederick Douglass as president and Willie Cook as director. However, it failed within a year.

In 1898 Cook composed the musical *Clorindy: The Origin of the Cakewalk* in collaboration with poet Paul Laurence

Dunbar. According to *DC Jazz: Stories of Jazz Music in Washington, DC*, Co-authors Maurice Jackson and Blair A. Rumble explain, "(Cook and Dunbar) got together in the basement of a rented house on 2232 Sixth Street NW just below Howard University at about 8:00 p.m., where without a piano or anything but the kitchen table, the composition was finished—all of the songs and the libretto and all but a few bars of the ensemble—by 4:00 a.m. the following day."

Cook was critical to the early development of Duke Ellington, both in Washington and after he moved to New York. In his autobiography, *Music is My Mistress*, Ellington wrote, "Well, Marion Cook, His Majesty the King of Consonants. I can see him now with that beautiful mane of white hair flowing in the breeze as he and I rode uptown through Central Park. When I was browsing around Broadway, trying to contact with my music, I would run into Dad Cook."

One of Duke Ellington's most enduring legacies is the **Duke Ellington School for the Arts** (DESA), located two blocks from Georgetown University. The school was founded in 1974 by activists and artists Mike Malone and Peggy Cooper-Cafritz. Their main goal was to provide equal opportunity and access to literature, art, music, and dance education for the talented youth of DC, regardless of background or ability to pay. Notable graduates include: Comedian **Dave Chappelle**, activist **Angela Davis**, R&B singer **Johnny Gill**, actor **Corey Hawkins**, dancer **Tracy Inman**, singer **Ari Lennox**, trumpeter **Wallace Roney**, author **Adam Serwer**, singer **Tony Terry**, and actress **Samira Wiley**.

Other Duke Ellington School Alumni include:
Taraji P. Henson - Award-winning actress, known for her roles in films such as *Hidden Figures* and the TV series *Empire*.
Samuel L. Jackson - Legendary actor, known for his roles in films like *Pulp Fiction* and *The Avengers*.
Chris Dave - Renowned drummer and producer, known for his work with artists such as D'Angelo and Adele.
Phylicia Rashad - Actress and director, best recognized for her role as Claire Huxtable on *The Cosby Show*.

Capital Acts: Washington DC Performing Arts

Ossie Davis - Actor, playwright, and civil rights activist, known for his involvement in numerous films and plays.
Meshell Ndegeocello - Grammy-nominated singer, songwriter, and bassist.
Tinashe - Singer, songwriter, and actress, known for hits like "2 On" and "All Hands on Deck."
Tituss Burgess - Emmy-nominated actor and singer, known for his role in the TV series *Unbreakable Kimmy Schmidt*.
Eric Benét - R&B singer-songwriter, known for hits like "Spend My Life with You" and "Chocolate Legs."
Jason Moran - Jazz pianist and composer, recipient of numerous awards, including a MacArthur Fellowship.
Renée Elise Goldsberry - Tony Award-winning actress and singer, known for her role as Angelica Schuyler in the musical *Hamilton*.
Daveed Diggs - Tony Award-winning actor and rapper, known for originating the role of Marquis de Lafayette/Thomas Jefferson in the musical *Hamilton*.
Lamman Rucker - Actor, known for his roles in TV shows like Tyler Perry's *Meet the Browns* and *Greenleaf*.

Jerry Seinfeld and Dave Chappelle walking next to the big chair outside the Duke Ellington School.

© Comedians in Cars Getting Coffee.

"You know, when I was growing up, I was probably about eight years old, and at the time, we were living in Silver Spring. Yeah. Yes. Common misconception about me and DC, a lot of people think I'm from the 'hood.' That's not true. But I never bothered to correct anybody... because I wanted the streets to embrace me. As a matter of fact, I kept it up as a ruse. To be honest, when (friends) talked about the projects, I used to get jealous. Because it sounded fun. Everybody in the projects was poor, and that's fair. But if you were poor in Silver Spring, it felt like it was only happening to you."

Dave Chappelle
Double Feature

Blanche Calloway

Born in Baltimore, Maryland, on February 9, 1902, Blanche Calloway was a charismatic and remarkable performer known for her vibrant personality and distinctive stage presence. She significantly influenced her younger brother, **Cab Calloway**, who became an internationally renowned jazz musician; it was Cab who inspired **Billy Eckstine** to impersonate him at the Howard Theater talent show.

Blanche's journey began at Morgan College, which she left to tour with various cabaret groups. In 1921, she made her professional debut in "Shuffle Along," the first all-Black musical hit on Broadway.

Blanche formed her own orchestra in the 1920s and 1930s becoming the first African American female to conduct an all-male Jazz orchestra.

Her first recordings in 1925 with her Joy Boys included a young Louis Armstrong on his Cornet playing songs she wrote herself, including "Lonesome Lovesick Blues."

Intermission - Native Cast

The DC area has steadily nurtured a solid number of actors and actresses who have impressed audiences on stages and screens. Many of our hometown thespians have captured the spotlight worldwide. Some were natives and some simply born to run elsewhere to make their mark. Join us on this star-studded journey as we present the charm and charisma of some of our talented neighbors who called the District of Columbia area once their own.

Edwin Booth (November 13, 1833 – June 7, 1893) toured throughout the United States and the major capitals of Europe, performing Shakespearean plays. Introduced to acting by his London-born actor father, Junius, his actor brother was assassin John Wilkes. They were raised on a farm in Hartford County. Some theatrical historians consider him the greatest American actor.

Edmund Flaherty, known as Pat Flaherty, was born on March 8, 1897, and attended Eastern High School on 17th and East Capital Streets. A popular DC athlete he went on to Princeton and served in the US Army as a pilot in World War One. He next played both professional baseball and football, notably in the 1921 World Series for the New York Giants and kicked for the Chicago Bears.

Following sports, Pat Flaherty befriended Joseph Kennedy, JFK's dad, who was then making much money by reorganizing and refinancing several Hollywood studios. Kennedy hired Flaherty as a studio producer who parleyed that opportunity to a successful film career racking up supporting roles—usually muscle-bound—in more than 200 films. These include *Mutiny on the Bounty* (1935), *Sergeant York* (1941), *Yankee Doodle Dandy* (1942), and *The Pride of the Yankees* (1942).

At Eastern High School and in the movies. © KSPD

In 1943 he returned to service as a US Marine captain in the Korean War. After that it was many more movies including playing a policeman in ten films, including *Harvey*. He passed away in 1970 from a heart attack.

Publicity shot, White House visit, and Glinda. © PD

Mary William Ethelbert Appleton Burke (August 7, 1884 – May 14, 1970) found fame in silent and sound movies, on Broadway, and in radio as **Billie Burke**, taking the name of her internationally famous clown father.

The future actress, born "somewhere around K Street," would spend most of her early years touring European circuses with her Dad before her family settled in London. Billie, the actress, returned to her native DC on November 10, 1927, while appearing at the National Theatre in Noel Coward's *The Marquise*, visited President Calvin Coolidge and First Lady Grace at the White

House to thank them for having attended the previous night's performance.

Ms. Burke was glad to be "back again with the home folks" in Washington; she told the press, "It is thrilling to think I am able to tread the same walks once sauntered by Lincoln."

It was in the comedy drama, *Dinner at Eight* (1933), that Billie would find the character that she would play the rest of her career. It is the hapless, feather-brained lady with the unmistakably high voice who would be more interested in little details than what was at hand. She married Florenz Ziegfeld, the American Broadway impresario.

Maryland's vaudevillian, Brooke Johns reported that when Ziegfeld's safe was opened following his death of pleurisy in 1932, his wife discovered it empty. He had lost his wealth in the stock market crash of 1929. Billie needed to work as an actress to pay the bills. She is today immortalized as the good witch Glinda in the classic *Wizard of Oz* film.

Rufus Mackahan; b. Feb. 10, 1899 in Washington, DC. **Alan Hale Sr.** studied to be an opera singer and is best remembered as the sidekick to the famed Errol Fynn, and father of Alan Hale Jr., the skipper in TV's *Gilligan's Island*.

Helen Hayes MacArthur nee Brown; October 10, 1900 – March 17, 1993 (See Chapter 21)

John Astin, b. March 30, 1930, in Baltimore, MD. His father, Allen Varley Astin, was a physicist director of the National Bureau of Standards. The actor's family lived on Battery Lane in Bethesda, Maryland. He studied drama at John Hopkins university and is remembered today as Gomez in *The Addams Family* TV series and/or Patty Duke's ex-husband.

Alison Hayes, Born Mary Jane Hayes in Charlestown, WV, on March 6, 1930. She moved to DC and was in the class of 1948 at Calvin Coolidge High School. She won the title of Miss District of Columbia and represented DC in the 1949 Miss America pageant. She played lead in the 1958 film, *The Attack of the 50 Foot Woman*.

Frances Sternhagen (January 13, 1930 – November 27, 2023). Her mom was a homemaker who served as a nurse during World War I. Her father was tax court judge John M. Sternhagen. Educated at the Madeira and Potomac Schools in McLean, VA, she went on to work at Washington's Arena Stage from 1953-1954, and then made her Broadway debut in 1955 as Miss T. Muse in *The Skin of Our Teeth*.

Dolores Conchita Figueroa del Rivero (Jan. 23, 1933 – Jan. 30, 2024), known professionally as **Chita Rivera**. She was the daughter of Katherine (née Anderson), a government clerk, and Pedro Julio Figueroa del Rivero, a clarinetist and saxophonist for the U.S. Navy Band She co-starred as Anita in the first West Side Story run in Washington, DC a critical and commercial success.

Madlyn Rhue (née Madeline Roche) b. Oct. 3, 1935 – Dec. 16, 2003) was a film and television actress born in DC. Despite multiple sclerosis she appeared in films and many TV series such as *Rawhide* (1959), *Cheyenne* (1955), *Star Trek* (1966,) *Hawaii Five-O* (1966), and *Fantasy Island* (1977 including performances in a wheelchair.

Michael Learned (b. April 9, 1939) is an actress, known for her role as Olivia Walton in the long-running CBS drama series *The Waltons* (1972–1981).

David Birney (April 23, 1939 – April 27, 2022) was an American actor and director.

Bonnie Blair Brown (b. April 23, 1946) is an American theater, film, and television actress.

Charles Elmer Taylor Jr. was born in DC on January 13, 1931. He attended the Congressional Page school until he served in the Korean War. He became the comedian, **Rip Taylor**.

Peter Thorkelson was born at DC's Doctor's Hospital on Feb 13, 1942. His father, Jack, was an economist and the family lived in a stately house on 16th Street, NW. They moved to Detroit when Peter was a year old.

> **Peter Tork** became a Monkee. They both appeared together on one *The Monkee's* TV episode.

Edward Kirk Herrmann (July 21, 1943 – December 31, 2014) was an actor, director, and writer. He was known for his portrayals of Franklin D. Roosevelt in both the miniseries *Eleanor and Franklin* (1976) and 1982 film musical *Annie*, Richard Gilmore in Amy Sherman-Palladino's comedy-drama series *Gilmore Girls* (2000–2007), and a ubiquitous narrator for historical programs on The History Channel and in such PBS productions as *Nova*.

Benjamin Jeremy Stein (b. November 25, 1944) is a writer, lawyer, actor, comedian, and commentator on political and economic issues. He began his career as a speechwriter for U.S. presidents Richard Nixon and Gerald Ford before entering the entertainment field as an actor, comedian, and game show host. He was Mr. Rooney in *Ferris Bueller's Day Off*.

Leigh Taylor-Young (b. January 25, 1945) is an actress who has appeared on stage, screen, podcast, radio, and television. Her most well-known films include *I Love You, Alice B. Toklas* (1968), *The Horsemen* (1971), *The Gang That Couldn't Shoot Straight* (1971), *Soylent Green* (1973), and *Jagged Edge* (1985). She won an Emmy for her role on the hit television series *Picket Fences*.

Goldie Jeanne Hawn (b. in DC November 21, 1945) and raised in Takoma Park, MD, is an American actress. Goldie's dad was Edward Rutledge Hawn, a DC musician and conductor who was a descendent of the youngest signer of the Declaration of Independence, E. R. Rutledge. Her Mom was Laura Steinhoff, a jewelry shop/dance school owner. They lived in a brick duplex and Goldie's wedding reception with first husband, Gus Trikonis, an actor and director, was held in the back yard.

Goldie graduated from the old Blair High School in Silver Spring, MD, in 1963: "I used to ride my bike there all the time and I knew all the cracks in the pavement... Gifford's, the best sundaes in the world." Goldie said in a 2002 documentary film *Silver Spring: Story of an American Suburb*. She attended American University in DC.

Bonnie Blair Brown (b. April 23, 1946) is an actress with high-profile roles including the play Copenhagen on Broadway, the film

Altered State, and the title character in the TV series *The Days and Nights of Molly Dodd*, running from 1987 to 1991.

John Heard (March 7, 1946 – July 21, 2017) was an actor, a son of Helen (Sperling), a member of the Art's Club. She also appeared in community theatre. Her husband, John Heard Sr., worked for the Secretary of Defense office.

The son graduated from Gonzaga High School in 1964 and entered Catholic University studying for a Masters, while working as a plumber's assistant. However, he dropped out of CU for acting full time, including in productions at Arena Stage. He told the press, "I was lazy and was just looking for a way to make a living, I guess, and I decided I didn't want to teach drama, I wanted to do it."

His film credits, including *Big*, *The Trip to Bountiful*, and *Deceived*, are impressive and lengthy. He became part of our culture after playing the forgetful father in *Home Alone* and its sequel.

Jonathan Banks (b. January 31, 1947) is an actor raised in Chillum Heights, MD. His mom once worked as a secretary for the CIA. He graduated from Northwood High in Silver Spring, MD, and was classmates with Kevin Kline at Indiana University. His many film roles from 1974 to the present include *Stir Crazy*, *Airplane*, *Beverly Hills Cop*, and *Without a Trace*. His TV role of Frank McPike in the series "Wiseguy" earned him an Emmy nomination.

Robert Hays (b. July 24, 1947) is an actor, known for a variety of television and film roles since the 1970s. He came to prominence around 1980, co-starring in the two-season domestic sitcom *Angie* and playing the central role of pilot Ted Striker in the hit spoof film *Airplane* and its sequel. He was raised in Bethesda, MD.

Samuel Jackson (b. Dec. 21, 1948) is one of the most widely recognized actors of his generation, with films he's done collectively grossing over $27 billion worldwide, perhaps the highest-grossing actor ever. However, baby Samuel didn't stay in DC for long, and moved with his family to Chattanooga, Tennessee where he was raised.

Debra Monk (b. February 27, 1949) Monk was born in Middletown, Ohio, but was voted "Best Personality" by her graduating class at Wheaton High School in Silver Spring, MD. In 1973, she graduated from Frostburg State University. Monk was awarded a Master of Fine Arts from Southern Methodist University in Dallas, Texas. Monk garnered first attention in theatrical circles as one of the co-writers and co-stars of the musical *Pump Boys and Dinettes* (1982). She won the Tony Award for Best Featured Actress in a Play for performance in *Redwood Curtain* (1993). She was nominated for a Tony Award for roles in *Picnic* (1994), *Steel Pier* (1997), and *Curtains* (2007). In 2000, she won an Obie Award for *The Time of the Cuckoo*.

William Hurt (b. in DC March 20, 1950 – March 13, 2022) was an American actor. His Dad worked for the state department. He received various awards including an Academy Award, BAFTA Award, and Cannes Films Festival Award for Best Actor, but had few adventures in DC.

Robert Wisdom (b. September 14, 1953) is an actor. He is known for his roles as Howard "Bunny" Colvin in *The Wire*, Norman "Lechero" Saint John in *Prison Break*, and Harold Conway in the 2021 Hulu film *Vacation Friends*. Wisdom was born to Jamaican parents. He is a graduate of Saint Albans School.

Daniel Stern (b. August 28, 1957, in Bethesda, MD) is an American actor, artist, director, and screenwriter. He is best known for his roles as Marv Murchins in the *Home Alone* films. Stern played in several productions at his Bethesda-Chevy Chase high school, and when he went for a lighting engineer job at a DC Shakespeare Festival, he got hired for a walk-on spot in their *Taming of the Shew* production starring Glenn Close. He abruptly quit high school and moved to New York. His brother, David Stern became a noted TV screenwriter working on *The Wonder Years* (which Daniel narrated) and *The Simpsons*.

Clifton Powell (b. March 16, 1956) is an American actor who primarily plays supporting roles in films, such as in Ray (2004), for which he received an NAACP Image Award for Outstanding Supporting Actor in a Motion Picture nomination.

Damian Young (b. October 27, 1961) is an actor notable for his appearance in the Hal Hartley film *Amateur* (1994). He also featured in Hartley's earlier film *Simple Men* (1992), and has appeared in theatre, television and film.

Christopher Meloni (b. April 2, 1961) is an actor. He is best known for playing NYPD Detective Elliot Stabler on the NBC legal drama *Law & Order: Special Victims Unit* (1999–2011, 2021–

present) and its spin-off *Law & Order: Organized Crime* (2021–present).

Michael Nouri (b. December 9, 1945) is a screen and stage actor. He is best known for his television roles, including Dr. Neil Roberts on *The O.C.* and Phil Grey on *Damages*.

Michael Sylvester Gardenzio Stallone **(Sylvester Stallone)** was born July 6, 1946 in New York City. He moved to Silver Spring, MD, with his father when he was five. His childhood nickname was "Binky." I met with his father, Frank, in his Potomac home in 1984. Frank mainly talked about himself but I did learn that Sly made his first movie in the Maryland woods he called *Horses*. And when he had to choose between playing *Rocky* and perhaps losing a movie contract or selling the rights to the *Rocky* script he wrote and not playing *Rocky*, his Dad told him "Tell that producer you'd rather eat the script then let someone else play your character." His brother is the musician, Frank.

Kathy Lee Gifford was born Kathryn Lee Epstein in Paris, France, to American parents, Joan (born Cuttell; January 20, 1930 – September 12, 2017), a singer; and Aaron Epstein (March 19, 1924 – November 19, 2002), a musician and former US Navy Chief Petty Officer. Her father was stationed with his family in France at the time of Gifford's birth. Gifford grew up in Bowie, Maryland, and attended Bowie High School. During high school, Gifford was a singer in a folk group called Pennsylvania Next Right, which performed frequently at school assemblies.

Tony Todd (b. December 4, 1954) is an American actor who is perhaps best known for portraying the title character in the *Candyman* film series (1992–2021).

Richard Schiff (b. May 27, 1955) is an American actor. He is best known for playing Toby Ziegler on *The West Wing*, a role for which he received an Emmy Award.

James McDaniel Jr. (b. March 25, 1958) is an American stage, film and television actor. He is best known for playing Lt. Arthur Fancy on the television show *NYPD Blue*. He played the role of Paul in the hit Lincoln Center play *Six Degrees of Separation*.

Matthew George Frewer (b. January 4, 1958) is a Canadian American actor and comedian. His dad was Captain Frederick Charlesley Frewer, a Royal Canadian Navy officer. Raised in Canada, with no other DC connections so far, but for the record, he's a native DC-born actor who is the first to play an artificial intelligence character, Max Headroom. Go Matt!!!

Julia Scarlett Elizabeth Louis-Dreyfus was born January 13, 1961, in New York City. Four years after her birth in NYC, her family moved to Washington. After moving to Washington, DC, when Louis-Dreyfus was four, her mother married L. Thompson Bowles, dean of the George Washington Medical School; Louis-Dreyfus gained a half-sister, Lauren Bowles, also an actress. In 1979, she graduated from the all-girls Holton-Arms School in Bethesda, Maryland. She later said of the school, "There were things I did in school that, had there been boys in the classroom, I would have been less motivated to do. For instance, I was president of the honor society."

She has received more Emmy and Screen Actors Guild awards than anyone and is the daughter of the late French billionaire Gerard Louis Dreyfus.

Bowles has appeared in numerous TV shows, including *Arrested Development*, *CSI: Crime Scene Investigation*, *Judging Amy*, and *Private Practice*. She has appeared with Louis-Dreyfus in programs such as *Seinfeld*, as a waitress at the diner; *The New Adventures of Old Christine*, *Watching Ellie*, and *Veep*.

Erik King (b. April 21, 1963) is an American actor, best known for his portrayal of Sergeant James Doakes on Showtime's television series *Dexter*. He is also known for his roles as Moses Deyell on *Oz*, and as Bobby Davidson in *Missing Persons*.

Sandra Annette Bullock (b. in Arlington 1964) Her father worked for the Department of Defense, settling in the DC area after serving in Germany in the Army in the '50s. Her mother was a German opera singer and continued to perform but took a day job as a professor of music at Mary Washington College down in Fredericksburg. During her high school years, Sandra became president of the German Honor Society, a member of the Thespian Honor Society, and a varsity cheerleader. During a TV interview, Sandra said she had no idea what she was cheering about since she had minimal knowledge of sports, but a classmate said she provided comic relief as the "class clown, the funniest girl at Washington-Lee."

After high school graduation, Bullock left DC for East Carolina University, where she earned her Bachelor of Fine Arts degree in Drama in 1987. NYC is where stage roles served as steppingstones toward her eventual film career and accolades including an Academy Award, Golden Globe Award and Screen Actors Guild Award.

Wanda Sykes was born on March 7, 1964, in Portsmouth, Virginia. Her family moved to Maryland when she was in the third grade. Her mother, Marion Louise (née Peoples), worked as a banker; and her father, Harry Ellsworth Sykes, was a U.S. Army colonel employed at the Pentagon.

Martha Maria Yeardley Smith (b. July 3, 1964) is an American actress. She stars as the voice of Lisa Simpson on the animated television series *The Simpsons*. Born in Paris she came to DC at the age of two where her father became the first obituary editor for the *Washington Post*. After a number of school plays she joined the Arena Stage with an apprenticeship.

Kathleen Charlotte McInerney (b.1965) is also known by her stage name **Veronica Taylor**. She is an American voice actress known for her dubbing work in English-language adaptations of Japanese anime.

Jeffrey Wright (b. December 7, 1965) is an American actor. He has received numerous accolades, including a Primetime Emmy Award, a Tony Award, and a Golden Globe Award, in addition to a nomination for an Academy Award. Wright began his career in theater where he gained prominence for his role in the Broadway production of Tony Kushner's *Angels in America* (1993), for which he won a Tony Award for Best Featured Actor in a Play.

Wendy Davis (b. June 30, 1966) is an American actress. She is best known for her role as Colonel Joan Burton in the Lifetime television drama series *Army Wives* (2007–2013), for which she received three NAACP Image Award for Outstanding Actress in a Drama Series nominations. Davis grew up in Joppatowne, MD. She graduated with a degree in Theater from Howard University.

Louis Alfred Székely born September 12, 1967, in DC, and known professionally as **Louis C.K.**, the comedian and actor was an infant when his family moved to his father's Mexican homeland. At seven they relocated to Boston where Louis C.K. began his comedic career.

Ana Gasteyer, born May 4, 1967, is an actress, comedian and singer. The daughter of an artist and DC lobbyist who became the mayor of Corrales, New Mexico. Gasteyer grew up on Capitol Hill.

She graduated from Sidwell Friends School where she was childhood friends with Amy Carter, then daughter of the President. "I was at the White House often," she told Kelly Clarkson in 2023. "I have a picture of us tobogganing together outside, and I don't remember any photographers around."

She and Amy were together when the secret negotiations were made at the presidential retreat, Camp David, that led to peace between Egypt and Israel. There Ana played the violin for Egyptian President Anwar Sadat.

Today best known for her six-year work on *Saturday Night Live*, creating characters, including NPR radio host Margaret Jo and impressions of Martha Stewart and Hillary Rodham Clinton.

Edward Harrison Norton (b. August 18, 1969, in Boston) was raised in Columbia, MD. His father was an environmental lawyer and federal prosecutor in the Carter administration. His mother, Lydia Robinson "Robin" Rouse, was an English teacher.

At age five, Norton and his parents saw a musical starring his babysitter at the Columbia Center for Theatrical Arts (CCTA) and watched movies with his father. He has said his initial interest was in film cinematography but later reflected he was fascinated with theater, not films; hence, theater inspired him to act.

He made his professional debut at the age of eight in the musical *Annie Get Your Gun* at his hometown's **Toby's Dinner Theater**, directed by Toby Orenstein Carter.

David Khari Webber Chappelle (b. August 24, 1973) Chappelle is a stand-up comedian and actor. (see Duke Ellington School)

Whitney Cummings (b. September 4, 1982) is a comedian actress, writer, producer, and director. Cummings graduated from Saint Andrews Episcopal School in Potomac. She interned at WRC TV on Nebraska Avenue, and studied acting at Washington, DC, Studio Theater. Her mother worked at Neiman Marcus at Mazda Gallery.

Jonathan Edward Bernthal (b. September 20, 1976) is an American actor. Beginning his career in the early 2000s, he came to prominence for portraying Shane Walsh on the AMC horror series *The Walking Dead* (2010-2012; 2018).

David Michael Bautista Jr. (b. January 18, 1969) is an American actor and retired professional wrestler and mixed martial artist. He rose to fame for his several stints in WWE between 2002 and 2019.

Rick Yune (b. August 22, 1971) is an actor, screenwriter, producer and martial artist of Korean descent. His most notable roles have been in the movies *Snow Falling on Cedars*, the first *Fast and Furious* film, the James Bond movie *Die Another Day*, and *Olympus Has Fallen*. He was part of the main cast of the Netflix original series *Marco Polo*.

Olugbenga Enitan Temitope Akinnagbe (b. December 12, 1978) is an American actor and writer, best known for his roles as Chris Partlow on the HBO series *The Wire*, and as Larry Brown on the HBO series *The Deuce*.

Kellie Shanygne Williams-Jackson (née **Williams**; b. March 22, 1976) is an American actress. She is best known for her role as Laura Lee Winslow, the middle-born child of Carl and Harriette Winslow on the ABC/CBS television series *Family Matters*, which ran from 1989–1998.

Betty Gabriel (b. Jan. 6, 1981) is an American actress. For her work in horror films, particularly Blumhouse films, Gabriel has been established as a "scream queen." She has been nominated for two Black Reel Awards, a NAACP Image Award, and a Screen Actors Guild Award.

Regina Lee Hall (b. Dec.12, 1970) is an American actress. She rose to prominence for her role as Brenda Meeks in the comedy horror *Scary Movie* film series (2000–2006). She has since appeared in the television series *Ally McBeal* (2001–2002), *Law & Order: LA* (2010–2011), *Grandfathered* (2016).

Katherine Heigle (b. in DC, 1978), actress, but raised in CT.

Archie Kao (b. 1973) is an American actor and producer. He is best known to American audiences for series regular's roles on *Chicago*, *Power Rangers Lost Galaxy*, as well as long-running hit *CSI: Crime Scene Investigation*.

Eden Sonja Jane Riegel (b. Jan. 1, 1981) is an American actress. She portrayed Bianca Montgomery in the daytime drama *All My Children*, and propelled the character into a Gay icon, as well as a popular figure within the medium.

George Owen Gore II (b. Dec. 15, 1982) is an American actor and comedian. He is best known for portraying Gregory "G" Williams on the FOX series *New York Undercover* from 1994 to 1998 and Michael Kyle Jr. on the ABC sitcom *My Wife and Kids* from 2001 to 2005. He was also one of the main characters in the cast of the comedy *Second Generation Wayans*.

Samira Denise Wiley (born April 15, 1987) is an American actress. She is best known for her starring role as Poussey Washington in the Netflix comedy-drama series *Orange Is the New Black* (2013–2019) and as Moira in the Hulu dystopian drama series *The Handmaid's Tale* (2017–present), for which she won the Primetime Emmy Award for Outstanding Guest Actress in a Drama Series.

Bibi Osterwald:

Her last screen appearance was Jack Nicholson's neighbor in "As Good As It Gets" (She mouths 'Son of a Bitch' at Jack). She grew up in DC, studied theater at Catholic University, did five years at Rockville Roadside Theater and played at the Willard Hotel. The Central High School graduate appeared on Broadway and in films, TV and commercials. She was Carol Channing's first standby (understudy) in *Hello Dolly* and appeared in such Broadway shows as *Gentlemen Prefer Blondes*, *Bus Stop* and *Look Homeward Angel*. She passed away January 2nd, 2002 at age 83. She last played DC in 1984's Road Company of *42nd Street* at the National Theater.

Chapter 15 - Dinner with Mr. B.

Billy Eckstine and Miller Dixon at Charlie's club in Georgetown during our dinner interview. © S. Moore

Billy Eckstine first arrived in Washington, DC, from his hometown of Pittsburgh, PA, to attend Armstrong High School and then Howard University, majoring in General Education. He aimed to return home with a degree and teach like his sisters. His education goals changed because of a surprise win at a Howard Theater amateur contest. Billy used his rich, almost operatic baritone voice to impersonate Cab Calloway.

William Clarence Eckstine (July 8, 1914 – March 8, 1993) became an American jazz and pop singer and historic bandleader during the swing and bebop eras.

In 1985, Eckstine was appearing at Charlie's Club in Georgetown for two nights. Bill Reichenbach, Charlie Byrd's drummer, was backing him up. Margaret and I arrived the first night with a legal envelope of Xeroxes of my published articles and a personalized letter to Billy describing my *Capital Acts* project with an interview request. His show was beautiful, and I gave him the envelope after he left the stage. We returned to our table, and a few minutes later, he came over. He had read my letter and asked me to join him for dinner the next night if I could. "I'll be with an old friend, Miller Dixon, and we will talk about old times," he said. I went home that night very excited.

The next evening, I joined Billy and Miller. They both ordered fish, and I quickly learned they were once a team "taking the girls out on date night." Eckstine lived at 1752 Oregon Ave N.E. The house had belonged to Reverand Charles Wallace and became an after-hours club after Billy moved out.

Billy began chatting with my cassette recorder running: "We'd go to the Howard Theater every Friday. It was mainly listening and hearing and being exposed to new things. As far as my music was concerned, it was here at the Howard. But of course, I wasn't thinking of it as any career at that time. I thought I would probably be a teacher like my sisters were. But I always liked music I sang in the church choir in Pittsburgh when I was at Holy Cross Church. I never thought I wanted to be in show business. That never happened. *The Howard Amateur Show* was a case of doing something I thought I would enjoy. I went on the show for fun."

Billy won second prize on his first attempt, and a week later, he was the first prize winner. Miller, a retired DC police detective, added that the award was ten dollars. "He split the prize money with his friends and probably got a dollar. Later, when Billy played the clubs, we would line up on the stairway. He'd go and sing, and they threw money on the dancing area, and we would split." Billy remembered that the money then "was very shallow, but we had a lot of fun."

Billy continuously won several Howard amateur contests. "After those, I was hired as the vocalist for the Howard Theatre pit band. It was headed by Tommy Miles with a very fine band and famous musicians like James 'Trummy' Young (trombone), Elton Hill, Benny Turner, and Jimmy Mundy. I started hearing things I wanted to do when I got into that band. That time I was just all 'Big Eyes.' This was 1935. I decided to make music a career while playing in the pit band. My local popularity was increasing. Duke Ellington heard me and encouraged me to continue singing. Ellington was THE escape as far as music was concerned then."

It was 1935 when Billy returned to Pittsburgh without a degree and began singing in local clubs. Eventually, he shuffled off to Buffalo, wheeled into Detroit, and finally made Chicago his kind of town with his "first important professional gig" at the Club De Lisa.

"At De Lisa, I decided to study music and understand more about this craft. It was interesting enough that I got the old show business bug. Show business decides whether you have enough guts to stick with something you want to do. Show business decides it. The main thing you got to do is be honest with yourself. Then if it happens for you, then OK!"

Two years after his De Lisa club engagement, Earl "Fatha" Hines hired Billy as vocalist with his band. Eckstine gained national recognition through successful recordings "Jelly, Jelly" and "Stormy Monday Blues" which he co-authored with Heinz. Billy stayed with the "Fatha" for the next four years. Many of the young players in The Earl Hines Band would shift their allegiance to Billy during these years.

Photo: Eckstine and female fans inside Life Magazine (May, 1946)

"After I left 'Fatha' Hines, I played in clubs on New York's 52nd Street as a solo player. Then I decided to assemble my own big band," he said. The first band he organized after his initial hit song successes featured John Malachi (piano), Wardell Gray (sax) Charlie Parker (sax), Dizzy Gillespie (trumpet), Gene Ammons (tenor sax), Dexter Gordon, (tenor sax), Miles Davis, (trumpet), Kenny Dorham (trumpet), Fats Navarro (trumpet), Gene Blakey (drums), and Sara Vaughn (vocals). "It was my band. I organized the band, and Dizzy was the first musical director," Billy told me.

Historically, this group has been considered the first Bebop Jazz band. Ironically, it was Dizzy Gillespie, a frequent visitor to DC to see personal friends, whom I literally bumped into a few years later in Olson's record store. We talked briefly, and when I mentioned Eckstine, he said, "There was no band that sounded like Billy Eckstine's. Our attack was strong, and we played bebop, the modern style."

According to the Miles Davis documentary *Birth of the Cool*, the real pivot point for a young Miles Davis during the summer after his high school graduation is when he was invited to sit in with the Billy Eckstein Band. "The greatest experience I had in my life with my clothes on was sitting in with that band," said Miles. "I was eighteen years old. Right then and there, I decided I had to be in New York on 52nd Street, where the action was. It was a laboratory—the future of modern jazz right there in that new band."

John Malachi, Jazz pianist

Born in Red Springs, North Carolina on September 6, 1919, Malachi moved to Washington, DC when he was ten years old. I was able to interview Malachi shortly after my dinner with Mr. B. He was then a music professor of Piano and Jazz Studies at Howard University. He is famous for helping Billy make history in The Eckstine Bebop Orchestra. The following is a detailed history he was so kind to give me. He passed away just a few years after we talked.

"I was ten years old when my parents moved to Washington. We began by living in the 1000 block of P Street and next moved to 1344th Street And then up to the 1700 block of 8th Street. We did a lot of moving. It was during the Depression. My father was working a job making thirty-five dollars every two weeks at a secondhand furniture place on 7th Street. And he drove a truck.

"One evening my father and uncle came home with the truck and started unloading a piano. I had two brothers and two sisters. And my uncle said to us, 'I will give five dollars to the first one of you kids to learn how to play this piano. My father's making $17.50 a week, so you can imagine what five dollars meant.

"My grandmother had an old pump organ down in North Carolina when I was very small. I liked to get up there and fool with it. But on this evening. I started fooling with the piano. And by the end of the night, I was playing a little piece with two fingers. The idea came so easy it just fascinated me and after that I couldn't wait to get home from school to get back to my new toy. And that's the way it's been ever since."

Malachi accompanied numerous jazz groups in the 1940s and 1950s. After first performing in the band of Trummy Young, Malachi went on to play, compose, and write arrangements for the Billy Eckstine Bebop Orchestra from 1944 through 1947. He toured with Creole musician Illinois Jacquet whose sax solo on "Flying Home" is critically recognized as the first R&B saxophone solo. Malachi also accompanied singer Pearl Baily who lived in DC for a while when she first started and attended Georgetown when I was there. She got a theology degree in 1985 at age 67.

Malachi and Eckstine both had attended Armstrong High School and knew other from various gigs in the Washington clubs. Malachi said, "The members of the band, Dizzy, Charlie, Sarah, and all of us, were disgruntled about the money we were making. Earl Hines wasn't sharing the wealth. Billy Eckstine was making all these hits (with the Hines band), and the players would just get paid for the record date."

Professor Malachi continued, "Because we were playing these 'record huge' crowds, the band decided we'd leave Hines and Billy would take over. Billy had a pretty fair name at that time. He was standing ten feet tall but no one knew what it was going to be like without Earl Hines." When asked if he was writing music at this time, he reported, "yeah, as a matter of fact, I wrote the first recording date we had. They recorded a composition of mine. 'Open Sax.' I was more surprised than delighted because I thought I had much better music at the time. But I think they felt it was more commercial. It was an orchestral piece. I wouldn't even attempt it on the piano alone."

Decades later, **Shirley Horn**, **Buck Hill** and many other city musicians would follow their leads. The history is rich and beautiful. The following books are recommended which feature more DC musicians.

DC Jazz: Stories of Jazz Music in Washington, *by Maurice Jackson and Blair Rubble:*
(Georgetown University Press)

Washington, DC, Jazz
By Dr. Reginia N. Williams and Rev. Dr. Sandra Butler-Truesdale. Foreword by Willard Jenkins.

Chapter 16 - Come Gather Round People

An ardent music union supporter and relentless advocate of traditional music, Mary Cliff is a key witness and longtime instigator of Washington's enduring folk music revival. Few people can claim "I was there" like Mary. A lifetime resident of Arlington, VA, she got into the budding DC folk music scene just as the "Great Folk Scare" erupted in America—an inside joke that circulated among musicians as "old-timey" folk songs like "Tom Dooley" became commercial radio hits. Banjos and guitars started popping up on American campuses.

Cliff first came in tune with this folk music revival during high school at Immaculate on Washington Circle from 1957 to 1961. She didn't like the rock and roll of her time, finding no substance in tunes like "Louie, Louie" and "Surfin' Bird." Her folk epiphany came through the car radio as she and her father heard "Tzena, Tzena, Tzena" by Pete Seeger's group, The Weavers.

She was then listening to emerging folk impresario, Dick Cerri's 1960 radio show, *Music Americana, the Folk Music of America* on WAVA-FM radio. As a student at Catholic University in 1961, she soon became a familiar face singing in hootenannies at the Cellar Door. She took a part-time job at the Cellar Door, There she became close friends with many of the club's regular performers including a teen-age Emmylou Harris, Virginia, bluesman John Jackson, and Donal Leace when he was a protégé' of local Roberta Flack. Dave Harrington, now known as Richard, sang "'Bob Dylan's Dream' there every other week," Mary remembers smiling.

Mary Cliff, with friend Richard Harrington in 2017. © S. Moore.

For over five decades Washington's easily identifiable

voice of Mary Cliff has promoted ubiquitous folk music on DC on her acclaimed show.

Mary Cliff introducing the 2024 DC Legends Tribute at the Strathmore. © S. Moore

"She has been the leading light regarding folk music on the air for decades here in this market, not only espousing nationally and internationally known artists, but being extremely supportive of local and regional artists, too," said Michael Jaworek, promoter at Alexandria's Birchmere music venue in a *Washington Post* interview with John Kelly.

In interviews, Mary describes herself as a cultural mediator, highlighting her role in bridging different cultural expression through music and events. She doesn't see herself as a political activist, because she has been too busy programming music and enjoying concerts to attend protests. Instead, she sees herself as a cultural mediator. She was one of the original members of the Folklore Society of Greater Washington founded in 1964 and served as president for many years. In an interview with Richard Harrington, she tactically embraced the entire folk spectrum: "I have a foot in all camps, which makes me an octopus," and she has joked with journalists about her programming, which featured bluegrass, blues, folk, gospel, and traditional music from around the world.

For decades, her detailed *Whose Where* weekly rundown of venues and performers has been a precious guide to the rich music found across America and the DC area.

"When she was on the air on a powerful station, we could feel the difference here in terms of ticket sales," adds Jaworek,

Each program of *Traditions* is an example of honoring, preserving and transforming musical culture. Cliff has won multiple Washington Area Music Awards (Wammies) for supporting local folk performers. Mary was inducted in the Folk DJ Hall of Fame for Folk Alliance International in 2018 and has kept *Traditions* going on Arlington's community radio station WERA.96.7 via Arlington Independent Media.

Using music to unite people around a common cause—a key characteristic of patriotic and protest events—dates to the US colonial period and has been a powerful tool for advocating ideas and inspiration throughout American history. Some of the earliest protest songs are "The Liberty Song" (1768) and "John Brown's Body" (1861).

1775's "Free America" is one of the earliest "patriotic" songs composed by Dr. Joseph Warren, a physician, accomplished writer, and an early casualty of the Revolutionary War. It begins with the lyrics, "Come, join hand in hand, brave Americans all, and rouse your bold hearts at fair Liberty's call. No tyrannous acts shall suppress your just claim or stain. In freedom, we're born; in freedom, we'll live; our purses are ready, steady boys, steady."

Protest songs have been a vital part of American culture, evolving over time to address a wide range of social, political, and economic issues, including abolition, the labor movement, civil rights, Vietnam war involvement, feminism, LGBTQ rights, and more, using performing arts as a tool, especially in the Nation's Capital. In general, protest—from gentle to radical—is intensely American.

"Yankee Doodle Dandy" is familiar to all but was initially sung by the British troops to mock Americans. "Doodle" was a slang phrase then meaning "simpleton." Over time, the colonists embraced the song and transformed it into an anthem, reflecting the resilience and spirit of the American people.

The March on Washington for Jobs and Freedom—attended by 200,000—is one of the most significant events in the civil rights movement. It was successful in pressuring the administration of John F Kennedy to initiate a strong federal civil rights bill in Congress.

The protest was envisioned by A. Philip Randolph, a long-time civil rights activist dedicated to improving the economic condition of Black Americans. On August 28, 1963, the march featured some of the most influential musicians of the time, performing in front of a crowd of over 250,000 people. It's been called the most peaceful demonstration of its size. Reverend Martin Luther King, Jr. gave his "I Have a Dream" speech at this three-hour program at the Lincoln Memorial. Other speeches from prominent civil rights and religious leaders include a young John Lewis, then with the Student Nonviolent Coordinating Committee [SNCC] and Cardinal Patrick O'Boyle.

The day ended with a meeting between the march leaders and President John F. Kennedy at the White House. The musicians that day included folk singer and activist Joan Baez, who performed multiple songs, including "We Shall Overcome," the anthem for the civil rights movement. Peter, Paul, and Mary sang "If I Had a Hammer" and "Blowin' in the Wind," Bob Dylan's first hit as a songwriter, thanks to their successful cover version. Dylan sang "Only a Pawn in Their Game" and "When the Ship Comes In." His "Freewheelin" album (which opened with "Blowin in the Wind") arrived in record stores only two months earlier.

Odetta, the folk singer and civil rights activist known for her powerful voice, sang "I'm On My Way" and "I'm Gonna Let It Shine." Folk-blues musician Josh White delivered a rousing performance of "Freedom Road." Mahalia Jackson, the powerfully voiced gospel singer delivered a stirring performance of "I Been' Buked and I Been Scorned" right before King took the podium.

Opera singer Marian Anderson opened with "He's Got the Whole World in His Hands." The crowd did not miss the significance of her performance. She was scheduled to perform at DAR Constitution Hall in 1939 but the "white-artist-only" clause printed in every contract issued by the DAR was enforced. Like the city itself, the DAR was segregated then.

First lady Eleanor Roosevelt was angered by this decision. She sent DAR her letter of resignation and wrote in her weekly column "My Day," syndicated nationally in over forty newspapers, that the "DAR has taken an action which has been widely criticized in the press. To remain as a member implies approval of that action, and therefore I am resigning."

However, the DAR did not relent. Walter White, then the executive secretary of the National Association of the Advancement of Colored People [NAACP] suggested the Lincoln

Memorial, a national monument, be used for the concert. Secretary of the Interior Harold Ickes invited Anderson onto the stage on April 9, 1939. She started her concert with "My Country, 'Tis of Thee"—also known as "America." When she got to the third line of the beloved tune, she changed "of thee I sing" and sang *"to thee we sing."*

> A pastel drawing of the Lincoln Memorial concert done for the Works Progress Administration (WPA—a depression-era federal program—by Joseph Schwarz, the father of my late wife, Margaret Moore

The largest mass arrest in American history occurred on May 1, 1971—also known as "May Day"—when 7000 protesters were rounded up. The single goal of the protest was to bring traffic to a total halt in the nation's capital. Guess who played the concert held at the monument to galvanize the event.

It was the Beach Boys who were trying to jumpstart a career that went sideways when group genius Brian Wilson fell mentally ill. They were promoting their *Sunflowers* album released in August, just three months after the Kent State shootings, and during a summer of campus protests and rallies in response to bombing raids in Cambodia.

A new song, "Student Demonstration Time," wasn't much of a protest but rather a message for protesters to stay safe. Love asked the concert promoters to let the Beach Boys play first at the May Day concert so the group would be gone "before any riots broke out."

In 1980, with Brian recovered from his setbacks, Mike Love had an idea to return to the National Mall to do a July 4 free concert. Love recruited corporate sponsors and intended to invite different genre bands to join them, including Earth, Wind, and Fire. According to Love, the National Park Service said no to EW&F "because Black bands had caused crowd-control problems in the past."

The Beach Boys 1980 concert drew more than 500,000, their largest crowd ever, and more than 400,000 the following year. The Beach Boys had never endorsed a political candidate, but the country was recovering from the Iran hostage crisis, and Ronald Reagan was rolling out his "morning in America" theme. The Beach Boys' positive image seemed a better fit for the country's mood. And their shows were popular.

Enter James Watt, the U.S. secretary of the interior, who had unilaterally decided that the Beach Boys would *not* be performing at the 1983 Fourth of July concert because they played "hard rock" which "attracted the wrong element," and the Nation's Capital wasn't going to "encourage drug abuse and alcoholism as was done in years past."

Nancy Reagan phoned Love to apologize, and Watt became the most unpopular member of her husband's administration. The Beach Boys played on the White House grounds for a benefit for the Special Olympics that year. Wayne Newton played the next Fourth of July gig, and it rained. The crowd celebrated their new umbrellas.

Watt resigned soon after making the following remark in a lame attempt to boast about his advisory committee for a coal-leasing program: "I have a black woman, two Jews, and a cripple, and we have talent."

The Beach Boys triumphantly returned to the Mall on July 4, 1984, and brought along Ringo Starr and Justin Haywood of The Moody Blues. When Ringo came on, the band played "Back in the USSR." It was exhilarating.

There were four **Human Kindness Day** concerts on the Mall from 1972 to 1975, honoring (in order) Roberta Flack, Dick Gregory, Nina Simone, and Stevie Wonder.

Muhammad Ali and the Pointer Sisters joined in for the Nina Simone tribute. After the 1963 murders of civil rights activist Medgar Evers in Mississippi and the tragic bombing at the 16th Street Baptist Church in Alabama that claimed the lives of four young black girls, Nina Simone was inspired to pen a powerful protest song, "Mississippi Goddam". This song emerged as a fiery anthem of black political protest during this turbulent time in American history. Serving as a resolute response to the calls for "going slow" in the face of movements like desegregation, the song defiantly called out systemic injustices and condemnation of everyday racism.

Simone's 1974 appearance at the Kennedy Center, one year before her tribute, was a significant event in the venue's history and her illustrious career.

Fat City, Sea Train, The Staple Singers, Donal Leace, Archie Stewart, Bill Seligman, Mr. Rhythm, Frank Bullard, Drop of Blue, Lorraine Rudolph, the New Generation, Zulu Nation, the Colmenares, the Mighty Wonders, Calvert Crusaders, Flying Nesbit's, Capitol Ballet Company, Ebony Impromptu Company, 3rd World Revolution, and the Wayne Davis Company were some of the artists who took the stage for the Human Kindness shows. Crowds ranged from 25,000 to 55,000 during the four years.

However, the last Human Kindness Day honoring Stevie Wonder, hosted by Bob MacAlister of the local TV show "Wonderama," turned into a devastating fiasco.

One young attendee remembered visiting her family in Maryland. She talked her mother into taking her fourteen-year-old brother and twelve-year-old sister down to the Washington Monument grounds for the show. It was an unfortunate mistake.

Things turned ugly, when her little brother was surrounded by a group of boys pushing him to the ground. She managed to throw enough of these boys off and pull him out of the crowd. She grabbed the hands of her brother and sister and ran for several blocks until she felt they were safe. On the way home, she made them promise not to tell their mother!

By the time it ended, there had been an estimated 500 robberies, 150 smashed windows, forty-two looted refreshment stands, seventenn stoning's of uniformed officers, thirty-three fires, 120 cases of public brawling, and fourteen cars demolished. 600 injuries were reported, with 150 people being treated at hospitals. Police made 600 arrests.

On a brighter note a 1979 concert protest was called the Coalition Anti-Nuclear Rally, with a large blue "No Nukes" banner next to the Capital. Joni Mitchell changed some "Big Yellow Taxi" lyrics to "They paved paradise and put up a nuclear hot spot." Prompting the protest is when the Three Mile Island nuclear-generating station near Harrisburg, Pennsylvania suffered a partial meltdown of their Reactor 2. This was close enough to Baltimore to scare the sh*t out of many people.

News in 2024 is that Three Mile Island will be reactivated in 2028 to exclusively provide power to Microsoft.

I took this picture with of Joni Mitchell, Jackson Brown, and Graham Nash at the No Nukes concert with a borrowed Polaroid camera © S. Moore

Chapter 17 – The Big Three First

Timothy Alan Patrick Rose was born in Washington, DC, on September 23, 1940. He, his mother, and aunt lived in the Fairlington neighborhood of Alexandria. Tim Rose graduated in the class of 1958 from Gonzaga High School. His grandmother played piano in silent movie houses when she was young. His mother also played piano, and his aunt sang opera in the house.

At Gonzaga, he won a best musician prize but lost a college scholarship to a tuba player. His instruments then were banjo and guitar. Tim met another student, Ellen Cohen, in the fall of 1962, and they started singing with a friend, John Brown. They called themselves The Triumvirate. While touring, they met guitarist Jim Hendricks and became The Big Three, producing two albums.

Tim told UK's Brian Mathieson in 1998: "Cass was very difficult to work with. She was always right because a fat girl's never wrong, so in any musical disagreement, everybody would side with Cass. I wanted to go rock. I wanted to take the folk genre and put in electric guitars, bass, and drums; Cass said she would never do that with her music—she never wanted to be a rock singer."

Ellen Naomi Cohen was born in Baltimore on September 19, 1941, but her early life was spent in Alexandria, Virginia.

She took the name "Cass" (she admired TV actress Peggy Cass) while attending George Washington High School (with fellow student Jim Morrison) and later assumed the surname "Elliot" in memory of a friend who had died. She became interested in acting and was cast in a production of the play *The Boy Friend* at the then Hilltop Theater in Baltimore.

Cass took a full-time job working at the *Baltimore Jewish Times* newspaper to make a living while parts (hopefully) opened. She covered the society bits like weddings, bar mitzvahs, classified ads, and obituaries. "It didn't teach me about the newspaper business," she admitted to a UK reporter, "but the mothers would send me gifts to list their daughters' weddings first, so I learned about graft."

Moving to NYC in 1962, she toured in *The Music Man* and almost won the part of Miss Marmelstein in *I Can Get It for You Wholesale* (Barbra Streisand got it). Then, she moved back to the DC area to attend American University (not Swarthmore, as mentioned in the Mammas and the Pappa's song "Creeque Alley." At a Georgetown party, she met Tim Rose and began singing with him.

Philip Wallach Blondheim III was born on January 10, 1939, and grew up In Alexandria, VA, where he became friends with **John Edmund Andrew Phillips** (b. August 30, 1935 on Paris Island, S.C., but also grew up in Alexandria). Together they were Scott Mackenzie and John Phillips. Scott met John at his apartment on Ramsey Alley in Old Town, near the Torpedo Factory on the Potomac waterfront. Phillips was seven years older than McKenzie and already an accomplished singer and songwriter. With friends, Mike Boran and Bill Cleary, they created a doo-wop group called the Abstracts. McKenzie had sung with classmate Tim Rose in their first high school group, the Singing Strings.

In 1961, Phillips and McKenzie encountered folk musician and later noted historian and author Dick Weissman during the peak of the folk music craze. They formed the group The Journeymen, and went on to record three albums and seven singles for Capitol Records. Some of their best songs were "500 Miles" and "San Francisco Bay Blues" which they popularized. As the Beatles rose to fame in 1964, The Journeymen disbanded. McKenzie and Weissman pursued solo careers, while Phillips formed a new group with Cass, Denny Doherty, and Zal Yanovsky named "The Mugwumps," who often played in DC at the Shadows and later Cellar Door.

A Mugwump, by the way, is someone, especially in politics, who "sits on the fence," although Mama Cass became a strong supporter of 1972 presidential candidate George McGovern before her death by heart failure in 1974 at the age of thirty-two.

The group disbanded, and John and Cass, with Denny Doherty and Michelle Phillips, created The Mamas and the Papas relocating to California. Scott McKenzie declined John's invitation to join the new group, citing in a 1977 interview that he wanted to pursue his own path due to feeling incapable of "handling the pressure." He moved to New York two years later and signed with Lou Adler's Ode Records. John Phillips wrote and produced "San Francisco (Be Sure to Wear Flowers in Your Hair)" on which McKenzie played guitar, while Hal Blaine from the Wrecking Crew played drums—a single that sold over seven million copies and today is remembered as a theme song for the "Summer of Love."

John Phillips, the son of a fully disabled thirty-year Marine veteran, lived in the DC area, and did four years at the Linton Hall School in Manassas. Linton Hall, a Catholic Church-affiliated military school back then. John hated it.

In his autobiography, *Papa John* (co-written by Jim Jerome), Phillips says he initially was excited to hear, "When the nuns take you to the office to beat you, they do it to you naked." He was disappointed, however, when a classmate explained, "They're not naked; you are!"

John was happy to return to Alexandria for high school and to escape a place where even comic books and records had been forbidden: "After the rustic isolation at Linton Hall, I was happy to be back in the Del Ray neighborhood. George Washington High School was like a non-stop party after Linton Hall."

Thanks to a musician relative, John started playing guitar and visiting various live music venues in the DC area, including "one all-black dive just over the 14th Street Bridge in

Washington, at 7th and O Streets." (Probably the Stage Door restaurant near the Howard Theater). "[We were] two white kids from Virginia checking out the Cajun and blood music."

After high school, John "managed to enroll and leave American University, George Washington University, the University of Virginia regional branch in Arlington, and Hampden-Sydney College in rural Virginia." After discovering rock' n' roll, John dropped out of college and moved into an apartment of his own in Old Town Alexandria. He worked various sales jobs while playing music at night and starting writing songs.

Before long, he landed a postal route for better income. He was a terrible mail carrier, getting in big trouble by trashing a load of mail, so he went back to playing music for a living.

He formed a quartet in Alexandria that eventually included lifelong friend Scott McKenzie, a group with strong vocal harmonies. One of the other members was "Mike Boran, a tall, younger kid who played piano in a notorious DC-area party band called the Capital City All-Stars."

John made trips to New York to sell his songs at the Brill Building, but he had little success.

Back in DC, "George Wilkins, a co-owner of Edgewood Studios in Washington, gave us a break on studio fees and let us record there." Under the group name The Smoothies, their first single got them exposure on Philadelphia's *American Bandstand*, then a local Philly show hosted by Dick Clark. The more significant break came the following year in New York: "We played Folk City as The Journeymen for six weeks in the spring, and each of us pulled down $125 a week...sharing the stage with great acts like the Clancy Brothers and the venerable Mississippi blues legend Lightnin' Hopkins...and a scruffy, anemic-looking kid by the name of Bob Dylan."

The New York exposure landed him a deal with California-based Capitol Records, leading John to depart his East Coast life for a life of California dreaming for the rest of his sixty-five years—passing from heart failure on March 18, 2001.

Jim Morrison's high school home in Alexandria, VA © KSPD

Halloween of 2011 found Jim Morrison's old bandmates, Robby Krieger and Ray Manzarek, landing again in Alexandria, Virginia, for a Birchmere concert performed soon after the 50th anniversary of Morrison's graduation from the city's high school at 1005 Mount Vernon Avenue, the same side of the same street as the Birchmere. The building is now called George Washington Middle School. During the show I attended that evening, Krieger told the crowd that he and Manzarek drove by Jim's old high school to do their soundcheck at the legendary hall.

During Morrison's adolescent days living in the area, he developed his love for literature and poetry, spending countless hours at the local public library and much of his free time visiting various bookstores in the DC area. As a result, Jim Morrison amassed a library of around 1,000 volumes while the family lived in Alexandria. Jim's bedroom was the basement of the house, with his astonishing book collection for a teen of that era. His first public appearance is reported as "a poetry recital at a beatnik joint known as Coffee' n' Confusion" (925 K Street NW).

So, it's clear that his time in the DC area during those formative years, with easy access to various bookstores in Georgetown and other parts of the DC area, helped fuel the fire of Jim Morrison's growing intellect and poetic muse. Washington DC writer **Mark Opsasnick** has published two Morrison books, *The Lizard King Was Here* and *Orange Brick in Warm Sun - Jim Morrison in DC*" (Booklocker). Excellent accounts of Morrison's DC adventures, with many interviews with folks who knew Jim.

Charles D. Young

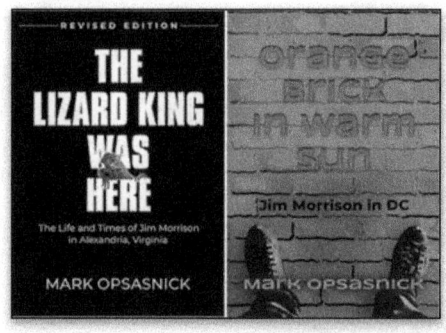

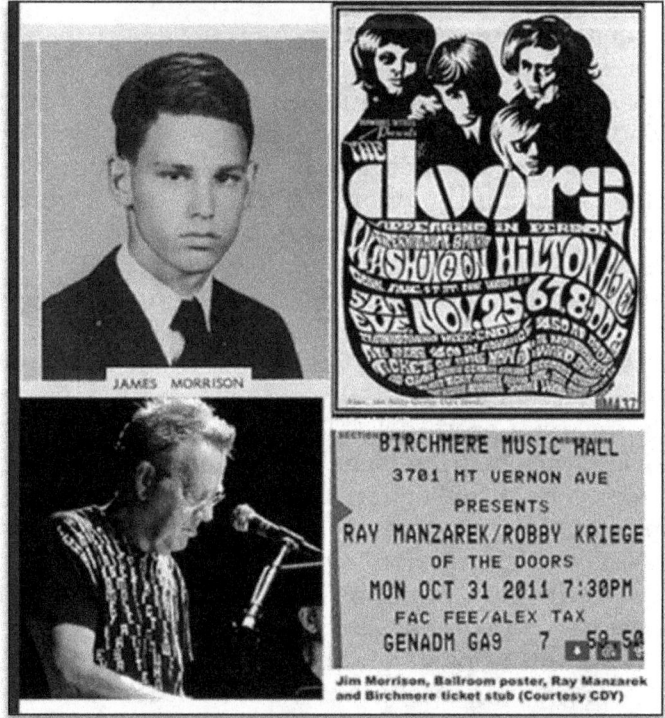

Jim Morrison's high school picture, Washington Hilton poster, Ray Manzarek, and a Birchmere ticket. © KSPD

Chapter 18 – DC's Comic Beat Goes On

The Langley Punks (l-to-r) Larry Zabel, Pat Carroll, Bob Young, Jim Phalen © 1979 Bill O'Leary

Dave Nuttycombe has performed, produced, and written about comedy since the Nixon administration and most recently was co-producer of the extraordinary *Feast Your Ears—The Story of WHFS 102.3 FM* documentary about the legendary progressive radio station in Bethesda, MD. I became a fan in 1984 when I heard my favorite joke of all time on one of his group's Travesty records.

© Linda Bangham

Unfortunately, the joke is so hilariously offensive on multiple levels that it cannot be included here.

However, on my way to one of the premiere showings of *Feast Your Ears*, now my favorite documentary film of all time, I thought it might be funny if I bit his ear in the theater lobby when I arrived. *Feast [On] Your Ears*—get it? Dick Bangham, the genius behind the digital visuals in the film, ignored my joke, which is often his cool move. He frequently did the same when he was playing in Root Boy Slim's Sex Change Band.

The Bayou: DC's Killer Joint, Dave's PBS documentary, was nominated for an Emmy Award, but the judges must have been drunk or something. He remains bitter. We thank Dave for writing his section, to which we have added tiny editorial changes to make it appear it is written by us Capital Acts authors.

* * *

In the early 1970s, three friends from Our Lady of Good Council, an all-boys Catholic high school in Wheaton, MD, began making short black-and-white films. Borrowing one of their dad's 16mm cameras, Pat Carroll, Bill O'Leary, and Larry Zabel spent weekends filming themselves running around in fields and basements, mimicking the antics of their comedy heroes, the *Three Stooges*, who they had grown up watching after school on WTTG Channel Five's *Cap 'N Tugg* program. The youngsters named their endeavor Travesty Films.

Then, with the addition of some more Good Council friends, Bob Young, Jim Phalen, and Jim's friend Tom Welsh, they created a series of films featuring The Langley Punks, three—and then four—suburban burnouts without a clue. The Punks took their name from the then-rundown suburb of Langley Park, MD, where the group would watch movies at the Langley Theater and buy beer.

When the Biograph Theatre announced the Expose Yourself film festival in 1974, a showcase for student and independent filmmakers, Travesty found an outlet beyond just projecting their efforts at parties to friends. Amid such earnest offerings as *Nude Dune* and works by professionals eager to showcase their corporate work, Travesty's shorts, like *Invasion of the Paramecium Men* (1975), *Cloning Around* (1976), and *Curse of the Atomic Greasers* (1976), proved to be regular crowd-pleasers. Pat Dowell described the films in the *Washington Star* as "epic fits of adolescent buffoonery" and "boisterous lunacy." On the other hand, Gary Arnold wrote in the *Washington Post* that Travesty's work was "more than a little sophomoric" but added that the group "continues to improve as a performing unit."

Indeed, Travesty's output was directly related to the Expose Yourself screenings. When the Biograph announced a date, the group would gather over a few weekends, pool their money for beer, film stock, and processing (mostly beer), and create another often improvised and manic production. "Shoot it and show it" was Pat Carroll's motto.

When Travesty's *Neurotic Psychotics* (1978) took the top prize over the dramatic work of director Rich West, West decided that if you can't beat 'em, join 'em and teamed up with the ragtag crew. The result of the collaboration was *Intestines from Space* (1978), the first Travesty film with synced sound and another winner with the public.

At the same time, Dave Nuttycombe was playing drums around town in the band The Dogmatics, performing original satirical songs and parodies of Top 40 tunes. (Songs such as "I Struck Out at the Disco" and "New Gym in Ohio," a parody of Neil Young's "Ohio," based on a then-current scandal.) Yes, this is exactly like Weird Al Yankovic, but a few years before he became known. Dave and Travesty would later open for Weird Al at the Wax Museum club after their "Rock and Roll Doctor" became a hit on the Dr. Demento. But we're getting ahead of ourselves.

In 1977, a *Washington Post* profile of Expose Yourself focused on Travesty and Pat Carroll ("A shy, shuffling young man.") drew Dave to the show. After watching Insurance Salesmen from Saturn and realizing he was among kindred spirits, Dave approached Pat and Larry in the lobby and asked them to screen their films during breaks at Dogmatics gigs. Thus, the video bar was invented, which would not become popular for another four or five years.

In 1979, forty years after Hollywood introduced color to motion pictures with *Gone with the Wind* and *The Wizard of Oz*, West and Travesty decided to make a movie in color for the first time. And make it a musical. Or, as the poster for *Alcoholics Unanimous* read, "a semi-musical."

Pat reached out to Dave to produce what "would climax the film," "When the Red, Red Robin (Comes Bob, Bob, Bobbin'

Along)." Dave rounded up his musician friends and got a sweet deal at Omega Recording Studios, then in Kensington, MD, and the resulting film was yet another Expose Yourself favorite. Dave was asked to officially join the group.

While waiting to go into production on their next film, *Hyattsville Holiday* (1981), the group would gather at Rich West's production studio in Arlington, Musifex. Dave, in particular, had years of scripts he'd written with nowhere to produce them. With West again supplying a professional sheen, the team began work on what would become the album *Teen Comedy Party*, which the New York Times called "a truly funny recording." The album featured probably the last recording of the Starland Vocal Band, friends of Dave's, and the aforementioned Dr. Demento Show hit, "Rock and Roll Doctor." That cut would be included on two comedy anthology records, Demento's Mementos and the Rhino Records box set, World's Greatest Novelty Recordings.

Pat Carroll, Jim Phalen, Bob Young, Larry Zabel, Rich West, Don Hogan, Tom Welsh, Dave Nuttycombe
© Bill O'Leary

In 1983, the cable TV provider for Prince George's County offered Travesty its yet-unfinished Hollywood MD studios to produce whatever they wanted, within limits. "The Travesty Show was a half-hour homage to early television programs like *The Honeymooners*. It featured Root Boy Slim, the Wanktones, and Ron Holloway. Though the show was shot on videotape, the idea was to screen it as a kinescope—a filmed copy of a television broadcast, which was the only way to have a copy of a live show back in the early 1950s. The group spent $1,500 filming the video to achieve the desired degraded effect.

The success of *Rock and Roll Doctor* and the more professional look of the films drew the attention of such publications as *People Magazine* and *Fangoria*, which did profiles of the group. Local radio and TV stations reached out for interviews. NBC4's Arch Campbell was a particular supporter, often to the annoyance of anchor Jim Vance. The Washington Post's Richard Harrington wrote a feature profile group interview. In 1983, the *Biograph* offered to screen a retrospective of Travesty shorts. The group produced new introductions to each film, featuring Dave as the pompous and ill-informed "noted authority" Prof. Maurice duMontage. The retrospective ran for a week and was popular enough to be held over as a midnight movie for several weeks, until receipts fell below what the regular X-rated screenings had yielded.

When the *Biograph* closed in 1996, Travesty was asked to be part of the final screenings. They produced a faux-documentary about themselves, *From Here to Obscurity: The Films of the Langley Punks*. Again, Prof. duMontage provided specious commentary. In 2011, the AFI Silver Theatre came calling and Travesty again screened *Obscurity*, with new interstitial material and some re-editing of the original films. The show was a sellout. In 2017, AFI offered another screening, and the group managed to produce a new short, *Curse of the Atomic Greasers 2: Last Bus to Bladensburg*, forty-one years after the original Atomic Greasers.

> In the movie, *No Way Out*, there's a scene where Kevin Costner jumps off the Whitehurst Freeway and lands onto the roof of the Bayou. Dave Nuttycombe tried that once, but he didn't quite make the impact he was seeking. * So, he co-produced the film *The Bayou: DC's Killer Joint* in collaboration with Director Dave Liling, and co-writers, the former DC 101 producer Bill Scanlan, and former Washington Post staffer, Vinnie Perrone. *The Washington City Paper* summed up an interesting review: "*The Bayou: DC's Killer Joint* may not convince the Bayou's many critics that the place was a treasure, but that's probably not what it aspires to do. It serves as a valuable document of the venue's long, influential history as a DC pop-cultural center—-not to mention its simple, timeless importance to some as a boozy refuge."
> The Capital Acts co-authors say, "Trust us. Anything connected with Nutttycombe is gold. It features so many musicians we love.

> Watching this film is also cheaper than therapy, and way more entertaining."
> https://www.concertarchives.org/venues/the-bayou
> is an online history of the Bayou
>
> Steve M.

* Mr. Nuttycombe suggests that this never happened, though he is happy to be mistaken for Kevin Costner, which has also never happened.

* * *

Lewis Black was born on August 30, 1948, in DC and grew up in the Burnt Mills neighborhood of Silver Spring, Maryland. He graduated from Springbrook High School in 1966. In his 2005 autobiography, *Nothing's Sacred*, he cites attending Martin Luther King "I Have a Dream" speech.

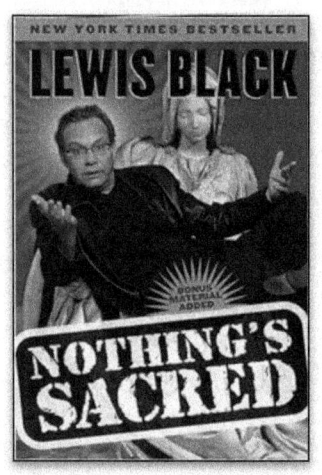

"I was a hundred yards from him. I may not have fully comprehended the moment, but I knew I was in the presence of greatness. My finest moment was probably when my friends and I took off our clothes and strolled buck-naked around the Jefferson Memorial. Even if people noticed, they didn't seem to care."

He was in 10th grade when President John F. Kennedy was shot, and notes at this time, when his world began to crumble, his sense of humor blossomed. "Nothing develops one sense of humor more than the hard reality of trauma. Humor is how we find comfort in the totally illogical. For it is the bridge back to the logical."

Black cites, Paul Krasner's satiric magazine, *The Realist*, as one influence. "It taught me never to trust anyone who doesn't have a sense of humor."

The top SAT student in his high school graduating class, he applied to Yale, Princeton, Brown, Amherst, Williams, and Georgetown. He was rejected by all except Georgetown. He then realized he didn't want to go there, as that was too close to his home. He wanted to go to a college where his parents couldn't get to him on the weekends.

Yet, he enrolled at the University of Maryland for his freshman year. He dreamed of killing his high school guidance counselor, who he blamed for the college rejection letters. His mission was to transfer to a better school. "The highlights of the year were the times we would head to a rock club to listen to a group called The Great Dames. The band consisted of four beautiful, tall women who would transport me out of my ever-present depression. Sadly, they were nearly the sum of my sex life. I never had the nerve to speak to any of them. I would just constantly fantasize about our lives together. It's amazing how little it takes to keep a man going."

About Washington DC, he added in his bio: "The problem I always found living so close to DC as a kid was that the government was always in your face. It could make you crazy. The morons start spouting nonsense, and because you're close by, you just want to drive downtown, find them, and start screaming at them. If I had lived there as an adult, I probably would have lived over a grate near the Capitol building so I could yell at them every day."

Chapter 19 – Everyday Holliday (Stage One)

© Geoffrey S. Baker

I first met Johnny Holliday in 1986 at the WMAL radio station near the intersection of Jennifer Street and Wisconsin Ave NW for an interview for the Journal newspapers. I watched him prepare his twice-daily sports report for the syndicated ABC Information Network. He was alert but easygoing and appeared much younger than his then forty-seven years old.

He exchanged good-natured banter with passing colleagues and a few guests between phone calls, gathering information. Following a last call from New York and a two-minute forefinger blitz at his manual typewriter, he slipped into a small studio just down the hall. And with the flick of a switch, his familiar voice was broadcast to 400 stations coast-to-coast. That could be about two million listeners then. *Wow, he made that look easy*, I thought.

Johnny was celebrating thirty years on air at that time. "Looking back at everything I've done," he told me. "I guess I've managed to cover all the bases."

In fact, he had covered not only the bases but also the end zones, basketball courts, putting greens, and racetracks. He was also a play-by-play announcer for WMAL, ABC radio, and Home Team Sports cable TV. Holiday had painted audio and video pictures of more than 1,300 games then, including University of Maryland and basketball and football, Bullets, Orioles, NCAA, USFL Masters, golf, even the Kentucky Derby.

"It's not a job." He said, "After all, how many guys would love to get on a plane and fly to South Bend, Indiana to broadcast the play-by-play of a Maryland-Notre Dame football game?" He paused, then answered his question. "Why? They'd give their left arm to do that, and I'm getting paid. There's no way to beat a combination like that."

Also frequently seen and heard on TV and radio commercials, Johnny had then starred in thirteen dinner show productions at the Harlequin Dinner Theater, including *Company*, *Bye Bye Birdie*, and *How to Succeed in Business Without Really Trying*.

Johnny Holiday Bobbitt (his real name) is a native of Miami, where he played baseball, football, and basketball in high school and went out for drama as well. "I always felt that the more well-rounded you are, the better off in life you would be," he explained, adding: "The more you do, the more audience you'll have."

Later, on the interview day, a quiet Holiday was set in a silent studio. He sipped a can of grapefruit juice. His broadcast responsibilities had Most guys settle for ticker-tape play-by-play, but Johnny finds the human-interest angle. "No matter what town we're in, the phone rings, and it's one of his buddies. No matter where it is, it's Johnny's town."

In 1986, Johnny got to the WMAL studio at 5:30 a.m. for morning sports reports and returned at four for his afternoon spots. When he was doing dinner theater. He didn't get home until 11:00 p.m. And when he wasn't doing dinner theater, he often played benefit basketball games after hours at local high schools with his Radio Oneders basketball team. In 927 games, Holiday estimated that his team had raised more than $1.4 million for community causes.

And then, of course, there were his "play-by-play" sports broadcasts of Maryland University basketball and football games at home and away. "I have no social life," he laughed. But it didn't look like Johnny Holiday would have it any other way.

* * *

The Journal article was well-received. I felt lucky to have met Johnny. Fast forward fifteen years. I was asked at my GU job if I knew anyone in broadcasting who might speak to students about careers in the field. I called up Johnny, and he agreed to come and speak to the students. Ben Fong Torres (the once *Rolling Stone* magazine editor and author) had then featured Johnny in his new book about radio, *The Hits Just Keep on Coming*: "Johnny was proud to be mentioned but I told him that he should write his own book."

He shot back, "I will if you'll help me." And we were off and running. Our 2001 book, *Johnny Holliday: From Rock to Jock* with a Foreword by Tony Kornheiser (and still in print), was applauded, documenting his legendary, award-winning sports broadcasting career with the University of Maryland basketball, the Olympics, and other adventures.

Ben Fong Torres wrote a cover endorsement for us: "You think Johnny Holliday is a great sportscaster? You should've seen him on the court as a blazing point guard on various radio station basketball teams. And you should've heard Johnny as a rapid-fire DJ, spinning stacks of hot wax at topflight Top 40 stations from San Francisco to New York City. *In Johnny Holliday: From Rock to Jock*, Stephen Moore slows him down just enough to tell you Johnny's amazing story."

In 2001 and our book. © S. Moore

For starters, in our early book research, Ben Fong-Torres told me how much he loved Holliday in San Francisco, listening to him on KYA radio. "Johnny emceed the last Beatles show in 1966 at Candlestick Park," Ben reported. But when I mentioned this to Johnny, he replied, "No, I didn't do that."

Further research proved that Johnny was indeed there with the Beatles. Confronted with the truth, he replied "I guess I forgot about it."

"You FORGOT you emceed the last US Beatles concert," I yelled. I couldn't believe it, but as he regaled me with rock and roll encounters and even more impressive sports stories, I understood how his rich life with so many unforgettable moments could cause selected amnesia.

In Johnny's words: "By age fourteen, I was captivated by Miami radio. Especially by Jerry Weitzner of WINZ 940. Because I thought it would be fun, I called Jerry at the station and asked whether he needed an assistant. I ended up working for him and helping to file his records away. And running his errands after school.

"In 1956, I tried the Miami radio market and came up sucking air. The only two stations that I didn't try or that hadn't rejected me were Rhythm and Blues and R&B formats."

This was nearly seventy years ago, and Miami was fiercely segregated. The pre-Elvis R&B music was still regarded as race music and hadn't yet crossed over to find acceptance by a white audience. Nat King Cole was enormous then and could easily sell out his engagement at the Fountain Blue Hotel. However, when the show ended, he had to travel back to the Lord Calvert Hotel in the Black community to get a room for the night.

"But what the heck, I thought with no job offers from the white stations, I had nothing to lose by trying R&B. I liked the. I got the job on WFC. The listeners were very supportive and accepted me. We did some remote broadcasts from the rooftop gardens of the Lord Calvert Hotel with performers like Lena Horne and Louis Armstrong.

"From Miami, I went to Rochester, NY radio and from there to WHK in Cleveland. A series of 'Crusin" records was released in the early 1970s that featured the Top 40 DJs from the late 1950s through the mid-60s. My WHK work is heard on the Crusin' 64 album.

"When Washington Post music critic Richard Harrington reviewed '64' as the best of the series, I phoned Richard to offer my thanks, he replied. 'That's you? I thought it was some other guy in Cleveland.'

"After five years in Cleveland, my next radio gig was 1010-WINS in New York City. I relished the excitement of New York City immediately. I love being on 50,000-watt WINS with Murray the K, just in time for The Beatles' American invasion.

"Years later, when I was at WWDC in 1975, management sought to generate some strong publicity by hiring my old mentor, Murray the K, 'the fifth Beatle.' The mistake that Murray made when he took the job here is that he never related to the local audience. All he wanted to do was tell his listeners about his New York adventures. Murray's ratings suggested that Washington listeners didn't give a damn about his schmoozing with Tom Jones or his weekend parties in New York.

"He. never caught on at WWDC and later jumped to DC's pioneer alternative music station, WHFS. But he didn't do well there, either. He finally made his way back to New York to his old station WOR until throat cancer claimed his voice and his life."

In the mid-60s, Johnny became the announcer for TV's "Hullabaloo," which was broadcast at Studio 8H, the same one now used for *Saturday Night Live*.

"My favorite highlights from doing that show were Marvin Gaye's 'Ain't That Peculiar,' and Chuck Berry's 'Johnny B. Goode.'

The Four Seasons with Johnny in NYC. © J. Holliday

"When I next moved to San Francisco's KYA, I continued doing 'Hullabaloo.' This meant I'd leave San Francisco at 8 a.m., arrived in New York City at 4 p.m., with a car waiting to go to NBC. We taped two shows. I'd be back on a flight to San Francisco at 11 p.m. that night. I did this every week except when we did the show from NBC Burbank, CA a few times.

"KYA was the 'Boss of the Bay,' and yours truly became the Baron of the Bay. KYA was involved with whatever was happening musically in San Francisco in 1967. We sponsored shows at the Cow Palace and the other local venues. One of the first big shows I emceed featured The Rolling Stones, The Byrds, The Beau Brummels, and Paul Revere and the Raiders.

Sly and Johnny © J. Holliday

"One of the most talented jocks in the city was Sylvester Stewart, also known as Sly Stone, working at K-Soul programming to the city's Black audience. I listened to Sly with guests like Billy Preston who dropped by to jam with him on the air. Sly had a great set of pipes and a soothing radio style.

It was Sly's idea to add tunes by The Beatles and Bob Dylan to the K-SOL playlist.

"After I became friendly with him, we cooked up an idea to put together a television show. Sly would be the Black guy, and I'd be the white guy. We called our show 'Salt and Pepper.' The show never got off the ground, but we had fun dreaming it up. By February 1967, he performed locally with his own group, the Family Stone.

"My San Francisco experiences would prepare me for life in Washington, DC." (Continued in Chapter 47)

Mary Clare and Johnny on their wedding day, and at a 2021 Johnny tribute.
© J. Holliday

Chapter 20: Roberta's First Take

"If anybody asks me where I'm from, my first inclination is to say Washington, because that's where I grew up meaningfully. I had to sign Roberta Flack to our Atlantic Records label because listening to her sing and play the piano gave me a sense of an ever deeper meaning to my life. Where I was from and where I could go."

Ahmet Ertegun, *Atlantic Records: The House That I Built*

Roberta Cleopatra Flack was born in 1937 in Black Mountain, North Carolina, to a musical family but raised in the Green Valley neighborhood of Arlington, Virginia. She started piano lessons at age nine and sang and played organ and piano for the first time publicly at her home church, the Lomax AME Zion, where her mother, Laron Flack, was the organist. Laron's love for music and devoted involvement in the church significantly shaped her daughter's musical interest and talent. The Flack family allowed young Roberta to attend concerts by the Queen of Gospel, Mahalia Jackson, and the pioneering Soul Stirrers, whom Alan Lomax had recorded in 1936 for his Library of Congress American Music project. Sam Cooke began his career in this group in 1958, and Roberta was greatly inspired by his music.

Flack attended the Hoffman-Boston High School—then the only school available for African American children in Arlington—until age fifteen, when Roberta expanded her musical range to classical, winning second place in a Virginia statewide piano competition. With this prize, she became one of the youngest—but undoubtedly the most famous—students in Howard University history to be admitted with a full music scholarship.

After graduation, she began student teaching in DC; her father's death called her back to Farmville, NC. She accepted a teaching position in a segregated school district. As the solo music teacher responsible for 1300 students ranging from kindergarten to twelfth grade, she told journalist Philip Jackson that she experienced significant weight loss and even suffered a nervous breakdown throughout that challenging period. However, despite the hardships, she did some good things that year. Returning to the DC area with her bachelor's in music education, she taught music at Browne, Banneker, and Rabaut Junior High Schools and gave private piano lessons in her house on Euclid Avenue, where she moved from Arlington.

Co-author Charlie Young's college friend Jo Spiller and family lived next door to Roberta in Arlington. Jo says she was friendly and kind, occasionally inviting them to catch her performances at DC venues, including the elegant Tivoli Club, where Roberta accompanied Opera singers on piano while they sauntered around the room. During their breaks Roberta would play folks songs, blues, and popular tunes. She graduated to the 1520 Club for a few nights weekly singing solo with her piano, and then—most notably— to Henry Yaffe's Mr. Henry's restaurant on Capitol Hill.

There she played five nights a week, three sets per night, and prominent musical faces began to turn up in those Mr. Henry's audience as word spread about the talented schoolteacher who sang and played piano by night. High-profile entertainers appearing in town would come in late at night to hear her sing. Visitors identified include Johnny Mathis, Ramsey Lewis, Burt Bacharach, Woody Allen, Bill Cosby, Ramsey Lewis, and Less McCann.

McCann was knocked out by her act. He told PBS affiliate WNET, "Her voice touched, tapped, trapped and kicked every emotion I've ever known." He arranged for Roberta to record an incredible thirty-nine demos in one nine-hour session with Atlantic Records, who signed her in 1969. Her debut album, "Take One," recorded in a ten-hour session, included the Eugene McDaniels song, "Compared to What," released as a single. It is an extraordinary debut album that deserves recognition as a timeless masterpiece. Exquisite production. Captivating song selection. It showcased Roberta Flack's tremendous talent.

A year later, her second LP was released. It marked her first work with Donny Hathaway, who became a frequent collaborator. Then—thanks to its inclusion in Clint Eastwood's 1972 *Play Misty for Me* film three years after its release—"The First Time Ever I Saw Your Face" (from her debut LP) was released as a single and became an international hit, shooting to number one in the US within seven weeks.

The song was a 1957 folk song written by British political singer-songwriter Ewan MacColl for his wife Peggy Seeger (Pete's half-sister), who grew up in Washington. Roberta taught this song to her high school students and regularly performed it at her residency at Mr. Henry's. Elvis, Peter Paul & Mary, and Johnny Cash had recorded it, but Roberta's voice made it a hit.

Mr. Henry's

Henry Yaffe was a hairdresser in his native Baltimore and Washington, an Army Air Forces bombardier during World War II, and an Air Force cryptographer during the Korean War. In 1965 Yaffe bought the 601 Club, a country-western bar at Pennsylvania Avenue and 6th Street SE and, without closing, remodeled the space to the wood-paneled pub that became Mr. Henry's.

Yaffe said, "Roberta told me if I could give her work there three nights a week, then she would quit teaching." She did, and Jaffe successfully converted the apartment above the bar into a dedicated space known as the Roberta Flack Room with oak paneling obtained from the now defunct Dodge Hotel near Union Station. He added church pews and a Mason & Hamlin piano to create a more intimate energy. The decor included tastefully crafted upholstered chairs exuding a conservative aesthetic reminiscent of the 1950s. He designed the acoustic system catering to Roberta's specific requirements. He became a concert promoter and once brought trumpeter Miles Davis to DAR Constitution Hall. Roberta became known around town for her unwavering pursuit of perfection.

April 22, 1972, was declared Roberta Flack Day with a weekend celebration, including receptions at the Kennedy Center and the Congressional Caucus Room. She was honored with the Top Female Vocalist Award from Downbeat Magazine and performed a public concert at the Lincoln Memorial. Her days as a teacher were long behind her; she was on her way to four Grammy Awards, including a Lifetime Achievement Award.

As she told *Ebony Magazine*, "Once I realized music—any kind—can feel holy and sacred, I knew I'd found my religion." In Roberta Flack's 1953 senior yearbook at Hoffman-Boston, she was listed as "most musical" in the class superlatives, and in the "Class Prophecy," her classmates predicted she would play piano at Carnegie Hall. This prediction eventually came true when Flack performed there in 1971 and again in 1981.

Photo is Roberta Flack Day poster © Lou Stovall & Lloyd McNeill

Donny Hathaway

Born and raised in Chicago in 1945 Donny Hathaway received a scholarship to Howard University to study music. There he met his roommate, Ric Powell, a drummer and they formed the Ric Powell Trio with pianist Harold Wheeler, "I had approached Donny about joining us but he was cautious." Ric told MusicManKevin (Kevin Gowens) in *Soulful Conversations*

(2016). "Donny's family had warned him about getting involved in music that was 'away from the church' so there was pressure there that he might end up like Sam Cooke and others who had strayed from the church. Donny knew 'Maria' from *West Side Story*, 'Georgia,' and 'The In Crowd' by Ramsey Lewis. So he agreed to join us. There was a club called Billy's on Vermont Avenue who hired us and we began playing the Black clubs around the Howard and the white clubs on Capitol Hill. And when Dr. Martin Luther King was killed, Donny wrote 'The Ghetto' with his Howard roommate Leo Hutson, 'Trying Times' and most important, 'Thank You Master for my Soul.'

"Curtis Mayfield came to DC and offered Donny an opportunity to work with the Mayfield singers as a producer for Curtom Records. Donny moved to Chicago but he was like Duke Ellington with his arranging in a studio and Curtis wasn't using his talent. He could go into a studio late and night and in the morning emerge with a masterpiece. Some of the musicians would complain that his arranging with violins and horns were so lovely that they were stronger than their voices."

One of the Mayfield singers was Guy Draper, also a Howard University friend of Donny's who helped organize more Howard U music pals: Marvin Brown, Tom Fauntleroy, Bob Hayes, George Roland and Al Johnson, first as Al and the Vikings, originally, and finally The Unifics' *Draper* produced their 1968 hit songs, "Court of Love," "It's a Groovy World," and "Toshisumasu."

Hathaway would team with Roberta producing two hit singles, "The Closer I Get to You" and "Where is the Love?" It established them in a romantic, almost erotic setting, highly appreciated by their fans. But they were only drawn together by friendship. Roberta Flack commented, "People compare him to Otis Redding. But Donnie is greater. He's not only a singer, but also a composer, arranger, conductor, singer and teacher."

Donny Hathaway, then thirty-three-years-old, unexpectedly died on Saturday after he plunged from the fifteenth floor of his Essex House room at 160 Central Park South. The singer had recently returned from dinner with Roberta with whom he had spent the day recording, according to Edward Howard, a business associate. "We suspect suicide," was the police's verdict. His room was bolted shut and no visitors were present, he added. But Mr. Howard, vice president of David M. Franklin & Associates, an Atlanta-based concern managing Hathaway and other prominent Black entertainers, disagreed saying "he was in good spirits, having just written new music and having performed with Roberta all day. He hadn't been drinking heavily or taking drugs of any sort."

According to his estranged wife, Eulalah, he was hospitalized for emotional problems on two occasions in 1972. The day after he died she said, "He was troubled." She said his trouble was his quick rise to success and the anxiety it had produced. Eulalah, also a singer met when they were students at Howard University. He was a straight-A student although he never graduated. She said her husband did not use drugs.

At the Birchmere © K.C. Alexandria

Lalah Hathaway is the daughter of Donny. In 1991, Lalah, with saxophonist Gerald Albright, and keyboardist Joe Sample, played two sold-out R&B/light jazz shows at the Birchmere music hall in Alexandria, VA. Promotor Michael Jaworek cites this show as a pivotal event for the hall as it began to draw crowds that appreciated R&B to the Birchmere then better known as a bluegrass, country, and pop venue.

The Washington Post's Mike Joyce wrote about her performance: "The daughter of the late Donny Hathaway displayed a big, sultry voice, plenty of poise and often improved upon the recorded versions of the songs she drew from..."

Both Sample and Lalah Hathaway later collaborated in 1999 on the successful album *The Song Lives On*. Lalah has returned annually to the hall since then.

Donal Leace

West Virginia song writer Donal Leace began singing folk songs in local DC coffee shops while a freshman at Howard University in 1960. "On a good night, I could make $60 and on bad nights, I was guaranteed $10," he told me in 2013 sitting in his office at Duke Ellington School of Performing Arts.

Donal then served as Chair of the Drama Department at where he taught and mentored young artists including comedian **Dave Chappelle** and opera mezzo-soprano, **Denyce Graves**, who made her debut at the Metropolitan in 1995.

© Photo: Connie Brandt Smith

Among his many contributions, Donal served as a judge for the National Theatre Helen Hayes Awards. In 2000, Donal was named to the Washington Area Music Awards Hall of Fame and was inducted into *Washingtonian Magazine's* Music Hall of Fame in 2003. He met fellow musicians Carolyn Hester, Mike Seeger, and Dave Van Ronk. They helped him get a gig at the Showboat.

Donal remembers, "In 1961, Van Ronk invited me to Gerde's Folk City in New York City to meet the new folksinger, Bob Dylan. I was most interested in Bob's arranging then, on songs like 'House of the Rising Sun.' It was interesting when Bob later came down to do the Showboat Some guy kept giving Bob the Nazi salute during his set until he was thrown out. Bob's new original songs were a little off-putting because most of us were trying to perfect the traditional folk songs."

Leace was offered the opening spot at Georgetown's Shadows Club in 1962 by then-owners Jack Weiss and Bob Covallo. Donal says, "I gave up a sure thing—one night a week at the Showboat for six nights a week at a club that might not work out. It was a Georgetown University hangout. Lots of students. I moved into the upstairs apartment and went to work. The Showboat was known as the 'Home of Charlie Byrd' so they hung a sign outside the Shadows, 'The Home of Donal Leace,' which was an ego boost and also literally true. The first acts that came in were The Journeymen (Scott McKenzie, John Phillips, and Dick Weissman), Josh White Jr., and someone I had lobbied for, Judy Collins."

First Dylan show in DC: Bob Dylan sat in with a University of Virginia folksinger friend, **Paul Clayton**, on September 24, 1961, at Charlie Byrd's and Pete Lambros's Showboat Lounge for a Sunday night hootenanny. Dylan has acknowledged that "Don't Think Twice..." was a riff that Paul [Clayton] had. Donal Leace talked with me about attending that show: Dylan's arrival in Greenwich Village was in January 1961. Paul Clayton was a University of Virginia folksinger who later committed suicide. Paul Clayton's out of print *The Folksong Revival* book also talks about Dylan as they were very close friends in those early days. It now appears that Bob's "original" "Don't Think Twice" was a reworking of Clayton's song, "Who's Gonna Buy You Ribbons When I'm Gone?" (A quiet lawsuit settlement was done later by their publishers.)

In a 1964 interview with folk fanzine *Gargoyle*, Dylan said "[Folk music] goes deeper than just myself singing it, it goes into legends and Bibles, it goes into curses and myths, it goes into plagues, it goes into all kinds of weird things that I don't even know about, can't pretend to know about. **The only guy I know that can really do it is a guy named Paul Clayton**, he's the only guy I've ever heard or seen who can sing songs like this, because he's a medium, he's not trying to personalize it, he's bringing it to you... Paul, he's a trance."

S. Moore

Note: Here's the YouTube link for Clayton's song. https://www.youtube.com/watch?v=dTZ_hMiI8Tg
Bob clearly ripped this one off.

David Pitts, author and journalist, said in his tribute: "Donal was known as 'Washington's Favorite Folk Singer,' working for over nine years at the famed Cellar Door in Georgetown. Over the years he performed with many of the musical greats, including quite simply an American treasure whose music speaks to all the world. He earned his undergraduate degree at Howard University in where he served as President of the Howard Players. Donal earned graduate degrees from Georgetown University and George Washington University; he was also honored as both a Fulbright Scholar and US Presidential Scholar. During the 60s John Denver, Odetta, Nina Simone, Judy Collins, Ramsey Lewis, Keter Betts, and Emmylou Harris, as well as comedians Dick Gregory, Bill Cosby and Richard Pryor. Donal recorded for Franc, Gateway, JBL and Atlantic Records, touring nationally with Nancy Wilson and internationally with Roberta Flack. He recorded his first album *Donal Leace* in 1972, and later released CDs *Leace on Life* in 1992 and *Leace Renewed* followed in 2002. Donal's music inspired many, including Kanye West, who sampled 'Today Won't Come Again' on his 2005 hit, 'Hey Mama.' Donal was deeply committed to the Washington theater community. Among his many contributions, Donal served as a judge for the Washington Theater Awards Society's Helen Hayes Awards. In 2000 Donal was named to the Washington Area Music Awards Hall of Fame and was inducted into the *Washingtonian Magazine*'s 'Washington Music Hall of Fame' in 2003. Donal Richard Leace, passed away from COVID-19 on November 21, 2020."

Ahmet Ertegun
"I came close to signing Elvis Presley. I offered 25,000 for his contract and they asked for 45,000 and I just didn't have the other twenty grand. I should have gotten The Beatles, but one of my lawyers kind of messed up."

A. Ertegun

Date of Birth: July 31, 1923
Place of Birth: Istanbul, Turkey
Family Background: Moved to Washington, DC, in 1935 when his father was appointed U.S. Ambassador of the Republic of Turkey.

One brother: Nesuhi, introduced him to jazz music at an early age: First exposed to the music of Duke Ellington and Cab Calloway at the age of nine.

At age fourteen, he received a record cutting machine from his mother, which sparked his interest in composing lyrics for instrumental tracks. He developed a passion for music, particularly jazz, which led him to the heart of Washington DC's soul district to watch renowned artists like Duke Ellington, Cab Calloway, Billie Holiday, and Louis Armstrong.

Education: Attended an all-male private school, Landon School, in Bethesda, Maryland. Graduated from Saint John's College in Annapolis in 1944. Continued his education with graduate courses in medieval philosophy at Georgetown post-graduation.

Ertegun has said he gained deeper insights into the struggles faced by Black people in America while studying at Howard University fostering empathy for those facing discrimination.

Cultural Reflections: Although Turks were never enslaved, he saw recognized parallels in the discrimination faced by Muslims in Europe, particularly during historical conflicts.

DC Music: With his brother he amassed a substantial collection of over 15,000 jazz and blues 78 records and frequently visited Commodore music shop a pivotal time in American history.

Stereophile Review: Ahmet Ertegun's legendary stewardship of New York–based Atlantic Records made him one of the most powerful figures in the music industry, but he began his career with the small, unsuccessful DC label Quality Records. Ahmet and his older brother Nesuhi lived in DC, where their father served as an ambassador from Turkey. The brothers were avid traditional jazz fans, well-versed in the local music scene. In '46, Ahmet partnered with Herb Abramson of Jubilee Records and Max "Waxie Maxie" Silverman, owner of the Quality Music Store. They named the label Quality Records after Maxie's store.

Bo Diddley was also in DC during the late 50s, cutting sides in his home studio. That's Diddley on guitar with his band backing up the great Washington vocalist Billy Stewart on "Billy's Heartache"/"Baby You're My Only Love" (1957). Diddley also plays on the '57 Marquees releases "Wyatt Earp" and "Hey Little School Girl."

(See Chapter 30: Bo Diddley and Disciples)

Chapter 21 – Lady Helen Hayes
by Donn B. Murphy and Stephen Moore

Helen Hayes. Portrait by Furman Finck, 1966. National Portrait Gallery, Smithsonian Institution. The actress's favorite portrait hangs in the Helen Hayes Gallery of the National Theatre in Washington, DC.

Helen Hayes reigned on Broadway for nearly fifty years and in the hearts of Americans for much of the 20th century. The petite actress began her career as a child, and performed as an ingenue, serious actress, and character comedienne, enriching the stage, films, radio, and television in every part she played.

She garnered a Best Oscar award—and was the first stage actress to do so—in the 1931 film *The Sin of Madelon Claudet*, playing a hapless, wrongly accused woman who tragically descends from virtuous mother to blowzy prostitute. The actor playing her husband was native Washingtonian Alan Hale (later the real-life dad of Alan Hale, Jr., the Skipper in *Gilligan's Island*).

In 1971, she won her second Academy Award as Best Supporting Actress for the film *Airport*, playing the endearing but wily little old lady. This captivating comic portrait brought her to the attention of young audiences unfamiliar with her stage career.

    Helen's portrayal of the grave Queen Victoria in the Broadway play *Victoria Regina* was a tour de force. Her performance, alongside then-newcomer Vincent Price, captivated audiences for two years on Broadway and continued road tours. Her dedication to the role, performing it well over one thousand times, left a lasting impression on the theater world. Producer Gilbert Miller estimated that her performance was witnessed by a staggering 2 million people, a testament to the power of her art.

* * *

    Helen Brown was born in the nation's capital on October 10, 1900, the only child in a boisterous Irish clan. Her father was Francis Van Arnum Brown, a traveling salesman for the Auth North Provision meat processing plant on Bladensburg Road not far from New York Avenue. Helen was his eager companion at baseball games. Together, they were thrilled at concerts by the United States Marine Band under the baton of John Phillip Sousa. Her mother, Catherine Estelle Brown, was called "Brownie" and named after her father's cousin, Catherine Hayes, a professional singer celebrated as the "Swan of Erin" and well-known in her native Ireland. Helen would eventually adopt Hayes as a stage name.

    Helen was just four when she was discovered one day by her mother while in the bathtub, wearing a towel headdress and waving a rattan fan. Playing her first role, the tot announced grandly that she was "Clee O' Patrick in her bath."

    Enthralled by the budding talent of Sarah Bernhardt, Brownie promptly took Helen to her first play. They paid a quarter each for grand seats in the front row of the top balcony of the National Theatre, just two blocks from the White House. The performance left the young Helen spellbound, clinging to her seat, and hoping against hope that the actors would reappear. Standing on the stage of the National eighty years later, Hayes looked back with a mix of nostalgia and longing, telling a captivated audience, "I didn't want to leave the theater—and I guess I never really have."

Brownie took Helen to every possible stage show and concert she could, the two of them often standing in queue for hours to acquire the best available or least expensive seats. They also went to flickering silent movies at the Star Nickelodeon Theater on 9th street, NW.

Brownie enrolled Helen in the Holy Cross Academy grade school when she was five and make her private stage debut as Peaseblossom in a children's version of Shakespeare's *Midsummer Night's Dream*. Brownie enrolled her in the fashionable and popular dance classes conducted by Miss Minnie Hawke, who staged an elaborate May Ball each fall, and sometimes a musical spectacle with a storyline.

Helen's first public performance was doing an Irish jig dance, but after a few faltering steps, she withdrew in panic. Hayes commented in 1990, "I was to do an Irish jig. I came on and saw the audience and just kept on going in a circle and off. Then I collected myself in the wings, and I wanted to go back, but they wouldn't let me. They had had it with me."

But the next year on January 22, 1909, Helen Hayes was a showstopper at Washington's Belasco Theater on Lafayette Square across from the White House. In a matinee performance of *Jack, the Giant Killer* she impersonated the currently popular music comedy star Annabelle Whitford in her Gibson Girl Bathing Beauty number from the Ziegfield Follies. Helen accurately simulated Whitford's routine. *The Washington Post*, *The Washington Star*, and *The News* called her "most clever," "perfectly delightful," and "among the biggest hits of the afternoon."

New York actor-manager Lou Fields was in the audience and invited Mrs. Brown to contact him when she was ready to bring her daughter to New York. Several years later, she did just that. In the meantime, however, Hayes joined the Columbia Theater Players where she made her professional debut as Helen Hayes Brown on May 24th, 1909, portraying the young Prince Charles in a royal family. Newspapers called her "another star...And one of the hits of the evening...already a warm favorite." Next, just eight years old but small for her age, she played Claudia, age five, in *The Prince Chap*. And again, she scored.

Behind the scenes, Hayes grappled with her self-image, feeling she was plain and uncomfortable in the ruffled frocks and oversized hair bows she had to wear for her early performances. This insecurity persisted even at the peak of her career when she intended to purchase a fur coat but instead splurged on an impressionist painting. She once overheard two matinee ladies discussing her, but they dismissed the idea that it could be her due to what they perceived as the dullness of her appeal.

However, she was captivated by the artistry of Hollywood's makeup artists. She took it upon herself to learn the craft, a skill she would use to her advantage both on and off the stage throughout her life. Her transformation from a pubescent Princess to a Dowager queen in her greatest role, Victoria Regina was particularly lauded. She even held cotton pads in her cheeks during the final scene to achieve the puffy visage of the ancient monarch.

In the fall of 1909, Brownie decided it was now time to take her daughter to New York to see what Broadway had to offer. They were welcomed by Lou Fields, who was himself preparing to star in *Old Dutch*, a Victor Herbert musical.

She was paid thirty-five dollars a week, nearly what her father was earning and made an immediate success as the little mime in the show, which opened on November 22, 1909, at the Herald Square Theatre. Hayes toured with the show.

Old Dutch marked the Broadway debut of Helen Hayes Brown, a momentous occasion that drew the attention of celebrities Lillian Russell and Diamond Jim Brady, who sat in boxes on opposite sides of the theater on the opening night. In the *Evening World Newspaper*, reviewer Charles Danton called her out, "In this clever tot, Mr. Fields has the greatest leading woman of her size. With a youngster only a head taller than herself, she tumbles the house into laughter as she goes through the soulful pantomime of a sentimental song." This early recognition and praise from the industry and the public alike, is a testament to her talent and the impact she was already making in the theater world.

From 1915 to 1917, she returned to DC to act with the Poly Players, and back to Broadway with the renowned John Drew in *The Prodigal Husband*. That same year, she made a film, *The Weavers of Life*, dubbing this this "one my first and my worst." She also graduated that year from the Academy of the Sacred Heart high school on Park Road NW.

Dynamic Broadway producer George C. Tyler became her primary mentor. He sent her back to Washington in the summer of 1919 to join a new repertory company he had established at the National Theatre and appear with Alfred Lunt in *On the Hiring Line*. Coming to maturity, Hayes mastered the flapper genre, which used such ploys as a hand-on-the-hip pose, pursed lips, and come-ons like "Oh, you naughty boy!" And almost overnight, she became Broadway's Darling Ingenue. For several years, she could do no wrong.

And then, in Bab, she received her first star billing, with her name in lights on a huge electric sign. The producer chose her name because it was shorter than the playwright Booth Tarkington's and could, therefore, be set up in larger letters. Hayes was only twenty but still learning her craft.

Her success story extended to the late 1920s, when she found her niche in radio. Not only did she become the star of several series, but she also took on the role of a producer. Her leading men included the brilliant Orson Welles, who was not only her producer but also her co-star for a season. The title "First Lady of the American Theatre" was first bestowed upon her by a sponsor for one of her series. Over time, she inherited the title without any rivals, a testament to her unmatched talent and dedication.

To her mother's dismay, she began encountering Charles MacArthur, a former Chicago journalist who would become an elegant Manhattan writer and playwright Friends thought theirs was an unfortunate mismatch. Helen was too naive, they reasoned. Charlie was too worldly and cynical. He already had a string of girls, and Dorothy Parker had nearly committed suicide on his account. He was a generous drinking companion, and an irrepressible practical joker, and Helen adored him. His writing partner and close comrade was Ben Heck, and their play *The Front Page* was about to open on

Broadway. If it succeeds, Charlie promises that he and Helen will be married. It was clear that the play was a roaring success, and Charlie and Helen were married.

Charlie told Helen, "with me, you may never be rich, but you'll never be bored." A pledge that was fulfilled. And which sustained their marriage. He proved to be her great and only love. Her daughter, Mary McArthur, was born the morning after Valentine's Day in 1930. In that year Hayes supported the congressional campaign of socialist Haywood Brown, a friend from the Algonquin Roundtable. After that, her politics veered to the right, and she eventually became a dedicated Republican.

In 1932, Helen Hayes starred with Gary Cooper in Paramount's *A Farewell to Arms*. The film had been slashed by the censorious scissors of the Hays Office, a powerful industry self-policing agency. And one "offensive" climactic seduction scene was relegated to the cutting room floor, diminishing the credibility of the drama. Helen Hayes told us she was "brokenhearted and depressed" some sixty years later when she recalled that an attempt to restore the film to its whole failed because the excised footage had been lost.

Helen knew that sex and glamour, on screen and off, were not her strong qualities. She lacked the long, slim legs, broad shoulders, fanfare, bust and blockbuster cheekbones sought by the producers, and favored by cinematographers for silver screen sirens in that era. MGM mogul, LB Mayor was determined to solve that when he ordered for her a slinky white satin gown in which he had successfully showcased Norma Shearer. It will be very revealing, he told Helen. She retorted, "What it will reveal will not help."

Donn, Helen, and Steve in 1990
© Richard Coe

Donn Murphy had another theory on why she

wasn't a movie star. And we took photos to an ophthalmologist to get his opinion. Donn suffered from strabismus, the tendency of one eye to drift wide of alignment.

Unremarked on in thousands of articles about her, and perhaps respectful interviewers ignored this, but our expert eye doctor agreed with us that Helen also had this eye ailment. It helped her onstage with a certain wide-eyed and inquisitive look, as if her mind were focused on distant vistas of contemplation. But the close-up cameras of film and movies were not equally complimentary, and camera operators may have minimized the problem.

No longer a child, she still stood five feet tall in 1933 when she sought to play Mary Stuart, one of the tallest queens in history in Maxwell Anderson's *Mary of Scotland*. When she was told by a producer that she was "too short" for the role, "How short is the roll?" Helen shot back.

Helen told us that on a cold rainy night in Columbus, Ohio she had the most satisfying single performance of her entire career in this play. During the run of *Mary of Scotland*, she was hailed as a major American star, and she came into her own as a tragic actress of regal stature. Audiences in city after city rose in standing ovations.

In 1935 Helen opened the day after Christmas 1935, in another historical drama, *Victoria Regina*.

On her porch running lines for us in 1991. © S. Moore

Audiences were wildly enthusiastic, and this second royal portrait proved to be her great public triumph and centralizing apex of her long career. Invited to the White House, with numerous other awards that followed.

For her scholarly biography, Donn Murphy and I convinced her to let us write it with her providing the Foreword in 1989, and we all met together at her Nyack, NY home and talked with her extensively. Sitting on her backyard porch overlooking the Hudson River she would act out passages from her favorite plays for us over iced tea. Up close and personal, she was amazing.

Helen and Charlie's son, James arrived on December 8, 1937. Both were adopted by the MacArthur's soon after. Jamie made his stage debut at eight years old with his sister Mary, in the play The Corn Is Green. Later educated at Harvard, he continued acting in both film and television, notably in the series Hawaii Five-O, which ran for twelve years from 1968 to 1980. Jim played Danny ("Book em") Danno.

Throughout the 1940s, Helen Hayes toured the country in the plays *Happy Holiday*, *The Glass Menagerie*, *Victoria, Regina*, and *Good Housekeeping*. Mary McArthur appeared again with her mother in a try-out of *Good Housekeeping* in 1949. It was during this run that Mary fell ill and died soon thereafter of polio. James was eleven at the time of this family tragedy. The shocked parents were grief stricken beyond consolation. Hayes suffered pervasive guilt for having been on the road so much while her children were growing up. She was seized by an uncharacteristic paralysis of will while Charlie surrendered to dark despair and drinking. "The very worst thing that can happen is to bury your young," Helen told us.

She was touched by the condolences of many strangers who had lost children but who had somehow survived. She came to see the "need to be strong" for her son. Eventually she took up the battle against the disease which had slain her daughter and her charitable work helped to lead The March of Dimes campaign to cure polio. Overwhelmed with grief, Hayes's husband began drinking heavily and died in 1956.

In 1964 Hayes starred at the Catholic University of America in Washington, DC, in *Good Morning, Miss Stub*, playing with an all-student cast while living on the campus. In 1971, her longtime friend Fr. Gilbert Hartke invited her to return. She chose again to live with the students in the campus dormitory. During rehearsals, she was hospitalized with the recurrence of her dreaded asthma-like attacks. She recovered and the show went on. Helen received congratulations from Mrs. Richard

Nixon at a White House luncheon. But a Washington physician diagnosed her as allergic to backstage dust, cautioning that continued stage work would be dangerous to her health. At her final curtain call of this run, she announced, this time accurately, that she had given her final live performance—on the stage of a Catholic school in Washington, DC, she noted, where her career had begun some sixty-five years earlier.

Helen had previously disparaged television as that little breadbox, but now she said, "'God bless TV" and moved into TV in 1972 included Harvey with James Stewart. She began taping a TV miniseries called *The Snoop Sisters*. In 1971 she won the Academy Award, her second as best supporting actress for the film Airport. She had previously earned the distinction of being the first stage actor to win the award in the 1931 *Sins of Madelon Claudet.*

The last time we saw Helen was in Nyack, when we were wrapping up the *Helen Hayes: A Bio-Bibliography* book and finalizing her Foreword for us. We asked her for some final words about her career.

She told us, "I always thought that the secret of my success is that I am like somebody down the street who lives in the neighborhood." She described herself as plain and unimpressive, endowed with the quality of being average, which created a recognition and a kinship as one of the family. Rather, she was what her fans wished to be humble homie yet worldly, wise, assertive but not unbearable, and pragmatic but alluringly hopeful. She was majestic without being haughty and neighborly, but not commonplace.

Our book *Helen Hayes: A Bio-Bibliography* was published on March 1, 1993, one week before her death. Foreword by Helen Hayes.

Foreword

I am not one to sit and ponder about the past. There is too much in the present demanding attention. So much to see! So much to encounter in the world!

And so I have never stopped to keep scrapbooks. I've been terrible about that one thing and I am sorry. I apologize to the world for it.
I guess I haven't had any great sense of myself as history because as I lived my life, that was enough for me. I never kept my notices, good or bad. They came through and then passed out of my hands and out of my life.

But it is good to know what the past has been: that enables you to enjoy the present. Therefore I appreciate this assembly of such a host of names of my fellow players and such a grand recording of past events. The memories rush back! I appreciate the research effort which went into this volume which will remind me of so much I had forgotten in my long and overcrowded life. Donn Murphy and Stephen Moore remember more about me than I do, I can tell you that! This project has been a delight to me.

But the best part was living it, and for that I give thanks!

Helen Hayes

Helen Hayes

Nyack, New York
October 10, 1991

Richard Coe, Washington Post theater critic, was Helen's close friend. She would stay with him when she visited Washington. Helen died on Saint Patrick's Day, 1993 of congestive heart failure.

© S. Moore

Capital Acts: Washington DC Performing Arts

> 235 NORTH BROADWAY
> NYACK, N.Y. 10960
>
> September 1, 1983
>
> Dear Mr. Moore:
>
> You have my blessing and enthusiastic support in what looks like a very important project.
>
> I ask only that you let me buy a copy of the book whenever it comes out.
>
> Give my best regards to Father Hartke.
>
> Sincerely,
>
> Helen Hayes

First letter from Lady Helen on Capital Acts project: 1983

Favorite signed photo

Chapter 22 – Byrd's Nests

"The road to success in anything is always the fun part, isn't it?" I always told students that the fun is in the 'getting there' and the doing. After you get there, you find out all the things that are wrong."

Charlie Byrd

In 1986, Charlie Byrd finally invited me to his Annapolis condo to discuss his career. Hundreds of thousands of Washingtonians had seen him play live when he finally agreed to meet me for an interview.

A true guitar genius—knighted by Brazil's government for contributing to samba music and owner of a twenty-six-foot boat called "I'm Hip." He greeted me in his boxer shorts at the door of his Annapolis condo, and we proceeded to his kitchen table. He was happy and relaxed—he never put his pants on—and when I turned on the tape recorder, he just started talking: "I'm from Chuck-a-Tuck, Virginia. I came to Washington in 1950 to study with **Sophocles Papas**. I lived in a residential apartment. between 19th and 20th Street. They had some musicals coming through at the National Theatre, and I worked on a few in the pit orchestra. *Silk Stockings. Damn Yankees.*

Carol Channing played about flappers or something like that about the movie industry (It was *The Vamp*.) That was a total flop. They spent tons of money and had a big orchestra and rehearsed it, and it was a big flop. And the show she did before. *Hello, Dolly*. She brought that back and hit the jackpot.

"When I first came to DC, the Capital Theater was still operating, but I never worked there. I did some club work but was swamped as a student with Sophocles then. I didn't want to be too involved in working in clubs, but I did some, also with acts at the Blue Mirror.

"I used to go to the Howard Theater when I first came to town. The first job I had in Washington was 7th and T, which is right by the Howard.

This was the Stage Door restaurant at 618 T Street. Cecilia Penny Scott was a pioneering Shaw community activist, philanthropist, and mentor. In 1953, Scott opened Cecilia's at 2002 12th Street; she later purchased the Stage Door restaurant at 618 T Street, NW, across Wiltberger Street from the Howard Theatre, and renamed it Cecilia's.

Before it closed in 1969, its many celebrity customers included James Brown, Cab Calloway, Sam Cooke, Redd Foxx, Billie Holiday, Joe Louis, Sugar Ray Robinson, Dinah Washington, and Jackie Wilson.

Ken Avis

"I played with bass player Benny Fonville and T. Carson on piano and Bertell Knox on drums. The singer was Laura Joy. There was a musician, Bernie Miller who wrote a tune called 'Bernie's Tune.' This song got recorded a lot. Recorded by Mulligan. It's a standard jazz tune, and Washington's Bernie Miller wrote it. I had been playing at a Connecticut Avea place called the Vineyard. There was a musician-entrepreneur named Tony Williams, a drummer in Washington. He wanted to get something started on a slightly grander scale. He wanted to get something shaking, so he rounded up a couple of backers. One was Toby Green, and the other was Pete Lambros.

"And they were looking for a place to open a nightclub featuring jazz. They came up with The Flame on Connecticut Ave. which was already owned by someone else. Then they formed a partnership with the owner. And we opened there

"Felix Grant started plugging the place on his show. And Jack Nimitz who was a baritone saxophone player, was still in town then.

Photo: Charlie at The Birchmere
© Oelze

"And he had just put out his first recording. He had been with Woody Herman and a lot of big bands.

"But he had just done his first recording on his own, and we were both in this group, and business started to be really good. But the owners couldn't get along, and we were really moving into an established business. So, they agreed to disagree, and we started looking for a place to move this club.

"Pete Lambros's father had this place on Columbia Road. which was the Showboat. And we went into the Showboat temporarily, just to keep us employed. That's kind of what happened. It was a smoky little room in the basement and it took off. Super. It was doing so good that we decided to stay there. We opened there with a small trio, Tony Williams (on drums) and Keter Betts (on bass This was the first trio I had. So that's pretty much what I know about that whole thing.

"And I did my very first recording there, which was in 1956. Felix Grant (on WMAL radio) played it. Jack Nimitz was on baritone saxophone. He had just put out his first recording. although he had been with Woody Herman, and a lot of big bands. But he did his first recording here in DC on his own. And business became good.

"And Felix started his *Nightcap* TV show. He had been interested in the jazz scene in Washington and had been a booster when we were at the Flame. He continued to be a booster when we moved over to the Showboat. This was

October of 1956. And the television show was Felix's idea. Business had been pretty good from the beginning of the Showboat, but once the TV show started. it really assured lines around the block. The TV show was the icing on the cake."

"You must have felt great at that time, Charlie," I interjected.

He answered "Well, I felt super. The Showboat was a very 'in' place in a way that contemporary people wouldn't understand. Washington in the '50s didn't have that many restaurants or clubs that people went to. Kind of a small-town thing. So it was the in place when there weren't many in places. Robert Redford used to stop by. The Arena Stage crowd used to be regulars. The Washington Post was in about twice a week.

"I met Kate Smith. I knew she was from Washington, DC. We did a television show in California. She was a nice lady. It was much after her prime, though. She still had an apartment in Northern Virginia that she kept and regretted not getting to spend more time in it. It was in Roslyn, one of those first tall buildings."

Birth of Bossa Nova

The upbeat, samba rhythms of Brazilian music began to take shape in the late 19th century, particularly within the Afro Brazilian communities in Rio de Janeiro, samba became more defined and popularized especially during the 20s and 30s when it began to gain prominence in Brazilian society and culture, especially during the Carnival celebrations.

The samba song "Carioca" was featured in a 1933 movie *Flying Down to Rio* with Fred Astaire and Ginger Rogers. In the 1950s, Brazilian composers such as Antonio Carlos Jobim and Luiz Bonfá slowed the samba into smoother and more tuneful music. *Black Orpheus*, a 1959 film by Brazilian director Marcel Camus, featured this new music now called bossa nova, or "new beat." Winning the Academy Award as best Foreign

Language film in 1960 helped introduce bossa nova music Internationally.

A few American musicians were playing this new music, including Bud Shank and emerging music from Brazil. As early as 1953, Brazilian guitarist Laurindo Almeida and Bud Shank, a California saxophonist and flutist, were recording music that, would now recognizable as early bossa nova.

In 1961, Byrd with his trio, drummer Buddy Deppenschmidt and bassist Keter Betts, went on a State Department-sponsored tour of South America for three months. One-night Keter persuaded Charlie to go down and listen to the music by the local musicians. Charlie told me that Keter asked him he if wanted to see the local folks do the bossa nova dance, and Charlie responded, "I don't care what the bossa nova dance looked like." But he went with Keter.

I asked him, "What did it look like?"

He replied, "Like people doing whatever they wanted to do dancing to jazz music. By the time I heard bossa nova, it was a blend of Brazilian music and jazz."

When they returned to the States, saxophonist Stan Getz played a DC club and discussed the bossa nova with Charlie in December of 1961. And two months later they came together at All Soul's Church in DC to record *Jazz Samba*.

Musicians on the session were Betts, Deppenschmidt, and Bill Reichenbach on drums. Bill, born and raised in DC, joined Byrd as his trio drummer afterward from '63 thru '72. He then became the house drummer at Blues Alley. Byrd's younger brother Joe Byrd also played bass and rhythm guitar on the *Samba* session.

Byrd paid $50 bucks to rent Pierce Hall at All Souls Church on New York Avenue for the recording session. He had attended services there a few times and knew the minister and also the beautiful acoustics of Pierce Hall's thirty-foot ceiling. Verve producer Creed Taylor, born and raised in the Blacksburg, Virginia area, produced the album and named it *Jazz Samba*.

Released in 1962, *Jazz Samba* would launch bossa nova in America through critical acclaim and huge popularity to reached reaching number one on the *Billboard* jazz record charts.

Hanging with Duke Ellington

"I met Duke Ellington several times and got to know him pretty well. Duke didn't talk about Washington very much, except in a casual way. He knew he was from Washington and he knew that everyone else knew it, so it was a very casual thing with him.

"I think the nicest experience I ever had with Duke, aside from experiencing his music in my own personal way. But the nicest I had with Duke was to play with him. They would now call it 'opening for him.' I opened for him at an affair at the Palladium. It was a private thing in Los Angeles that took us to the Palladium, and we played first. And we played an intermission. And it was a combination dance and concert, the way the things had been in the 30s, of course. Because that is the kind of thing it was.

"After one concert, we were talking backstage. Duke took his jacket and his tie off. His tuxedo shirt was on but open. He was undressing while we were talking. And he complimented me on my music and the trio. He spoke 'You know what you should play? Come on, I'll show you.'

"We went back on the stage and the piano was still there, and he sat down at the piano and was showing me this tune that he thought I should play. It was called 'The Single Petal of a Rose' Lovely Title. About an hour and a half later, he was still sitting there showing me tunes. A very private concert from him, showing me things that would sound good for me. I didn't play my guitar. I just listened. That was in the mid 60s."

Sophocles Papas

"He was my reason for coming here," said Byrd. "I had met Bill Harris, who was playing with a carnival in Upstate New York. And Bill started talking, and I found out he was also interested in classical guitar, which was my passion at the time. I had been studying some in New York City, and he told me about Papas.

"I found out that Papas was the only classical guitarist approved by the GI Bill in the US. So, I packed my bag and came to Washington to study with him. He was one of the pioneers of the classical guitar in this country back in the 20s. He came from Egypt but he was Greek. He's living in Northern Virginia. He's ninety, but lucid. Last time I saw him was six months ago. Give him a call. His wife's name is Mercer. I'll give you his number."

Charlie ended up phoning Mr. Papas from our kitchen table and they chatted with me listening. I turned the tape recorder off.

Ken Avis and **Lynn Veronneau** commemorated the 50th anniversary of the recording of *Jazz Samba* with their band, Veronneau performing it in concert at All Souls Church. A panel discussion about the legacy of *Jazz Samba* followed.

Avis said "Washington, DC, is often overlooked as a music town, yet it has been the backdrop for so much musical history. This city truly served as a crucible for this groundbreaking album, and it's wonderful that we are taking the time to celebrate it."

(L to R) Pete Walby (drums), David Rosenblatt (guitar) Lynn Veronneau (vocals), Ken Avis (guitar/vocals) Jim McFalls (trombone) and Jeff Antoniuk (sax), © Veronneau Music.

Ken and Lynn run the **Creative Cauldron** theater, founded by their Producing Director, Laura Connors Hull, in February 2002. Since its incorporation Creative Cauldron has grown and has called the Little City of Falls Church home since taking up residence in ArtSpace Falls Church in 2009.

Charlie, Bill Reichenbach, and Keter Betts. © C. Byrd.

William Frank Reichenbach Sr. (December 18, 1923 – May 16, 2008) was born in Washington, DC, and attended McKinley high school. With Byrd he developed the jazz-samba drumming style. During World War Two he played with the Navy band, and later toured with The Dorsey brothers, After working with Byrd he became the house drummer at Blues Alley.

Bill Reichenbach and his son, Bill Reichenbach Jr. © KSPD

His son, Bill Jr., was born in 1949, and raised in Takoma Park, MD. He is the renowned trombonist and versatile horn player on Michael Jackson's *Thriller* and *Bad* albums and also over 1000 recordings including sessions with George Benson, Cher, Christopher Cross, Joe Cocker, Céline Dion, Aretha Franklin, Natalie Cole, Elton John, Michael Jackson, Dolly Parton, Barbra Streisand, and Aaron Neville.

I visited Bill Sr. at his Takoma Park house in 1986 and he told me with a smile that he was disappointed that his son, then thirty-five years old, was playing rock and roll music. I'm certain from his heavenly drum seat he's very proud now.

Chapter 23 - Bob Berberich's Beats

Saint Camillus students wait for Grin's show. © B. Berberich

Bob Berberich is a beloved musician and one of the most accomplished drummers from the DC area and beyond. His iconic drumbeat begins the song "What a Girl Can't Do" by his first group, The Hangmen—a fabled regional hit on Monument Records.

The Hangmen's 1965 song knocked the Beatles' single "We Can Work it Out/Day Tripper" out of the number one spot on local radio charts. 1200 fans appeared for a Giant Record store band appearance, creating a chaotic situation. Jack Shaver, then the owner of Giant Record stores, told the media, "A mob of teenagers turned out to hear the Hangmen. The police cleared the store because the crowd created a fire hazard. Police rescued the band with an exit ride in their patrol car."

I've been enjoying Bob's drumming for six decades from Hangmen, Grin, Rosslyn Mountain Boys, and through today in bands he plays with at great venues like Hank Dietle's in Bethesda. I feel close to him because we have similar backgrounds growing up in DC where our mothers encouraged us learn about and enjoy music. Thanks, Bob for contributing to Capital Acts.

Q: How did it all start with you, Bob?

A: I'm a fifth-generation Washingtonian. The first Robert Berberich came over from Germany around 1860. He was a cobbler who joined the Union army to get citizenship and came to DC. After the Civil War, he opened a shoe business, Berberich's Shoes, on 7th Street. That's my great-great-grandfather. Shoes were a big deal in DC back then. But the Depression closed the store down. If it wasn't for that, I'd probably be selling shoes, and we wouldn't be here talking.

Q: When did the music start?

A: My Mom turned me on to music. The first singer I remember is Johnny Ray, who had an intense style. I was three or four years old when my Mom used to take us to the Connie. B. Gay shows at the National Guard Armory.

One of the reasons my mother loved music was because she was from the South during the fifties. All these people, white and Black, were moving up from the South for jobs during World War II. And they brought that musical influence with them, so I grew up loving country music. My sister, Carol, a few years older, grew up in the era of early rock and roll. By the time she was in eighth grade, my mother would have sock hops in our house on Klingle Road in DC.

In the living room, we would roll up the rug and have a stack of 45s with chips and Coke. There was a basket for the boys' switchblades.

I heard all the Little Richard and Chuck Berry records. So here I was as a kid, listening to country music and rock and roll. By the time I was a teenager in the early sixties, rock and roll sucked for the most part. So we were all listening to the R&B station, WOOK. We listened to soul music.

> Note: In 1947 WOOK was launched in Washington, DC, as the first US broadcast radio station to feature African American broadcasters serving African American audiences. Originally located at 1580 on the AM dial, the station swapped call letters and channels with WINX AM moving to 1340 AM in 1955. S.M.

I went to the Howard Theater and saw James Brown when I was thirteen years old. The other thing DC had was the drinking age for beer and wine, which was eighteen, but everybody, by the time they were fifteen, had a fake ID, and nobody cared. I started working in bars playing drums when I was fifteen. First with The Reekers. Then we played teen club-type gigs and when somebody would throw a party. And bars.

Q: How did you decide to play drums?

A: We moved to Silver Spring when I was seven. My older sister was dating a guy in the neighborhood who played drums. He was the first person I could stand next to and watch. On my fifteenth birthday, my parents got me an old beat-up set of Slingerland drums, which are right now in my car. It's the set I still play mostly. Slingerlands, which are now in my car. It's the set I still mostly use. I learned to play along with an old Magnavox Hi-Fi record player—pre-Beatles. I was playing to Ventures, Little Richard, and Ray Charles records. And very soon after I started playing with the Hangmen,

Q: Who was your first most influential drummer?

A: Earl Palmer was the New Orleans drummer who played on all the Little Richard and Fats Domino records. He was my first influence. I didn't even know his name back then. I was playing to these records he was playing on and learning. I never met him, but Pete Kennedy tells a good story about meeting him once in LA.

> **From Tone, Twang, and Taste: A Guitar Memoir**: Pete was invited to play at Dante's Jazz club in the late 70s and complimented an older drummer he heard there. "You sound great, Earle," Pete complimented him. "Do you ever play R&B?"
>
> The drummer replied, Well, I played on all of Little Richard'' hits, "Willie and the Hand Jive" and "You've Lost That Lovin' Feeling." Pete then realized he was talking to Earl Palmer, one of the original inventors of rock n' roll.

Q: Where and when did you start to see local bands in DC?

A: I was fifteen and still going to Saint John's high school. We used to go see Roy Buchanan at the Silver Dollar. Somebody gave my name to the guys that were forming the Hangman, within a couple months pre-Beatles. Tom Guernsey was the leader of two bands, the Hangmen and the Reekers. I joined the Hangman, but when the Reekers played a gig and needed a drummer, then I was their drummer.

For the holidays, we also played Bard College. Josh Brooks, Sara Vass and Mark Gorbulew (early WHFS radio folks) and Chevy Chase went to Bard College. Tom Guernsey had gone there also, as did Mike Henley from the Reekers and Mac McCune. We would drive there and play. I knew all those people and were friends with John and Tom since I was fifteen.

After, after the Hangmen broke up, I played in a house band called The Button for a while in Georgetown. That band with me moved to Greenwich Village in 1967 playing in New York at the Cafe A Go-Go and Steve Paul's. Once we were doing our set there and somebody comes up and grabs a set of drumsticks and starts playing along with me. I'm getting ready to punch the guy, and it turned out to be Keith Moon, drummer for the Who. Moon and I played a song together. And on our break, Who bass player John Entwistle, Keith Moon and Jimi Hendrix sat in our equipment and played.

John Hall and I with friends Vince Williams and Mac McClure moved into a beautiful old Victorian house on the corner of Cedar and Eastern Ave in Takoma Park, MD, afterward. We called it Toad Hall. It was absolutely fantastic with stained glass windows. Donald Fagan (later of Steely Dan) and his girlfriend spent the summer of '68 at that house.

Q: Is this when Grin began?

A: Yes. George Daly, who was the rhythm guitarist and lead singer for the Hangmen began playing bass with me and with Nils Lofgren, who George had discovered playing at the Ambassador Light Theatre.

This was the line-up for our new band. Dolphin. Paul Dowell was the bass player from the Hangman. He became the lead singer and rhythm guitar player. George Daly became Dolphin's bass player, and George brought Nils on board. Bob Dawson his recording equipment from Bias over to the house and set it up on the porch looking through looking through the front window. The recording at Toad Hall was a Car Dealership ad and Nils's original "Grubbs Blues."

We played some local shows and P Street Beach and shows like that. We were kind of a hippie band but we broke up after six months. Paul left and became a roadie for the Jefferson Airplane.

And that's how we formed Grin. Neither Nils or I had ever sung in a band before. And I mean, we learned to sing just by doing it.

This was 1969.

It was then that Nils went to see and meet Neil Young at the Cellar Door. He went up the back stairs and got into the dressing room, and said "Hey Neil, I'm a singer songwriter." Neil handed him his Martin and said, "Play me a song."

Neil was so blown away with what he heard that he literally paid for us to travel to California and rented us a house first in Hollywood, and then in Laurel Canyon. He was going to produce Grin. That was the plan.

We eventually moved to Topanga Canyon. We became the house band at Topanga Corral, which is a famous biker roadhouse club at the top of Topanga. And Neil Young would bring his guitar and amp and sit in with us all night long.

When Grin first went to California, we played for Bill Graham who used to have those nights where it was up and coming unsigned bands. We played the same night with (Springsteen's first band) Steel Mill. That was their Bruce and Nils's first contact.

And somebody was on the side of the stage tooting people up. I thought it was cocaine. I take a hit before I get on stage. It was acid.

It was something more than acid. It was a psychedelic because it had instant effect. And I had an out of body experience while I was playing. I was literally up in the ceiling looking down on myself playing.

Q: I've loved Nils since Grin. I saw you guys open for the James Gang at Maryland University, and Nils and I worked together on the Birchmere book about his donating his family's player piano to the club. He's in charge, a real hands-on guy. Was he like that in those early days?

A: In Dolphin not so much because he was still in high school and he was playing with another band. But by the time we formed Grin, he had a one-track mind. And you were pretty much along for the ride. He's focused on what he wants to do. He's in charge.

And that's a great thing to have for a leader of a band. That's what Nils had that Springsteen saw in him, you know, and why they were together because Bruce Springsteen is like that, too.

Q: What happened with The Hangmen and Grin?

A: The biggest regret I have with the Hangmen—and I wasn't involved in the business end. I'm the drummer. But the Hangmen ended up firing Dave Ottley, our original singer, who was great. And that was pretty much the end. We went downhill from there.

We were in California and preparing for Neil Young to produce Grin. It's 1969. We're opening up for the acts at the Topanga Corral like the Flying Burrito Brothers and Taj Mahall. And Neil calls us up and says "I can't produce you. I'm going to Woodstock."

When Neil joined Crosby, Stills, and Young and couldn't produce us, we got his producer, David Briggs, who we were really tight with.

We were really clicking again when Grin got dropped.

Nils had no choice. Nils was the star. And (my next band) The Rosslyn Mountain Boys became a popular band. And I'm really proud of that first album in particular. The only regret I have for the Roslyn Mountain Boys was that we broke up at all.

Lofgren goes for gold with Springsteen
By STEPHEN MOORE

Q: In 1984 I wrote a Journal article announcing the news of Nils being tapped to join the E Street Band. I wrote, "Three weeks into his senior year at Walter Johnson High School, Lofgren formed the critically acclaimed rock trio Grin and dropped out of school to pursue a professional career in music...Grin disbanded in 1974. Nils however, rebounded with a solo recording contract. And the opportunity to audition for the Rolling Stones as a replacement for their guitarist, Mick Taylor. Although Nils lost the job, his stature within the music industry was greatly enhanced and his reputation as a musician spread. Stones guitar Keith Richards at that time called Nils a real survivor." And I called you for a quote and you added, "Those early songs that Nils wrote for Grin, 'Rain,' 'If I Were a Song,' and 'Outlaw" were great.'"

Berberich married local rocker **Martha Hull** in 1986, a versatile vocalist and songwriter hailing from the Washington, DC, area, and together they started the Vinyl Acres record store in Frederick, Maryland. Hull is known for her dynamic transition from punk to folk, blending her hard-edged experience with a heartfelt approach to songwriting and performance. Starting in 1975 she performed with various bands including The Slickee Boys, D.Ceats, Steady Jobs, Dynettes, and Ottley. Her rendition of Tex Rubinowitz's "Feelin' Right Tonight" with D.Ceats caught Tex's attention and gave her a recording opportunity with Ripsaw Records.

Monument Records

"What a Girl Can't Do" was released by Monument records. The label's founder, **Fred Foster**, left his farm home in Rutherford, NC, in 1958 at age seventeen for DC. He started writing country songs while working at the Connecticut Avenue Hot Shoppes—a primary sponsor of Milt Grant's WMAL-TV *Bandstand* show—and then he drove a food service truck in DC. He later sold records at Irving's Music, where he met Ben Adleman an early DC music publisher. Through Ben, Foster met Jimmy Dean and produced and wrote Dean's first hit song, "Bummin Around," recorded at Sounds Studio on 1124 Vermont Avenue, with "Picking Sweethearts" on the flip side.

So, yes, the Monument record logo on the labels of subsequent hit songs by Roy Orbison, Dolly Parton, Willie Nelson, Ray Stevens, and Kris Kristofferson, Charlie McCoy, Boots Randolph, and the Hangmen, was inspired by the Washington Monument.

The success of "Bummin Around" landed Foster in Nashville, where his next project was recording a newcomer, Roy Orbison. Roy was shy, and Fred moved him behind an acoustical barrier that would not only better record his soft singing style but also pick up far less of the band's sounds. Nashville began using this new technique of Fred Foster's "Isolation booth."

Capital Acts: Washington DC Performing Arts

© Roy's Boys LLC

Bob Gordon, Bass, Nils Lofgren, Vocals, Guitars, Keyboards, and Bob Berberich on Drums

An ad for the 1971 Grin's debut album: Dedicated to Roy Buchanan with "special thanks" to Neil Young and Crazy Horse.

Berberich's Shoes on 7th Street.

The Giant Music riot over the Hangmen's record.

Chapter 24 – Slickees, Nighthawks & Razz

In 1975, punk, garage, and psychedelic music propelled a rock band hailing from Bethesda, Maryland, to emerge with Martha Hall as the lead vocalist, guitarists Marshall Keith, and Kim Kane, Andy Von Brandt on bass, and drummer Chris Rounds. The band calling themselves **The Slickee Boys** became regulars at The Keg in Georgetown.

"The first 'most impactful, memorable, and important concert' for me was in 1986 when the original Slickee Boys played a concert at the 9:30 Club with the then current Slickees. It was Kim Kane, who was in both bands, and I who called all the other members and they agreed to do one show. Martha Hull, the original singer coordinated with Marshall Keith and Kim Kane on what would be sung. That was a great show and everyone had a blast.

"'Gotta Tell Me Why,' their cover of 'Pictures of Matchstick Man,' and 'When I Go to The Beach' are some of their best songs. I ran their fan club for twenty years. My radio show, *Forbidden Alliance*, is the name of one of their songs."

Robbie White
Forbidden Alliance
WOWD Radio

Robbie White with Kim Kane
© *R. White*

By 1978, the band, comprising of Keith Kane, drummer Dan Polensky and bassist Emery Alexa placed an ad in Unicorn Times, searching for a vocalist to complete their new lineup.

DC native Mark Noone played in bands while attending Gonzaga High School in the 70s. "I went to the Berkeley College of Music, for a year after Gonzaga, and came back here to DC, got in a Virginia band called Crossroads. It was a good band. All fun guys doing cool covers, like Steely Dan.

"I had seen Razz, and the Slickee Boys with Martha Hull at The Keg. I lived right near there. I knew there was an original music scene going on. And that's what I wanted to do. So I proposed some of my original songs to Crossroads And they say 'no.' 'Tell me why,' I asked. They said, 'Because there's only three chords in them.' Well, I'm like, 'Alright, okay. We won't do them.'

Mark Noone at home and at 2024 DC Legends show. © S. Moore

"Then I see the ad in *Unicorn Times* that the Slickee Boys are looking for a singer. I thought 'I'm gonna get this gig!' It was a regular ad with Kim Kane's number. I had moved to Bethesda and I lived near him. So, I call him. Kim picked me up and I drive to Dan Polensky's house for my audition.

"And then later I'm at a Ramone's show in the back room of the Varsity Grill. Dan comes over and says, 'Well, we decided you are going to be the singer.' Totally unceremoniously. I said, 'OK...Alright.'

"The Slickee Boys then were basically Marshall Keith and Kim Kane's baby. They were new, weird, and different. Both had great quirky ideas. Kim's father was in the Foreign Service, so he had lived in Burma and Korea. He had that kind of total Asian influence, with a kind of a Zen attitude towards everything as Disco was fading.

"And Marshall was so artistic. Nobody around DC was really doing anything like this. There was the band Razz, one of the best live bands I ever saw. They were a real rock and roll band like the Rolling Stones. With Abaad Behrens and later Tommy Keene, *Razz* was a great band.

> Speaking of the late Tommy Keene: Here is an "interview quote" on how his career took off:
>
> You were really a band guy and sideman playing in New York in the early '80s, then you suddenly became a solo artist.
>
> "After I was in New York, **I moved back to DC** I didn't know a lead-singer type—or another songwriter who I thought I could get a band together with. So, I thought, 'Why don't I do a solo thing? I have a kind of different, distinctive voice. Maybe it'll work.' I was thinking of it almost as a gimmick. But I didn't think I'd be doing it twenty-five years later. I always figured I'd put out a solo record and then join a band, but it never happened. If there would've been a Michael Stipe character, or if I'd found my Roger Daltrey, I would've joined up with them."
>
> SM

Mark Noone continues: "And the Slickee Boys came along with something that was completely different. Marshal Keith was the real genius of the Slickee Boys. Kim Kane was more like the spiritual leader. Dan, the drummer was like the king of comedy. He was the brotherhood of the group. I was the front man character, a charismatic connector with the audience kind of thing.

"We had original material and it was just a different kind of rock and roll even before I joined the band. They started a new wave thing—whatever you wanted to call it.

"Many who started other bands would come and see the Slickee Boys. We seemed kind of inspirational to a lot of the local scene here, which I'm very proud of.

"There's always been great music in DC you know? And I say this often. Baltimore knows it. Richmond knows it, and DC knows it. Some people outside of DC look at the government here and are surprised there is great music. Bands here? Really?"

"So, I'd like to see The Slickee Boys known as being the beginning of something affirmative, something different."

On May 29, 1980, Seth Hurwitz and partner, high school teacher Rich Heinecke, booked their first concert, the Slickee Boys at Adams Morgan's Ontario Theatre, for the local premiere of *The Punk Rock Movie*. Seth is today the founder and chairman of I.M.P.

and co-owner of the iconic 9:30 Club, a key figure in the evolution of live entertainment in Washington DC.

Noone continues: "I listen now to our tapes of old live performances. It's really the Marshall Show. We never would've gone anywhere if we didn't have Marshall's talent and not just because of the way he played guitar, but what he played. He would just figure stuff out on songs that I wrote. He'd come up with the parts if I didn't come up with them. He would play these perfect parts. He and I wrote tons of songs together. He wasn't that big on writing lyrics much. So, I wrote lyrics to a lot of his songs and it was just a joy to write lyrics to his music because his music was just so cool."

Marshall Keith

Marshal Keith and Patty Ferry © Beth Harrison (Thank you Patty for great help!)

"I was a teen in Rockville, MD, in the '70s listening to my brother Rusty play guitar and sing," says Marshall Keith in 2024 from his Maryland home. "I would play whatever else I could—bass or maybe a lead break and sing harmonies with him. That really got me used to just sort of figuring out how music is put together.

"Besides all the normal stuff that you'd hear on the radio, I started, listening to albums by Jefferson Airplane and Frank Zappa and the Mothers of Invention. I liked all the normal stuff, but I, especially liked the music that was, off to the different sides of the spectrum. I liked harsh sounding things like Zappa and the pretty things like the beginning of 'Strawberry Fields Forever.'

"And I really liked the keyboard called the mellotron that was used. It was an early keyboard that used taped loops of recorded sounds to produce musical notes. In my brain the mellotron sort of defines that era. It was used in the Moody Blue's 'Knights of White Satin,' 'Space Oddity' by Bowie and the beginning 'flute' notes of 'Strawberry Fields Forever.'

"But at the same time, I also liked the harsh stuff. Like when The Kinks came out with 'You Really Got Me.' I love that too. Probably my favorite Rolling Stones album is *Their Satanic Majesty's Request*. The Stones never did anything like that again, but I just love it. It combines harsh stuff and then they use the mellotron in the song '2000 Light Years from Home.'

"When Martha left, and we didn't have a vocalist, I thought maybe we'd do what we wanted, and perhaps we'd quit the Slickee Boys. But then I listened to (Georgetown's radio station) WGTB (punk was starting to happen). And the music they were playing was great like the Ramones. The Slickees had played at Max's Kansas City. WGTB's Steve Lorber made sure we got there. We played well, but overall, the experience wasn't great.

"But the music on WGTB was excellent, and I thought, well, maybe now we should really get back together and really try—full steam ahead. We auditioned some women singers, but we were the Slickee boys, so that didn't work out. And then we found a bass player named Emery Alexa. And he was good, really energetic, and could play the fast speed, and also throw in very unexpected stuff.

"Emery, Kim Kane, Dan Polensky and I started working on the TV melody since we didn't have a singer. I always loved TV theme songs like 'Twilight Zone,' 'Mission Impossible,' 'I Spy,' and 'The Man from Uncle.' We spent a lot of time on this medley of TV songs. That was right up my alley. There are weird jazz chords and stuff.

"We only worked on this TV medley, and then Mark Noone came to audition. He was the first person who we said, 'Man, this guy can really belt it out,' and he sings in tune very well.' He knew music well, how to write it for our band, what the rhythm guitar player would do, and what I would do.

"And, by this time, we started to want costumes on stage, not just come in our street clothes. Kim did the gypsy thing with scarves and bracelets. And I went for a mod thing, checkerboards and polka dots and that kind of stuff. And so that was always a big thing with us.

"Kim Kane began designing our album covers as we wanted to have a lot of visual stuff and so Mark comes along. And he had to have an image. He went on stage with a formal kind of a thing: a suit coat and a tie maybe. And the suit coats became sparkly. We were starting over again with Mark. Since there was punk music happening, people had been hearing that music so it was easy and accessible by that point.

"Mark told us 'You got to move around on the stage.' And we started playing out with a lot of euphoria. Some of our music is hard to play because you are going so fast, but when we would be tight and had a good set, it just felt great."

Mark Noon adds: "Well, we all wrote songs. There were songs that Marshall and Kim and I wrote together like 'You're Automized.' Kim came up with part of it. Marshall came up with the other part, and then I wrote the lyrics. Then there's plenty of songs like 'When We Get to the Beach' that I wrote myself.

"And then things like I would come up with a lick, in 'Life of the Party' and Marshall would say 'that's great' and he'd play it just the way I wanted. That was the real luxury with the Slickee Boys. I would write a song and Slickee Boys would do it exactly how I imagined it when I was writing it. Ah that's a luxury. I'd never had that since I've started writing songs. I've had bands do them and do great jobs. But the Slickees had this thing, you know, it was just like, 'Wow, That's how I imagined it when I was writing it.'"

* * *

"Joey Romero was a drummer with Jr. Cline and the Recliners. Yeah, great guy. We were good friends for a long time. When I lived in Takoma Park, we both lived within blocks of each other and we were hanging out a lot. He's a good guy. We were at a great party once. A band was playing. There's beer everywhere.

"Joey's says, 'Let's get outta here. This party sucks. I'm leaving this party.'

"I said, 'Dude, man, this party is raging.'

'This party sucks. I'm outta here,' he insisted. I thought, 'I've got to write this song.'"

The Slicky Boys achieved legendary status by opening for U2 at the Bayou on two occasions in 1980 and 1981. Their music video for the single "When I Go to the Beach" secured second place in MTV's Basement Tapes competition in 1983, making history as the first DC band to have a music video aired on the popular, pioneering MTV network.

Jan Zukowski

Jan holds a special place as one of our favorite local bass player. Hailing from Forestville, Maryland and a graduate of my Suitland High School, where I first knew of him, playing in various rock 'n' roll bands and notably, one of DC's favorites, The Cherry People, with Punky Meadows, Doug and Chris Grimes, and Rocky Issac. During the period spanning 1967 to 1973, The Cherry People were one of our National bands. Their single "And Suddenly" made number forty-five on the Billboard's Hot 100.

"My first band," says Jan, "was the Night Owls, and we played the Francis Scott Key elementary school during the lunch afternoon talent show. And then I met schoolmate Dennis Boone and we ended up being in a band called Adams Apples. This became Nobody's Children. That's when I switched over from guitar to bass. The band played some festival in Upper Marlboro and the WPGC disc jockey Harv Moore decided to take us under his wing. He became our manager.

"We did a bunch of shows. I backed up Neil Diamond when I was like 16. We did records: 'I Told Santa Claus I Want You,' which Harv wrote, and the backside was 'Stuck in the Chimney' recorded under the name Surf Boys, because we were also under contract with United Artists. Many bands did that. They had studio guys or they would record things under a pseudonym because of contractual things. So these were the first bands that I was with. And we played many shows. I backed up Jimmy Johnson, who did 'Handyman' and Lou Christie. I was fifteen years old the first-time playing bass in Georgetown. I also played the Peppermint Lounge, downstairs and I think it was called The Frog upstairs. My mother had to drive me."

In 1974, Zukowski transitioned into a blues stalwart by joining The Nighthawks. Over the course of three decades, he entertained audiences and contributed to more than twenty albums during his tenure with the band.

(l to r) The Night Owls: Dennis Boone, Mark Mouhtouris, William (Lee) Travers and Jan Zukowski: Inside cover of the *Suitland 1967 Yearbook.*

Following The Nighthawks, Jan became one of the Fabulous Hubcaps, an oldies band dating back to 1972 with a roster of DC musicians playing storied bars and clubs. And for the resume prize, Jan played bass for George Thorogood & The Destroyers at Live Aid May 13, 1985.

(l to r) Bo Diddley, Jeff Simon (drummer in shades), George Thorogood, Hank Carter (top) with horn, Jan Zukowski, and Albert Collins © KSPD

The Destroyer's drummer Jeff Simon explains, "Everyone was on board with Live Aid, and it worked out schedule-wise that Bo Diddley and Albert Collins could play with us. But (bassist) Billy Blough was vacationing in Europe with his wife and we had no way to get in touch with him. So, we called our friend, Jan Zukowski, who played with the Nighthawks to fill in."

Jan remembers it as, "The Nighthawks had the same booking agency as George and they couldn't get ahold of Billy. I got up at the crack of dawn, flew out of Buffalo into Philly, did the Live Aid and then I flew out then I around six or something to Rochester and played with the Nighthawks opening for Taj Mahal that night."

Mark Wenner, Jan Zukowski, Greg Allman, and Jimmy Thackery.
© KSPD

Pete Ragusa, drummer, The Nighthawks, Razz, et al.

Q: You've played with so many DC groups. Please tell us how it all started for you, Pete.

A: I was born at Doctors Hospital which eventually became Howard University Hospital and I grew up in NE over by DC Stadium. My father Peter, and his oldest brother Frank were sax players in a band. Their brother-in-law was the drummer, doing 40s tunes in local clubs.

Here's a remarkable story. I had been in the Nighthawks about seven years and our name was well-known in the DC area at that time. One Sunday I went over to my parents' house for dinner because my Dad's brother was going to be there. After we ate my Uncle turned to me and says, "You know your father and I had a band." And I said, "yeah, I know all about it."

My Uncle added: "And we were called the Nighthawks."

I looked at him and I looked at my father. My father had waited years to tell me this. They were called Jarboe and the Nighthawks. My uncle was the front man. Jarboe was his middle name.

We would have family get togethers, when I was little, and I'd, sit in front of the bass drum when they were playing and just absorb all the sound., watching them play. You can get a guitar and learn how to play it using a music book. But the drums is really a mechanical thing. If you don't see it, you don't get it.

Q: When did you get your first kit?

A: Well, I was about ten years old. I was begging my parents for a drum. kept saying, no, no, no. Not happening.

Q: Why do you think your father wouldn't want you to play?

A: Well, I think it was mostly my mother. Yeah, she was probably so sick of the drums. Anyway. our grandmother lived around the corner from us, and I had an uncle and cousins lived on the other side of Cheverly, MD, from us.

Before Christmas, they would bring all the gifts that they bought for the kids and leave them at my grandmother's house. So, I was on the second floor of the house, and we could look down the stairs to the front door. Me and my brothers were just peeking around the corner and I hear it. They bumped into something and it was the drum. Yeah, it was a snare drum with a little symbol attached to it. It was a Kent from Montgomery Wards.

So that, that was my start. And until high school, I kind of self-taught myself how to read music and how to play drums. My dad had a collection of big band music that was astounding. Really cool. I would put records on and play along with them in the basement rec room.

Q: Would that be Woody Herman and Duke Ellington?

A: More like the Dorsey Brothers.

Q: Did you see any live music?

A: We used to go down to the bandstand near the water across from the Watergate. And see the Army Big Band, and the Navy band. Yeah.

Q: When did you decide 'Now I am a drummer? I'm a musician.' When did you think that really clicked?

A: I think it was the moment my dad played the Benny Goodman Quartet At Carnegie Hall album. And hearing Louis Belson play drums. It was thunderous. I thought 'man, that is too cool.' And that was a point that really grabbed me.

The Beatles came, and I liked them. They were good but kind of simplistic to me. They had the elements there, and the one thing that linked both styles was that they made people dance. And that's something that my father's band instilled in me. People want to dance. And I realized that was an important aspect of playing music.

Q: Did you listen to Bebop?

A: I missed it all. Had I heard that I probably would have ended up going a different direction.

Q: Where'd you go to high school?

A: Bladensburg High School. I'm a PG County Boy. When I got to high school it was the R & B—rhythm and blues—and soul music that really pulled me in. I mean, all of it. Motown, Stax. I just really dug it. I couldn't put it down. My first album I ever bought was Junior Walker and the All-Stars Shotgun. The first 45 I ever bought was the Everly Brothers. And all the teen shows and all that stuff, they were all soul bands, because that's what you danced to. Larry Kidwell whose band Lawrence and the Arabians, and their drummer, **Mike Zack**, was the biggest influence on me. When Mike started to play with rock bands, I would go to Georgetown and follow him.

(Photo) Pete with me at Hank Dietle's club in Bethesda, MD.
© Sarah Bonner

Now here's another iconic moment for me. It was at the CYOs, when Lawrence and the Arabians were playing. there. I don't think I missed a show from 10th to 12th grade. The Arabians were originally like a five-piece band, but there was one show at a high school, in Mount Rainier and it was a battle of the bands between the Hangmen against Lawrence and the Arabians.

And the Hangman came out, and they rocked their ass off and everybody loved them. Everybody knew who they were. Then there the Arabians are setting up and they're getting ready to play, and the whole room goes black.

From the upper deck there is a single spotlight. And the spotlight goes on Mike Zack's cymbals and he's got symphony mallets. And he starts from a whisper to this screaming roar of a symbol roll. And he holds it. He's holding it. It's just blitzing loud. And he counts off in his face 1-2-3-4 and they go into "Goldfinger." Whoa. This was their first gig with horns. They had three horns. It was unbelievable.

With two guitars, a bass and a drum, you can get some cool stuff out of that, but you can't beat the harmonies on those horns.

I mean, it's just blows it away, doesn't it? And Larry Kidwell and his brother Mike were two of the best singers I had ever heard. They were so soulful. You close your eyes and you thought they were Black, and they were wearing the matching suits and everything. It was a real show. And that's what I wanted to do. I eventually ended up in a soul band in my senior high school year We had three horns and were called the Manchurian Candidate. I didn't see the movie, so I didn't know what it meant. I next went to the Prince George's Community College and University of Maryland and studied music with Frank Scimonelli. Yes, that's our friend Paul's father. He ran the music department at PG

College. And I met vocalist **Mike Reidy** and guitarist Bill Craig there. They were starting a band and asked me if I wanted to come over to Mike's house one night and just jam around and see what we could do. So that was the beginning of **Razz**. I was their first drummer.

> "Imagine if Mick Jagger and Keith Richards had simultaneously fathered a child with a Bollywood actress. The result would be Abaad Behrens who moved with his parents from India to Northern Virginia in 1969, when he was 15."
> John Kelly, *Washington Post*

Abaad Behrens singer-guitarist, with Razz, Artful Dodger et al.

While attending Washington Lee High School, in Arlington, VA in the '70s he played in a rock 'n' roll band called Sway, which specialized in covers of the Rolling Stones. In 1972 he joined the band **Razz,** a group that delivered big fun and excitement in 1972. The lineup featured Behrens, with Mike Reidy, Bill Craig, Pete Ragusa, and bassist Ted Nicely— basically a rock 'n' roll dream team!

After Razz he became lead guitarist in the band Artful Dodger a group from Fairfax, Virginia. Behrens went on to play for the Smash band and Johnny Bombay and the Reactions. He has been active in Razz reunions, the Howling Mad, and others. Abaad is also a cancer survivor, special education teacher and—in our book—one of a kind.

Capital Acts: Washington DC Performing Arts

Our conversation began with:

Q: Why do people love what you do?

A: I think it's because of how I feel about what I play. I am 110 percent all out, not worrying about anything else I serve. The Indians have a term—*puja*—I'm not religious, but stepping on a stage is a sacred space for me. When doing so, I have to exercise everything and connect with the audience. Right? And that is like the one piece of fire I have, so I must use it. You know? So maybe that's how I'm special —or it's them saying, "look at this crazy guy." <laughs> I think the audience has a reverence for the puja.

I was in a movie theater once watching the ending credits for a film called *The Departed* by Martin Scorsese. The music rolls in, and I hear this fade-in guitar. It stunned me. It was Roy Buchanan's "Sweet Dreams," which is such a deep cut to put at the end of a movie like this one. It made me regret I never saw Roy live.

But when I was in Razz, we were playing in a place called the Act 4 in Georgetown. During a break, somebody said, hey man, Danny Gatton is playing down the street at the Keg. So, during the break, we walk down and walk in, and I hear him sounding like a keyboard, but it's Danny mucking around on the guitar. I understand I'm watching something very special. That was a powerful moment.

Q: For guitar heads what's your favorite go-to rig?

A: I'm going under the wave on this question. When I grew up in India, we had no decent equipment whatsoever. My first acoustic guitar, I think the strings were about like this (holds his hand a foot over the neck). When I came to America, my mother bought me a guitar that was also terrible. It had a whammy bar that, when you pushed it down, would take its time coming back up.

So, here's what I learned. It's not the rig; it's you. I can get a sound out of anything at any time. I don't care. Gimme something. I'll find a way to make it sound musical. I have taken that bad guitar and played it at the 9:30 Club."

***

Mark Wenner
(with Weasel and Cerphe)
© S. Moore

"It was a time when Elvis was in the army..." begins Mark's story that includes over forty-plus years of singing and playing harp for his band, **The Nighthawks.**
See: Interview @
https://www.unstarvingmusician.com/ump-30-mark-wenner/

In 2023, WTOP Radio's Neil Augenstein announced that DC filmmakers **Jeff Krulik** and **Richard Taylor** would screen an extended director's cut of their *Razz (The) Documentary* film at AFI Silver Theatre and Cultural Center in Silver Spring, Maryland.

"When you saw Razz at a small place, like The Keg (in Georgetown, or Childe Harold (in Dupont Circle) or the Psyche Delly (in Bethesda), the experience was 'this is incredible—this is national talent in a small room," Taylor told Neil.

Krulik agreed: "They left a lasting impression, which is why there's still a fan base today."

Jeff's movies are surprisingly cool and include **Heavy Metal Parking Lot** and **Led Zeppelin Played Here.** And also:

- *The Scott And Gary Show* (1983–1989)
- *Forestville Rocks* (1985)
- *TVs From Outer Space* (1985)
- *Memories of Elvis* (1987)
- *You Gotta Get a Gimmick* (1987)
- *An Afternoon with Zippy the Chimp* (1988)
- *Boxing Night* (1988)
- *Monster Truck Parking Lot* (unfinished) (1988)
- *Rock 'n' Roll Psychosis* (1988)

- *Show Us Your Belly* (1988)
- *Twenty-Five Cents Before Noon* (1988)
- *We Need a Staple Gun* (1988)
- *Public Access Gibberish* (1990)
- *Ilana Solomon Sings* (1993)
- *?* (1995)
- *Mr. Blassie Goes to Washington* (1995)
- *Hop On The Bus Gus* (1996)
- *King of Porn* (1996)
- *Most Entertaining Person on Planet Earth* (1996)
- *Meet Fanboy* (1996)
- *Ernest Borgnine on the Bus* (1997)
- *Go-Go Girls Don't Cry* (1997)
- *Katie Bar the Door: The Goodwill Book Sale* (1997)
- *King of the Freaks* (trailer) (1997)
- *Neil Diamond Parking Lot* (work in progress) (1997)
- *Thank You Roma* (1997–2000)
- *Follow That @#*! Torch* (1998)
- *Heavy Metal Parking Lot: The Lost Footage* (1998)
- *Legend of Forrest Tucker* (trailer) (1998)
- *Neil Diamond Parking Lot* (1998)
- *I Created Lancelot Link* (1999)
- *Jewish Film Festival Trailers* (1999)
- *Memo from Reidy* (1999)
- *First Edition Barbara* (2000)
- *Harry Potter Parking Lot* (2000)
- *Jeff's People* (2000)
- *King Of Porn 2: The Retirement* (2000)
- *Obsessed With Jews* (2000)
- *Pancake* (2000)
- *Urology for Big Daddy* (2001)
- *Jeff Krulik Picks the Weasel* (2002)
- *Hitler's Hat* (2003)
- *Heavy Metal Picnic* (2010)
- *Kentucky Confidential* (2011)
- *Tales of Belair at Bowie* (2019)
- *We Are Fugazi from Washington DC* (2023) (co-curated by Joe Gross and Joseph Pattisall)
- *Razz (The) Documentary* (2023) (co-directed by Richard Taylor

© S. Moore

Walt Starling grew up in Hyattsville, MD. I met him in 1970 when we both started at the University of Maryland. He was Walter back then. I phoned the famous Walt to ask for an interview in 1983. We met at the College Park Airport and realized we knew each other.

He did the afternoon traffic radio report on stations *WASH* (97.1 FM), and WPGC (95.5 FM) and owned his own airplane. I took this picture after we circled the city for two hours. It was thrilling. He was the first radio fly guy to use a plane to do traffic reports in DC.

From 1974 until 1995, he orbited the Beltway at 1,300 feet, reporting traffic twice a day. He thought he logged over 2 million air miles before he died at age 52 of colon cancer on Jan4, 2005.

He was a really good guy.

Chapter 25 – Connie B. Gay's Country Club

Connie Barriot Gay was born in Lizard Lick in 1915, a small North Carolina farm town about eighteen miles from Raleigh. Gay, the youngest of ten children, became the top country music promoter in Washington, DC, during the early days of television and radio.

Connie discussed his life with me in 1987, sitting in the grand living room of his McClean, Virginia, home. It was the most impressive residential home I had ever entered at the time.

Mr. Gay, a founder of the Country Music Association, greeted me in a white suit for an afternoon chat. At first, he seemed happy yet cautious about me wanting to talk with him about his rise from rags to auspicious riches in the music business. We began with an off-the-record discussion about the problems of alcohol with country music, and then he talked generously about his career.

"My father was a dirt farmer," he began. "Money was something we didn't own. We knew everybody around Lizard Lick was poor." It was the depths of the Great Depression when Gay hitchhiked to the North Carolina State University with $2.25 in his pocket. Always a good talker, he convinced the school's treasurer to let him enroll. "If you haven't got any more sense to come down here to go to college on $2.52, then I haven't got any more sense than to let you try," was the treasurer's response.

Gay worked his way through school, doing any job he could get, from feeding hogs to working the school's switchboard. He studied from library textbooks and ate the cafeteria food tagged to be thrown out. After graduating with a degree in Agriculture, Gay grabbed a New Deal government job in soil erosion work for the Farm Securities Administration. He became an organizer of small farm cooperations to combat rural poverty, where farmers could jointly buy necessary machinery and tools.

With the outbreak of World War II, Connie was sent to the Caribbean islands to organize similar farm cooperatives. "I arrived in Washington DC in the early 1940s as a writer for various government officials, including President Roosevelt, and landed a job as the radio voice for the Department of Agriculture's *Farm and Home Hour*." Another show was *Fashions and Rations*, and he wrote slogans for the war's patriotic Victory Garden effort.

Connie took to the streets of Washington during the first years of World War II, a story which I now consider introspectively as my interview scoop with the "Hillbilly Impresario." Gay told me about those early days, "I'd buy these 'Keen-Edge' knife sharpeners and sell them for fifty cents on the street. I had this live Gila monster in a case, and I'd hold it up and shout, 'I'm gonna eat this thing!' to attract attention. Then I'd sell the sharpeners. There would always be one person hanging around after I'd finished and say, 'I thought you were gonna eat that thing!'

"When I started my radio show, *Farm and Home Hour*, I began to get repeated requests to play hillbilly music. Music on the radio then was either pop music or tuxedo music. There was the *Grand Ole Opry* and *Louisiana Hayride*, but by and large, it was an ethnic phenomenon and neither recognized nor promoted by radio networks. Hillbilly's music was about booze, broads, and broken hearts. When FDR died, I decided to leave the government and went to Arlington Radio Station WARL."

On November 6, 1946, Gay brought hillbilly radio to a substantial metropolitan area for the first time. The success of Gay's half-hour show, *Town and Country Time*, soon expanded to the station's entire format. Although WARL in Arlington was slightly less in transmitting power at one thousand watts, the station benefited from a clear signal this side of the Shenandoah

Mountains, and the music traveled across DC, Maryland, Virginia, and even reaching parts of West VA, Pennsylvania, New Jersey, and Delaware.

"It went over like gangbusters, and we were successful from the minute we went on air," Gay asserts. He called it "country music," and gradually, the term defined the genre of rural music as the irreverent "hillbilly" term died out. As television took over from radio in the early 1950s, *Town and Country Time* moved to local DC TV Channel 7, and the popular show was eventually syndicated to forty stations nationwide.

Connie demonstrated country music's respectability by selling out Constitution Hall for 27 straight Saturday nights in 1948 with his country music shows, a record that still stands. Some called the place "Connie's Barn."

(l to r) Buck Ryan, Mary Klick, Jimmy Dean, Dale Turner, Marvin Carroll, Alex Houston w/ Elmer, Scotty Irwin, and Herbie Jones.

A Few Firsts by Gay

First country music airshow: He rented the Bailey's Crossroads airfield and hired a flying circus, while a country music band played to the crowd on the ground. 55,000 people attended while local firefighters enforced a single entrance and exit, and Gay charged $1.00 per person.

First country music picnic: He made a deal with a local fried chicken dealer, charging one chicken dinner per patron for admission. "That way," he said, "I didn't have to pay admission tax on ticket sales; there were no tickets."

First country moonlight cruises on the Wilson Line on the Potomac River out of Washington. "The boats would hold [about two hundred] people, and I'd charge two dollars a head. After we got beyond Coast Guard jurisdiction, I'd sell shots of whiskey for the then-outrageous price of a dollar, beer for fifty cents, and nickel colas for a quarter. And I'd turn off the water fountains as soon as we left the dock. It was hotter than the binges of hell out there."

It was Gay who brought Elvis Presley to the Wilson Line for Presley's first and only Washington DC appearance on March 23, 1956 [although Elvis did play Landover, Maryland's Capital Centre twice in 1976 and '77].

Elvis Presley and his Blue Moon Boys, as they were billed, were booked on Friday March 23, 1956, to launch the new season of the '56 Country Music Moonlight Cruise concerts, but the four-deck, 200 ft. S.S. Mount Vernon blew a valve that the crew couldn't repair by show time. Some of the hundred folks waiting in line on the Maine Avenue dock asked for their two dollar admission back. But the show went on—for an unexpected three hours.

Opening for Elvis was Jimmy Dean. Elvis dropped by before his 1956 Wilson Line concert to provide Jimmy Dean with a slightly nervous interview on Jimmy's TV show.

The twenty-one-year-old Elvis had released "Heartbreak Hotel" two months earlier—his first million-dollar record. His back-up studio band included Chet Atkins on guitar and Floyd Cramer on piano. This record was No. 1 on the Country and Western charts when Elvis boarded the old ship that night, accompanied by his classic trio of Scotty Moore (guitar), Bill Black (bass) and D.J. Fontana (drums).

Writer Peter Golkin creatively chronicled the evening in a Washington City Paper article (2/15/2007). Peter cleverly ended his story with, "The show, unlike the boat, rocked."

In 1958, Gay helped found the Country Music Association and became its first president. He later helped organize the Country Music Foundation, which runs the Country Music Hall of Fame, where Gay himself was finally inducted in 1980.

Connie moved to entrepreneur with the success of these country music acts in the nation's capital. Known for their restrictive policies, He next set his sights on the Daughters of the American Revolution (DAR) Constitution Hall as a venue for the kind of music he wanted to promote to DC's audiences.

"The DAR was kind of tippy toeing around the word 'hillbilly.' The old biddies of the DAR didn't want to taint their hall with cow droppings," Gay told me. "They were very selective. They wanted Toscanini, not Marian Anderson. They called our first show 'Folk Music.' October 31, 1947, we went in for one night with Grandpa Jones, Kitty Wells, Eddie Arnold, and Minnie Pearl. We sold out two shows, setting a house record for gross receipts. Over 10,000 people were turned away. After twenty-six consecutive sell-outs, the hall got the nickname 'Connie's Barn.'"

On April 7, 1948, Gay's Constitution Hall program became the world's first network-televised country music show. Gay explained, "This television thing needed sounds and entertainment, and what we were doing was right down their alley. NBC was five stations: Boston, New York, Philadelphia, Baltimore, and DC. They televised it, and the response was good. Of course, there were only a minuscule number of TV sets back in those days. NBC brought their cameras in with a truck out back. It was live, and it was fun."

He became "the man to know" for aspiring country and western performers. He helped launch local DC musicians Jimmy Dean, Roy Clark, Patsy Cline, and American University graduate George Hamilton IV to fame.

In addition, Connie was responsible for Charlie Pride's first recording contract. "I gave Charlie his first square meal in Nashville. He had made a demo tape making the rounds. One night, I was playing pinball in an airport with Chet Atkins, who was the head of Nashville's RCA operations. I told Chet we should bet on the games and said, 'If I win the next game, you'll have to sign Pride to RCA, and if I lost, I'd pay him $50. I won.'"

Gay was highly proud of his success with the phenomenal Charlie Pride. He told me, "Although I'm a Southerner, there's never been a drop of bigotry in me. The closest we ever came to bigotry was our mother saying, 'Never let a Negro be nicer to you than you can be to him.'"

Connie soon became known as a star-maker and began buying radio and television stations around the DC area. He once owned eleven, "And everyone was a dog when I bought them. This was an era we'll never see again. It was after World War II. People were moving South to the North, and they were homesick for nostalgic, sentimental back-home tunes."

One of Gaye's many deals was purchasing an AM station for $464,000 on the back of a Shoreham Hotel menu with a $1.00 contract for the FM rights. "Nobody thought that FM would amount to anything at the time, and I got several million dollars back for that one dollar a few years later."

The call letters were already WGAY before he bought it, but Connie admitted that his ego caused him to buy the Washington radio station. He sold the station in 1973, and it turned away from bluegrass.

My grandfather took me to my first concert when I was five. It was at the National Guard Armory, and I only remember standing in line to meet the show's star, Jimmy Dean. Patsy was standing next to him.

Patsy Cline

In 1932, in Winchester, Virginia, Hilda Patterson was to be married to forty-two-year-old Sam Hensley.

Signed Jimmy Dean. Patsy Cline's national debut on Arthur Godfrey.
And Gay's picture: I sneaked a pic from my car when I was leaving his house.

A week later, Virginia Patterson Hensley was born. The world would come to know the little Ginny Hensley as Patsy Cline. A few months later, her mother, Hilda, turned seventeen.

The Great Depression was on. Patsy saw dark times. Her family moved nineteen times as her father sought places to work. A fortunate job occurred when Sam became the boiler man at Washington and Lee University, a small Liberal Arts school in Lexington, VA, and the ninth oldest college in the United States, even older than the U.S. Constitution.

The young family found housing on campus. When Patsy opened her window, she'd sometimes hear big bands perform at the school. Most of them had a girl singer. She would start to sing along, and her fascination with pop music began there.

When Sam lost this job, Patsy's mom, Hilda, left him, packed up Patsy and her two siblings, and moved to a Winchester home without electricity or water. She didn't attend school past the eighth grade. On Saturday mornings, Patsy listened to a country music radio show hosted by deejay Jim McCoy, whose wife Angie met Hilda and Patsy and invited them to the station. Following that visit, Patsy began singing in local bars at age thirteen, doing pop and country music.

After this local success, she managed a trip to Nashville's *Grand Ole Opry* for an unsuccessful audition the following year. She was underage but made an impression. She returned to Winchester and worked at a meatpacking place by day. By night, she wore bold lipstick and men's jeans, singing country music in the bars. She graduated from the chicken job to cleaning buses and restrooms at the local Greyhound station. Patsy also entered numerous talent contests then but never won.

When Patsy turned twenty, she joined local musician Bill Peer, singing with his band, and traveled to Washington DC to become a regular performer at the Famous bar beside the Greyhound bus station. It was here that she worked with Jimmy Dean, Roy Clark, and others to develop her unique style.

Patsy made her national television debut on Arthur Godfrey's *Talent Scouts*. His CBS show aired from New York City on Monday nights. The Godfrey format featured agents and managers presenting their latest artists. Her friend Ray Rainwater chose a more conventional dress for this opportunity instead of the cowgirl top and men's jeans she typically wore. On January 21, 1957, Patsy's mom, Hilda, pretended to be her manager.

Cline captivated the country with an impressive performance of "Walking After Midnight" which she recorded the previous year. Patsy said she didn't like the song much, but the studio audience did, ringing Godfrey's studio's applause-o-meter decidedly. "Don't go away, Patsy, honey," Godfrey told her. "You done won this."

Decca enthusiastically released the song as a single. It was Cline's first hit song at number two on the country charts and number twelve on the pop charts. It sold a million copies.

After this success, Hilda started making her daughter a pink outfit with record-shaped wool patches featuring the names of Patsy's singles in pink rhinestones: "Poor Man's Roses" on the right shoulder, "Come On In" on the left shoulder, "Yes I Understand" on the right leg," "Stop the World" on the left leg, and "Walking After Midnight" on the back. Patsy became one of the most influential vocalists of the 20th century and was one of the first country music artists to cross into pop music. Her first *Billboard* number one hit was 1961's "I Fall to Pieces," followed by "Crazy" penned by Willie Nelson, her most famous song. Originally called "Stupid," Nelson wrote "Crazy" in less than an hour.

Patsy's producer, Owen Bradley, suggested Patsy not to use Nelson's singing style but rather her own, which was more like the big band and jazz performers she heard on the radio growing up. The studio musicians took a lot of time getting the tracks in place, but Patsy nailed the vocal in one take.

Almost endlessly covered by other artists, Patsy Cline's recording of "Crazy" was inducted into the Grammy Hall of Fame for fundamentally changing country music.

Patsy Cline's radio debut was recorded at the WMAL radio studios in DC in August 1954 during Connie's radio program *Town and Country Time*. The United States armed forces then sponsored and distributed the recordings. The recordings were pressed onto LP format and mailed to thousands of radio stations to encourage military recruiting.

She had just won the National Country Music Championship contest in nearby. Warrenton, Virginia, and her prize was the radio appearance on *Town and Country Time*. Jimmy Dean, not Connie, hosted Patsy's first appearance, and they had an immediate on-air ease together. For her first national radio exposure, she sang a fun tune called "Walkin' the Dog" and the country classic "It Wasn't God Who Made Honky-Tonk Angels."

Jimmy encouraged listeners to send requests for encore appearances by Patsy directly to the United States Army Band in Fort Myer, Virginia. They did that since she appeared on the show many more times. One of these shows included a song Patsy sang with these words: "Here they come, straight and tall, they're the proudest of them all—the United States."

In conjunction with her last appearance in 1962, Patsy performed at Quantico Marine Base in Virginia soon afterward. My father was stationed there then and met her after the performance. He'd grown up just a short distance south of Patsy's Virginia hometown of Winchester and loved her music. The only record album I recall him owning was Sentimentally Yours, Patsy's August 1962 final studio album, released just months before the plane crash that silenced her extraordinary voice.

Charles D. Young

And Now..... Chapter 26 – Best in Show

We encouraged our community to share a cherished memory from a performance or event that holds a special place in their hearts—not necessarily the most significant but one they recall with love.

Abaad Behrens Guitarist w/Razz, Artful Dodger et al.

"The Stones in 1972. Their Exile on Main Street Tour at RFK stadium. Tickets were $5 and opening was Stevie Wonder. I got my guitar chops from Keith all along, and this was my first time to see the band and my hero in action. I cut school to get tickets at a department store. I ran into the vice principal back at school, and he says, 'Aha I got you.' I said 'I don't care. Put me in detention. I got my Stone's tickets.' And I sat in the pit not far from the stage. I was the moth to my flame."

Bob Berberich, Drummer, w/Hangmen, Grin, Roslyn Mountain Boys.

"After the Hangmen broke up, I played in a house band called The Button in Greenwich Village in the summer of '67 at the Cafe A Go-Go, Once we were doing our set and somebody comes up and grabs a set of drumsticks and starts playing along with me. I'm getting ready to punch the guy, and it turned out to be Keith Moon, drummer for the Who. So, Moon and I played a song together. And on our break, Who bass player John Entwistle, Keith Moon and Jimi Hendrix sat in on our equipment and jammed."

Cathy Ponton King, Blues vocalist, guitarist, and songwriter.

"I don't want to start crying but it was the last time Levon Helm came to Wolf Trap, just before he died. John Hiatt was the opening act and although Levon's voice was ravaged they both came out and sang 'I Shall Be Released.'

"Amy Helm, Levon's daughter, sang a whole verse acapella. And it was like, you know, dear God, take me now."
Cathy with Mark Segraves © CPK

Bill Starks, Singer/songwriter, keyboardist, WAMA winner, currently with Ruthie and the Wranglers and an alumnus of Rhythm Method, Smalltalk, Jr Cline & the Recliners, Cathy Ponton King band, and the Dynettes bands.

"It was 1968. My social studies teacher, Mr. Sipe, was the faculty sponsor for our Earle B. Wood Junior High teen club. He got us all tickets to see Gladys Knight and the Temptations at the Shady Grove Music Fair. I was thirteen in eighth grade and my first rock concert. It was a spiritual experience like going to church.

"Their showmanship impressed me on all kinds of levels. I loved all the music. I hadn't been to a show like that before. You can picture the Temptations and they're all dressed alike, and doing their incredible dance moves, singing with the ensemble and in harmony arrangements.

"But not only that, they worked the audience completely. And if you remember Shady Grove, it was a theater in the round and had aisles that divided the sections of the seats that extended like spokes of a spokes of a wheel. And the Temptations would run out in those aisles and with the mics and sing right in front of the audience. I was completely mesmerized. It blew my mind."

Photo: Bill sitting at his parents player piano, the very place where he taught himself to play.. "I started when I was just five years old," he recalls. "I was captivated by how the keyboard worked as the rolls turned. It helped me visualize the music and understand elements like voices, chords, arpeggios and such. The music from those rolls truly inspired me." © B. Starks

Roger Mudd, broadcaster.

"Hans Kindler was the National Symphony's founder and music director (in 1928.) One favorite DC memory growing up is going to the Constitution Hall back in the '30s to hear his children's concerts when he conducted the mouse-poor National Symphony."

Ken Ludwig, playwright and many more.

"It was a production at the Arena Stage called *The Razzle* by Tom Stoppard. Doug Weider directed it. It is one of my favorite comedies. And it was done so wonderfully at the Arena. It was a time for me that made such a huge impression. I watched it and thought 'now there is the way to write a modern comedy.'"

Daryl Davis, R&B and blues musician, and author.

"Chuck Berry's original piano player Pinetop Perkins and Muddy Waters would come to my house when they toured DC and once Muddy was opening for Eric Clapton at the Capital Centre. I drove Muddy to the show and he and Eric hadn't seen each other for a while. Muddy and Pinetop, and I are backstage when Clapton comes up.

"'Hey Muddy, good to see you again, my brother,' and hugs Muddy.

'I got something for you.' And he hands Muddy the gift. Muddy opens it up, and pulls out a bottle of Hennessy Cognac, which is Muddy's favorite drink, and Pinetop's too.

"Muddy says, 'Oh Eric. I'm on the wagon now. I stopped all that.' Eric's like, 'I'm sorry, man. I didn't know.' And so Muddy looks at me, and asks, 'Is it OK if I give it to my boy here?' meaning me. And, Eric says, 'Sure.' So Muddy hands me the bottle. Tennessee Hennessy Cognac.

"'I don't drink, but I accepted it. Why? From Eric Clapton to Muddy Waters, to Daryl Davis.'"

Michael Oberman, Music journalist, wildlife photographer, former manager of Claude Jones, Rosslyn Mountain Boys, and others.

"Picking one memory that stands out...difficult but not impossible. Having interviewed over 300 musical artists from Joni Mitchell to James Brown, Jim Morrison to Curtis Mayfield for my

weekly column in the (Washington, DC) *Evening Star* newspaper…I decided not to choose one of those memories.

Instead, David Bowie spending his first day in the U.S. with me, my brother, and our parents in Silver Spring, MD…magical. January 1971. Bowie is brought to the U.S. by my brother Ron for a promotional tour of radio stations and to meet music journalists. I was under no pressure to interview him. Instead, we had dinner in a restaurant and then David came to my house in Takoma Park. How did that trip in January 1971 influence David to adopt the persona of Ziggy Stardust? You will have to read my book, *Fast Forward, Play, and Rewind* to find out." © M. Oberman

Ron Newmyer, Musician, producer, and concert organizer.

"I watched the Beatles on Ed Sullivan and joined the Beatles Fan club shortly afterward. I saw their ad in the Evening Star newspaper. I sent in my two bucks, and my membership got me an early alert that the Beatles were coming to the Baltimore Civic Center in the fall. The Feld Brothers managed the Carter Barron Amphitheater and produced the Beatles show in Baltimore, so they arranged a bus at the Amphitheater parking lot to take us DC fan club members to the concert.

Ronnie and Louie © The Newmyers

"I was only ten years old, but I told my parents, 'I have to go to this,' and used my money that I earned shoveling snow to get two tickets. I told my older brother, Louie: 'I got two tickets to see The Beatles. You want to come with me on the bus?'

"'No,' he answered

"'Why not?'

"'Because I'm a Dave Clark Fan,' he said proudly. And he turned it down. He didn't go!

"Fortunately, another friend, Bobby Cahill, a year older than me could, so my parents drove us to the bus at Carter Barron. It was drizzling, and my bus window was down. My mom and dad were outside waving to us. My dad asks, 'You got your ticket?' And I reached into my pockets, and I didn't have it. The bus was idling. He yelled, 'Get off the bus. Get off the bus.' I made a death march down the aisle, realizing I would not see the Beatles. I screwed up. I lost my ticket.

"As I stepped off the bus, I saw a white envelope floating in a puddle at the foot of the stairs. I picked it up, and it was the ticket. And we got back on the bus. Oh, man!

"The bus stopped three blocks from the Civic Center. My friend and I followed the crowd, walked into the Civic Center, and saw the Beatles show. It was life-changing, my first concert and the excitement level was through the roof. I watched the girls going crazy for the Beatles and thought this looked even cooler than playing sports. Two years later, I saw the 1966 Beatles show at DC Stadium. Louie, still buying Dave Clark 5 albums, went with me this time. He had learned his lesson."

Adele Abrams

Attorney, Safety Professional, WHFS DJ (1974-88).

"I was a sophomore at the University of Maryland, majoring in journalism in 1971. I had never heard of the Allman Brothers before coming to college.

"Dame and Mark, my two very good friends, were Allman

Brothers fanatics and they turned me on to this music. I had just started working at WMUC, the U-MD campus radio station.

"I loved the Allman Brothers by the time I heard they were coming to Painter's Mill music hall on my birthday. Dame and Mark got me a ticket as my gift. It was an amazing show and we celebrated. That was the last show of that tour, and the band went back home to Macon, Georgia.

"Two weeks later Duane Allman was on his Harley-Davidson Sportster when a flatbed truck carrying a huge crane boom made a left-hand turn in front of him. He slowed his bike toward the center of the road so he could swing around the truck, but it stopped short. The crane's weight ball knocked Duane off his Harley. He had a few visible bumps and scrapes, so it looked at first like he wasn't severely hurt, but he had massive internal injuries and died in surgery that evening."

Recorded on a hand-held cassette machine by then eighteen-year-old radio journalist Sam Idas, this concert was released as a CD by the Allman Brothers Band recording company in October 2020. The tracks are "Statesboro Blues," "Trouble No More," "Don't' Keep Me Wondering," "One Way Out," "In Memory of Elizabeth Reed," "Hot 'Lanta," and "Whipping Post."

In 1978, our DC area had a surprise encounter with Greg Allman. I covered this story for the WHFS *Pipeline* newsletter (with the motto: "Published Monthly Upon Occasion.") Here's what I wrote about the promise of Greg joining our own Nighthawks:

"Gregg Allman was in Atlanta looking to reestablish a home base when he was turned onto the Nighthawks in March by Twigs Lydon, a former roadie with the Allman Brothers and currently road manager of the Dixie Dregs. At the time while hopes were high for an Allman Brothers reunion, Twig suggested a night out, so Gregg could hear a hot blues band from DC playing three hours away in Jacksonville, Alabama. Although less than enthusiastic Gregg agreed and wound up sitting in on the last Saturday night. He then told the audience, 'I'm here to hire these guys and get 'em to play with me.'"

The guys in question, of course, were the Nighthawks. Plans for the Allman Brothers reunion was shelved, and Greg showed up in town two weeks later for a landmark appearance with the Hawks at the Bayou. Since then, he's performed with them, both in and out of town, and plans for a southern tour are solidifying.

"The music provides the common ground and the Nighthawks renowned energy is proving contagious. It's hard to say where this turn in the road will lead, but all signs point to some good music coming out of the merger. Greg ain't wasting time no more. However, Dickie Betts's call to Greg for an Allman Brothers reunion ended Greg's Nighthawks future."

Jay Schlossberg Owner, Media Central, LLC—and Producer: WHFS: Feast Your Ears film.

"It was June 20, 1983—the first time the Grateful Dead played Merriweather Post Pavilion. My friend Bob and I had seats in the center section near the back row.

"There was an evening of Washington DC thunderstorms, one after the other. We were undercover, of course, so we stayed dry. But it was just pouring rain and thunder and lightning. And they played a really good first set. They took their intermission and came back. It was getting dark, but still on and off pouring rain. The lawn was turning to mud because all the deadheads were dancing on the lawn. The mud started to come down off the lawn and run behind the seats. We went up to get a drink with mud everywhere.

"The Dead returned for their second set. They were doing fine with the thunder and lightning. People were still partying. During their song 'War Rat' there's a part four and a half minutes in where they sing 'I'll get up and fly away' four times. On the last chorus line three lightning bolts converged into one and hit the middle pole of the pavilion.

"The lights went down and then came back on and we hear Brent Midland's organ go 'boom.'

"I've heard the board tapes. The lightning strikes exactly four minutes and forty seconds into the song and you hear the 'pop.' It gives me chills because I remember that exact moment so unusual and specific—involving the band, the audience, and nature all converging in the same little moment. The crowd lets out a roar for the next fifteen seconds like you've never heard anywhere. Everyone on stage got shocked but nobody got hurt. And they continued to play. It calms down and they finish the song. I have to say that t was the most moving moment in any concert I've ever been to. And believe me, I've seen some amazing shows."

Uncle Rick Harmel

"When I first got out of the Navy, I met Jim Radcliffe, who was a drummer in Southeast DC and gave lessons," says my Uncle Rick.

Uncle Rick, my son Charlie Moore, also a drummer, and me.
© S. Moore

"He was teaching me and brought a young guy named Danny Gatton over to my house. Danny had just graduated from Anacostia High School. This was around 1962, and we started jamming at Pop's house on 36th Place. No song that I recall, but Danny could play the crap out of his guitar just doing lead riffs then.

"Danny brought in Richard Creighton on bass, Jan Rhodes on sax. And Dick Heintze on organ, and that became our band for years. I kept the band book for contacts.

"For a Christmas party, Danny once got Jack Casady, a bass player he knew. Dick Heintze, Jan Rhodes, Danny with Jack Casady and I did the gig.

"Heintze and I got Chick Hall Jr., "Little Chick," we called him. and all did gigs around town as the Neons. Danny became a sheet metal worker and still went on with his music. He'd help me on elevator jobs and gigs. One day he came by the job telling me he was quitting sheet metal work because he was afraid he'd hurt his hands. I tried to talk him out of it.

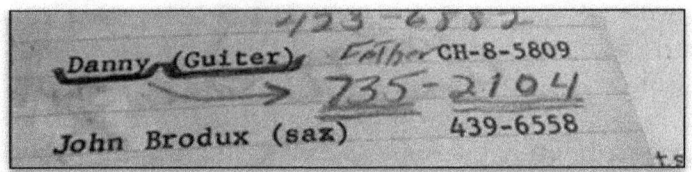

Photos from Uncle Rick's band book, Danny on (Guiter)

L. Susanne Gordon, WHFS's first news broadcaster; Founding Director at American Center for the Integration of Spiritually Transformative Experiences (aciste.org); Faculty, University of Maryland.

"It was in the mid-70s, so I had heard Bruce Springsteen and the E Street Band's music, of course. But I'd never heard Springsteen live.

"I had no interest in hearing him live. I didn't get what the big deal was, other than that his was a good rock and roll band, like a lot of other bands. But what made him 'The Future of Rock and Roll'?

"I was surprised to get a phone call from a former boyfriend, a Springsteen fan. We hadn't been in contact for months. He had two tickets to a Springsteen concert at DAR Hall, he told me, and he invited me to go with him. I needed to see Springsteen in person he said, to understand what all the buzz was about.

"Turned out our seat numbers were A-1 and A-2, and the former boyfriend was right. I was blown away. All the way away. It was one of the best concerts, maybe the best concert, I've ever seen. All the band members were outstanding musicians, playing great songs, but it was their dynamic, their collective energy, and the joy they were taking in playing together that was so amazing. It took me several more E Street Band concerts to understand how incredible the band was, to notice that they never seemed to play the same song, or the same set, the same way.

"That concert was special in another way. The partner of one of the band or crew members was a violinist and, throughout the concert, she and Bruce played a number of joint lead parts that were absolutely transcendent. So, I confess, once I started paying attention to the band, their albums, and the liner notes, to being disappointed to realize that this had been a one-off; the violinist wasn't actually part of the E Street Band.

"Even so, I left that concert a dedicated Springsteen fan."

Bill Clinton, Musician and former Leader of the Free World.

"One of my haunts in Georgetown was the Tombs, a beer hall in a cellar below the 1789 restaurant. And the Cellar Door just down the hill from my dorm on M street. They had great live music. I heard Glenn Yarborough, and jazz organist Jimmy Smith. And a forgotten group called the Mugwumps, who broke up shortly after I came to Georgetown.

"Several weeks into my first semester, I went to the Lisner Auditorium to hear Judy Collins sing. I can still see her standing alone on the stage with her long blonde hair, floor length cotton dress, and guitar. From that day on, I was a huge Judy Collins fan.

Photo: Bill with Jerry Jeff Walker © Oelze

"In December 1978, Hillary and I went on a brief vacation to London after the first time I was elected governor. One day as we went shopping down Kings Road in Chelsea. The loudspeaker of a store blared out Judy's version of Joni Mitchell's 'Chelsea Morning.' We agreed on the spot that if we ever had a daughter, we'd call her Chelsea."

Steve Houk Musician, *Living on Music* broadcaster.

Steve began his music journalism and TV careers in 2004 and started singing two years later. His Tommy Lepson interview is Chapter 44. Steve's favorite personal experience to share for us is meeting his high school music idol, Peter Frampton.

"*Frampton Comes Alive* was Peter's 1976 live album that turned him into a superstar," explains Steve, "as well as being a seminal part of my early musical admiration. Being a huge longtime fan, our 45-minute radio discussion on his life, career, and new Grammy-winning instrumental album *Fingerprints* was incredible."

Photo: Peter with Steve

"Later, I saw him play The Birchmere, and Peter was happy to meet me at his tour bus after the show. It was wonderful meeting the man I listened to decades earlier.

"We chatted about our radio interview, which he said he loved, and his show. As I said goodbye and walked away, he saw his live album I had brought for him to sign sitting on a bench. 'Hey Steve, you want me to sign that?' 'Oh my, yes, of course!' I replied, so he signed it, we hugged, and off I went, delighted. Baby, I still...love your way."

DC area musicians that Steve has interviewed for *Living on Music* include:

Alcantara, Arch	Fox, Melissa	Lloyd, Juliet
Anito, Flo	Quinn, Francis	Lockey, M.
Baxter, Jeff	Hamburger, A	Logsdon, R.
Berigan, Lisa	Harvey, Carly	Moore, Stephen
Campbell, Sela	Heck, Brad	Mystic Chicks
Carroll, Jon	Helms, Neeta	Naked Blue
Chappell, Dave	Holliday, J.	Newmyer, Ron
Cline, Daryl Jr.	Indigo, T.	O'Brien, Sio
Coulter, Billy	Jaworek, M.	O'Connell, E.
Davis, Daryl	John David	Oelze, Gary
Davis, Kara	Kalish, Bill	Oelze, Susan
Ditoro, Cathy	Kasdorf, Julia	Paris, Dan
Ebert, Jim	Kibel, Seth	Previti, John
Elliott, Dave	Kurt, Scott	Ray, Annie
Everett, Cal	Langer, Jenny	Reed, Tim
Fishell, John	Lisi, Nancy	Reese, Patty

Roots, Sol	Tash, Michael	Wright, Ryan
Schumer, Arlen	Taylor, Linwood	Wright, Todd
Schwartz, Danie	The Sidleys	Starks, Bill
Scott, Eric	Thomson, Dess	Wyland, Dede
Selby, Eric	Timbers, Chris	Zukowski, Jan
Smallwood, G.	Trawick, Justin	
Sullivan, Chuck	Tsaggaris, L.	

Al Petteway, Grammy Award-winning guitarist, who passed away on September 25, 2023.

A great friend to the Birchmere, who sent me several of his CDs after he generously contributed to that book.

His lovely instrumental music was inspirational and comforting, especially while writing alone late at night. He was the first musician I contacted when this Capital Acts book's publication was certain, and he sent me this Facebook message:

"Capital Acts should be an interesting project. So much has happened in the DC area in my lifetime. And from the time I was in high school, I was taking advantage of all the musical entertainment DC had to offer. I was like a sponge. These are many concerts I attended that really changed my life musically. Later I was playing clubs and giving concerts myself. But these early days were pretty interesting, from hanging out backstage at the Blind Faith concert on the night of the first moon landing, to singing 'Early Morning Rain' with Peter, Paul and Mary and Gordon Lightfoot backstage at Carter Barron.

Just after returning from Woodstock that same year, Peter Yarrow had also attended so we had lots to talk about. I was seated on stage with a folk group who were guests of Peter, Paul and Mary. Years later Pete Kennedy and I discovered that we had both been there on that stage, seated very near each other, but we hadn't met yet.

We later played together and became good friends. Pete wrote a wonderful book (*Tone, Twang, and Taste: A Guitar Memoir*) about his experiences and would be a good resource for Capital Acts. DC was such a great place for the study of all kinds of music from the 1950s on. Good luck. Al."

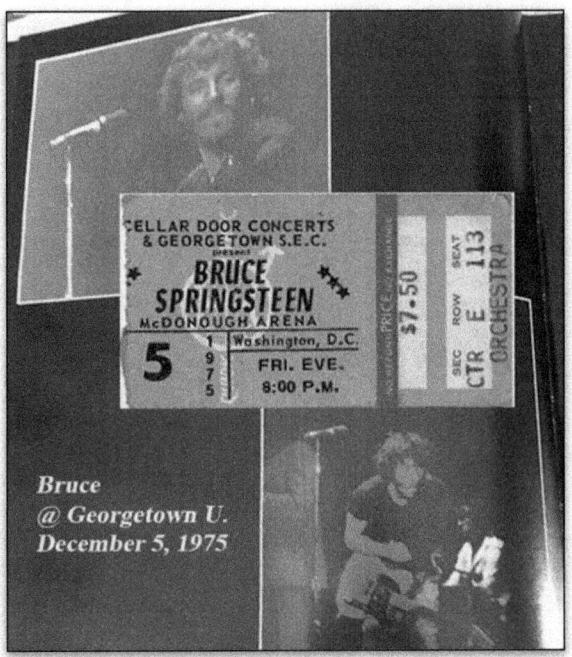

Georgetown University Yearbook

Chapter 27 – Chapin, John J. & Joan

© Connie B. Smith

Writing a song is like cracking a safe. It takes deaf manipulation and gentle coaxing to get the tumblers, or the words and musical notes to slip into place. Often the doors refuse to open, and the gold remains elusive. But talent makes the difference, and talent abounded in singer-songwriter Mary Chapin Carpenter's 1987 CBS album *Hometown Girl*. The country-flavored folk singer's vinyl debut was the first release of a multi-record deal with CBS.

"I'm real proud of this record," Mary Chapin Carpenter, a then 28-year-old resident of Takoma Park, Maryland and ten-year veteran of the local music scene told me when I interviewed her for one of her first newspaper profiles (the *Journal*'s "Tempo" section on March 20, 1987).

"CBS is going to aim the record to the country market. Hopefully there's a place for me," she said. That Carpenter still had doubts about achieving national prominence led some observers to call her "the reluctant star."

"I cried when the CBS offer came," the blonde singer confided. "I just couldn't believe it. I still feel that it's beyond my wildest dreams. Maybe when I see my face on the album jacket, I'll be convinced that it's happening."

Hometown Girl actually began as a demo tape made with John Jennings, her long-time guitarist and producer. "I've been confident about Mary for a long time," said Jennings in 1987, who served a decade with local singer Bill Holland and his Big Yankee Dollar band before settling into session work at Bias Recording Studio in Springfield, VA. Jennings is the one who motivated the reserved singer to transition away from relying on covers and start performing her own, which harmoniously combined folk and country influences. He would continue producing her first eight albums.

Also important to her story is Bill Danoff (of the Starland Vocal Band, and famously co-composer of "Take Me Home, Country Roads"). He introduced her to John Jennings, and found her day-job work and a place for Chapin, as her friends knew her, to write and rehearse songs. She and Jennings performed briefly with his Bill Danoff and Friends group in 1982.

"I'm no prophet, but anyone with ears and heart can tell that Mary's got it. It's difficult to fail with her," Jennings told me for my article.

Hometown Girl began as a simple four-song demo tape produced by Jennings. It eventually found a hearing with record industry executives.

"John encouraged me to record my own songs," said Carpenter. And my manager, Tom Carrico said, 'We've got nothing to lose if we shop it around a little.' So I said, 'Sure, why not?'"

Enter Gary Oelze, owner of Alexandria's Birchmere Club, local Mecca for acoustic musicians and their devotees. "Mary Chapin Carpenter was very shy when I first met he," said Oelze

"She was playing at open mics around town and opening for my headliners. She once came to a Rosanne Cash show. She asked me if I would give a tape she had made of her songs to Rosanne. I said 'No,' but asked her to wait while I went to the green room to arrange for Rosanne to meet her and accept the tape in person. Of course, Roseanne agreed. But when I went back to get Mary Chapin, she had left the building leaving her tape on the soundboard."

Oelze had the ear of CBS vice presidents. He told me by phone in my first conversation with him on his helping Mary Chapin Carpenter's career: "They asked me what was hot in Washingto. I said Mary. Songwriting is her strong card and she's so darn good." The CBS people listened to Gary and soon thereafter we're listening to the Carpenter tape, which they had overlooked. "I take it as a personal compliment to John's production of the tape that CBS didn't ask us to re-record it," added Mary. "We were three days away from signing with an independent label when CBS called," Carpenter confessed. "I was already the happiest girl in the world."

Carpenter arrived in this area with her parents and her guitar in 1974 from her native New Jersey. "My earliest musical influence was Judy Collins," she explained, but The Band and Emmylou Harris provided stronger inspiration as Carpenter matured. Her family lived near Gallagher's Pub, where Open Night Mic Night became her portal to local fame. "My father got tired of hearing me play my guitar in my room and finally told me why don't you go down to that bar and play?"

Returning from Brown University with a degree in American studies and a sharpened desire to perform, she aimed her sensuous alto voice at patrons of a dozen local bars. "I played the Joni Mitchell and Bonnie Raitt roles for five years and got so burned out that I almost quit music."

Once she realized that a few clubs like Washington's Food for Thought and Kramer Books and Afterwords would allow her to focus on her own music, Carpenter found she could play fewer gigs and fewer cover songs, shaping her act to her own image. Soon, the local music community began taking notice. Of the personal singer with the down homie wisdom in their lyrics.

"One of the greatest nights of my life was playing the Kennedy Center, Carpenter said. I got to be on the show with Jonathan Edwards and a whole group of real good people like Jesse Winchester and John Hiatt. It was the week of contrast, one night on stage at the Kennedy Center and the next night passing the hat at Food for Thought events."

April 1987 surpassed those memories. Carpenter, Jennings, and the rest of her band opened for Kris

Kristofferson at New York's Famed Bottom Line on April 6, and again headlined the Birchmere on April 25 and the release of her album. She still sounded cautious:

"I'm one of those people who dilute their excitement. It's nice to finally get some notoriety, but at the same time, I'm a little intimidated by it. It is scary."

Mary Chapin Carpenter won five Washington Area Music Association Awards, "Wammies," in 1985, including Best Female Vocalist in both the Bluegrass Country and Folk Acoustic categories and Best Songwriter to boot.

Gary Oelze recalled in the beginning: "John Jennings would come in with Pete Kennedy in different configurations of bands that I would use as opening acts. I became friends with John Jennings and met Chapin through him. We all called her Chapin back then. I admired her talents as well as John's. She had a voice like an angel. But she was very shy on stage. Often, she would look down when she sang and wouldn't look up at the audience. I think she opened for or joined in on about thirty shows. And then she would sing something she wrote, and I remember thinking that I would rather publish her than record her.

"I knew she and John were working on that album together when I traveled to Nashville to negotiate the potential sale of the Seldom Scene's 15th Anniversary concert at the Kennedy Center in 1986 to CBS. I was talking with Larry Hamby, then vice president of signing new acts."

Oelze mentioned Carpenter and got Carrico to send Hamby a tape. Oelze said, "Larry would drop by the Birchmere when he was in DC to catch the O' Kanes and others. Larry asked me what was going on in DC musically and I mentioned Chapin's name. I told him I was hiring her off and on while she was working on her songs. I reminded him that I had sent him a tape.

"And he replied, 'Do you know how many tapes I get, Gary? Thousands.' He finally found the tape and took it to Roy Wunsch, President of Sony Records Nashville Division. This led to Carpenter being signed to Columbia. Larry sent me a letter adding, 'I think of you often as I see Chapin's career blossom. You must be so proud.'"

Although Columbia didn't re-record the debut album, *Hometown Girl*, they did provide advance money needed to get the album to market. It sold 60,000 copies but did not recoup its costs. "Some labels might have dropped her then, but I think everyone saw the promise of what would come," Tom Carrico said. "They kept her on because they knew how good she would be." Her follow up 1989 album *State of the Heart* was a blockbuster success generating four top ten singles.

In 2020, for Gary Oelze's Birchmere history, Chapin added this about her former musical partner: "John knew what a special place the Birchmere was and he played with me many times and on his own there. He revered it the same way I do. For those of us who have known the club, it's so important that they always put the music first. Obviously, there are some very special clubs around the world that take the same approach, but the Birchmere is unique."

John Jennings with Chapin. He passed away from metastatic cancer in 2015. Lyle Lovett said "John always had a smile on his face. He was so articulate in his playing. His personal joy always came through his music. The way he played sounded like the way he spoke to me. Jennings brought all of his positive energy that he had in life to his music."   © Oelze

***

Mary Chapin Carpenter and Joan Jett are at opposite ends of the musical spectrum. Jett's family moved to Rockville, MD, in 1967, the same year the Carpenters family arrived in Takoma Park, MD. Joan attended Randolph Junior High School and Wheaton High School.

By 1987, Joan was an established star while Carpenter nervously awaited the release of her first album.

Here is an article our friend Jayne Blanchard wrote when she was a *Journal* staff writer in the 80s. Our thanks to Jayne for letting us reprint her piece which appeared on the front page of the *Journal*'s "Tempo" section when my Mary Chapin Carpenter piece entitled "Reluctant Star" appeared below the fold.

Joan Jett: She's living her life for rock and roll
by Jayne Blanchard. Friday, March 20, 1987

Followers of rocker Joan Jett know that she favors dusky leather clothing teamed with sneakers and the sounds emanating from her guitar can rival any chord work from a hairy-armed ax man band. Here are three things you might not know about Joan Jett.

One: The first song the Rockville, MD teen learned when her guitar was "On Top of Old Smokey." She was thirteen at the time and wanted to play T Rex.

Two: The female performer who wielded great influence on her was not Susie Quattro, Grace Slick, or Janis Joplin. It was Liza Minelli. (*Cabaret* had a big influence on me," she says.).

Three: She is gorgeous. Photos of Jett portray the twenty-six-year-old as raccoon-eyed and as hard edged as an Arrowhead. In person, Jett has the dark, smoldering looks of someone as mysterious as Egyptian statuary.

Her spiky hair is as glossy as blackened egret feathers. And her dark, doe eyes are onyx as her skin glows opal. The secretive, knowing eyes draw you closer to Jett, as if diamonds were tumbling from her mouth rather than words delivered in a steel-wool rasp from too many nights howling "I Love Rock and Roll."

Jett dresses for her interview with the subtlety of a rock star—black reptilian leather pants, brocade jacket, enough silver bracelets and necklaces to create sterling place settings for twelve and black boots dripping with silvery leaves.

For all the finery, Joan Jett keeps her life as stripped down as a Springsteen spiritual.

She lived in Rockville, MD, from 1968 to 1974 until her insurance salesman father moved the family to Southern

California, where Jett channeled her rock and roll yearnings not to get backstage to smooch Humble Pie band members but to start her own band, The Runaways.

Since her debut at sixteen with the notorious all-girl band, The Runaways. Jett has dedicated her life to loving rock and roll.

With several solid albums behind her (and another one on the way) and a reputation for mega-tours that last for years, Jett has earned a hard-won success as a basic rocker who can more than hold her own with the big boys.

Jett began another tour in January and it is rumored she is to appear in the Washington area again—possibly in "surprise concerts" at the Bayou in April.

She can now add another notch to her studded belt. Last month saw the premiere of Jett's first movie, *Light of Day*, a Paul Schrader film about a brother and sister who work out their family problems by playing in a bar band. The film, starring Michael J. Fox as the brother, garnered so-so reviews. Most critics, however, singled out Jett as one of the brightest aspects of *Light of Day*.

Indeed, Jet may not have the control of a Streep or a Fonda. but she has an intensity that sears the screen. When Jett is in a scene, the other actors seemed to grow paler in her wake.

"I had a lot of preparation," Jett says. "My acting coach, Sondra Lee, worked with me since I read for the part. I also have high energy, period. When I lock myself into something you can't tear me away. I'm very focused and concentrated."

It was Jett's ease with the rock life that first suggested her to director Paul Schrader.

"I knew from the get-go that I couldn't cast an actress," he says. "Four or five films have tried to use actresses as musicians and they were resoundingly rejected. It was very clear audiences didn't want it. I had to get a rock and roller."

Jett feels that her contribution to the film to "give a feeling of what it's like to play in a band, to make everybody comfortable with it. But honestly, I don't think an actress could have played the part of Patty. Rock and roll is a very get your hands dirty job."

Rock 'n' roll is one thing Jett knows about.

She remembers attending rock concerts like Black Sabbath, Grand Funk Railroad, and T Rex at the Baltimore Civic Center in those pre-Capital Centre days. And quote sitting in the crappy seats in the back and seeing 18,000 people going crazy and thinking "that's what I want to do. I want to be up there making people happy."

To achieve this, Jett became a rebel. "My rebelling is against people telling me: Girls can't play rock and roll Are you crazy? It's not your place."

"That was a motivating thing to prove people wrong," she continues.

"At sixteen, I was angry when people would ask me, 'Don't you feel your guitar sounds different with female skin touching the strings?'"

These questions frustrated Jett and gained her an unruly reputation in her Runaway days.

"I was very angry and violent. I'd get to the point where I'd grab people by the coat and drag them out of the room when they would ask right off the bat, 'So are you girls sluts?'

"Now I realize how angry I can get over ignorance. Instead of being mad, I just sit down and talk to people about it."

Jett feels she has a lot of explaining to do.

"People have so many misconceptions about rock and rollers," she says. "Everyone thinks it's 'grab a guitar, grab a beer, grab a blonde.' But it's very athletic. You have to get a lot of sleep and take care of yourself and get your priorities straight. I'm serious."

She formed The Runaways consisting of guitarist, Lita Ford, singer Cherie Curie, and bassist Jackie Fox in 1976 under the guidance of producer Kim Fowler, who fueled the band's undeserved slatternly reputations with exclamations of "Mothers. Lock up your sons."

"It took tenacity to endure The Runaways years. In 1976 it was unheard of for girls to be playing any kind of electronic instruments. We were looked on as freaks."

The thing that threatened most people in Jett's view was the honesty of the four suburban girls.

Friend Sharon Johnson with Joan.
© S. Johnson

"People didn't want to know that girls in America smoked, drank and had sex. They just didn't want to know."

"The band broke up after we realized no one was going to take us seriously. Anyone who saw us in concert knew we weren't the jailbait band with the reputation we were slapped with. People didn't want us to explain, they just had their perceptions."

The bad years—and ensuing alcohol problems behind her ¬Jett can afford to be introspective. "I think the Runaways now would be much more intense than the Bangles or the Go-Go's. But I think we really opened doors for other all-girl bands."

After The Runaways, Jett met musical producers Kenny and Merrill Laguna and "got my priorities straight." Under their guidance (The Lagunas are now her managers) Jett formed the Blackhearts. With her new band, she recorded *Bad Reputation*, which was snubbed by every major record company until the Lagunas pressed and produced the album for Boardwalk Records.

Jett was eventually picked up by Casablanca Records. Where she recorded such albums as *Glorious Results of a Misspent Youth*. The Blackhearts are not known as much for their recordings As for their raucous, sweaty live act. "The best part of being a musician—other than playing the music you love—is making people happy. The audience is everything to me."

She describes the feeling from the screaming fans as "pure love tinged with a sexual vibe. And love as in respect because your music gets them through tough times."

Jett lives for that "oneness with the audience. "You're all one person. You're on automatic pilot don't have to think about anything. It's all spontaneous. You don't feel like a jerk. It all glows."

Varsity Grill's Back Room

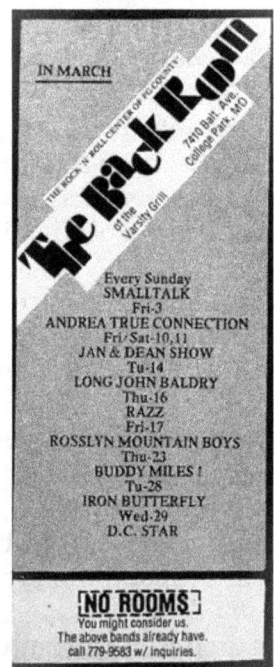

(Courtesy of Andrew Reader)

Chapter 28 ~ Songwriters' Delight

And then there was when my wife Margaret and I hung with Taffy Danoff in 1985. Margaret graduated from Wheeling Jesuit University in West Virginia, and "Take Me Home, Country Roads" came to mind. Taffy told us her detailed story of how this anthemic song came to be:

Taffy: The song began when Bill and I drove to Boyds, Maryland, for a family reunion. I was driving, and Bill had his guitar, riding shotgun. We were on Clopper Road, and he started singing "Country Roads" repeatedly because that's how Clopper Road goes up and down Route 270. And we got to our family reunion at the Isaac Walton League cabin and returned home.

So, "Country Roads" became one of the things we were working on. 'Country Roads, Da, da, da – up and down." The next few months this started to become a song. With songwriting, you can't just finish a song if there's nothing there, so it sometimes just sits there.

And then we did a second version of it, and it became West Virginia because, one, it's easier to rhyme than Maryland, and two, a friend and fan was writing us letters from a commune in West Virginia, saying how wonderful it was there. I don't think he said, "almost heaven," so Bill is responsible for that.

And then the lyrics became, "Country roads, take me home to the place where I belong, West Virginia."

In 1971, John Denver was hired at the Cellar Door. It was his first time headlining as a single solo artist. John had persuaded Mary Travers from Peter, Paul, and Mary to listen to "I Guess He'd Rather Be in Colorado," and she recorded that on her first solo album. This was our first actual (cover) recording. John was singing it at the Cellar Door, so Jack Boyle, who owned the club, knew this and hired us to be John's opening act, thinking this would be perfectly compatible because he was doing one of our songs.

During that week, the plan was John would come over to our Macarthur Boulevard basement apartment to listen to what else we had written because he liked Colorado. We were all going to meet at 3702 Q Street. We went home after the gig and waited.

Chris O'Connor, a manager of the Cellar Door and eventually became John's road manager, had a night deposit at the bank. And then he and John Denver were going to come. But they didn't show up. And they didn't show up, and they didn't show up.

We had left the Cellar Door at midnight, and by 2:30 a.m., we were ready to call the police. And then there was a knock on the door. It was them. They had been in a car accident. When they crossed Wisconsin Avenue, somebody hit them broadside. John Denver had broken his thumb. He had a cast on it. Bonnie, Chris's wife, had hurt her back and her side. They were at Georgetown Hospital ER getting everything fixed up.

They were like a sprung coil because of the adrenaline of coming off a gig and an accident. John was in a lot of pain and nobody could go to sleep anyway, so they decided to come and explain why they weren't here earlier?

John said, "I won't sleep because it hurts too much. So what music have you got?"

I said to Bill, "Show them 'Country Roads.'" Bill said, "No, it's not finished." I said I didn't care if it was finished because we knew it was hot. And so, we showed him what we had of

"Country Roads" and John went crazy. We all thought it would (at least) be a regional hit.

We sang it over and over, and it sounded real good with us singing with him. John took care of the lead, and we wrote and rewrote the second verse and then wrote that bridge: "I hear her voice in the morning hour she calls me." So that was the three of us collaborating. We stayed up until 7:00 a.m.

And the next night we sang it at the Cellar Door. John didn't yet know the words, so he read them off a piece of paper. We had known from the onset that it had something special. We sang it, and people went crazy. There was a five-minute ovation.

Next, John called his producer, Milt Okun, and told him, "I've got the hit, and I'm bringing Bill and Taffy up [to New York City]" because he happened to have recording time at his RCA studio.

We had never been in the big time and now we are singing with the famous Milt Okun producing. Paul Stookey of Peter Paul and Mary dropped by and listened to the playback and said, "That's the next 'Hey Jude.'"

Afterward, Milt took Bill and me out into the hall and asked us, "How do you see the division in terms of the publishing and writing credit on this particular song?"

And we said, with hesitation, "Well. We don't know. How about fifty-fifty with us and John?"

And Milt says, "Uh, John doesn't see it that way."

"Uh oh," I thought, "Here it comes. They're going to steal it. He has Mafia connections. We're going to be killed."

Milt says John sees it as John "will have a third, Bill will have a third, and Taffy will have a third." In fact, we ended up getting 75 percent of the royalties, and 25 percent went to John.

So, we signed an exclusive deal with Milt Okun and his Cherry Lane Music company on the spot.

"No one is a finer person than Milt Okun, And nobody has ever been finer or fairer to us in the business than John Denver. Every good thing that happened to us after that for a couple of years was directly related to John Denver. He would take us on his gigs so we could sing the song with him. We played Carnegie Hall and the biggest rooms in the country. John's manager, Jerry Weintraub got us outrageous record deals. John took us to England in '73. We did a television series on BBC. It was a totally rich experience. And I've heard almost everyone sing, "Take Me Home, Country Roads."

L to R) Lucy Kirkland (daughter of Lane Kirkland AFL-CIO): Raphael from Dupont Circle: Best buddy, Bruce Adams, the Cellar Door bartender who first told me about Taffy at Clyde's; Susan Warren, one of Taffy's friends; Taffy's younger brother, Eddy; a great character; Norman Welles, who played drums with us; "Big Jim," who called himself the mayor of Dupont Circle; Taffy and me; Helen Dapney, a woman Taffy worked with. Phil Keats, Bill's roommate at Georgetown; John Hall, from WHFS; Howard Freidman, a lawyer from downtown.

Bill identified their friends on
Fat City's first album *Reincarnation*

I first met Bill Danoff and Taffy Nivert at Mike Schreibman's Emergency club performing as Fat City. I was fifteen and struck by the beauty of one of Bill's songs, "There's a Man in China." I bought their first album, *Reincarnation*, and learned that song on my guitar.

During a break that first night at the Emergency I talked with Bill outside the club, suggesting they "improve their act" by playing some Hendrix songs. I thought their act was too folkish for the times.

Bill patiently explained his ideas for a gentler approach to music. He clearly had confidence in what he was doing. I remember less about what he told me, then feeling gratitude for his tone and patience in talking with me. I was a stupid high kid in high school and I loved Fat City after that night.

When reminiscing once about my Hendrix comment, Bill added, "It would be difficult paying Hendrix on my acoustic guitar with Taffy on kazoo."

Bill was a Georgetown student who "started in show business" as a temporary doorman at the Cellar Door. Taffy grew up in Falls Church. VA. I was thrilled when Starland Vocal Band with Bill, Taffy, Margot Chapman, and Jon Carroll hit the jackpot with "Afternoon Delight." They filmed their acapella version of Paul Simon's "American Tune" on the Georgetown campus for their summer TV show, and I watched with pride. This photo is from when I interviewed Bill for the 2016 Cerphe's Up book.

* * *

A few other notable songwriters with a Washington DC area connection include **Huddie William Ledbetter** (January 20, 1888 – December 6, 1949), better known as Lead Belly, who wrote and recorded "The Bourgeois Blues," during his visit to Washington, DC, on June 22, 1937. As a first impression of Washington, it was an incisive, damning indictment of the city's rampant Jim Crow segregation conveyed in three minutes of rippling 12-string blues.

Alan Lomax described the encounter years later in an PBS documentary: "He came to stay with me in Washington, which at that time, was a Jim Crow town, and Blacks weren't supposed to enter white hotels or houses. Well, I lived in a little apartment across from the Library of Congress, and Lead Belly and his wife, Martha, came up to spend the night with us. The landlady objected, and Lead Belly and Martha, at the head of the stairs, heard the argument that I had with the lady—she said she was going to call the police and have us all put out. So, we finally had to get in a car and find a hotel. But Lead Belly made a song about this called 'Bourgeois Blues.'"

His other songs including "Irene Goodnight," "The Midnight Special," and an interpretation of "The House of the Rising Sun" helped get him inducted in the Rock & Roll Hall of Fame in 1988.

Photo: *William P. Gottlieb, Library of Congress*

In 2015 to celebrate the 125th birthday of the Huddie Ledbetter, Todd Harvey interviewed Lead Belly family members Terika Dean and Alvin Singh on his contributions to American culture and world music with an overview of the significant Lead Belly materials in the Library of Congress.
https://www.youtube.com/watch?v=xbymD5b-B7Y

* * *

Lyricist **Ted Koehler** was born in Washington, DC, on July 14, 1894. His early career as a pianist during theatre films led him to write special material for vaudeville singers and eventually produce his own nightclub shows. In the 1920's, working in Manhattan, Koehler contributed to Broadway musicals such as *9:15 Revue*, *Earl Carroll Vanities* of 1930 and 1932, *Americana*, *Cotton Club Parade*, and *Say When*.

Moving to Hollywood in early 1930's Koehler worked on several successful film musicals including *Manhattan Parade*, *Let's Fall In Love*, *The Big Show*, *Happy-Go-Lucky*, *Dimples*, *Hollywood Canteen*, *Up In Arms*, *Rainbow Island*, *San Antonio*, and *Weekend At the Waldorf*.

In his collaborations with the great Tin Pan Alley composer, Harold Arlen, Koehler produced such memorable standards as "Stormy Weather," "Get Happy," "Kickin' the Gong Around," and "I Love a Parade." Ted Koehler died in Santa Monica, California on January 17, 1973.

Don Raye was born Donald MacRae Wilhoite Jr. on March 16, 1909. In Washington, DC, after graduating from New York University, Raye began his career appearing in vaudeville shows, touring extensively throughout the United States and Europe. In 1935, in began writing his own material for a nightclub act and earned a contract with Hollywood film studios in 1940. Raye joined the Army during World War II and would return to songwriting and produced a catalog of hit standards after the war.

Throughout his career, Don worked with several collaborators, most notably, Gene De Paul, also a war vet who arranged for Hollywood films. The Raye catalog includes "He's My Guy," "I'll Remember April," "You Don't Know What Love Is," "Irresistible You," "Music Makers," "The House of Blue Lights," "Down the Road a Piece," "Gentle Is My Love," and "Boogie Woogie Bugle Boy." Don Raye died in 1985.

***

In general, a distinctive guitar solo is not mentioned in songwriting credits for a tune. However, in Skunk Baxter's case, his guitar solos are so iconic they become integral to the composition. I often take more interest in his songs waiting for the lead to elevate and make them memorable. His contributions are key in defining the songs themselves.

Therefore, we mention:

Jeffrey Allen "Skunk" Baxter
b. December 13, 1948, in Washington, DC.
Skunk @ The Birchmere 2022.
© S. Moore

He was inducted into the Rock & Roll Hall of Fame as a member of the Doobie Brothers in 2020. You can hear Skunk's innovative leads on the recordings of bands he's played with, including Steely Dan and Sprit. Dan's "Rikki Don't Lose that Number," "My Old School," Donna Summer's "Hot Stuff," and the Doobie's "South City Midnight Lady," are examples of his dexterity.

Baxter also worked as a defense consultant and advised U.S. members of Congress on missile defense so there are many Washingtonians who know him more as a computer systems analyst than a guitar slinger.

Baxter also played bass with DC-born songwriter, **Timothy Charles Buckley III** (b. Valentine's Day, 1947), although Tim grew up in New York City.

DC's **Johnny Gill Jr.** (born May 22, 1966) was the "G" in the Rhythm and Blues supergroup **LSG**, (Gerald Levert and Keith Sweat were the others.) LSG's 1997 self-titled debut album, titled was certified platinum with the chart-topping single "My Body." Gill attended Kimball Elementary, Sousa Junior High, and Duke Ellington School of the Performing Arts.

Before his Mickey Mouse club fame, **Jimmy Dodd**, won a Motorola songwriting contest with his "Washington" song.

He travelled from Hollywood to receive his award. The song was recorded by Sam Jack Kaufman and his Capital Theater Orchestra (Sam was the President of the Local music union) The singer was a local, Roy Roberts. The song didn't catch on. (Thank you DC writer Lori Wysong for this one).

Hear his song at:
https://www.youtube.com/watch?v=OoTCwcvtCIc

While I was working at Georgetown our President, Father Leo O' Donovan, was elected to the Board of Directors of Disney, whose CEO Michael Eisner's son, Breck, was a student. They visited Williamsburg, and Eisner came up with a $650-million project idea (equivalent to $1.21 billion in 2023): It was called "Disney America," a theme park dedicated to the history of America thirty-five miles west of DC in Virginia. However, Haymarket, VA, residents mouse-trapped the plans, and bibi-di—bobbi-di blocked the project.

The Clovers began at Armstrong High School in 1946 with Harold Lucas, Billy Shelton, and Thomas Woods. The trio expanded to a quartet with the addition of John "Buddy" Bailey (lead) and then joined by Bill Harris in 1950. The most popular R&B vocal group of the first half of the '50s, with nineteen hits on fifteen singles, including "Love Potion No. 9," "Fool, Fool, Fool," and "Lovey Dovey."

Ruth Alston Brown was born January 12, 1928 in Portsmouth, VA. American singer-songwriter, and referred to as the "Queen of R&B," she brought a pop music style to R&B music in hit songs for Atlantic Records in the 1950s, such as "So Long," "Teardrops from My Eyes," and " He Treats Your Daughter Mean." Ruth Brown was inducted in the Rock & Roll Hall of Fame in 1993. Her trademark song in later years was "If I Can't Sell It, I'll Keep Sittin' on It." Amazing talent!!!

Chapter 29 – Daryl Davis: Roots & Blues

© Journal Papers

A motto for Daryl Davis is "Don't let things discourage you from doing the things you want to do." He cites his biggest musical influence as pianist Pinetop Perkins, who got his name from Pinetop Smith, the first to record a Boogie-woogie song in 1928.

In 2024, Daryl remains a much-in-demand musician with four Washington Area Music Awards including "Best Traditional Blues/R&B Instrumentalist."

Born in Chicago, Daryl's father was the first Black Secret Service Agent and had a subsequent career in the US Foreign Service. After living in various foreign countries, including African nations, his family settled in Potomac, MD. As a teenager, he attended Wooten High School in Rockville in the mid-1970s and practiced boogie-woogie piano in the school's music room.

His first band, Darrell and the Day Rails, played '50s rock and roll locally. They were hired to open for the Coasters and Drifters at Waldorf's Stardust Inn in Southern Maryland.

There, the Day Rails backed up the Shirelles, Platters, and Rosemary Clooney, among others.

He majored in jazz performance at Howard University, earning a BA in jazz. John Malachi, the late jazz pianist of Billy Eckstine's ground-breaking be-bop orchestra, was Daryl's piano instructor, John Malachi was very fond of Darrell, but he never made an effort to change Darrell's style. I had interviewed Malachi and first met Davis at a Smithsonian piano concert that John did in 1985. I immediately felt a sense of trust in Daryl. I could also see he loved Malachi, and I did too.

After Howard University, Davis moved to Vienna, Austria, for three months, where he played with American jazz singer Rozza Wortham. He returned to the Washington area with experience and more confidence in his ability to remain a professional player.

"Nowadays, piano players (sometimes just play chords with their left hand because they have a bass player," notes Daryl, "but my style is to keep rhythm with the left hand, playing several notes at a time while my right-hand plays the melody and solos." One of his first Darryl Davis bands included Mark Chandler, formerly of the Northern Virginia rock band The Road Ducks, and drummer Adolf Right, a band director at Howard. In the 80s, Davis played piano with local blues bands, including The Wild Cards and Johnny and the Headhunters.

* * *

In 1981, he began playing piano for Chuck Berry, an association that lasted more than thirty years and included numerous East Coast and Midwest tours.

In addition, Davis performed with Little Richard, "Who danced on my piano while I played 'Good Golly, Miss Molly,' and he often filled in for the retiring Pinetop Perkins with the Legendary Blues Band."

Meanwhile, Daryl and the Day Rails were regulars at DC nightclubs Desperados, Cellar Door, Wax Museum, and the Bayou. Daryl also worked with many of DC's top country and western groups. In 1988, his group became the Daryl Davis Band, and he'll reach 150 gigs for 2024.

His essay on the late Danny Gatton is in Chapter 29.

With pioneering Chuck Berry © D. Davis

Singing the Blues

"Back in the day, people like Eric Clapton, the Rolling Stones, and other British rockers were opening for black artists like Muddy Waters and Howling Wolf, who were touring in the UK. However, in the States, the radio stations weren't promoting these original black artists, so when the English groups came over to the States, they were skyrocketing, while the black originators of this music were not. We sometimes couldn't even get played on the white radio stations.

"Not all the artists, but most would give credit where credit was due and say, 'Hey, I got this from Muddy Waters. I got this from T-Bone Walker, Howling Wolf, and Robert Johnson.' Some of the other artists—and I'll name them like Led Zeppelin stole the music. And let me explain the difference between cultural procreation and stealing. A lot of it was racism because this country was not promoting black artists like it would promote white artists. We sometimes couldn't even get played on the white radio stations.

"The British rockers doing the black blues artist music were skyrocketing, while the black artists who created it stayed down. Borrowing music is to be shared regardless of who creates it, whether country, blues, rock and roll, jazz, reggae, or whatever. It's to make people happy and positively affect people, so it should be shared. And if you play a song, and I like it, I should be allowed to play it.

"If it's a classical piece, like Beethoven's, I will play it exactly as it is written because you don't interpret classical music your way. You interpret it the way the composer intended it. Beethoven says 'crescendo,' you crescendo. But with jazz, country blues, etc., you have artistic liberties to play the song as you feel it.

"Take Stormy Monday, for example; Muddy Waters might sing it one way. T-Bone Walker and Ella Fitzgerald will sing it some other way. They have that freedom. Alright.

"But if you write and I do, I will credit it as 'written by Stephen Moore,' and I will put that on my record. I'm not going to say 'written by Daryl Davis' if I didn't write it but Led Zeppelin did that. Not once, but several times. Other artists like the Stones and Clapton would give credit where credit was due.

"However, Led Zeppelin played Howlin Wolf's 'Killing Floor' on their first American tour in 1969, and then later recorded it as 'The Lemon Song' on their album Led Zeppelin II with songwriting credits given to Jimmy Page and Robert Plant. 'Whole Lotta Love' another example is very close to 'You Need Love' by Willie Dixon. To compare, Cream credited Robert Johnson on 'Crossroads.'

"Many people might say that Elvis culturally appropriated Black music, but no, he did not. He gave credit where credit was due. Eric Clapton became a humongous super rock star, but he wanted people to know where he got his music. Eric brought Muddy Waters on tour with him.

"And so Muddy was exposed to a new audience, and his career was revived. Clapton also did an album with B.B. King, Riding with the King."

In 2024, Davis said, "I have ramped up my work in racial reconciliation. The country has become more polarized, and I've reached a point where I can pick and choose what gigs I play. And a lot of my time is spent today on giving lectures and working with white supremacists to help them see another path, another ideology. It will be forty-two years that I've been doing this."

As a race relations expert, Dr. Daryl Davis has received numerous awards and high acclaim for both his book, *Klan-Destined: A Black Man's Odyssey in the Klu Klux Clan*, and his award-winning film documentary, *Accidental Courtesy*. He is the first Black author to write a book on the Ku Klux Clan based on in-person interviews and personal encounters.

Capital Acts: Washington DC Performing Arts

White House BMA Concert

President Carter hosted the first-ever Black Music Association Concert at the White House on June 7, 1979. He also decreed June as Black Music Month. His VIP guests included Andre Crouch, Evelyn Champagne King, and Billy Eckstine. Chuck Berry did his "duck walk" and changed the lyrics from "Oh Carol" to "Oh Amy" (to honor Carter's young daughter).

Daryl recalls, "I was Chuck Berry's guest and I also played the 2003 American Achievement Awards," where Chuck gave the Academy's Golden Plate Award to guest of honor Bob Dylan. "One of Dylan's biggest writing influences was Chuck Berry. Bob called him 'the greatest poet.'" In fact, Dylan's song "Subterranean Homesick Blues" is based on Chuck's "Too Much Monkey Business."

Chuck Berry and Cerphe

"Part of Chuck's contract called for the promoter of the event to supply a backup band for him and two Fender Dual Showmen amplifiers. I was seventeen years old when Mike Schreibman and his New Era Follies booked Chuck into the McDonough Arena at Georgetown. I didn't start playing piano with Chuck until 1981.

Chuck made it very simple to follow him. He'd cue you. Like I do. And if you watch me, you'll be able to follow.

Steve Wolf was Chuck's designated bass player at this gig but he wasn't understanding what Chuck wanted. Wolf, a jazz bassist, played with Danny Gatton, Linwood Taylor and many other DC performers but he was playing this time like Chuck did it on those early Chess records. Cerphe who was

announcing the show understood that Berry wanted. Simpler bass. So, he asked Steve to borrow his bass.

"Cerphe played and he was good. He knew exactly what Chuck wanted," says Daryl.

> The McDonough Gymnasium opened in 1951 giving the Georgetown University Hoya sports teams a home. Great music has been held at the Arena including shows by Count Basie, Ray Charles, The Byrds (w/ Clarence White), The Who, Grateful Dead, and the Bruce Springsteen 1976 *Born to Run* show. I saw the Boss then in the same week that I first started my career at GU.
>
> S. Moore

Daryl, Johnny Castle, paying tribute to Bo Diddley at Bandhouse Gigs **DCLegends** concert at the Strathmore in 2024 © S. Moore

Chapter 30 – Bo Diddley and Disciples

With the steady thumping blues groove played out on his homemade cigar-box electric guitar, more than Bill Haley or Elvis, Bo Diddley has a singular claim to being the legitimate "Father of Rock n' Roll."

Born in 1928 in McComb, Mississippi, and raised in Chicago, Bo transformed the rural and urban music he grew up on into our modern American electrified art form. Diddley laid the foundational stones of rock and roll by blending blues, country, and R&B with innovative amplification styles.

In 1959, Bo moved to Washington, DC, only a few years after his 1955 Chess Records hit "Hey, Bo Diddley" introduced the world to his signature bomp-a-bomp-a-bomp BOMP BOMP beat. ("Shave and a haircut; two bits" is how Richard Harrington captured it in cold type in a 2006 interview with the then seventy-seven-year-old legend.)

Bo explained what made the town attractive, "I just wanted to be in Washington, DC, around the Howard Theatre...I did everything from DC. At that time, I was driving all the time—I didn't start flying until 1968—and it was close to New York and the South."

Bo lived at 2614 Rhode Island Avenue NE, where he built a recording studio in his basement. Unbelievably he made his classic *Bo Diddley is a Gunslinger* album there. He also recorded a doo wop band, The Marquees: Chester Simmons (bass) with Reese Palmer (first tenor) and James Nolan (baritone) with Marvin Gay (second tenor). Marvin would change the spelling to "Gaye" when he became a soloist.

Marvin was born in Washington, DC, on April 2, 1939, at Freedmen's Hospital (now the location of the Howard University communication school and radio station WHUR). With his minister father on piano, Gaye started singing at four years old in a Pentecostal church, and at Cardozo High School he sang soprano in the choir.

Marvin once said, "I hope to refine music, study it, and find some area I can unlock. I don't know how to explain it, but it's there. These can't be the only notes in the world, there's got to be other notes some place, in some dimension, between the cracks on the piano keys."

Social justice issues often drive Gaye's music, as indicated by his disillusionment about life in DC. Growing up in housing projects and disaffected with school, Gaye dropped out from Cardozo before graduating. Biographer David Ritz quotes Gaye as saying, "I hated Washington. The place filled me with a feeling of hopelessness. Nothing happened in Washington. Nothing was made, produced, or sold. It was all government, papers, bureaucrats, and bullshit. Here was a city blessed with musical talent and no place to record, no real labels, promoters, or distributors."

Photo: Marvin in the 1964 T.A.M.I. show

For Marvin Gaye, music became a way to escape the nation's capital and his life with a domineering father.

As a member of the Marquees, Marvin performed at many venues on 14th Street NW. But he left DC in 1957 for a brief stint in the Air Force before landing in Detroit in 1961, where his hits like "Never Let You Go" soon earned the title "Motown's "Prince of Soul."

In 1971 Gaye released *What's Going On*, inspired by police brutality against anti-war demonstrators; the songs tell the story of a Vietnam veteran who returns home to find only hatred and suffering.

The overtly political album happened to coincide with the "Spring Offensive" May Day anti-war protests in DC. It spent weeks at the top of Billboard R&B charts, and its success let

Gaye break away artistically and financially from Motown producer Barry Gordy. *Rolling Stone* magazine proclaimed *What's Going On* Number One in their Greatest 500 Albums of all time.

Tragically, Gaye lost his life when his father shot him during a fight at his L.A. home in 1984. While Marvin Gaye was somewhat ambivalent about DC, he is specially remembered through his Marvin Gaye Park, Marvin Gaye Day, and the timeless music he created in his hometown.

The Jewels were a girl group that Bo also recorded in his studio. "It was not a big studio, but since we didn't know anyone else who had a studio in their house, that was a big studio," recalled Jewels' singer Sandra Bears for John Kelly's *Washington Post* column in 2015. The Jewels sang backup on the song "Bo Diddley Is a Lover" and, around 1960, recorded a few of their own tunes in his Rhode Island Avenue basement studio, including "I Need You So Much" and "For the Love of Mike."

"Bo Diddley was a really nice man who liked to help people," Sandra told Kelly. "For him to reach back and help different artists, I thought that was really nice."

Diddley obviously felt DC's mix was a good fit. DC is a cultural crossroads between North and South and Appalachia. The nation's capital has always been self-conscious about its "Southerness" and is a welcoming city to cultural transplants.

The first recording studios in Washington, DC, were established in the early 20th century. Some of the notable studios include:

1. **Columbia Recording Studios**: Opened in 1931, this was one of the earliest and best-known studios in Washington DC. It was later renamed to Omega Recording Studios.

2. **WORL Recording Studios**: Opened in 1946, this was one of the few studios in Washington DC that catered to African-American musicians.

3. **Edgewood Recording Studios**: Opened in 1948, this studio was known for recording gospel music and became a popular destination for artists in the 1950s and 1960s.

4. **Track Recorders**: Opened in 1963, this highly regarded studio has hosted many famous artists over the years, including Jimi Hendrix, Marvin Gaye, and Stevie Wonder.

5. **Bias Recording:** Bob Dawson has been producing music professionally at Bias since 1972 and he's never wavered from his goal of helping artists capture their best performances, while having a whole lot of fun doing it. That comfortable, easy-going atmosphere created in Bob's studio brings out the best for singers, instrumentalists, arrangers, composers, and other producers. These studios, along with many others, played a significant role in the development of the music scene in Washington, DC, and continue to be an important part of the city's cultural history.

While living in Washington, Diddly showed off his technical innovations in electric amplification. Musicians often rub shoulders with political celebrities in DC, and in 1961, Diddley was invited to play at a fancy debutante party for a diplomat's daughter, Dede Buchanan. While an orchestra played upstairs, Bo Diddley rocked the younger crowd in the downstairs party room by demonstrating his new gizmo that let him trigger recordings directly from his hand-built guitar. The always astonishing guitarist could use it to accompany himself, playing both live and recorded music simultaneously.

Bo showed off another of his own recording inventions to violinist Eddie Drennon who met Diddley when asked to record string parts on his songs while a student at Howard University. It was a Y-cord cable that let you split the signal from an electric guitar and get boosted sound out of two amplifiers at once. Drennon told Post reporter John Kelly, "When we played the Avalon Theater in San Francisco in 1966, Big Brother and the Holding Company with Janis Joplin were the opening act. When they heard the sound, they were amazed what was coming off the stage. They came back the next night and had electric everything. They didn't realize it wasn't only the equipment, but it was the person who created it."

In 1962, Bo was invited to the White House to perform a private performance for President Kennedy and Jacqueline, but he later told the *L.A. Times*, "Yeah, but Kennedy wasn't there. He was out talking to Castro or something."

Bobby Parker and Bo Diddley on "Ed Sullivan show" in 1956.

Diddley continued to tour regularly after leaving Washington in 1966 for California. But as with many rock and roll originators, Bo struggled to get the financial rewards for his profound influence on modern American music, playing paid gigs internationally into his late seventies to survive. Others had more commercial success with songs Diddley was forced to sell royalty rights to make some needed cash.

The distinctive three-stroke/rest/two strokes rhythm of the "Bo Diddley beat" can be heard in the hits of Buddy Holly, The Rolling Stones, Bruce Springsteen, The Who, Tom Petty, U2, and rapper B.o.B.

In 1986, cultural recognition started to come due when he was inducted into the WAMA Hall of Fame, just one of many career accolades, including induction to The Rock & Roll Hall of Fame in 1987, and was given the Grammy Lifetime Achievement Award in 1998. Diddley eventually settled in Florida, where he died in 2008.

Bobby Parker

"Watch This Step" was a hit in the United States—reaching #51 on Billboards Top 100 in 1961. The song's repetitive riff, which Parker said was inspired by a Cuban jazz song found a fan in Liverpool, England. In a 1974 radio interview on WNEW, **John Lennon** admitted "Watch This Step" was the basis for the guitar riff in "I Feel Fine." On air, John said, "'Watch your Step' is one of my favorite records. The Beatles have used the lick in various forms. The Allman Brothers used the lick straight as it was."

The blues guitarist-singer **Bobby Parker** was born in Lafayette, LA, August 31, 1937 and died October 31, 2013 in Bowie Maryland.

Raised in Los Angeles, he toured in bands with Little Richard and Chuck Berry but settled in DC to play and record with Bo Diddley.

Bobby appeared on the TV show with Bo Diddley. Parker His "Blues Get Off My Shoulders" in 1958 and "Watch This Step" in 1961 was recorded at Edgewood Studios at 16th and K Streets for V-Tone Records.

In a March 1990 interview with George Harrison in *Musician Magazine*, George said, "We were crossing Scotland singing 'Matchbox' by Carl Perkins in three-part harmony, and it turned into 'I Feel Fine.' The guitar part was from 'Watch your Step'—just a bastardized version."

And Carlos Santana told Guitar Player Magazine in 1996, "Bobby Parker is a musician of the same caliber as Albert King and Albert Collins. He's one of the few remaining guitarists on this planet who can pierce your heart and soothe your soul. He inspired me to pick up the guitar."

(Our thanks to for these Beatles and Santana citations: houseofrockinterviews.blogspot.com)

In the 1990s, Parker returned to the national scene with two CDs for the New Orleans label Black Top records, *Bent Out Of Shape* (1993) and *Shine Me Up* (1995), and later toured with Carlos Santana at Switzerland's 2004 Montreux Jazz Festival, later released as a DVD.

Cathy Ponton King is a DC favorite singer/songwriter (see Chapter 39) and remembers "one of the best shows I ever did was with Bobby Parker, who I became close friends with. We were both playing Madam Organ's about one day a month and on an Adams Morgan Day here comes Bobby. He jammed with me and my band.

"I thought I'd died and gone to heaven. I knew about his legacy and we developed this close relationship, like young white girl protégé, but more like close friends. A cousin of mine bought the Bethesda movie theater and turned it into the music club, and on my birthday. Bobby agreed to open for me.

"Shortly after this I was talking online to one of Bobby's best friends, Omar Ashaka, who was a real estate agent. And he said all his life, Bobby wanted to own a home, but nobody would lend him the money to be a homeowner. All the mortgage companies told him 'no.' But Omar was able to get him a home finally.

"Bobby was on top of the world. He was living in his Temple Hills, MD, home. He was seventy-six. The cause of his death was a heart attack. The house had wooden floors that required this special cleaner so he went to the Walmart to buy some. Bobby never smoked because he had asthma, but when he got to the store, he had forgot his inhaler.

"And suddenly he couldn't breathe. And then the next thing you know, he goes into cardiac arrest and drops dead. And this was right after he played the gig with me. Everybody in the Walmart freaked out. They took his cell phone out of his pocket, and pressed the button for last number called, and they got Omar. And they said, 'Do you know a man named Robert Parker?'

"Omar answered, 'Yes.' They said 'Well, he died here at Walmart. And he's at an emergency facility here in in Bowie, MD. Come and get him.'"

Howlin' Wolf, Muddy Waters, and Bo Diddley

Chapter 31 – Fahey's Sonic Frets
by Steve Lorenz

© S. Moore

"All I have ever done with music was to depict various emotions in an organized and coherent musical language, especially hate, fear, repulsion, grief, depression, or feeling nothingness."
– John Fahey, liner notes to *The Legend of Blind Joe Death.*

When "going on the road" meant South instead of West, guitar prodigy John Fahey emerged as DC's version of Kerouac's anti-hero—a real Beat. Alienated and dislocated in a postwar suburb striving for "normalcy," Fahey sought a lost, more authentic America through its darker musical roots.

Today, with a cult following of acoustic enthusiasts and a spot among the top one hundred guitarists of all time according to *Rolling Stone*, Fahey is celebrated for his raw, instinctual "American primitivist guitar" style and his eclectic, tragic life. His influence extends beyond his own music to mentoring guitar giants like Leo Kottke and Robbie Basho.

As a key figure in the "DC Blues Mafia," Fahey played a crucial role in reviving the careers of Skip James and Bukka White in the early 1960s. He helped shine a light on forgotten bluesmen in Washington, DC. Drawing inspiration from DC's record collectors, beatnik coffeehouses, and hillbilly music shows, Fahey ventured down Route 61 into the deep South, bringing Delta blues masters back to cosmopolitan Washington.

Born in 1939, John Fahey's family moved to a house on New York Avenue in Takoma Park, Maryland, in 1944. Takoma Park, with its tree-lined streets and neat Victorian houses, was one of the first planned commuter suburbs along the B&O Railroad. By the 1950s, it embodied the promise of postwar America.

Fahey's father, Al, worked at the National Institutes of Health but was reportedly distant, spending much time away. In contrast, his mother, Jane, who worked at the US Geological Survey, was devoted to her son. On a fishing trip, Fahey met Frank Hovington, a Black singer and guitarist, who inspired him to purchase his first $17 guitar from the Sears-Roebuck catalog.

As a teenager, Fahey often played by Sligo Creek, a place that would later inspire his rolling, haunting fingerpicking style in the song "Sligo River." Turtles he found later appeared as a guiding theme in his work, including his 1968 album *Voice of The Turtle*, recorded under the fictional blues persona Blind Joe Death. [Note: his album *The Transfiguration of Blind Boy Death* is prominently featured in Stanley Kubrick's cult film *A Clockwork Orange*.]

Psychological issues that would later plague John Fahey are hinted at in his surreal and factually dubious autobiography, *How Bluegrass Ruined My Life*. The book offers a colorful critique of his culturally stifling suburban upbringing in Takoma Park during the 1950s. Fahey describes his local gang's antisocial antics, such as throwing rocks through neighbors' windows and turtles at passing cars on Piney Branch Road.

Like many White suburban kids in DC, the talented Fahey quickly became a bluegrass fanatic. His early exposure to "primitive" music included Bill Monroe's "Blue Yodel No. 7" on Don Owen's WARL show and hillbilly groups at the Rising Sun, Maryland music park. In his memoir, Fahey recounts attending a Hank Williams show on one of promoter Connie B. Gay's riverboat excursions on the Potomac. Williams, drunk and irate, lashed out at the audience, saying, "Why don't y'all go straight to hell?" Fahey had hoped to hear his favorite song, "The Singing Waterfall," but Williams instead performed "Alone and Forsaken," which Fahey described as "the most distressing desolation song" ever written.

A chance meeting in 1956 at a Unitarian church in Northwest Washington with Richard K. Spottswood, a respected collector of "obsolete music," redirected Fahey's focus to the blues. Both Fahey and Spottswood were part of a small network of DC blues and bluegrass enthusiasts, trading rare records and tapes with other aficionados like Joe Bussard and Tom "Fang" Hoskins.

In an interview with *Washington City Paper's* Eddie Dean, Spottswood told how Fahey had an epiphany after they found a rare record in Baltimore. A scratchy copy of Blind Willie Johnson's "Praise God I'm Satisfied" left Fahey emotionally devastated, as if struck by lightning—a transformative experience with slide guitar. Interestingly, Spottswood's own awakening came a few years earlier when he discovered Skip James's "Hard Time Killing Floor Blues" for a dollar in an Adams Morgan record shop. Fahey was later instrumental in "rediscovering" the barrel house bluesman languishing away in a Bentonia, Mississippi, hospital before helping revive his career in clubs around DC and the folk circuit.

Together Spottswood and Fahey hunted for old 78s around the Washington area, including treks into Black neighborhoods, knocking on random doors looking for old records to buy. Though naive, in their own way Spottswood and Fahey crossed Washington's 1950s racial boundaries to get at forgotten relics of Black musical culture.

By the late 1950, John Fahey transformed himself into a virtuoso blues guitarist, but with notorious stage fright usually ameliorated by alcohol he also began disguising himself behind mythological aliases. A recent graduate of Hyattsville's Northwestern High School and a philosophy student at American University, Fahey began recording under the pseudonym Blind Thomas in a makeshift basement studio at Joe Bussard's parents' house.

Bussard was pressing custom 78 rpm discs on a second-hand cutting machine for his Fonotone label, selling these "rare" records to collectors while keeping Fahey's identity a secret. Early in his career, Fahey's Beat side emerged as he cleverly impersonated bluesmen from the 1930s, deceiving buyers who were none the wiser. Few buyers where any the wiser when Bussard labeled Blind Thomas recordings in his mail-order catalog as "authentic Negro folk music." In the early Sixties, as Fahey frequented record shops and DC coffeehouses like the Unicorn on Dupont Circle, he became part of the emerging "DC Blues Mafia." This small network of beatnik country blues enthusiasts aimed to hone their performance skills syndicating with a few affluent collectors of rare "obsolete" records motivated to preserve what they saw as a vanishing art form.

Members included Dick Spottswood, Bill Givens, Nick Perls, Mike Stewart, Gene Rosenthal, Mike Ochs, E.D. Denson, Fahey, and Hoskins. Alongside Gayle Wardlow, Dick Waterman, and others in New York, they managed rediscovered blues artists such as Skip James, John Hurt, Son House, Lighting Hopkins, and Muddy Waters. Through their close relationships and legal control, they became known as the DC arm of the "East Coast Blues Mafia." But their rediscoveries were wary of patronage too. Rosenthal recalled that Skip James would intentionally play badly in front of audiences that applauded without knowing better.

Rosenthal, founder of Silver Spring's Adelphi Records, recalls in a *City Paper* interview with David Dunlap a loose collective of enthusiasts and collectors known as the Thong Club. "We wore leather thongs around our fingers and wrists," he said. "To join, another member had to put a thong on you. [John] Fahey put mine on. We wore them until they were stinky and scuzzy."

Rosenthal, who was fortunate to have a recording studio in his parents' house, recorded John Hurt for Spottswood's Piedmont label and Skip James for Fahey's Takoma label in 1964. Inspired by Takoma, Rosenthal founded Adelphi Records in 1968, naming it after Fahey's song, "The Downfall of the Adelphi Rolling Grist Mill."

In 1964, Fahey sent a postcard to a town mentioned in a Bukka White song, addressed to "Booker T. Washington White - Old Blues Singer." This led him to Memphis, where, with E.D. Denson's help, he convinced White to move and set him up with coffeehouse gigs and a release on Fahey's Takoma label, Mississippi Blues.

That same year, Nick Perls, a blues collector from American University, found Son House near Memphis. Meanwhile, just a few miles away in Tunica, Mississippi, Fahey discovered Skip James in a hospital bed with an undiagnosed tumor. James later praised the better treatment he received in DC in his song "George Washington Hospital Blues."

The "rediscovery" of Delta blues legends by DC record collectors and aficionados like John Fahey made the capital a crucial, though often overlooked, center of the postwar blues revival. Tom Hoskins's 1963 rediscovery of Mississippi John Hurt inspired others to seek out living blues legends. Though often unequal partnerships, Fahey and the DC Blues Mafia's work in rediscovering and relocating these blues artists ultimately helped pave the way for local talents like Archie Edwards, Flora Moulton, John Cephas, and Phil Wiggins to gain recognition.

During the Civil Rights movement, understanding the blues as a gateway to Black culture and consciousness gave the blues revival crowd a special kind of cross-racial access and influence. In an interview with Joel Slotnikoff, Spottswood described Fahey as a "down-at-the-heels version of James Dean. Except Dean looked suave and Fahey looked tough."

Fahey's image as a Beat anti-social loner resonated with the country blues albums he studied relentlessly. He founded Takoma Records in 1959 to release his debut album as Blind Joe Death, a deep dive into "primitive" instrumental blues. [With only ninety-five original copies pressed, they are now worth thousands on eBay.] More successful for others, at Takoma Records Fahey helped launch the career of propulsive finger picking phenome Leo Kottke and hidden talents like Robbie Basho. Many of DC's top blues and bluegrass talents recorded at Takoma, who like Fahey applied traditional fingerpicking to neoclassical compositions, including Peter Lang, Max Ochs, and Mike Auldridge.

Fahey also played a key role in Canned Heat, introducing Bob Hite to Al Wilson, who contributed to a Fahey album in 1965. Moving the label to Los Angeles while studying for his master's at UCLA under D.K. Wilgus, Fahey wrote a groundbreaking thesis on Charley Patton, titled "The Masked Marvel."

Throughout his career, Fahey released numerous albums blending blues, bluegrass, Indian Ragas, and pop music. Musicologist Barrett Eugene Hanson, known as Dr. Demento, noted that Fahey "was the first to show that traditional fingerpicking techniques could express non-traditional musical ideas—harmonies and melodies akin to Bartok, Charles Ives, or Indian music."

Fahey sold Takoma to Chrysalis in 1979 but continued to record and tour, though his live performances were erratic. He played Wolf Trap Farm Park with Taj Mahal in 1971, but at a 1973 show at GWU's Lisner Auditorium, Mark Spivak of the *Washington Post* reported that Fahey abruptly left the stage despite the crowd's ovation and cheers.

A cantankerous guitar genius marked by the highs and lows of a blues player's life; Fahey faced significant struggles. In 1986, he contracted Epstein-Barr syndrome, which, combined with alcoholism and diabetes, drained his resources, and strained his relationships.

By the mid-1990s, he was living in poverty in Seattle, selling his guitars and rare records to pay rent. A fortunate inheritance and a 1994 Rhino Records retrospective revived his profile. Fahey began working on a definitive package of Charley Patton's work, expanding on his Berkeley master's thesis. As a skilled composer, he provided a detailed musical analysis and biography of Patton's repertoire. Spottswood noted in an interview, "John Fahey loved music with a tragic component, and southern rural music was always much franker about tragedy than popular music."

Fahey died in 1997 during heart surgery, just before the release of Revenant's compilation *Screamin' and Hollerin' the Blues: The Worlds of Charley Patton*, which won three Grammy Awards in 2003.

Mississippi John Hurt and the "DC Blues Mafia"

Many blues aficionados know the legend about the "rediscovery" of Delta bluesman Mississippi John Hurt in early 1963 by DC guitarist and blues fanatic Tom "Fang" Hoskins. At a time of voter registration and Freedom Rides, at an American University party just before Spring Break, Hoskins convinced an unknown co-ed girl to "borrow" her father's Dodge Charger and go on a road trip down to New Orleans with a quick stop in Mississippi. The fast-talking Hoskin's erstwhile plan was to use the excursion to find out if the country blues master was still alive in the Mississippi Delta, the land where the blues began.

A close friend of John Fahey, Hoskins was also an enthusiastic blues player and collector who associated with audiophile Richard Spottswood in finding rare recordings of old blues "race" records. (Two of Hurt's other songs appear on Harry Smith's seminal *Anthology of American Folk Music*, one of the first albums in the official Kennedy White House collection.)

Spottswood acquired a tape from Australian ethnomusicologist Jonathan Edwards which revealed clues about Hurt's location heard on a Okeh 78 rpm recording of Avalon Blues, which the pair pinpointed on an old map of Mississippi. Hoskins fortunately found the aging John Hurt in his small sharecropper shack in Carroll County, Mississippi, on that trip with his unknown companion, but managed to get reported for violation of the Mann Act on the excursion across state lines.

Few have heard about Hurt's very first performances in Washington once he arrived in the capital city from the Delta. Though not enrolled, Hoskins was occasionally on campus at George Washington University, and with another notable folk music collector friend **Gene Rosenthal** who founded Adelphi Records, showed up regularly for meetings of the GWU Folk Music Club, a central gathering point for students from across the city who wanted to learn and play traditional folk songs and bluegrass. Several members went on to form the Folklore Society of Greater Washington [FSGW] including long time "folkie" Sheila Cogan, who claimed it was "the most integrated club" on campus because it had one Black member. She recalled Civil Rights activist and SNCC organizer Stokely Carmichael showed up to some of their dormitory "hoots" to sing spirituals like "Michael Rowed the Boat Ashore."

In contrast to his early days when he was playing farm parties and had a few unsuccessful recordings, much of Mississippi John Hurt's "revival" took place before audiences of white college-age folk music lovers. He received his first enthusiastic response from folk music fans at GWU, and in a personal interview Sheila Cogan claims that the first place Tom Hoskins took John Hurt when he came to Washington was WRGW, the university radio station created by students to highlight folk music.

However, Cogan did admit, "It had limited range; it only broadcast to the dormitories." With help from the student club's unofficial media sponsor, WAVA's "folkie" disk jockey Dick Cerri, they arranged John Hurt's first concert appearance at the Red Cross Auditorium on F Street near campus. Cogan recalls that Mississippi John Hurt was warmly welcomed by the audience but was stunned by where he found himself: "It was interesting because Hurt, to my knowledge, had not been performing in public for the last thirty years, so he was suffering a kind of stage fright, and he asked a group of us on stage, and we formed a semi-circle around him. And he asked someone else to tune his guitar, that he was not able to his own satisfaction..."

Unsurprisingly, Cogan's early encounter confirms reports of Hurt's humble, "buddha-like" and grandfatherly persona, always finding easy rapport with the young, civil rights conscious folk and blues music fans of DC and elsewhere as he did on many college campuses and coffee houses during his "revival."

Dick Cerri interviewed Hurt soon after the show on his *Music Americana* folk program, another new experience for the former sharecropper. Cerri complained with a smile, "I started asking him questions on the radio, and he would answer by just shaking his head. I said to myself, 'we have got a problem here.'" Eventually, Hurt recounted for Cerri the story about when Hoskins and Mike Stewart, another white blues fanatic from DC, knocked his on his cabin door: "I thought they were revenue men and were going to take me to jail!"

Hoskins and Stewart traveled on their own trip into the South, playing with and recording Hurt at his humble Mississippi home, confirming he still had his performance skills. [The small wooden house, planned as a museum, unfortunately was the victim of arson in 2024 soon after opening]. A few weeks later, Louisa Spottswood helped move Hurt and his wife to DC with promises of a new recording career and made plans to open the Ontario Café and Gallerie' in Northwest DC, largely as a venue for the charming and talented elder bluesman.

It was there he met local barber and bluesman Archie Edwards beginning a deep and influential friendship between the two blues performers, Hurt's alternating bass style of playing already close to Piedmont blues of other locals Libby Cotton and John Jackson.

Spottswood used his connections at the Library of Congress to arrange a recording session at the Folksong Archive studio, and there was sense of urgency in getting this downhome blues talent in front of LOC microphones. Spottswood told researcher Bill Dahl that finding Hurt was "'Very nice. But my thought at the time was, look this guy could keel over tomorrow, and if he does, it will be a tragic thing. But it will be a lot less tragic if we have definitive recordings of these songs in place. I was thinking preservation.'" Through connections with fellow collector and promoter Ralph Rinzler, Spottswood also quickly arranged for Hurt to play the 1963 Newport Festival later that July where the "hippy grandfather" mesmerized the idealistic audience with his definition of the "real" country blues.

Chapter 32 – Kids in TV Wonderland

The unthinkable occurred on an otherwise ordinary day in 1961. Washington Cowboy Pick Temple led his pony off into the black and white TV sunset, never to return. After twelve years and several thousand broadcasts of his popular children's program, the *Pick Temple Giant Ranch*, Lafayette Parker "Pick" Temple, a native Washingtonian folk singer turned television personality, packed up his puppets, cased his guitar, and became a pure and gentle childhood memory.

"It's been over twenty years since I've appeared on TV," Pick told me in 1984 for a *Journal Newspaper* article. Then retired and living with Jeanette, his wife of forty-eight years, in Sun City, AZ, he added, "And I'm certainly not a legend in my own mind."

Not a legend? A quarter of a million Washingtonians who grew up with Pick Temple, Ranger Hal, Bozo, Cap 'N Tugg, Pete and his Pals, Claire & Coco, Cousin Cupcake, and other local kiddie shows of the 1950s and early 60s would disagree.

Pick Temple was Washington's original TV superstar.

Collage. Pick on TV. After the *Journal* article Pick and I began exchanging letters. His costume at the TV and Radio Museum, and publicity photo. © S. Moore

Together with his fateful dog Lady, his pony Piccolo, puppets galore, and occasional Popeye cartoon, humor games, and folk songs captured the fancy of area youngsters who watched faithfully and were eager to enlist in his Giant Rangers club.

Lucky "Rangers" could appear with Pick on the show if their postcard requests were chosen. And he highlighted as many individual kids as airtime would allow. (He couldn't accommodate all his fans, however. One young lady waited eight years for her chance to sit in the studio hayloft and was a college sophomore when her big moment finally arrived).

"I enjoyed the children," says Pick. "But I never considered myself an actor. I was more of a participant, so to speak. Then WJLA TV newsman, John Harter, and Pick's son, Parker Temple, were puppeteers on the show. Behind the deceptive simplicity of the format, they remembered a larger process at work.

"On the air Pick would frequently quote Shakespeare," recalls Parker, then an Air Force major at the Pentagon. "The reason that Dad is so well remembered is that he never talked down to the kids, never played the buffoon. He was the inveterate teacher. The kids would just be having fun, but the parents would appreciate what was going on."

"If it were a nice day," added Harder. "Pick might turn to the camera and say, 'You kids ought to consider going out to play instead of watching TV.'" That kind of honesty vanished down the vast TV wasteland trail not long after Pick's Ranch closed.

Temple was never really a cowboy. Before he donned his chaps for television as a young man during the 30s, he had taken an interest in American railroad songs. Riding the rails and box cars and sitting at hobo campfires, he heard the work songs and the "out of work" songs of common men caught in the throes of the Great Depression. He recorded some of these for the music archives of the Library of Congress in 1948. That same year he first appeared on local television.

"I had been playing folk around town at banquets, talent shows and such," Temple recalled. "WTOP called and asked me to perform on their *Stars of Tomorrow* amateur show. At that time, I didn't know a single person who owned a TV set, and I had never even seen one." The success of his TV debut convinced Temple to abandon nineteen years of civil service with the Census Bureau for a full-time commitment to the tube. It was a happy move, as evidenced by Temple's forty-three volume diary, which chronicles his long career in the infancy of the new broadcast medium. *The Pick Temple Giant Ranch* playing live seven days a week, ultimately proved too expensive for its sponsor, Giant Foods. The show folded and Temple returned to government as an audiovisual expert, producing motivational films for the Volunteers in Service to America's Vista program.

In 1984, at age seventy-three, Temple was enjoying a laid-back Southwest lifestyle and the wide-open prairies he had not yet seen in his TV cowboy days. Golf and swimming kept him fit. And the railroad memorabilia which crowded his home reflected his continuing lifelong affair with trains.

Of course, he clearly liked reminiscing with his old Rangers, but he was quick to put his TV accomplishments in an ever-humble perspective. He told me, "I never really thought our show was that good. The children had a great time. We did a lot of things, but we had some real turkeys too. Nostalgia is a great magnifying glass. People look back and say what a terrific show that was. But I believe it was terrific in their imaginations."

Maybe so, but it sure was fun.

(L-t-R) Me, Oswald, Hal, Dr. Fox, Margaret, Rosemary and Eager Beaver
© Karen Allen

Ranger Hal Shaw

For the local baby boomers, the memories of Channel 9's "Ranger Hall" show glow like campfire embers. The once wide-eyed audience of area youngsters may recall the rustic wood cabin and the Ranger's sidekick puppets "Oswald

Rabbit," "Doctor Fox," and "Eager Beaver" perched or more appropriately, stuffed, on the window ledge. The heard but never seen lookout scout, Scotty Irish, the grainy black and white Walter Lantz cartoons and always the affable Ranger Hal in relaxed command. This was another DC's vintage children's television in its awkward but golden simplicity.

"I loved being the Ranger," Hal Shaw told me in 1985, who still beamed the familiar grin and instant likeability that made him a Washington TV Kiddie Show hero. He wistfully added it was "freedom and creativity for thirteen years."

Margaret and I visited with the old Ranger at his Herndon, VA, home twice. It was an instant rewind to those nostalgic times. His accomplishments, however, didn't begin or end with Ranger Hal.

Shaw arrived in Washington in 1957 with a drama degree from the University of North Carolina and early fame as the first TV announcer performer in the state of Maine, where he ended up after exploring job possibilities in New York City. "In those days, people were so hungry for television that stations could get advertisers to sponsor test patterns," he recalled. As staff announcer at WTOP TV later, Shaw's break came that first summer when he substituted for the vacationing Pick Temple, whose Giant ranch was then a giant TV success. The advertising people at Schwinn Bicycles decided to sponsor Shaw in a new children's show and he developed the Ranger character. "I thought that a forest Ranger stood for everything right and good," Shaw explained. "And he had to know what he was doing." So in addition to standard kiddie fare, Shaw's program provided an imaginary window to an outdoor world of camping and nature. With fire prevention a perpetually hot topic, Smokey the Bear was a frequent guest of the US Forest Service, which made Shaw an honorary Ranger. Jackson Weaver was the voice of Smokey the Bear.

"I bought the uniform at Sears, but the hat is authentic" he smiled. And the uniform still fits. Weekends found the old Ranger packing a portable cabin into a station wagon and exploring the local shopping centers. A jittery line of 1000 anxious children waiting to meet Ranger Hal was not unusual at his countless personal appearances.

"I learned a great respect for children," he says. "They are true believers, and I was careful not to take advantage of their belief in me."

Unfortunately, Shaw success began to sour when the show left the air in 1969, bumped by a clown named Lorenzo. Shaw was also forced to close an unprofitable summer camp which he had established on the grounds of his six-acre Virginia estate. Adjustment into a new and adult role as sales manager for WTOP, was, he admits, difficult. Then a brain aneurysm ended his career and forced untimely retirement in 1978.

However, the cruelest blow to Shaw on Thanksgiving Day 1983, when he lost Rosemary, his wife of thirty-one years, to cancer. "Rosie was always the real talent of the family," said Shaw. Indeed, she was a gifted soprano who, with their three children, performed at many Christmas programs for the National Security Agency and the Department of Agriculture.

Neurosurgery slowed the old Ranger down, but didn't bring him to a halt. He went back to school at Northern Virginia Community College [NOVA] and graduated cum laude with a creative writing degree. And on Year's Day of 1983 he remarried. Shaw said of his new wife. "Joan is very attractive and very British."

He also avidly followed the careers of alumni of his show, including network newsman Max Robinson, who began his career operating the puppets. "I still get a thrill meeting and hearing from fans," he admitted, many of whom now have children of their own. "It excites me to know how much they enjoyed the program. I'm continually amazed at the recognition to think that I made that much of an impression, but I guess the fact that I was on the air for thirteen years I had to reach somebody."

Cap 'N Tugg

Harry Lee Reynolds was born on August 23, 1926, in Norton, a community in southwest Virginia. He created the seafarin character on the children's TV show *Popeye and Cap 'N Tugg* at WTTG playing all the characters: the ship's engineer, Mr. Flanigan, Coast Guard Commander Salamander ("We guard the coast, you know.") spy villains, Spike Marlin and

Axel Grackle, and his nemesis Captin Flash Flood. Tugg was always accompanied by his feisty parrot, Fantail (who was red and as everyone else voiced by Lee).

Willard as Bozo, Pete Jamerson, Claire & Coco. Bill Gormly, and Lee Reynolds © Kaptain Kidshow

Reynolds began in the army air forces in World War II, to pursue a career as a DJ and reporter for the American Forces Network (AFN) radio service in postwar Germany.

Transitioning into acting, he took on roles at the Barta Theater in Abingdon, Virginia, and later at DC's Arena Stage. In 1966, while working locally on stage, he finished his bachelor's degree in television and radio broadcasting and journalism from American University. Proficient in Arabic, French, and German, he occasionally engaged in sculpture and filmmaking endeavors.

Reynolds also directed *Milt Grant's Record Hop* when it began on WTTG-TV. (Later it was simply *The Milt Grant Show*.) He completed his career as announcer, writer, and director at the public broadcasting station, WETA, before he passed away from lung cancer at age eighty-seven on January 27, 2014. His *Washington Post* obituary headline was "Man With A Million Voices' Captained Children's Television."

My favorite kids show was WTTG's **Countdown Carnival** premiering on WTTG in August of 1963 when I was ten. The host was **Bill Gormly**, who had first been the "Pony Express Rider" on local Saint Joseph Missouri TV. His WTTG boss hired him as announcer and Bill was drafted to create a children's show. He did so by playing himself, with no budget for costumes. Gormly went to Al Cohen's magic shop and bought wigs and glasses and wore his own sweater every day. The studio had a rearview projection screen which allowed images to appear behind Bill walking in front of the screen.

He'd interview "guests" using the new video tape technology. He literally winged one of his first characters, Robin J. Finch, the bird expert who was inspired by a local birder; and Mr. Poucher, the mailman, "a grumpy, contentious fellow always berating the customers because their packages weren't wrapped correctly." After they had correctly repacked their item and walked out, Mr. Poucher would toss the package through a basketball hoop and the soundman would play a "crashing glass" effect.

And then there was Uncle Clyde, a Civil War veteran whose dialogue would invariably include the line "How 'bout them Redskins?" And don't forget A.C. Sparks, the electrician.

There was no audience for Bill's show. He played to the control booth and stagehand staff. "If they thought it was funny then that was good enough," he thought. The only kids who ever appeared in the studio were randomly picked from those who held carnivals for Muscular Dystrophy, which were coordinated by "WTTG-affiliated stations, with the main telethon held in New York City."

Bill Gormly and Mr. Poucher © Kaptain Kidshow

"Uncle Dave" Ginsburg grew up in Florida, where he started out with the *Tampa Times* covering theaters. He became a theatre manager and publicity man. Later, he travelled with a mind reading dog act. In the 1930s, he came to Washington to get a newspaper job but wound up working for Sidney Lust Theaters as a manager and publicity man. Ginsburg is well remembered in Hyattsville and Cheverly, MD for his *Uncle Dave's* kiddie show with his trained dog Rusty. "Uncle Dave" died in 1990 at the age of eight-six.

Officer Dick Mansfield

I attended Anne Beers Elementary School in Southeast Washington, DC, for my first two years. Dick Mansfield visited our class to teach us about safety. We didn't know he was a thirty-two-year retired Inspector with the DC Metropolitan Police.

He would invite a student to draw a random line on the large paper on his easel. He transformed that line into a picture with a safety theme. His creativity impressed me as if he were a magician. And we all absolutely loved him.

He taught us many songs, like "Remember Your Name and Address." While we sang, he drew his huge cartoons, which he'd give away to a lucky youngster who answered his "chalk talk" safety questions correctly. We also didn't know that his cartoons were published in newspapers and magazines, including the *Saturday Evening Post*. I was saddened that I never saw him again after I switched to Saint Francis Xavier catholic school on Pennsylvania Ave near Sousa Bridge.

But looking back, he was the first up-close "performer" I ever met. I started drawing cartoons for my school pals in the third grade, and I still look both ways while crossing the street. Thank you, Officer Mansfield.

Photo: A classroom photo of Dick Mansfield in 1922 © Kaptain Kidshow

Dick Dyszel: Bozo, Captain 20, and Count Gore DeVol

The incarnation of his media funhouse career began in 1969. The Illinois native surfaced first as a rock disc jockey at a radio station "way South of Saint Louis," he said. A scant year later, he was doing dual duty as a serious newscaster and Bozo the Clown at a newly established TV station in Paducah, KY. It was there—over a couple of brews with the production staff—that the character of Count Gore de Vol materialized. (the name is a twist on the writer's name, Gore Vidal)

"Soon I was playing Bozo, creating commercials during the 11:00 news, disappearing during the sports report to get into makeup, and going on at 11:30 as Count Gore De Vol hosting a horror film, he recalled breathlessly."

When he arrived at WDCA in 1972, the management at the Bethesda, MD, station decided that, in addition to the Count, Dyszel should become the amiable Captain 20, a promotional character. And continue the legacy of Bozo. Five years later, however, Bozo was becoming a bore. "By that time, I didn't think that a slapstick clown was what children needed or wanted," said Dyszel. "And I was relieved when the show was finally canceled." (Though his name was withheld from the credits at his request, Dyszel was Bozo longer than any of the other local actors, including Willard Scott, who played the role.)

In May of 1980, Dyszel's *Creature Feature* Saturday night spook show set a record as the first locally produced show broadcast in true stereo. His *Creature Feature* also showcased videos by local rock groups—one by rock group Mars Everywhere, and then ran the clip in its entirety backward "to see if there were any satanic messages," he joked. None appeared.

Dick was always looking for local films or videos. "It's nice to have the things besides my own wits and mind to play with. Makes for a better show."

These days, you can catch Count DeVol in person when he hosts horror films at AFI Silver Theatre in Silver Spring, Maryland. On October 26, he commemorated the 50th Anniversary of the release in 1974 of *The Texas Chain Saw Massacre*. https://www.countgore.com

Who is Kaptain Kidshow

"My Kaptainkidshow.com bio: Born on DC's Capitol Hill and a B.A. graduate of the University of Maryland (College Park), I realized in 2000 that details of the DC kid shows of my youth were missing from the World Wide Web. I subsequently created the <Kaptainkidshow.com> web site to salute the vintage TV kid shows produced In Washington, DC, and their hosts. The site is still very much a work in progress."

Bob Bell

Chapter 33 – Rumblers

Link Wray's earthshaking song "Rumble" was born on the fly at a record hop hosted by popular TV host Milt Grant. On a summer night in 1958, around fifty miles south of DC outside the Fredericksburg Arena on Route One, Wray and his band The Ray Men were among the guest performers onstage when someone at the dance party yelled out for "The Stroll," a 1975 hit song by The Diamonds, a Canadian band.

Fortunately, the Ray Men didn't know the tune, so Link improvised. The result hit the right chords with the crowd and became one of the most seminal sounds in the history of rock—one which required poking a couple of holes in a speaker when it came time to recreate the sound in the recording studio.

Fred Lincoln "Link" Wray Jr. (May 2, 1929–November 5, 2005) was an American guitarist, songwriter, and vocalist who became popular in the late 1950s. The way Link would describe the origins goes like this: "We'd been there all night long and the kids didn't pay a bit attention to us. And so, when I started doing this song, they started screaming over me, you know, because now there's something happening, right?

"[Drummer] Doug got so carried away, he just jumped off the drums. And I said let's finish the song. And he gets back on the drums and we played. We had to play this about four times for the kids. They kept hollering and screaming, banging on the stage, you know, play that weird song, play that weird song!!"

Link Wray passed away in 2005 at the age of seventy-six, but he finally got some of the recognition he deserved when the 2017 documentary *Rumble: The Indians Who Rocked the World* helped shed light on his contributions. Wray was a Shawnee Native American.

Then, in April 2018, the Rock & Roll Hall of Fame made a big move by starting to honor individual songs at their annual induction ceremony. Among the five songs they recognized that year was "Rumble."

When introducing this new category, Steven Van Zandt from the E Street Band mentioned how just one song can change the whole music scene. He emphasized how a three-minute track can lead to personal revelations and totally impactful experiences that stick with us. It's amazing to think about the kind of influence a single song can have!

Other guitarists agree. Here are a few quotes:

"Without Link Wray I would have not made "My Generation"
Pete Townshend
"Link Wray's influence is felt in almost every rock musician's repertoire, from the heavy riffs to the wild scrapes of the guitar strings." *Jeff Beck.*
"The best instrumental ever." *Bob Dylan.*
"Rumble is a game changer. It took guitar playing in a direction that no one had thought possible before." *Eddie Van Halen.*
If I could go back in time and see any band, it would be Link Wray and the Raymen." *Neil Young.*

"The name of the song originated from the stepdaughter of Archie Bleyer, the head of Cadence Records who was releasing the song after saying it reminded her of *West Side Story*.

Later dubbed by *Rolling Stone* magazine as "an invitation to a knife fight," the song was too raw for radio. It was banned in New York and Boston after concerns that it might incite gang violence and remains to this day the only instrumental song to ever be banned on radio.

The song greatly guided generations of musicians including Pete Townshend, Jimi Hendrix, Slash, and Jeff Beck. The forefather of punk, Iggy Pop cites it as one of his five most influential records. He remembers thinking "It's simple. I can do that. It's bad."

A young Jimmy Page first heard it on a jukebox and was stunned by the revolutionary sound. He spoke and then played "Rumble" in 2023 when Wray was inducted into the Rock & Roll Hall of Fame, sixty-five years after that Milt Grant dance party in Fredericksburg, Virginia.

This location witnessed 50,000 casualties within a ten-mile range during the Civil War. There's a move to have an official Virginia Historical Marker erected at this site where "Rumble" was born. *Charles D. Young*

Robert Ira Gordon was born in Bethesda, MD, in 1947. He attended both Bethesda-Chevy Chase and Walt Whitman High Schools. He was nine when he first heard Elvis Presley's "Heartbreak Hotel," which he characterized in interviews as "shocking and so new." He told *Rolling Stone* magazine about another pivotal moment in 1956: "I first saw Link Wray at a weekend show at Glen Echo amusement park in Maryland. My father took me and my brother there. He was doing "Rumble," and it blew me away."

Gordon would go on to find other early rockers to love, including Gene Vincent ("Be-Bop-A-Lula") and Eddie Cochran ("Summertime Blues"), and at sixteen in 1963, began attending the "exciting" R&B shows by Otis Redding and James Brown at The Howard Theatre.

At seventeen, inspired to take the stage himself, Gordon joined the local DC band The Confidentials as their lead singer. They recorded two singles and found some fans at the Bethesda Youth Center where they mainly played. His next local band was The Newports, with gigs at local DC bars, including The Keg, Rabbit's Foot, and Bayou.

He eventually became a lead singer for Tuff Darts, an early punk band based in NYC, that played the CBGB nightclub and other venues yet this music wasn't his real love. He told Joe Sasfy in the *Unicorn Times* in September 1977, "I would rather be singing positive songs. Let's face it, the words are pretty dumb." He later confessed to Variety in 2014. "I had split from my first wife, and punk worked for me. But I wasn't really into punk. I missed singing those old songs."

Danny Gatton and Robert appearing on a 1981 SCTV show.

The Strangeloves ("I Want Candy") record producer Richard Gottehrer, formerly evaluated a Tuff Darts rehearsal and, rather than working with the band, suggested teaming Gordon with Link Wray, creating two albums together—1977's *Robert Gordon with Link Wray* and 1978's *Fresh Fish Special*—earning Gordon a record deal with RCA, which housed the music of his idol, Elvis. The first time Wray heard Gordon sing, he said, "Hey, man, that's early Elvis!"

Mark McStea of *Guitar Player* magazine proclaimed, "Gordon kick-started the worldwide rockabilly revival in the late '70s..." Gordon's retro-sounding version of Bruce Springsteen's "Fire" featured The Boss himself on piano and pre-dated the hit version by the Pointer Sisters. Robert also got radio play with a remake of a 1955 gem called "Red Hot"—(by another vintage rockabilly artist Gordon admired, Billy Lee Riley), and Marshall Crenshaw's "Someday, Someway," a full year before Crenshaw's hit version. Gordon also collaborated with fellow rockabilly aficionado Danny Gatton on some of his best work.

Then followed nine more Robert Gordon albums: 1979's *Rock Billy Boogie*, 1980's *Bad Boy*, 1981's *Are You Gonna Be the One*, 1994's *All for The Love of Rock 'N' Roll*, 1997's *Robert Gordon*, 2004's *Satisfied Mind*, 2007's *It's Now or Never* with Chris Spedding, 2014's *I'm Coming Home*, and 2020's *Rockabilly for Life*.

Robert Gordon developed an international following, continuing to record and tour until his death from a battle with acute myeloid leukemia. He was seventy-five.

Linwood Taylor

According to his family, Linwood Taylor liked to entertain them. "My aunt said she knew I was going to be an entertainer because I would dance around the house and sing Elvis Presley's 'Hound Dog.' I was four years old." Linwood, an only child, said his ability to amaze his grandmother and cousins had a big impact on him: "I saw the Rolling Stones and a lot of the big groups but the one show that is my favorite was seeing Rick Derringer when I was twenty-one in a small DC club. He was totally rocking out. Rick hadn't released his live album yet. My friend's brother was across town with a date seeing the Eagles, We were like 'The Eagles? Forget them. This Rick Derringer was really rocking.'"

It's fifty years later and that experience is still with Linwood. He was born in Fort Lee, Virginia, but grew up in Lanham, Maryland., and started playing guitar at the age of twelve in the late 1960s, drawing inspiration musicians like Jimi Hendrix, The Animals, Booker T. & The M.G.'s, and Muddy Waters whom he had met and talked with at the Cellar Door already. He very fondly recalls saying "Pleased to meet you Mr. Waters, as I was drinking his champagne and smoking his reefer," Linwood laughs.

Linwood with the BC Rich guitar and on the cover of a well-known DC newspaper magazine. © Linwood Taylor

During his high school years at Archbishop Carroll High School in Northeast DC in the 1970s, his musical influences expanded to include Cream and Led Zeppelin, although Taylor first played guitar in an R&B horn band called **The Under**

Cues, covering artists like Curtis Mayfield and Chicago. His late 1970s bands in the Washington, DC, area, included The Patriots, a country rock group, and The Stags, a blues rock group.

In 1980, he formed his own blues rock group, The Linwood Taylor Band, where he served as the lead singer and guitarist. His band started when was going to these blues jam at a bar called Gentry near the Marine barracks. "I knew a guy I took a couple of lessons who had these blues jams there. He asked me if I had a band and I well, I totally lied and said, yeah. So I called my buddies up and we started playing blues and it was one of those situations where it just went on from there. The next thing I know I'm playing, opening for Johnny Copeland at the Gentry bar and for Rory Gallagher at this nearby place called the Saba Club. Randy Hansen, who was a Hendrix impersonator, played there with the real Hendrix drummer Mitch Mitchell."

The band gained popularity and headlined at various notable venues in Washington DC like the Gentry Club, Saba, and Bethesda, Maryland. Throughout his career, Taylor has shared the stage with esteemed musicians such as blues singers Albert Collins, Johnny Copeland, Coco Montoya, Luther Allison, Bernard Allison, and Joe Louis Walker, as well as guitarists Ronnie Earl and Eddie Kirkland, and harmonica player Anthony "Swamp Dog" Clark. He has released three albums: *Live at Colonial Seafood* in 1991, *Take This and Stay Out of Trouble* in 1993, and *Make Room for the Paying Customer* in 2000.

After that first impactful Deringer show Linwood bought a 1976 BC Rich Mockingbird guitar just like Rick's.

"This was very rock-and-roll-looking electric guitar, you know. I got rid of my Fenders and played that through a 100-watt Marshall amp. I was young and strong enough to carry it at that point."

Jorma Kaukonen & Jack Casady
Jack and Jorma with me @ the Birchmere

In 1960, two high-school pals formed their first band, The Triumphs, in their Northwest neighborhood of the nation's capital. By 1965, they were the lead guitar and bass players of Jefferson Airplane, psychedelic music pioneers and one of the first San Francisco-based groups to become *Billboard* hitmakers. Their blues-based Hot Tuna duo began as a side project in 1969, opening for their collective band, and a full-time endeavor when Casady and Kaukonen left the Airplane in 1972.

Both are longtime regular performers at DC venues and with a passion for the club, and their hometown. In late 2024, Hot Tuna was booked in December to return to the Birchmere.

Jorma remembers: "I left DC after I graduated in 1959. I went to Antioch College for a year and then I went to college for a year in the Philippines because my dad was stationed there. And then I came back and I worked in DC for a summer. Actually. I was the night shift manager of the Sunoco station on Connecticut Avenue.

"DC's my hometown. It was and always will be. I've played a lot of places in DC and would be hard pressed to remember all of them. There was Desperado's on M street in Georgetown. And I started playing the second Birchmere solo in the '80s which was like a house, and the one that's there now which I call Birchmere World.

"In a normal world, I'd be a great grandfather, but in this one, I've got a twenty-five-year-old son that lives in Arlington, Virginia, and my sixteen-year-old daughter is in high school in Ohio, where I live. My son and his buddies come to the Birchmere because they know they'd get a free catfish, beans, and maybe a beer."

"Or they could want to see Dad and his buddies playing music. But he's been coming to see me since he was a little kid. And now he's a grown man on his own. I mean, that's something right there.

"Returning to the DC area always reminds me of the early days we were starting. It's like going home. I remember the city back then before there was a Capital Beltway. Northern Virginia and Southern Maryland were country back then. We'd swim at Dickerson's Quarry [a deep and dangerous private lake surrounded by the steep rock in Montgomery County, MD.

"Now, we've played the Birchmere for so many years and know everyone. The sound just keeps getting better. When they have to invest in the sound system, they do. That's why I call it the Birchmere World. It's hilarious. It's got everything. It's got the statue of Pudge. It's got the store and the stages.

"Here's the deal. I'm eighty-two years old, and I've been in this game for a long time. And I feel blessed to be here. And not just to be able to play well—and I still think I can play well—but for the people who made the journey with us all over these years. That's something to be thankful for, you know.

"Check this out. My dad was in the service, so we traveled a lot, but I graduated from Wilson High School in 1959. My high school girlfriend and I are still buddies after all these years. She accompanies her elder son to see every gig I play in DC. Her name is Barbara…"

* * *

When arranging these interviews and I first told him I was going to interview his partner, Jack Casady, Jorma said, "People always think that Jack has a reputation for being mysterious. But he's a conversationalist MOFO, a real talker, with an unbelievable memory. And he was in DC longer than me." So, you're going to have a great time.

Jack Casady: "My advantage to be in Washington DC when I was twelve, thirteen, fourteen and just starting my just so-called ascend, I would go down to the Library of Congress to hear all the Alan Lomax collections of field music before it started to get put on LPs. I remember locking myself into those little booths with eight records or so. It would be called 'world music' today from all over, collected up and down the Appalachian states.

"And later I could go over to the Shamrock to hear Mac Wiseman, and then catch Ray Charles at the Howard Theater the next night, or see Louis Prima in the club circuit, and then head to the Dixie Pig bar over the DC line to play with Danny Gatton and a bunch of my pals....and all those influences I poured into the Jefferson Airplane and with Jorma in Hot Tuna."

* * *

Henry Charles Vestine (December 25, 1944 – October 20, 1997) Known as "The Sunflower," Henry was an American guitar player. Born in Takoma Park, MD, Henry was a childhood friend of John Fahey. They collected records and learned guitar together.

Henry's father was a geologist who discovered the "Vestine Crater" on the moon. He and his son went to blues shows in DC together. Henry, through the help of Fahey, went on to play in the group Canned Heat, performing "On the Road Again" at the Monterey Pop Festival.

Henry briefly played with Frank Zappa as a member of the original Mothers of Invention. The photo is Henry and Frank at the Whiskey a Go Go for a few weeks in October 1965 (before *Freak Out* was recorded).

Vestine's guitar work can be heard posthumously on Zappa's later 2004 *Joe's Garage*. Shortly before his death from heart and respiratory failure in a Paris hotel on October 20, 1997, Vestine recorded an album, *Guitar Gangster*, with native Washingtonian guitarist Evan Johns.

In 2003, *Rolling Stone* magazine ranked Vestine as 77th in the 100 Greatest Guitarists of all time.

© Link Wray Fan Group
https://www.facebook.com/groups/linkwrayfangroup/

Chapter 34 – Danny G, the Telemaster

(R to L) Jeff Wisor, Liz Meyer, Howard Scott Stein, J.B. Allison, and Danny Gatton. © DHTC

Danny Gatton can play anybody's music. No one can play his. And there's the rub: What do you do with someone who has no patience with boundaries and therefore obliterates them, who slips jazzy octave solos into a country tune, or finger-picks the blues bluegrass style, or plays complex chords where others might settle for single notes? In the age of specialized music, where it's easier to promote something that is blatantly one thing, how do you sell someone like Danny Gatton who is all over the map?
Richard Harrington, *Washington Post*, 1991

Essay on Danny Gatton by Daryl Davis

October 17, 1975, was the day before Chuck Berry's birthday. It was also the day of the grand opening of Veneman Music on Rockville Pike in Rockville, Maryland. To promote the event, the store brought in Les Paul with a big sale on musical instruments. Every young, aspiring guitarist knows if you want to play like Jimi Hendrix, you must have a white Fender Stratocaster. Though piano was my instrument, I was a young, aspiring guitarist at the age of seventeen and my guitar hero was Chuck Berry, I knew if I

wanted to play "Johnny B. Goode" like Chuck, I'd need a cherry red Gibson ES-335 despite the fact that I couldn't play a lick. A crowd had gathered to see Les Paul demonstrate some of his innovations on his Gibson Les Paul guitar. My friend spotted someone in the crowd with his eyes glued to Les Paul, and whispered to me, "Oh wow, that's Danny Gatton!" I was not familiar with the name and my friend proceeded to tell me Danny was one of the best guitarists around and I should get his autograph. When the demo was over, I walked up to Danny and introduced myself and said, "Mr. Gatton, may I have your autograph?"

He said, "You really need to get his autograph," nodding in the direction of Les Paul as he honored my request and gave me an autograph. At Danny's urging, I walked through the crowd and waited my turn and got Les Paul's autograph as well. Soon I began noticing the name Danny Gatton in the entertainment section of *The Washington Post* performing at bars and clubs all over the DC metropolitan area. I went and saw him at a place called The Childe Harold in Dupont Circle. He was performing with my rockabilly friend Billy Hancock. Billy invited me to sit in on piano and play a couple of songs with them, which I did. Danny's playing was out of this world. What he played all made sense, but what didn't make sense was how he was able to play all that on the guitar! I spent some time with him and Billy after the show and he was just as kind and humble to me as he was the day I first met him.

I continued going to see him at various places and once he showed up at a gig of mine in Baltimore and asked for my number. He called and said he was recording a new album and asked if I would play on two tracks and how much would I charge. I told him I wouldn't charge him anything as long as he would play on two tracks for me when I decided to release a CD. He agreed to do so.

I went to Big Mo Recording Studio and recorded the two tracks with Danny and his band. His lead singer was a great vocalist and rhythm guitarist named Billy Windsor who was also Danny's best friend. Billy was a real sweetheart of a man. Unexpectedly, Billy died before all the tracks were done. Danny took it very hard as anyone would when they not only lose a band mate but lose their best friend as well. He decided to take some time off from completing the recording session and get back to it later when his grief subsided.

I attended Billy's service and Danny walked over and spoke with me. During our conversation, he said he knew his project needed to be completed and he would eventually get back to it. Then he said, "When can I come and record on your songs?" I said I was in no hurry and it could be done after we finished his project. He said, "I don't know when I'll get back to it, but let's do yours soon." That was my last conversation with Danny Gatton. While I don't want to say what he said was prophetic, I will never forget those words. One of the tracks on which I played for him, "Ain't That Peculiar," was released posthumously.

What can I say and what did I learn from Danny Gatton? There are many great guitar players out there, but the bulk of them are assemblers. They take licks from multiple guitarists then and composite them into what becomes their style. However, guitarists like Les Paul, Jimi Hendrix, Chuck Berry, and Danny Gatton went far beyond compositing. They were innovators with their own licks and most importantly, their own sense of feel.

Danny has played my ES-335 and he sounded just like himself. I played on his Fender Telecaster and didn't sound a thing like Danny Gatton. Chuck, Danny, Les, and Jimi would sound like themselves whether they played their regular brand of guitar or if they were fooling around on a cheap guitar from Walmart. My advice to young, aspiring guitarists is listen to as much music and musicians as you can. You will not sound like your favorite guitar player just because you play a replica of their guitar. Learn the instrument and become the best you can be and it will manifest on whatever brand of guitar you happen to play. There will only be one Danny Gatton and what made him extra special was his kindness and generosity with his time and talent, never letting it go to his head. If you learn his licks, learn his humble demeanor as well.

Danny, Dave Elliott, and John Previti © D. Elliott

Danny Gatton's long-time bassist and collaborator **John Previti** shares this poignant story about Danny Gatton—via author and musician **Paul Scimonelli**:

"Many people who knew Danny described him as a real gentleman, very humble and soft spoken. Once, Chris Battistone, Barry Hart, and I were doing a gig with Danny at the Holiday Inn in Tyson's Corner. At one point between tunes, this young lady comes up to us and I want to put this the right way. I think she may have had some issues like maybe she was socially awkward or something like that. She was a very nice young lady. She came up to him and she had a triangle with her. This was unusual. I'm thinking, *Gee, she has a triangle*. She says to Danny, 'I'd like to play a song with you.' So, Danny, instead of looking at us and going, 'Oh boy, this is weird,' he took her completely seriously. He said, 'Hmm, I wonder what would sound good with the triangle.'

"He picked a song, she played it with us, and we did the whole tune completely. He didn't do it really quick to get it over with or anything like that. I think it was a Latin tune maybe. We finished the song, and she was very sweet. She gave him some pocket change and she said, thank you. And she went away. Danny didn't look at us, he didn't say a word or make any (negative) expression. He just took her as she was and treated her like a person. Here's one of the greatest musicians on the planet, and this sweet young lady coming up with a triangle and he just treated her with as much dignity that you could. And that was it. It sounds like a very simple thing, but it always made a huge impression on me."

> In his memorable memoir, DC guitar great **Tom Principato** recalled an evening in 1973 at the Childe Harold when he first saw Danny Gatton play as part of what in retrospect was a seminal if short-lived Americana band, one formed well before that genre had a name. The group was billed as "Liz Meyer and Friends" and featured a group-within-a group with Danny on guitar and banjo with his rhythm section of Dave Elliott on drums and Billy Hancock on bass. Liz provided acoustic guitar, most of the vocals and adjective Jeff Wisor on fiddle. The setlists included Liz Meyer originals as well as bluegrass classics and everything from rockabilly to jazz from Danny's part of the group.
>
> Principato says, "I sat there stunned as Danny ran through all those Les Paul, Charlie Christian, and Chet Atkins licks I was struggling to play—and he was doing it ever so nonchalantly on a 1953 Telecaster."
>
> Like Tom, I also saw the group play in 1973, in my case at George Mason University. I was so inspired by that performance I wrote my first published piece about music. Sadly, the group didn't last long as Danny formed Danny and the Fat Boys in 1974 and started his solo recording career.
>
> Liz Meyer, Danny Gatton, and Billy Hancock all are gone now, but nearly fifty years after that concert, I saw Dave Elliott play at the annual Danny Gatton birthday tribute concert at the Birchmere. I reconnected with him after that performance and asked a few questions including where and how he and Danny and Billy Hancock first played together.
>
> Dave explained he and Danny and Billy first met at the Hillbilly Heaven on Route One near Lorton, Virginia (then site of the infamous Lorton Reformatory prison, now an arts center). They essentially became the house band for a while at the country music roadhouse. Emmylou Harris graduated from nearby Gar-Field High School (where she was both a cheerleader and

valedictorian) and country music was the chosen genre there in an area that's now predominantly Hispanic."

Dave says, "The music at Hillbilly Heaven was just one slice of the musical pie the DC area offered. A lot of roots music, hillbilly music, big band and more that combined with the city's Black culture, both rich and poor." He also mentioned the "transient nature of the DC community, with the government and military people, so there were a lot of musical styles brought to the area that way, too."

On the other hand, Dave points out that "DC was called the bluegrass capital of the country at one time." That didn't last, of course. Liz Meyer eventually moved to Europe and became an award-winning bluegrass musician there, recording with stars of the genre including Bela Fleck, Sam Bush, and Jerry Douglas before her untimely death from cancer.

Dave says Danny and the Fat Boys could play bluegrass even if their roots were in 50s and 60s Rock & Roll, and they "liked all styles (even TV theme songs)." Although the majority of the local bands played Top 40 music and some country in the 60s, a lot of us enjoyed roots music more than Top 40, so "we were able to play what we liked" (listen to their incendiary "Harlem Nocturne" for an example). By the 70s, all those styles exploded and there were enough venues and opportunities in the area so anybody could play any of the different styles. Dave concluded that it wasn't always monetarily rewarding but "there were many musicians in the area that played for the love of music."

© *Charles D. Young*

Chapter 35 – Chuck Levin, The Music Man

Chuck and Steve © S. Moore

Amazement was my inescapable reaction during a 1985 interview visit to Chuck Levin's Washington Music Center. For many musicians it was a bit like "died and gone to heaven" for the mountainous array of instruments which crowded the vast showroom would seem to satisfy the wildest musical dream of neophyte or professional. Indeed, the beginners were there, gazing covetously at a glittery horde of guitars, keyboards, amplifiers, and other musical gear. And celebrity clients looked down approvingly from hundreds of eight-by-ten inch "glossies" which papered the walls.

I continued the article as, "The sound of instruments being tested blended with another kind of music in the Wheaton, Maryland, store. It was the buzz of a busy intercom, the ring of sixteen telephone lines and the staccato rhythm-and-chime of Mrs. Levin on the cash register in the front of the store. It was the sound of business. Big business."

"I think ours is the largest single-volume music store in the world," said Chuck Levin, between puffs on a cigar about the size of Chicago. "We really pump a lot of musical equipment through here." The public sees only a part of the pumping. Below the sales floor is a cavernous basement labyrinth of cartons, crates, and guitar cases. "Sometimes it even amazes me," smiled Levin, whose then $3 million-dollar inventory spreads into two warehouses as well. "We're big-volume dealers. We buy up other stores and other companies as liquidators." This, he explained, allowed him to give his customers exceptionally good discounts.

A flip through his stacks of past and present invoices revealed an astounding variety of customers. Among many rock stars to start with were Bruce Springsteen, The Who, and Stevie Wonder, who smartly endorsed his checks with a thumbprint. But the establishment is also solidly represented by such accounts as The Beach Boys, Woody Herman, the Ohio National Guard, the Army, Navy, and Marine bands and Walt Disney Productions, among others. Then there were the numerous universities and countless high school bands, the governments of Brazil, Peru, Argentina, and New Guinea, and the casinos of Atlantic City, not to mention the White House. The list went on.

It's an impressive clientele for a business whose only promotion is word of mouth and a tee shirt, given away with each "major purchase." Levin's own preferred brand of music is "Big Band." And the last advertising he did was in support of the "battle of the bands" segment on the local TV show called *Wing Ding* in the 1960s.

Chuck Levin, a native New Yorker whose nickname is "The Big Kahuna" estimates that approximately 250 local amateur and professional musicians—along with their friends—pass through his musical marketplace each day. It's not unusual for eight people to arrive together to purchase a set of guitar strings. The attraction says Levin is simple. "We've always dealt with name brands as a rule. We give a good price for our products, but far beyond the price is the fact that we service everything we sell. You can't offer junk or headaches to your customers and expect to generate any goodwill."

Indeed, eleven technicians staffed the store's woodwind, string, keyboard, and amplifier repair shops, and some fifty more people, most of whom are musicians sensitive to the special needs of the customers, are part of the operation.

Then the fifty-eight-year-old Levin and Marge, his wife of thirty-three years, opened their first Washington Music Center on H Street in northeast Washington in 1958. They had already purchased, made profitable, and sold their first business, the Bench Trumpet company. The original Center was burned in the 1968 riots following the death of Dr. Martin Luther King—a few charred embers of the building remained in a frame, hung over Levin's Wheaton desk. But it was silver anniversary time when this article was published and everything was coming up gold. The Levin sons, Alan (32) and Robert (26), then were partners, making this an operation under close family scrutiny.

"I'm real proud of Alan and Robert's involvement in selecting the best lines of sound-reinforcement and keyboards. The kids are knowledgeable in these areas and can choose the newer electronic instruments that are most of demand," beamed the proud Papa."

His offspring seemed to return the admiration. "He's the sharpest guy out there," said Alan.

Levin made a successful effort to make his large staff an "extended family" as well. He was a boss who was apt to arrive at the store with a big bag of submarine sandwiches for the sales force.

Though the store was officially the Washington Music Center, patrons soon tended to call it Chuck Levin's or Chuck's. He doesn't seem to mind. He wants all the customers to feel famous. "Some businesses rely on people dying or other misfortunes. What I like about the music business is that the people who come into our store are generally very happy people." The Big Kahuna made all the right moves to keep them that way.

* * *

After fort-four years of commanding the store, Chuck passed away on December 22, 2002. Following his passing, the family-run business continued under the leadership of Marge and Chuck's children, Alan, Robert, and Abbe. On March 2, 2010, the heart and soul of the store, Marge, passed away as did Robert in 2013.

Washington Music Center continued and celebrated its 65th anniversary in 2023. Today, Alan Levin presides as the "Son of Big Kahuna."

"We still try and do things the same way we always learned," Alan told us in October 2024. "My Mom, Dad, and younger brother are gone, but Robert's son, Adam, works here with nieces and daughters. It's a third generation of a family-owned business that brings new ideas to us. We still do the rentals and put the instruments into the hands of musicians. People travel to come here, so we're still a destination."

Alan signals his love of the DC area when he recalls James Brown playing Walt Whitman Fieldhouse when it opened each year. "And let me tell you, that was a band. They'd play an hour before James would take the stage. And the area musicians that come in the store today. Some for over fifty years. We laugh together. It's still like a candy store. Like my Dad said, it's supposed to be a fun business."

Paul Reed Smith

To the list of great guitar innovators like Les Paul and Leo Fender, we add the name of Paul Reed Smith, born and raised in Rockville, MD. In 1985, Paul was a veteran of the DC bar band circuit, having played guitar for the iconoclastic group Root Boy Slim, among others. But in his words then. "I always knew I wanted to make electric guitars."

Paul Reed Smith made his first guitar as an extra credit project while studying at Saint Mary's College in Maryland. He got an "A" and that's when Smith decided to follow his dream and make guitars for a living. His first solid body electric guitar in 1975 in an attempt to match—or better—the Gibson Les Paul Junior guitar he was playing in his band. This goal was achieved when Smith later teamed up with his mentor and partner.

His mentor and partner Ted Pritchard helped design the electric pickups which give a Paul Reed Smith instrument its kaleidoscopic range of sounds.

"Guitars are like your girlfriend or wife," said Smith. "Literally a friend you've got to feel really comfortable with and love. I make a deal with my customers. If they don't fall in love with their guitar, then I'll take it back and give them their money."

Rockstar Carlos Santana called Smith's PRS brand the Maserati of electric guitars, and bands such as The Cars, Aerosmith, and Journey were beating a path to his Annapolis, MD, workshop. Smith didn't have to worry about his customers not falling in love.

His crew then had ten assistants with his wife Barbara helping on the business end soon moving into a larger factory. And PRS guitars were in the music stores later that year.

1976
Paul Reed Smith builds his first guitar as an extra credit project while studying at Saint Mary's College in Maryland. He gets an "A" and decides to follow his dream and make guitars for a living.

2010
Inducted into Vintage Guitar Magazine's Hall of Fame

© Courtesy of PSRguitar.com

**Kindred Spirits
by Les Hatley**
is a pictorial memoir, with running commentary, of fifty-five years as a musician in the Washington, DC, area music scene. The book is based on a scrapbook updated continually from 1965 to 2020. The book goes to great lengths to celebrate musicians met and befriended along the author's musical journey.

The late Les Hatley was a long time Washington DC area guitar player, having started his music journey in 1965 and continuing for well over fifty years. His recordings charted both nationally and internationally. His music has been on soundtracks for shows on MTV, Animal Planet, Discovery, TLC, and PBS.

In 2015 he was inducted into the Maryland Entertainment Hall of Fame. He also won a Washington Area Music Association "Wammie." He was honored by the Songwriters Association of Washington with the Director's Award for Instrumental Music for his album *Chocolate*. His many, many friends miss him.

His book, which is an amazing 774-page treasure, is available at **https://store.bookbaby.com**

SM

Chapter 36 – Eva: Purity of Voice

© Blix Street Records

Eva Cassidy was born on February 2, 1963, at Washington Hospital Center in DC and grew up in Bowie, Maryland. A shy child with a passion for singing, she went on to sell over ten million records, most of which were released posthumously following her death from melanoma at thirty-three.

Keith Grimes played lead guitar in Eva Cassidy's band for five years. In a 1999 interview with Laura Bligh on Eva's website (https://evacassidy.org/keith-grimes-interview//), he shared: "Most of Eva's formative musical experiences took place in her childhood home. Her father taught her guitar, and family music-making was a big part of growing up in Bowie, which was semi-rural at the time."

As a child, Eva's musical influences spanned from Buffy Sainte-Marie folk songs to *The Wizard of Oz* soundtrack. Her first instruments were autoharp and guitar, though she was also familiar with the bass, banjo, and mandolin played by her father. Eva eventually discovered the music of the Wilson sisters and their band, Heart. She was known to perform Janis Joplin songs, contemporary hits like Bette Midler's "The Rose," and classics such as "Georgia on My Mind," along with other songs she heard at home.

When Eva was old enough to play in bands, she made her first amateur recordings with Method Actor, a soft-rock group that released their debut LP on Gaithersburg's BLP label. The album featured violin by Tom Prasada-Rao, now known for his "virtual world music ensemble." Eva provided vocals on every track and designed the album cover herself.

Eva's artwork was another facet of her talent that she didn't fully develop. Keith Grimes notes, "I think the principles she employed in her artwork informed her sense of musical composition."

"When I first met Eva, she looked like a pioneer woman. She probably just had come from work over at the tree nursery but looked like she'd just stepped off the Appalachian trail," said Grimes.

With a performing career that lasted only a few years, almost all her live performances were at clubs in the DC area, and many were noisy bars. Grimes added, "Eva was most relaxed and had fun on gigs where the audience was not paying rapt attention. Places like Blues Alley were tough for her, knowing the audience was listening intently."

Eva performed multiple times at Rock & Roll Hall of Famer Mick Fleetwood's short-lived venue in Alexandria, VA, where Fleetwood himself occasionally backed her on drums. He admired her determination to "go her own way," noting that she often chose public domain songs and others that seemed overexposed yet made them her own. "Eva was all about her music. She just wanted to sing. Eva had so much power and conviction," Mick said. He recounts how Eva went to New York to meet major record label executives but returned to DC disappointed, as they insisted, she conformed to the pre-packaged "diva" style and that her repertoire wasn't marketable.

Grimes notes Eva's remarkable skill in arranging old songs: "Once she got past the song's rudiments, she really chose her own interpretation using her musical aesthetic." He also mentions the "battle of the ballad," noting that if left to her own devices, she would have performed an entire set of ballads.

Washington writer Geoffrey Hines said it well in *Jazz Times*: "Cassidy was no diva; she didn't overload the songs with vocal gymnastics and stratospheric notes. Quite the opposite, she detached the songs from their genre associations, so that each one became a kind of folk-blues-jazz hybrid. She pared them down to their emotional core and glided into that essence with effortless confidence. As important as her calm, unfussy phrasing was the tone of her mezzo voice-so glowing and disarming that she seemed to be confiding in each individual listener."

Eva Cassidy released only two solo Record during her lifetime. The first was a collaboration with the late "Godfather of Go-Go," Chuck Brown, who likened their work to duets by Peggy Lee and Louis Armstrong. They covered Lee's signature song, "Fever," on the LP titled *The Other Side*. Their performance at The Birchmere remains a highlight in the club's history.

Eva's first solo release, *Live at Blues Alley*, in May of 1996 received good attention in the DC area. Grimes likes this record because "it gives a great sense of the breadth of Eva's enthusiasms," but he prefers the "stuff we did as a four-piece with no keyboards. The majority of our performances were done with that instrumentation. I got to play a guitar solo in every song!"

Eva and her family helped promote her music around DC receiving early support through Olsson's Books and Records, a small chain of independent stores started by John Olsson who managed the popular Records and Tape Ltd. on 19th Street Daniele Vargas worked in the Olsson's warehouse in the 1990s and recalls "Eva's mother delivering full boxes of CDs and cassettes" for distribution. Sara Krauss played a lot of Eva's music in the book section of Olsson's Old Town Alexandria store and got many requests from the music desk asking, "Hey, what CD were you just playing?" Catherine Hagman of the Bethesda Olsson's noted, "Eva's music had a place of pride in the Bethesda store," reflecting her life as a suburban Maryland hometown kid.

By the time it was too late, Ms. Cassidy lacked the medical insurance to cover her surgery and chemotherapy bills. In 1996, a benefit concert at the Bayou was organized to help with her mounting expenses. DC-area friends joined Eva for an evening of her favorite songs. Her final public performance was a deeply emotional rendition of Armstrong's cherished "What a Wonderful World." "It's one of my favorite songs," Eva said.

Mary Ann Redmond

Twenty-four Wammie award winner Mary Ann Redmond is a legendary musician who has been active locally since the 90s and has recorded remarkable albums and many original songs. "Love Me Anyway," with local musician and composer Todd Wright, for example, was covered as a duet on Celine Dion and Johnny Hallyday's 2012 Sans Attendre, selling over three million copies.

Mary Ann and Eva were friends who performed together and respected each other's artistry. When Cassidy was diagnosed with cancer, Redmond performed at the benefit at the Bayou in Georgetown to raise funds for her treatment. Redmond's vocals on a rendition of Cassidy's song "Hear" resulted in a cherished recorded duet that fans now treasure as a unique Eva track.

Born in Richmond, VA, she studied voice and opera at Virginia Commonwealth University while playing shows with the Jack Diamond band. Her CD, *Live At Blues Alley*, was recorded at her first gig there.

Jon Carroll, a founder of the Starland Vocal Band and long-time pianist for Mary Chapin Carpenter's band, produced Redmond's CD, *Here I Am*. The album includes a song written by Mary Chapin Carpenter for Redmond, "Alone but Not Lonely."

(On a personal note, Mary Ann is one of our favorite singers. Her shows are moving and special. Highly recommended.)

Eva and Chuck

Eva Cassidy's and Chuck Brown's destinies were linked by an undeniable thread of artistic brilliance, ensuring their influence on DC's music scene would endure for generations. Chuck Brown, known as "the Godfather of Go-Go," emerged from modest beginnings in Washington, DC, to forge a genre that became emblematic of the city's vibrant musical culture. His go-go music, a fusion of funk, jazz, soul, and pop, highlighted his remarkable talent for merging versatile percussion with a range of instrumental and vocal elements. At the same time, Cassidy, a modest singer from the Maryland suburbs, overcame stage fright to captivate audiences at the Cellar Door with her exceptional voice and heartfelt performances. Her close friends often described her as "the greatest voice you never heard of," underscoring her profound yet understated impact.

Cassidy's early career took off in the late 1980s in the local music scene, where she provided backup vocals for bands before fronting her own group, The Eva Cassidy Band. Her diverse range, from ethereal folk to lively jazz, attracted attention at venues like Blues Alley and Fatty's in Rockville.

This exposure led to a fortuitous studio meeting with Chuck Brown in 1992, resulting in the album *The Other Side*, a heartwarming collaboration on jazz, blues, and soul standards. Chuck's deep, resonant baritone perfectly complemented Cassidy's extraordinary vocal range, creating harmonies over Brown's signature rhythms that were both moving and distinctive. The album, featuring classic tracks like "Fever," "Let the Good Times Roll," and "God Bless the Child," showcasing both artists' exceptional talents and their ability to merge their unique musical backgrounds.

The Other Side duet album with Eva Cassidy allowed Chuck Brown to transition from the hectic 1980s club scene to explore jazz and cabaret blues. He knew Chris Biondo, who had inherited Black Pond Studio from a neighbor and recorded some of the emerging go-go bands like Rare Essence and Experience Unlimited [EU]. Biondo, who played bass in Eva's band, arranged for her to sing backup vocals with various groups and saw the potential in pairing her with Brown.

Brown recounted to Richard Harrington of the Washington Post that when Biondo played Eva's demo, featuring her warm renditions of "Stormy Monday" and "Take Me to the River," he was struck by her voice. "Chris put a tape on, and I heard this beautiful, honeyed voice coming out of the speakers. Her voice projected her feelings, and I could feel everything she was singing." Brown was surprised to learn Eva was not Black and recognized that her voice was a perfect fit for the sophisticated material he had always wanted to explore.

The smoky duet of classic jazz and blues standards on *The Other Side* highlighted the versatility and creativity of both artists. Although the album did not achieve commercial success, it was a significant artistic accomplishment for Cassidy and Brown. Cassidy's live performances continued to gain traction, and her band saw moderate success, performing with notable acts like the Neville Brothers at Wolf Trap Farm Park and drawing thousands at the Columbia Arts Festival and the annual *Taste of DC* right after Little Feat.

Eva's performances often favored smaller, more intimate audiences, allowing her to connect deeply with her listeners. She played at venues like Fleetwood's and the 219 Jazz Club in Alexandria, where she could engage with audiences on a personal level and reinterpret songs across genres—soul, blues, gospel, folk, or jazz—with remarkable skill. Her renditions of classics like Cyndi Lauper's "Time After Time" and traditional English ballads such as "The Wayfaring Stranger" showcased her acoustic guitar prowess and brought new dimensions to familiar material through her stunning vocals. But Eva was deeply skeptical of the recording industry that wanted to paint her as a cabaret singer. Cassidy determinedly resisted genre expectations and always remained true to her artistic identity and integrity, expressing herself best by staying authentic.

In November 1994, Eva Cassidy attended the Wammies in DC, where she won the award for traditional jazz vocals.

During the event, she performed a tribute to Quintin Footz, a Rare Essence drummer recently murdered, and Danny Gatton, who had committed suicide the previous month. Cassidy had taken guitar lessons from Gatton and recorded backup vocals on his album *Untouchable*. Reflecting on Gatton's death, she remarked, "Doesn't it feel like we've lost an uncle?"

After Cassidy's death in 1996, Chris Biondo continued to preserve and promote her music. He produced several posthumous albums on Blix Street Records, including *Eva By Heart* and *Songbird*. These albums highlighted her vibrant live and studio performances, serving as poignant reminders of Cassidy's extraordinary vocal and guitar talent, and the poignant sense of loss felt by her DC fans. Biondo remains a loving champion of her talent, believing her to be one of the greatest singers of all time—a sentiment shared by many admirers. Chuck Brown reportedly burst into tears upon hearing her unreleased material.

The Other Side exemplifies the refined tastes of DC, appealing to a diverse audience with a sophisticated appreciation for the city's unique, emotive music. Most recently, a 2023 theatrical effort entitled *When Chuck Met Eva* aimed to tell the story of the remarkable duo. However, rights to songs and production issues stalled the project, partly due to the challenge of finding singers who can truly capture the pure, majestic voice of Eva Cassidy.

Her evocative voice is the primary reason to listen to her renditions of familiar songs. One such classic, "Fields of Gold," was composed by Sting, whom Frank Zappa once dubbed "Mr. Sting." In a 2001 interview with the *Washington Post*'s Richard Harrington, Sting reflected on hearing Eva's version after her death: "A friend of Eva's sent me the recording after her death. I thought it was a beautiful rendition. I've rarely heard a voice of such purity. I was deeply sorry to learn of her death and somehow it gave the song another emotional level. I was very happy the work saw the light of day. It's an extraordinary success."

Within five years of Eva's death, *Songbird* an anthology of tracks from her first three independently produced albums, had sold over a million copies. By 2023, her recorded work had surpassed ten million albums sold worldwide. Her international acclaim was largely due to the airplay her version of "Over the Rainbow" from *Songbird* received on BBC Radio 2, two years after her death. The lead singer for the Police later commented, "I heard this voice, and it was so beautiful, so pure. And the next thing I hear, it's almost a year later, and Terry Wogan is playing it on Radio 2. Then lo and behold, it's number one in England, and I'm happy for her. Even though it's a sad, tragic story, it has kind of a poetry about it."

In 2023, a new release paired some of Eva's isolated vocals with new backing by the London Symphony Orchestra, created using AI. Despite strong sales, the release received mixed reviews. One Amazon customer noted, "Eva's interpretation of her repertoire is unsurpassed, but she has no need for a large orchestral accompaniment." Nevertheless, Eva Cassidy's pianist, Lenny Williams, believes she would have been recording with orchestral accompaniment if she were alive today. Eva was rare in every sense of the word and that voice endures on the home-grown DC recordings the world loves.

The artistic journeys of Eva and Chuck represent rich and dynamic periods in the cultural history of The Federal District. Eva Cassidy's soulful interpretations and Chuck Brown's revolutionary go-go sound continue to resonate with audiences, showcasing the diverse and vibrant music scene. Their surprise meeting and collaboration on *The Other Side* highlights the possible intersection of musical styles and backgrounds. Even though it took some time, appreciation for their work shows the inspirational impact they had on the world of music and the city they called home.

Capital Acts: Washington DC Performing Arts

© L. Hurley

Many Maryland residents knew Eva Cassidy but weren't aware of her musical talent. My wife, Margaret, was a Master Gardener and Eva worked at Behnke Nurseries at the Largo, MD, facilities. The Moore gang lived nearby in Greenbelt, MD, and we were there almost every weekend during the spring and summer.

Eva was chiefly a transplanter, especially tending to the immense poinsettias they grew every year for Christmas. Eva's sister Annette, also worked part-time at the nursery while she worked on her nursing degree, and their mother Barbara helped Eva in transplanting at Largo and also worked in the Christmas Shop at the Beltsville location. Eva was a shy person around Behnke's. I wish I knew that our garden associate sang. Beyond Behnke's is an interesting history:

https://beyondbehnkes.com/about-us/behnkes-history/

Our thanks to **Larry Hurley** for use of this photo of Eva when he was working with her at Behnke's.

SM

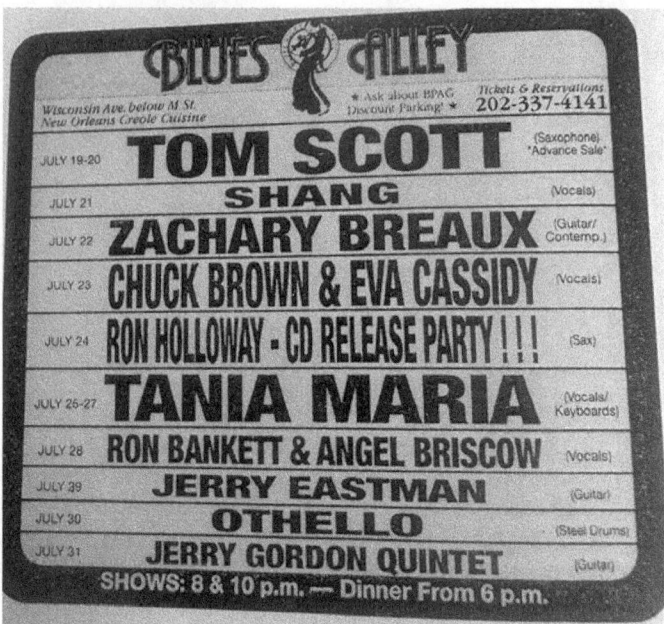

Chapter 37 – Chuck 2 Go-Go

Born August 22, 1936 in Gaston, North Carolina, Charles Louis Brown moved to Washington at the age of six lived in poverty with an absent father. As a boy Brown sang and played piano with his mother at Mount Zion Church in Fairmont Hills, a working-class suburb n Prince George's County. By fifteen he was living on the streets of the nation's capital, doing odd jobs and shining shoes where he once met Les Paul and Hank Williams. He sold the Washington Times-Herald and the Pittsburgh Courier (the great black weekly) in front of the Greyhound station downtown, but Chuck soon became involved in petty crime, and in a calamitous moment in the 1950s shot a man in what he said was self-defense.

Brown served the next eight years in Lorton Prison for manslaughter, and while there he taught himself to play on a guitar made in the woodshop by a friendly fellow convict. After doing his time Brown moved back to Washington, working as bricklayer in Capitol Heights, a truck driver, and as a sparring partner at local boxing gyms. Just as Eva Cassidy was being born, Chuck Brown was already starting to play gigs around DC, playing with jazz musicians, crooning with soul singer Jerry Butler, and joined the group Los Latinos in 1965.

Chuck Brown's creation of go-go is a musical history lesson, merging the cutting edge of urban sounds of funk, jazz, soul, and pop, rolling the best of high and low music culture into "the DC sound." Leading on guitar and vocals and putting together some of DC's top percussion and horn players, in 1966 he started Chuck Brown and the Soul Searchers. With his day job driving a furniture truck along the mid-Atlantic, Brown absorbed shifting rock and soul sounds of the decade. James Brown's funk mixed with Chuck's smooth and smoky baritone over layers of African-style percussion, and after pounding out new rhythms and lyrics from the road, Chuck would come and rock the homecoming at Howard University. This was the birth of go-go music, the unique sub-genre of funk using large brass sections of trombone, sax, and trumpet and innovative percussion with congas and rototoms, a constant back beat still heard on DC streets pumped out by kids playing on plastic buckets. Soon other bands like E.U. and Trouble Funk built on go-go to become substantial bands, and in 1979 Chuck scored a No.1 hit on the national soul charts with "Bustin' Loose" and go-go was putting the Capital City at the forefront of a new kind of Black music.

Brown died in 2012 at Baltimore's Johns Hopkins Hospital of a heart attack at the age of seventy-five, leaving his own indelible marks on DC's cultural landscape.

Other prominent go-go pioneers were Experience Unlimited [E.U.] formed in 1976 by Kevin "Pooch" Johnson and his friends. Their catchy party anthem, "Da Butt," released in 1988, brought go-go to a national audience, showcasing the genre's infectious rhythms and vibrant energy. E.U. became known for their compelling live performances, embodying the improvisational spirit of go-go. Jungle Boogie, another seminal band, emerged in the late 1970s and later transformed into Jungle, a go-go group noteworthy for their instrumental prowess and powerful performances. They gained popularity for their unique interpretations of funk standards and original compositions, contributing significantly to the genre's evolving sound.

The group Reese and the O.M.G also left an indelible mark on go-go. Led by the charismatic lead singer Tony "Reese" Harris, they were known for their engaging stage presence and ability to connect with audiences. Their sound blended traditional African rhythms with contemporary funk, creating a soundscape that captured the spirit of DC nightlife.

In the 1990s, the band Backyard Band rose to prominence, becoming one of the most successful go-go groups of the era. They were famous for their unique style, energetic live shows, and original hits like "Humpin'." Their music resonated with a younger generation and solidified their place in the go-go scene.

Lastly, The Junk Yard Band, which formed in the mid-1980s, introduced a new flavor to go-go. They became known

for their ability to meld humor with musicality in songs that portrayed everyday DC life.

These musicians and bands, along with Chuck Brown, have all played crucial roles in establishing go-go as a lasting cultural legacy of Capital City fostering a community defined by rhythm, energy, and creativity.

Because of Chuck, go-go is often called the "DC sound," and the Washington Nationals baseball team adopted "Bustin'

Loose" as its home run celebration song. In 2005 the National Endowment for the Arts gave him a National Heritage Fellowship award, and in 2009 the city gave the honorary name Chuck Brown Way to a block of 7th Street NW near the Howard Theater. © S. Moore

---

Chip Pie began taking photographs at a young age while he tagged along with his father, a newspaper reporter. He studied history at East Carolina University and moved to Washington, DC, in 1988. He has been shooting DC bands of all genres for over twenty years. One of his photographs is on permanent display as part of Chuck Brown Memorial Park. His go-go portfolio was acquired by the People's Archive of the DC Public Library in 2020, and the Washington City Paper gave him the Editor's Choice Award for his work in 2021.

His book **DC Go-Go 10 Years Backstage**, Chip Pye. Foreword by Greg Boyer was published by the History Press in 2022.

Chapter 38 ~ Groovin with Root

(l to r:) Winston Kelly, Ernie Lancaster, Miki Johnnie, Cherie Grasso, Ron Holloway, Root, Bob Greenlee, (and Walt Andrews out of frame on pedal steel). At the Bayou, early 1978.
© Courtesy R. Holloway

"I first saw Root Boy Slim at the Cellar Door. He blew me away. He was wearing a diaper and a leopard skin something over his shoulders, with those huge sunglasses. His Sex Change Band (with Dick Bangham, Paul Reed Smith, and Ron Holloway) was incredible. I loved his songs, "Boogie Till You Puke," and "I'm Not Too Old for You." We also ran into each other because we used the same pharmacy on MacArthur Boulevard. Offstage, he was Ken, short for Foster McKenzie. He was legally medicated every time I saw him, but like so many others, was into his own trip with additional substances."

Bill Danoff, Starland Vocal Band,

"I saw Root Boy Slim and the Sex Change Band in concert only once, at DC's Second Annual Homegrown Music Festival at George Washington University's Lisner Auditorium in 1977. An LP called *Direct Current: Washington Comes Alive!* (a title spoofing the then-current Peter Frampton goldmine of a live album) was released shortly after, loaded with highlights of that evening, including Root Boy, Tom Principato with George Leh and Powerhouse, the Nighthawks, Catfish Hodge, and Bill Holland and Rent's Due.

"I reviewed that *Comes Alive!* album for Unicorn Times and next received an advance copy of Root Boy's debut album for Warner Records, a collection produced by Gary Katz, best known for his work with Steely Dan. Root Boy received a reported $250,000 deal with the prominent label. An interview with Root Boy seemed in order.

"A new college grad, working in a Crown Books store while still living with my parents when the collect call from Root Boy Slim came in from a Massachusetts motel room. The most memorable line of that call came when Root Boy bragged, 'I took a shit on the Plymouth Rock this morning, Charlie.'"

A Graduate of Saint James (boarding) school in Hagerstown, MD, where he played varsity football, and a one-time African American studies major at Yale, where he was a member of Delta Kappa Epsilon with classmate George W. Bush a year older. He had spoken via collect call.

My parents told me about it when the bill for that call appeared on their phone bill. A bumper sticker still seen in the DC area to this day proclaims:

ROOT BOY SLIM OWES ME MONEY

Charles D Young

Dick Bangham, the co-owner with his wife Linda, of Rip Bang Pictures is a fun DC musician, masterful artist, and cinematographer who gave the look and animation to Feast Your Ears, the WHFS documentary film.

Also, a trombone player (although it's often difficult to hear any notes he produces in concerts), Bangham became a member and creative driver for Root Boy Slim. He recalls: "I was living in Takoma Park, doing album covers for the Nighthawks and the Roslyn Mountain Boys for Gene

Photo: Dick Bangham at 2024 DC Legends concert. © S. Moore

Rosenthal's Adelphi Records. Gene had moved his office into the back of Joe Lee's Record Paradise.

"This big Root Boy, in an overcoat looking like he'd had a couple of beers, came lumbering in. He had a demo tape he gave to Gene, who was spread kind of thin and couldn't afford a new act. I don't think Root Boy had made that big of an impression on him, so when he came out he was looking rejected.

"Joe Lee asked him what was up, and Root Boy said, 'Gene didn't like my tape.'

"'Well, let me listen to it,' said Joe.

"The next day Joe called Bangham and said, 'Man you gotta listen to this tape I got.'

"However, Dick wanted to do a record from the inside out. I had a whole plan for my Rip Bang Big Band and Review. I had been doing album packaging and covers but also working with producers; I was ready to do a concept album. This was before MTV.

"But Joe told me, 'Nah. Don't do that. Listen to this tape.'

"And I did and was blown away. The first song was 'Mood Ring.' It was like something from outer space. A garage tape with really good musicians on it. Joe asked, 'You want to meet him?' and I said sure.

"Joe and I were ruthless Scrabble players at that time, very competitive. So, Root met us at Joe's apartment and we played Scrabble. The Yale graduate held his own. He was wearing a blazer and sweater and looked very collegiate with his hair combed. He was a big six-foot-four, probably 250 pounds at the time. And he got bigger with eyes that could look right through you. And I remember him being funny that first meeting. We talked about politics and everything that night. He said, "Nice to meet you" on the way out, adding, **"I want you to help me get famous."**

In a 2006 Washington Post piece about the history of Joe's Record Paradise, John Kelly referred to store owner Joe Lee as "the black sheep of Maryland's Blair family and behind-the-scenes booster of DC music, involved with such acts as the British Walkers and Root Boy Slim."

Joe founded the store in 1974, running it while simultaneously booking acts in area clubs. Some touring musicians, including Sun Ra and Buckwheat Zydeco, stayed at Joe's home when they played DC. Joe also organized the concert in support of beloved WHFS on-air personality Damian Einstein, an event drawing over 10,000 people and resulting in Damian's return to the station.

Lee retired "to a mountain home in West Virginia" in 2008, and his son took over the store (which moved numerous times as rents escalated in the DC suburbs) just in time for the unexpected rebirth of the LP market. The store inventory eventually expanded to over 200,000 recordings, many by artists who owe a lot to Joe Lee.

He died from lung cancer on July 4, 2024. Among the many tributes to him following his death were several on WOWD radio in Takoma Park, the town where Joe had opened his first record store. One of the comments came from music writer Richard Harrington, who credited Joe with starting the "primitive movement" in the DC area because Lee welcomed and encouraged creative types who differed from typical DC residents, like Root Boy Slim.

Charles D. Young

Bangham's design genius helped fuel Root Boy's popularity. Dick created the glasses, album design elements, and co-vibes that propelled the enigma called **Root Boy Slim and the Sex Change Band and The Rootettes.** The Rootettes were Cherie Grasso, Micki Lee Jonnie, Kathe "Special K" Russell, and Marina "Mikki" Lee Jonne.

Photo: Root Boy and Richard H..
© KSPD

Dick Bangham, describes the band's epiphany: "When the Beatles started designing their own covers with *Revolver* and *Sgt. Pepper* I remember thinking, 'Man, I would like to do that. There's an art to this. The Beatles' designer was Peter Blake, the Andy Warhol of England."

Bangham's early influences were Spike Jones and *Mad Magazine*. His high school band was called "Peter, Paul, Almond, and Joy." He was doing freelance illustration work for the *Washington Post* then and took Root Boy down to the newspaper to meet some of the folks Dick knew, like Tom Zito and (then intern) Stephanie Mansfield. Dick proceeded and helped Root make demos which were first played on Georgetown's WGTB station.

"We were shopping them around. Joe Lee gave demo tapes to Weasel, who began to play 'Mood Ring' often on his WHFS program, and Josh Brooks, shared them with college friend Gary Katz, Steely Dan's producer. We got a call from Steely Dan's Walter Becker and Donald Fagen, and they came down to see Root Boy. They were impressed that it wasn't just a band. It was a show. They were recording their album, Asia, at that time. Katz called and asked if Root Boy wanted to record an album for Warner Brothers, so they 'discovered' Root Boy.

"Warner Brothers asked, 'Where do you want to record?' We could have gone anywhere. We said Criteria in Miami. That's where James Brown had recorded all his stuff. Clapton and the Bee Gees had recently recorded there. So that's where we went."

"Gary offered me the job of doing the Warner Brothers album (design and more) and I passed, which I really regret. The whole reason I got involved in this business was to do the art, and then I got a chance to design an album, and I said, 'Nah.'

"I'm still in touch with Gary. I've mentioned this to him a few times. He replies, 'Don't worry about it. You were having too much fun.'

"Often when Gary is interviewed, he'll be asked what his favorite and worst events in his career were, and he'll answer 'Root Boy Slim' to both questions.

"Why? Recording the Warners Brothers album was his best time, and subsequent 'album debut' Roxy show in front of the

Warner Brothers brass to present the album cuts was the worst."

Dick remembers that Root Boy "had been drinking all day, and was nervous, and he came on stage calling the Warner Brothers group 'corporate criminals.' He was sloppy. They hated him."

There wouldn't be a second Warner's album released, and they apparently paid him to go away.

On the flip side, however, Root Boy thrived and endured. Tim Craft was Bangham's friend and a Root Boy fan who was then appointed secretary to President Jimmy Carter. Dick took Root Boy to the White House, and they both sat in the Oval Office.

Sprouts

Tenor sax master Holloway recalls his first meeting with Root Boy: "The very first time I saw him; he was asleep on the couch at Track studio. I played on the song, 'Too Much Jaw Bone' about a woman who talked too much. It was the flip side of 'X-mas at K-Mark' first sat in with him at the Childe Harold in that summer of '76. I came down the steps from the dressing room, and whoa, the room was absolutely packed with two naked Go-Go girls on each side of the stage. We started playing and people went absolutely bonkers for that band. They loved Root Boy.

"Then I did few more gigs and 'X-mas at K-mart' got the band signed to Warner Brothers. I went down with them to Florida and started recording. I was there for that whole thing. We recorded the album in '77, and then sometime in '78 we did that significant gig in California. He went out there and made a very poor showing of himself. He was wasted. He had done a lot of drugs.

"He had an opening guy from DC area named David Franks (his old friend and late Fells Point MD performance artist. When Franks died, it was 'confirmed' by his friends that he had been the Poe Toaster, the secret guy who brought a wine bottle and glass to Poe's Baltimore tomb every birthday. The wine bottles stopped.)

"David opened the show in a wheelchair. He came out and his speech and the sound of his voice was very fragile. He's sitting in a wheelchair. He's telling jokes, trying to entertain all the bigwigs in the audience. Some people are like, 'I can't wait for him to get off.'

"We're backstage. And David, at one point in a very sheepish voice, said, something like, 'I hope you don't mind. I'm going to pass around a hat (to take up a collection).'

"And he does—and some gave generously. David acted like he was about to cry. He was so moved. And then he suddenly jumped up from the wheelchair and walked off stage. That's when certain people had had enough, even before they heard Slim.

"The Sex Change band broke up. Slim got tired of working with them in the early 1980s. He fired everyone but me because he didn't see me as being a part of that group. We continued in several versions of the Root Boy Slim Band, and they all had different names."

The Root Cause?

After Yale, McKenzie drove an ice cream truck in Washington, DC. One day, he experienced a psychotic break following a super high dose of LSD. He climbed over the White House fence. When they caught him, he told the U.S. Secret Service officers that he was searching for "the center of the universe." They took him to Saint Elizabeth's Hospital, our old local mental health facility in Southeast. His incident resulted in a diagnosis of schizophrenia, for which he was medicated for the remainder of his life.

Musicians during the six-album history of the band include Ernie Lancaster, Paul Reed Smith, and Steuart Smith, on guitar, bassist Bob Steel, Walter Andrews, keyboardist, Tommy Lepson, saxophonist Deanna Bogart, and drummer Tommy Ruger.

The band's original material includes "Boogie till you Puke," "I Used to be a Radical," "Christmas at Kmart," "Laundromat Blues," "Dare to be Fat," and "Mood Ring."

Foster Mackenzie III died in his sleep at his Florida home on Tuesday, June 8, 1993, at the age of forty-eight.

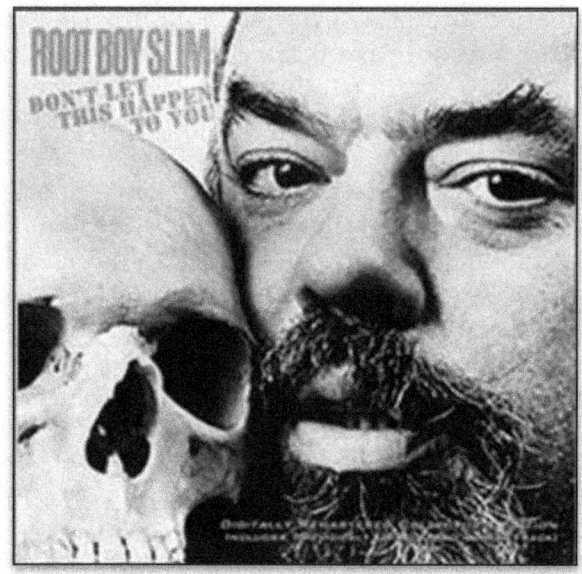

© Art/Design: Dick Bangham. Photo: Bill O'Leary

Visit https://rootboyslim.com/Store18.html
for albums and merch

Chapter 39 – Cathy Ponton King: Irish Fire

Native Washingtonian Cathy Ponton King says, "My family was from Ireland, and there were over forty families that lived in our Hyattsville, MD, area, and we'd have parties. I backed everybody up on guitar while they sang Irish ballads. I learned to play because of my Irish heritage. My grandmother was Margaret Coakley, an awesome woman who was awarded a Medal of Honor for promoting Irish music in Washington, DC.

Cathy recalls, "She had these amazing huge house parties packed with people drinking whiskey. They'd turn off the record player, and then every person had to sing—one by one. I sang these Irish rebel ballads, and the room would erupt in insane applause for me. I was just a kid, but I thought 'this is great' you know?

© Mike Peterson

© Mike Petersen

"The thing was that I had a great singing voice. The affirmation was, 'I'm worthy and I'm loved.' Everybody went crazy with applause for me."

She recalls, "Many of my friends who worked with me back then are amazing journalists today. For example, Jay Curtis was our WMUC program director and now a producer for CBS *Sunday Morning* and was a vice president of NPR. Adele Abrams was doing a WMUC rock and roll show—that's where I met her—and we decided to get an apartment together off campus around 1973. I remember all the hippies and streaking moving in to the 'Knox box' apartments on Knox Road adjacent to campus."

King became the news director and did a half hour student news show. "It was a tremendous experience learning this craft," she says. "When I first arrived the big news story was student drinking. The broadcasting studio was in Temporary Building FF (formerly the old journalism building)."

Maryland University radio was started by student, Gilbert Cullen, who built the first transmitter in 1942. Cullen went on to the Air Force in World War II and retired a successful dentist in Towson, MD, near his hometown, Baltimore. King adds, "The building was falling apart at the time I was there, so they moved us to the top of the dining hall."

Two concerts King remembers fondly in her senior year was a Root Boy Slim show, and a concert on the mall by David Bromberg, in front of the bronze statue of Testudo, the school's mascot.

After college, she landed a news job at the ABC bureau in DC. "It was around the Iranian hostage situation. I walked in one day and Barbara Walters was there working for TV and I was on the radio. I had gigs with my blues band, or I was hanging at the Childe Harold but needed to be at work at 5 a.m. The ABC night guard let me in and I took a two-hour nap on the couch. I loved every minute of it. What an opportunity."

"My next job was news director at WLMD in Laurel, Maryland. I had a radio show called *90 Seconds*. I was on the air six times a day with my radio interviews with famous people, like Chris Everett Lloyd, Julia Child, Joan Baez, Gloria Steinem, and more. I always let them say what they wanted to say."

And by the way she adds, "*The Humbler* DVD that Virginia Quesada made is brilliant. She began working on that in 1990. I went to the private premier for the DC people that were in it. I was in tears. I lost it. I was crying."

https://thehumblermovie.com/team

"However, I was working seven days a week back then but making $20,000 a year. I eventually was exhausted. I couldn't do it anymore. I wanted to be a musician and write songs.

My parents thought I was nuts giving up my job."

Danny Gatton, friend Jane, and Cathy.

Asked to name a sublime moment in her music career, Cathy says, "Playing Bethesda Blues and Jazz Club, and singing John Hiatt's song 'The River Knows,' one of my favorites to perform. It was a moment when everything was perfect. My vocal monitor. 500 people in this theater, and you could hear a pin drop. And I was singing acapella. It is profound when you hit that sweet spot. And the band came in on the second verse. It was one of those goosebump moments, and I adore John Hiatt."

Later she got the chance to open for Albert King's band at the Wax Museum in Washington, and he called her on stage to sing with his band.

She also opened for blues greats Albert Collins (shown in photo) Koko Taylor, Earl King, Bo Diddley, Hubert Sumlin, Buddy Guy, Willie Dixon, Son Seals, Paul Butterfield, Roomful of Blues (with Ronnie Earl on guitar), Marcia Ball, Sonny Landreth, the late Clarence Gatemouth Brown, and Delbert McClinton.

"My education and learning in the style and family feeling and affection with these musicians has left me with indelible memories and love for the musicians and their music and the sacrifices they made for the music. I got to know this passing generation at a time when their careers were ending, and mine was just beginning. Fortuitous timing," says Cathy, who now has four CDs of original blues, swing, rockabilly and ballads.

One of Cathy Ponton King's first pro gigs was playing Matt Kane's Irish bar at age seventeen. "It was the only Irish bar in those days where everyone went who was transplanted from Ireland such as my grandmother. Across the street from the *Washington Daily News*. Authentic Irish bar with many journalists hanging out. A guy named Frank was the manager and a week after I started there, he was arrested for running guns to JFK airport to give to the IRA."

While playing there the word got out there was going to be to be a new fancy Irish bar, called the Dubliner, with music. "So, it was only natural for me go audition. My father took me down there. He knew one of the owners who was this wonderful man named Danny Coleman.

"When I arrived for the audition there was Johnny Puleo, a famous harmonica player I'd seen on TV shows appearing with his harmonica gang. He was world famous, and he wanted the Dubliner job. But he lost the gig to Kathy. Back then Irish clubs would hire adult "little people" for entertainment because they were small like Leprechauns.

"Puleo, the 4-foot-11-inch little person (technically a dwarf) knew DC well, as he was born here on October 7, 1907. Once a local newsboy, he went on to play the Palladium in London, perform for the King and Queen of England, and entertain Presidents Roosevelt, Truman, and Nixon. He played "Max" in the film, Trapeze. He died of a heart attack at Holy Cross Hospital in 1983 at age seventy-four.

Cathy's group and Billy McComiskey, an acclaimed accordionist from New York City with his "Irish Tradition" group, started Irish music at the Dubliner. Cathy adds, "Billy lives in Baltimore now, but he still travels all over the world playing."

Chapter 40 – Crazy for Ken Ludwig

Arch Campbell is one of the best, and definitely the funniest entertainment critics this town has ever known. When asked to come up with his favorite theatrical experiences he offered, "Number one, the reworking of *Amadeus* at the National Theatre. It was wonderful to watch that coming together and how good it was. My second was the premier of *Crazy for You* by Ken Ludwig who became a good friend of mine.

"And, you know, if you're writing about DC you've got to talk to Ken Ludwig, our local playwright," insisted Arch, adding *Crazy for You* got a bad review in the *Washington Post*. "And of course I went on the air, but what Ken didn't know is that I grew up with a father who revered George Gershwin, the way people now revere the Beatles and the Rolling Stones. So, I loved his Gershwin play. I did my Channel 4 review that night and gave *Crazy for You* four stars. All the ads quoted me in it after that. The play went on to New York and did quite well. Ken credits me with saving *Crazy for You*.

"Of course, it always pays to follow Arch Campbell's advice so I made an appointment with Mr. Ludwig, and 'wowie zowie,' I met a playwright who is nothing short of astounding."

Ken Ludwig was born in York, PA, ninety miles from the Washington, DC, line. He completed his undergraduate work at Harvard and pursued further academics at Cambridge, but he always knew he wanted to be a playwright. "My parents said, 'You better get a day job because how can you support yourself being in theater?'"

"So, my day job became working for a big law firm in Washington, DC, called Steptoe and Johnson for four years.

And then one day I get a call from a friend of a friend who had given one of my plays to somebody in England. I next received a call in my little apartment from **Sir Andrew Lloyd Weber**. 'I love this play. I want to produce it,' he said. That call was exciting."

This news wasn't completely out of the blue. Ken explained, "I was talking to an English director at a party three days before the call. He told me, 'I hear you write good things and I'd love to read one of your works.' I had just finished *Lend Me A Tenor*. And he sent a copy to Andrew."

Prior to that fateful call which launched Ludwig's career to the West End he had success with two plays done in DC church basements and one—Sullivan and Gilbert—commercially done and produced at the Eisenhower Theater at the Kennedy Center and also for the National Theater of Canada. "That one had some wonderful people: Fritz Weaver as Gilbert, and Noel Harrison as Sir Arthur Sullivan."

Back to *Lend Me a Tenor*: "So Andrew flew me to London and next I'm working with him and staying at his house in London. He just kept me there for six months because we had to cast the play, choose the designers. We became friends. Your producer's the one who puts all the money up and makes the artistic choices. They need to be represented, And Andrew had only produced two other plays that weren't by him at that time.

"Your producer's the one who puts all the money up and makes artistic choices. They want to be represented. He produces *Lend Me a Tenor* and it opens at the Globe Theater (1986) now called the Gielgud Theater, to great reviews. It's a big, big hit, and Andrew produces it in New York on Broadway (1989), so I really felt I was on my way.

"The next thing that happened has a DC connection. I get a call out of out the blue from an American named Roger Horchow, who had started the Horchow Collection, the first luxury mail-order catalog with no brick-and-mortar presence that he had sold to Neiman Marcus in 1988. So he had made a good deal of money on that. Roger wanted to produce a Broadway musical, and he had acquired the rights to use the music of George and Ira Gershwin in a musical. He called me and asked if I would like to write it. I answered, 'I sure would,' so I wrote *Crazy for You* and we tried it out here at the National Theatre. We rehearsed in New York, of course, and brought it down here at the National. It ran for five years on Broadway Schubert Theater. And we won the Tony Award for Best Musical. And it was simultaneously then produced in London, where it played at the Prince Edward Theater for years. And we won the Olivier Award for best musical there."

I interrupted Ken and questioned whether he had any reservations about adapting the world's greatest music into his own play—a play that might not be worthy of this genius music.

He answered, "I do know what you're feeling. It is the greatest music. There were three great composers and lyricists in the *American Songbook*—Gershwin, Irving Berlin, and Cole Porter. It was a great responsibility, but it was a great joy. A great joy."

I asked him if he was confident he could do it.

Ken answered: "Yeah, I was good. And this was the first of what we now call the jukebox musicals. That is taking the work of a single artist and creating a new storyline and a new musical. *Mama Mia* then did it also. I've had six on Broadway, eight in the West End. My plays are all around the world. I fly around the world visiting my shows. Yeah. I hope I'm not boasting when I say at this moment, I'm the most produced playwright in the United States."

The list of Ken Ludwig's plays:

A Comedy of Tenors	*Shakespeare In Hollywood*
An American in Paris	*Sherwood: The Adventures of Robin Hood*
Baskerville: A Sherlock Holmes	*The Advetures of Tom Sawyer*
Be My Baby	*The Beaux' Stratagem*
Crazy for You	*The Fox on the Fairway*
Dear Jack, Dear Louise	*The Game's Afoot.*
Leading Ladies.	*The Gods of Comedy*
Lend Me a Tenor	*The Three Musketeers*
Midsummer/Jersey	*Tiny Tim's Christmas Carol.*
Moon Over Buffalo	*Treasure Island- Twentieth Century*
Murder on the Orient Express	*Twas the Night Before Christmas*
Postmortem	

Finally, I asked him what makes Washington, DC, special to him.

"I love it here," he states. "I love the community. It's a very artistic community. There's tons of arts and theaters. Friends all over town, I like being here. I don't like the idea of living in New York. I always felt there'd be too much pressure on me there. I would hear and see what other playwrights are doing all the time. I'd go, oh my God, I'd be comparing myself to them, and it would've put me into a tangle.

"By being here, I could ignore what's happening in New York. I'm not a big fan of big cities. I grew up in a small town. York, Pennsylvania. I like the smallness of it here in DC, I like the atmosphere, I mean, it's not small. I live in a house where I've got sidewalks all around me, and a big backyard. It was a wonderful place to raise my children. I like the schools. I like everything about it. I'm a huge, huge fan of DC. Mm-Hmm!

"And I've flourished here because of my happiness in living here. Wow. I would not have been happy (in the big cities). I came here and settled immediately in my twenties. I've never thought about living any place else."

Courtesy Ken Ludwig

Chapter 41 – Patty Reese: Showbiz Phenom

"With a voice like honey and sand, Patty Reese can hold her own with any other soul struck singers. Her sense of dynamics brings out the drama inherent in any good song—and she can write them too."

Michael Jaworek
Birchmere Promoter

The youngest of seven siblings, Patty Reese, grew up in a happy house where everybody played different kinds of music in everyone's bedrooms. "But for whatever reason, I was the only one who grew up wanting to play an instrument," says Patty. "I recorded myself singing, and I was in tears. I was so bad. I wasn't a singer. I became a guitar player and started a folk trio."

"I heard a lot of blues and soul, like James Brown. I loved classic blues and folk, like Simon and Garfunkel. They listened to different music, and I loved it all.

"Then, in the tenth grade, I met my choir director. Mrs. Hagyard taught me how to sing. I was just a sponge to how this French Horn player directed the choir, how she warmed us up and showed us how to sit and breathe and she taught me addition. She's ninety-seven now and we are still dear friends.

Patty and Mrs. Hagyard

"The music term 'addition' can mean expanding a singer's range, enhancing vocal agility, and incorporating new stylistic elements into their singing. Mrs. Hagyard was everything. She pulled me out as a soloist as time went on. I did all the talent shows. She's a legend from Springbrook. She touched so many people. Some days, she would say, 'We're not going to do music today at all. We will talk about life.' She'd go see the Ballet and take a cruise in the winter. I totally learned music from her.

"By my senior year, my first class was Madrigals, my second was music theory, and my third was choir. Then I had lunch. I took choir from a little lady named Lois Schultz, who was also my guitar teacher. I didn't like opera, but I sang classical music."

The Epiphany

"I woke up one morning and was listening to my clock radio. It was Cerphe Colwell on station WAVA, and he played a song by an artist I had never heard, Bonnie Raitt. When I heard Bonnie, I knew I could be a professional singer. This changed my life. I'm qualified.

© S. Moore

"When I graduated from high school, I sang in five languages and auditioned for the University of Maryland as a voice major—a first soprano. I also had a band called Island, so I sang classical music during the day and rocked out vocally at night. We worked fifty nights a year. I joined the band to see if I had the vocal stamina to do it.

"Meanwhile, my mother was trying to protect me. She had grown up on a Pennsylvania mountain. My real father was a police officer, and he had committed suicide before I was born. She had four children, and she remarried, and he had four children. We all moved in together. It was exciting. It was an eventful time. Lots of crying, black light posters, cops, and I was like Switzerland (neutral in times of conflict). Mom didn't really know what was going on sometimes. She thought we were just 'acting up.'"

Her acting over the years now has been recognized by the Washington Area Music Association with seventeen awards, "Wammies," including Album of the Year, Artist of the Year, Songwriter of the Year, Best Roots Rock Album, Roots Rock Vocalist, and Artist Website (www.pattyreese.com). Performances include significant venues and festivals including supporting international artists: Beth Hart, Greg Allman, Buddy Guy, Aretha Franklin, Little Feat, Ruthie Foster, and others.

Greatest Achievement:

When asked what her most significant achievements in life are. Why are you so important? Patty thinks for ten seconds and answers, "I think one of the reasons is because I just won't go away. I work a lot. I did over 200 dates in 2023. But I also tried to straddle the fence where I've done a lot of songwriting and albums, and I don't insist on just doing original shows."

Musician Magazine said it might be because of "the uniqueness and flexibility of her voice, combined with the maturity, polish, and professionalism of her songwriting...stirred in the cauldron of personal and performance experience, make her a triple-threat—*une chanteuse* extraordinaire...one special talent."

Reese is also a favorite of some of DC's influential and stellar artists, including David Chappell, Ron Newmyer, Tommy Lepson and scores of musicians live and on her albums. She is readily reciprocal because she always appears to enjoy praising others more than taking credit herself.

First Approach on Recording

"It's important to work with people you know what they will bring to the party: Their style and where they hang out musically. I bring them to my house first and kind of hash things out. I play them what I've written, and we get an arrangement with the rhythm section first. For example, Sonny Petrosky (drums) and Andy Hamburger (bass) do the rhythm tracks, and I sing and play, and we take it from there. I always make sure I keep my dummy vocal track because on a number of these, I kept that track as the real track because sometimes it's just the first time you do it, you're like, 'Hey, it's not going to get any better than that.'"

2024 DC Legends concert © Brooke Lowe

On guitarist David Chappell

This Washington, DC, native is one of the most sought after and respected musicians in the area. He has won Washington Area Music Awards,

"Wammies," for Musician of the Year, Rock Instrumentalist of the Year, and Roots Rock.

"David is a singer's dream. He surrounds what you're singing and knows exactly where to fill in and what coloration to play. He doesn't step on you. He's like a kid, too, because I don't think he's ever gotten burnt out or tired of playing. He just wants to play. He's a joy in the studio. And we just have an excellent rapport and a great time together. One funny adventure with David:

"We were playing the Cat's Eye Pub in Fells Point around 2010, and Ursula Ricks, a Baltimore legend blues singer, is in the room. I ask Ursula to come on up and sing, So while Ursula is singing—and unknown to me—Dave is behind me, mouthing off to some obnoxious drunk guy standing near the stage. They are in conflict.

"The guy is making comments on how Ursula should be singing. So, he comes up on the stage, but I think he has a pen and wants Dave to sign something. But no, he has a knife.

"Meanwhile, there's a guy outside who always walked up and down Fell's Point, where the musicians play. He is known as the Angel of Mercy. He's this black dude who looks like he lifts weights and always wears a weightlifting belt and wears a white tank top T-shirt. He usually waits around at night's end and helps everybody load out. He will make about five bucks, and he's a nice guy.

"So, this drunk guy comes up on the stage with a knife, and precisely at that moment—and I kid you not—the door busts open, and it's the Angel of Mercy of Fells Point. He walks in and shouts, 'In the name of Jesus Christ, I command you to drop that knife.'

"Meanwhile, the bartender and Ursula all have straight razors out—ready to go at this guy. Dave and I are the only people who don't have weapons.

"Then the guy with the knife and the Angel of Mercy leave the club. David and I just look at each other. What happened? And David is cool. He just wants to play."

Chapter 42 – The Stoneman Family

Many of the early country and bluegrass stars like Bill Monroe, the Stanley Brothers, and the Carter Family made regular stops in Washington, DC, on their tours. Luckily, the talented Stoneman family, known for their traditional mountain music roots, made DC their home. Their story is all about blending their rural music roots with city life and adapting their traditions to handle the changes of the modern world.

Ernest "Pop" Stoneman came from the remote Blue Ridge Mountains of southern Virginia, a region known as "The Crooked Road" with a rich mix of Anglo-Celtic music traditions and deep poverty. As a talented fiddler, Pop found some early success recording "old-timey" country and religious songs for Okeh Records during a prewar folk music revival. He caught the attention of famed talent scout Ralph Peer, who was on the lookout for genuine "hillbilly music," and Pop even went on to help Peer with the historic 1927 Bristol recording session that launched the Carter Family's career. His own plans were disrupted when musical tastes shifted from old-timey hits like Pop's song "The Titanic" to the newer country-blues style of Jimmie Rodgers, a change that made Washington, DC, a more attractive place for steady work and music gigs.

Although their farm was doing reasonably well, the 1929 economic crash hit large families like the Stoneman's hard. With little public assistance available, they left Galax in 1932, with Pop driving their old truck three hundred miles north to find work around DC. They first moved into an abandoned house at 1205 King Street in Alexandria but struggled with poverty and the large family faced frequent evictions. They lived in Franconia briefly before moving several times to homes across Washington. In 1938, a *Washington Times* reporter highlighted their struggle, noting, "Stoneman, a carpenter, can't find work either in his line or anything else."

Pop Stoneman took on odd jobs and carpentry work, while his musically talented children earned money by performing at grocery stores, car dealerships, and, if they were lucky, on local radio station WJSV. In 1932, Pop landed a radio gig where he did sketch comedy with family songs, introducing Washingtonians to the "Galax sound" while playing into popular hillbilly stereotype.

In 1941, they finally got a vacant lot in Carmody Hills, Maryland, near the southeast border of DC where Pop built a one-room house from discarded lumber to accommodate their large family. Even so, they were in dire straits, and the children had to steal coal from a nearby railroad yard to keep the house warm.

Fortunately, Pop found some success playing music regularly to support his family and keep their spirits up during tough times. Initially performing as Pop Stoneman and his Little Pebbles and later as the Blue Grass Champs, Pop and his gifted kids played at DC clubs and nearby music parks like New River Ranch. They brought authentic "hillbilly" music to Washington and left a lasting impact on the folk and bluegrass scene for generations.

The Stoneman family gained greater success thanks to country music impresario Connie B. Gay. In 1946 Gay was working as a promoter for the new radio station WARL, and while on his mission to make DC into "Nashville North," held a talent contest at Constitution Hall to find acts for his upcoming show. The Stonemans wowed the crowd and received regular spots on Gay's innovative country-music TV show. They also performed frequently at Club Hillbilly in Seat Pleasant for two years, where Gay had influence over the management. For many years, the Blue Grass Champs were regulars at many of DC's gritty honkytonks like The Famous and The Ozarks.

Family members occasionally teamed up with three key DC bluegrass musicians—John Duffey, Bill Emerson, and Charlie Waller—who would later form the Country Gentlemen. With Jimmy's powerful bass, Donna's bright mandolin, and Van's steady rhythm guitar, the Blue Grass Champs held their own with other local talents in Washington, DC, including Roy Clark, Patsy Cline, Link Wray, and Charlie Daniels. Historian Charles Wolfe notes that Scott Stoneman "single-handedly dragged country fiddle into the 20th century." Pop's many talented children eventually left an impact on modern country, bluegrass, and rockabilly.

> GENERAL carpenter would like to hear from home owners reg. to any kind rep. work; ref. Mr. Stoneman, WE. 3051 eve.

Washington Times, October 14, 1937

During World War II, the influx of military personnel with rural roots into Washington broadened the Stonemans' audience. They started playing bluegrass standards by Bill Monroe, hits by Johnny Cash, and even Bob Dylan covers. The Champs became regulars on local TV, performing a lively half-hour of country and bluegrass on WTTG-TV Channel 5. Their first album, *Blue Grass Champs: Live from the Don Owens Show*, featured both traditional tunes like "Little Cabin Home on the Hill" and the 1957 hit "Tequila." In 1955, Pop Stoneman won $20,000 on the TV game show *The Big Question* thanks to his geography skills, and a few years later, his daughter Roni Stoneman became a familiar face on *Hee Haw*.

Even as they struggled through the Depression and beyond, the Stoneman children continued performing in DC and in Galax into the 1980s, playing at college campuses and folk festivals, connecting with audiences who appreciated their traditional sound. Pop Stoneman and His Little Pebbles found they could at least partially thrive in DC, where local support helped the talented family through tough times. playing on the stage, radio, and TV. Forty years after his death, Pop Stoneman was finally inducted into the Country Music Hall of Fame in 2008.

DC Favorites

© S. Moore

Dudley Dale Connell (born February 18, 1956) is an American singer in the bluegrass tradition. He is best known for his work with The Johnson Mountain Boys, Longview, and the Seldom Scene. In Sept of 2020 Connell was inducted into the International Bluegrass Hall of Fame (IBMA) with the Johnson Mountain Boys.

Ruthie Logsdon is lead vocalist, rhythm guitarist and songwriter for critically acclaimed Ruthie and the Wranglers, and The Porch Delights. Along with her bands, she has racked up more than twenty-five Washington Area Music Awards including Artist of the Year, Best Country Vocalist, and Songwriter of the Year.

Chapter 43 – Back to Bluegrass

In 1986 I convinced John Duffey, original member and founder of Washington DC's pioneering bluegrass bands, The Country Gentlemen and The Seldom Scene, to give me an interview for this Capital Acts book. After months of pestering him at the second Birchmere where the Scene played every Thursday night, he finally invited me to his home. There I discovered a different Duffey from the stage artist. He talked slower. He was kind and relaxed. I had heard from others that John was a gentler person off the stage. They were right.

On stage he needed to be noticed, play astonishing bluegrass mandolin, and say things that made him stand out. But at his house that day—away from performing—there were few hints of the wise-cracking, slightly threatening Alpha male that some feared. We talked all day, and I left his house with four ninety-minute cassettes filled with his story in his own words.

These tapes became the basis of my 2018 book, *John Duffey's Bluegrass Life: Featuring the Country Gentlemen, the Seldom Scene, and Washington DC*, co-authored with G.T. Keplinger, with a Foreword by Tom Gray.

Opening the interview with a question about his father, a Washingtonian, John told me: "My father sang opera for twenty-five years and cut six sides for Columbia records in 1913. Dad was fifty-four years old when I was born and had long left the Met company when he moved back to Washington. I have the records by my father, but they are very old and thick 78 rpm's and are warped so badly. Plus, they play backward to the way records play today. I got to hear one of them at the Capitol Transcriptions recording studio on 11th Street."

Five-string Banjo

Duffey shared his bluegrass discovery: "One day I happened to be cruising the radio dial. I was about thirteen [1947] when I heard a banjo. A five-string banjo. I thought, 'Boy that's a neat sound.' And I started listening to that station. In those days they called it 'hillbilly music.'

"It was Bill Monroe and His Blue Grass Boys that really turned me on—music that caught my ear. And Flatt & Scruggs, Hank Williams, and Carl Smith. The music I'm involved with now.

"Other than just the sound of the banjo that appealed and fascinated me, I began to appreciate the fact that there was a lot of talent there. And once I saw an act that I'd been listening to on records, and then I went to see them live—gee, everything was right there. It sounded just like it did on the record. That's impressive."

John's saved paper route money allowed him to buy a Martin model 00 guitar to replace his warped Harmony. He couldn't afford the D model he preferred at the cost of $125, but his $70 did the trick for the Martin-00.

"My Martin made all the difference in the world and really got me interested in the music because I could play it and it sounded good, and it didn't come apart in a month."

In 1951, John was a junior at Bethesda-Chevy Chase high school. He'd catch the school bus at 7:30 a.m. on River Road a few blocks from his house. The school didn't start until nine, so he always arrived early.

"It was the last stop with miles to go and boy, that was a hike if you missed the bus. They opened the school cafeteria for us kids to hang out before school began so I start taking my guitar. Some kids began to gather around me and then 'lord' I find out there are about a dozen kids that could play guitar and one kid, **Sterling Ellsworth**, had a bass. So, we started these morning guitar sessions in the school cafeteria."

It was Doctor Sterling Ellsworth, an acclaimed clinical psychologist living in Eugene, Oregon, when we reached him in 2018 to contribute to *John Duffey's Bluegrass Life*. The then eighty-five-year-old Dr. Ellsworth noted this was the first time anyone had ever asked him about playing music with John Duffey.

Rainbow Mountain Boys

Dr. Ellsworth told us: "I was a senior, playing bass in the school orchestra. I had an old German bass fiddle but was getting tired of playing with a bow. I met John and we started in on learning bluegrass songs along with Bobby Slack on mandolin, and another student from Wilson High School named David Swann on banjo, with me plucking the bass. We called ourselves the 'Rainbow Mountain Boys.' I lived a few blocks from school, so John, David and I would go to my house for lunch, and practice with Bobby joining up after school."

When asked what kind of kid Duffey was, Ellsworth answered, "John was very shy. Shy people are not comfortable in social situations where impromptu communication is required. So, John concentrated on music and singing, which is set and predictable. He didn't do sports or have any girlfriends that I knew about. And I never met his folks. He was just a very nice kid dedicated to learning the music. Music was our fun. We practiced every day and got pretty good. John could play, sing and yodel very well. Finally, we entered a ten-school [Montgomery County, MD] talent contest."

"John sang and yodeled on a song called 'Chime Bells Are Ringing.' When we got to the end of the song Duffey extended the high note for as long as he could while Bobby played mandolin lines.

"When John finally ran out of breath, he ended the song. The audiences cheered. And we won the School Assembly talent contest and received a one-hundred-dollar war bond as the top prize." These talent shows were carried on two radio stations, WWDC and WASH on Saturday evenings. This was Duffey's first time on radio.

Sterling left for college in Chicago after high school to become a doctor, departing before the prized war bond arrived. When he returned to DC for Christmas break, he found out John had spent his share of the prize money.

The Rainbow Mountain Boys. 1951 (l to r) John Duffey, Bobby Slack, Sterling Ellsworth, and David Swann. They were playing on Saturday evening radio shows on WASH-FM and WWDC AM after winning the radio station contest.

Rather than duplicate the rich bluegrass history of the DC area here in *Capital Acts*, we offer the *Bluegrass Unlimited* review and free chapter of *John Duffey's Bluegrass Life* @ **https://assets.booklocker.com/pdfs/10346s.pdf**

> It is rare to come across a book that so perfectly matches its subject matter in content and style, but here we have it in a revealing, kaleidoscopic, entertaining biography of the great singer and bandleader John Duffey, written by Stephen Moore and G.T. Keplinger.
>
> I only knew Duffey as a fan, listener, and a one-time co-conspirator in trying to get money out of a promoter at a rainy festival our bands had played at. I still consider him the most complex, talented, entertaining personality ever to take a bluegrass stage. That's why I can recommend this book wholeheartedly. It's every bit as multi-faceted, funny, and entertaining as Duffey was. Using John's own words, along with contributions from eighty-two of his friends, associates and bandmates, this biography does not shy away from the

more difficult aspects of his life, which is as John would have wanted.

For the second generation of bluegrass artists, Duffey was possibly the most influential—not only in his recording and performing with seminal bands such as the Country Gentlemen and the Seldom Scene, but also with his inclusion of songs from other genres into the bluegrass repertoire while still retaining the unique tone and sound of bluegrass. He was the link from Bill Monroe to Sam Bush.

The book includes fifty rare photographs and a thorough discography of Duffey's recording career. I rarely use the word "essential" in reviews, but this one has earned it. Moore and Keplinger have written an essential and entertaining book on the larger-than-life John Duffey.

CVS. Bluegrass Unlimited

John and Nancy Duffey at the White House
© Theresa Williams

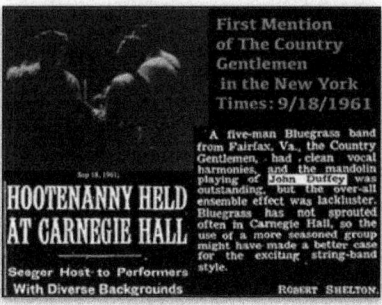

"First Mention of the Country Gentlemen," in national press.

John Duffey's name highlighted for our book.

Chapter 44 – Lepson & Crews
Featuring Steve Houk, Living on Music

Richard "Tommy" Lepson is a preeminent musician known for his versatility as a singer on keyboard and guitar. Born on April 22, 1951, in Washington DC, he grew up in Hyattsville, MD, and kick-started his career in junior high, where he first sang and played guitar. He knew music would be his life when he joined a local rock band, TL and the Barons, performing at regional teen dances.

By 1979, he had progressed to the local band "Cryin' Out Loud," whose lineup included Steuart Smith on electric guitar (now playing with The Eagles), Bob Coleman (on bass), and drummer, Steve Dennis. They earned a trusted reputation for covering classic soul by Al Green, Ray Charles, and local DC master Marvin Gaye.

In 2020, Emmy-winning TV veteran/music journalist Steve Houk, host of *Living On Music* on YouTube and lead singer with several DC-area bands, added Lepson to his twenty-plus year interview roster of both DC area musicians and world-famous ones like David Crosby, Derek Trucks, Steve Earle, John Hiatt, Richard Thompson, Paul Barrere, George Winston, and Herb Alpert. You can check out his list of DC-area musicians he's interviewed at the end of this chapter. We thank Steve for permission to share this edited version of their 2020 LOM discussion.

Q: You've been doing this music professionally since you were fourteen and have become a music institution as both performer, and studio musician with brothers and sisters like Patty Reese and Tom Principato, and appearing with national acts like the Kinks, Captain Beefheart, The Fabulous Thunderbirds, NRBQ, and the Righteous Brothers. You are in the Washington Area Music Awards Hall of Fame with a dozen Wammies.

I loved how one of the websites described you as being capable of "conjuring up James Brown, in one minute and Sam Cooke the next."

That's not a bad duo to have your voice compared to. I will say it is my great pleasure welcoming, one of my favorite local musicians and one of the real institutions around here. Tommy Lipson is here tonight. Hey, Tommy. How are you, man?

A: I'm doing good. Good to see you. Yeah. My daughter, son-in-law, and my granddaughter—they're listening right now. So, I'm saying "hi."

Q. How did music begin for you? How did you get that kind of musical thing in your heart and soul that early?

A: Well, I was always amazed at people that could play instruments. My Dad and I used to ride in the car and sing to the radio. I saw a band play when I was young. That really impressed me. I thought that was really cool. And then when I was about twelve years old, my cousin took me to University of Maryland to hear a live group called the Van Dykes from Baltimore. That really changed my whole view of things right there.

I remember standing there staring at these guys, and they all got off the stage and started talking to me. They were real nice to this this little kid. I didn't get in the way. I was good, you know? That made an impression on me. And then I ran into this guy who was played in the teen club, and he said he would give me instructions if I wanted to learn how to play something.

At the 2024 Bandhouse Gigs DC Legends show.
© S. Moore

So, I got together with him with an acoustic guitar. I learned the note names on the guitar, and that about as far as that got. He, he tried to show me (more) stuff, and I said, "No, no. I'll get it." I just wanted to know how to tune the thing. I figured out how to play it. And then a buddy of mine, Ronnie, lived behind me, and I started a little band when we were like thirteen. And, with a drummer, Kim Miller who lives two blocks from me now. And we played at Saint Andrew's Episcopal Church, parish Hall for the kids. That was a big, big hit then.

Q. One of the things you are most known for is playing the Hammond B-3 organ and those dazzling keys. Musicians like Danny Gatton and everybody love your playing. How did you evolve from guitar to keys?

A: I was sort of enthralled with the way the bass worked with the drummer. So, my first instrument was really bass guitar. I got that pretty much down and played that through high school and soul bands in high school.

Jimmy Cerone, the guitar player from that group, is no longer with us anymore. Jimmy and I went to The Byrd's Nest in Silver Spring. Charlie Byrd's place. We were underage but they let us in for the show: "Just sit there and listen and be quiet."

And I saw the Jimmy Smith Trio. He was playing a B-3 playing and the bass pedals, and I said, "Man. I gotta do that. That is it. Right there."

And then I heard Felix Cavalier play with the Young Rascals, and, and then it was all over. That's what I gotta do! I have to own an organ. You know? That changed me right there.

Q. Is it a big leap to go from guitar to keyboards, or were you able to pretty much evolve right through?

A: No, no. I kind of faked my way through a lot of it. I mean, I knew the note names on the piano, so I figured out the basic chords and stuff, and I moved my fingers a certain way, I'll get a certain sound. So I just sat and poked around on it until it felt right. And I started playing with people and nobody complained, so I guess it was all right.

Q. Yeah. I guess it's been all right. (laughs) I think it worked out.

A: I play by ear, but lately I've been trying to teach myself how to read music. So "look out," you know?

The Assassins (l-to-r): Brian Alpert (drums), Jimmy Thackery (lead guitar, vocals), Wade Matthews (bass, vocals), Tommy Lepson (lead vocals, guitar, keyboard), Bruce Harrison (keyboards, vocals) and Alex Holland (saxophones, vocals).

Q. Tell us about the music you started out with.

A: We were playing rock 'n' roll that was on the radio. Buddy Holly and some of the British music that was out. The guitar player and I wrote a song together. My dad drove us down to Edgewood Studios, and we recorded a 45 and asked the guy to make us a copy, and he said we'd have to record it again. We got two copies of our song. God knows what happened to those. We were fourteen.

Q. As you got in more into music down the line and, started to get things going, there was a band called The Assassins, that was really important to you. It was originally known as Jimmy Thackery and the Assassins in order to capitalize on the name recognition Jimmy had achieved after fourteen years of solid touring with the Nighthawks. Tell us how that band evolved and what it meant to you at that stage in your career.

A: I knew Wade Matthews, the bass player, for that group a long time. He told me they were looking for a singer. I didn't quite get that at first. But next they played a benefit at the Bayou for David Brinks, a great sax player and arranger who had passed away. And at the benefit I got up and sang Ray Charles's "I Got News For You."

After that everybody said, "Hey, who is this guy? He might be a good guy to get to sing for the Assassins, and they asked me to do it. I said, sure. Okay. Sounds like a cool thing to do."

Q Wow. How did that mold your musical like career. Did it give you a path?

A: So, there were a lot of bands that go way back go way back. But the Assassins were cool because we were traveling and playing around the country. I think in one year we put 1110,000 miles on a leased van. But I was with them for three years, and we did a lot of traveling, played some cool shows, played Robert Cray's birthday party for Polygram and in New York at the Hard Rock Café [in] New York. A lot of neat things.

Q. Tell us about Danny Gatton.

A: Danny was a great guy. I could sit and talk cars with him all day long about cars. He called me and said he was doing some recording, and he wanted me to come and play some organ on some stuff. And I said, "Well, how does it go? What are we doing?"

"You don't need to hear it. You'll be fine," he said. I thought *Oh, oh, look out!* So, I went to work with him in the studio, and this was for his *88 Elmira Street* record (1991). [The title is a reference to Gatton's Anacostia home as a child, and Tommy is credited playing a Hammond B-3 on the cut "Quiet Village".] I had a question about some chord in one of the songs. I asked "What's this chord you're playing here?"

And he says, "Well, I don't know, let's see. You got a G here and there' s a D down here, and you hold your hand this way. Just play that stuff you do on the organ. Just do whatever you do."

Danny was an easygoing guy to work with. And, we had gotten together before he left us. I was supposed to do a CD with him and join his group. Yeah. He said you know, if you do this CD with me, you are going to have to go out on the road and tour with me. And I said, "Yeah I know."

That would have been a lot of fun, and certainly a big thing for me. And, it would have certainly forced me to play a lot better. <laugh>

Q. That's for sure. I remember talking to Dave Chappell about his experiences with Danny and what an influence—cross the board—on a lot of different people.

A: Oh, yeah. Absolutely. And it's the kind of thing where you, don't realize the weight of the whole thing until it's gone. And you go, wait, wow. You know that's the way it is.

Q. Can you talk a little bit about Root Boy? He has an incredible reputation, both good and crazy. Give us some examples that make him live up to that reputation.

A: Well, some things I can't repeat on the air. It was a real thrill working with him. His name was Foster Mackenzie, and his nickname was Ken. So, I called him Ken.

The one thing that Ken taught me was to laugh at myself and don't take things so seriously. And that was a good lesson for me because before that I was very serious that I had to get everything perfect. And that's not the way it really goes.

Ken was a lot of fun to work with. Very unpredictable on a show, but the musicianship was great. Songs were a lot of fun to play. Nothing was sacred. He slammed everything. And he always had a very interesting way with words. It was a very good learning experience for me as far as songwriting goes, too.

Q. Oh, I bet. That had to be an experience and a half on several levels. Tell us a little bit about Urban Funk. They were a big part of your life your life back then as well.

A: Urban Funk was a cool band. Um, I was going to sing for them, but we needed a guitar player. Steve Long, the keyboard player, was a really strong soloist. There were several guitar players that were interested in playing at the time, but we had to rehearse and learn the songs. I said, "Well, I can play some of the stuff, you know, on the guitar, at least for us to learn the material." So that's what I did.

They didn't need a guitar guy doing all this flashy stuff. So, I just played some small rhythm stuff, a few leads here and there. Very abbreviated stuff. And it was good for me. It was, very, very enjoyable. But it got to be hard to book a seven-piece group at the time. But it was a good band. Maybe we'll get back together and play.

Chapter 45 - Select Radio Signals (AM)

It was Thomas Edison who led the US Naval Consulting Board in recommending that the US Congress establish a central naval research laboratory, charged with identifying and shepherding state-of-the-art military inventions. The Naval Research Laboratory [NRL] opened in July 1923, initially with a five-building campus on the east bank of the Potomac River at Bellevue in the District of Columbia.

The NRL played a significant role in advancing the field of radio technology and its applications. Some key contributions to the invention and development of radio technology include wireless communications and antenna design, frequency modulation (FM), radar technology, and satellite communication.

Arthur Godfrey

"The Old Redhead" was born in New York City on August 31, 1903. He served in the United States Navy from 1920-24. Additional radio training came during Godfrey's service in the Coast Guard from 1927 to 1930.

He passed a stringent qualifying examination and was admitted to the prestigious Radio Materiel School at the Naval Research Laboratory graduating in 1929.

His radio career got its start in a Baltimore beer emporium during the Prohibition Era from 1920 to 1933 while still an enlisted man in the Coast Guard. Godfrey, with several companions, heard a 1929 radio program featuring amateurs. His fellow Coast Guardsmen, who had heard him plunk a banjo, suggested he try out.

The group went to the WFBR radio station studio, which welcomed them as it did all comers, and offered Godfrey a trial. He was given a spot on the show, and soon a sponsor was found for him. The pay was $5 for a fifteen-minute weekly performance.

CAPITAL TO GET WJZ NETWORK BY WMAL

Operation of New Lease to Begin Tomorrow; Varied Features Included.

After several delays, the programs of the WJZ network will be brought into Washington, via WMAL, beginning tomorrow morning. The Federal Radio Commission authorized the leasing of the station to the National Broadcasting Co. yesterday.

Operation of WMAL under the NBC banner means a new set of programs, most of which have never been broadcast over a ..ashington station.

The first broadcast to be heard over WMAL Thursday morning will be the "Breakfast Club," a new feature to be broadcast daily, except Sunday, from 7 to 9. This program will feature news flashes, weather, time and temperature announcements, and music. Arthur Godfrey will be master of ceremonies.

Washington DC's WMAL AM station went live in 1933 with its first broadcaster, Arthur Godfrey. "The Old Redhead" as he became nicknamed.

Radio broadcasters of the time had a formal, somewhat aloof style, their stiff upper lips coming through the radio speaker. Godfrey recognized that a folksier approach would set him apart. What most traditional radio personalities didn't realize, he told *The Washington Post* in 1972, "The audience is one person sitting in a room, and if there are two, they're probably fighting. I saw that you have to talk to that one person."

In 1929, he earned $5 for fifteen minutes, and Godfrey ended his radio career in 1972 after forty-three years, except for a break after his bout with cancer.

Godfrey was married in 1938 to Mary Bourke. He had two sons and a daughter. His first TV show, *Arthur Godfrey Talent Scouts*, aired on Dec. 8, 1948. His program introduced Pat Boone, The Chordettes, Roy Clark, Patsy Cline, Vic Damone, Shari Lewis, McGuire Sisters, Barbara McNair, Johnny Nash, Carmel Quinn, and June Valli.

CBS bought a Broadway theater around 1950 and turned it into the studio from which Godfrey's and Sullivan's were broadcast. After both men were gone, they named it "The Ed Sullivan Theater," and David Letterman took over. Today, Stephen Colbert uses it.

The first commercial color program, presented by sixteen sponsors, was televised by the Columbia Broadcasting System (CBS) on June 25, 1951, in New York and was fed to stations in Boston, Philadelphia, Baltimore, and Washington. Among the performers were Arthur Godfrey, Faye Emerson, Sam Levenson, Robert Alda, Ed Sullivan, and Gary Moore.

He amassed a fortune that allowed him to fly airplanes to and from his estate near Leesburg, Virginia, as well as an East Side Manhattan apartment. He sold his Virginia estate in 1979 for more than $5 million. It's very appropriate that today Music Planet Radio, Cerphe Colwell's online radio station, is in Leesburg continuing a tradition.

Godfrey's flying once got him grounded by federal authorities for six months in 1954 over charges that he had buzzed the Teterboro Airport tower in New Jersey. He was king of the airwaves in the 1950s with two weekly prime-time series for CBS, as well as a daily radio show, playing talent scout and host to stars and occasionally singing in his trademark rusty rumbling voice. With Boy Scout sincerity, he chatted about his farm in the Blue Ridge mountains of Virginia and his favorite horses, but then shocked the nation by firing singer Julius LaRosa on the air.

One of Godfrey's longtime sponsors was Lipton Tea, but he often horrified sponsors by adlibbing his way through commercials and refused to push products he believed were pollutants. Despite that, he was reported by *Variety* to have been responsible for $150 million in advertising revenue for CBS in 1959.

Godfrey often said his secret of longevity as a performer was his ability to respond to new challenges.

"If you want to last, you have to grow," he said. "That little screen is merciless and if you aren't constantly more interesting and intriguing, they—the public—will drop you, ruthlessly."

Art Brown

Arthur William Brown was born in Granville, New York, and grew up in Burlington, Vermont. He attended the University of Vermont before becoming what he later claimed was the worst saxophone player in the U.S. Army during World War I.

In over forty-five years of dedicated work, he had evolved into a skilled pianist, organist, and disc jockey. Recalling his earlier days, people from the 1980s remembered him best as the talented pit organist at Lowe's Capital Theater, leading engaging sing-alongs between movie features with the iconic bouncing ball guiding the audience through the songs.

During our interview in 1985 at his Arlington, VA, home, Brown shared insights into his career, describing the synchronized performances he conducted during the sing-alongs at the theater.

"I was hired to work as an entertainer, doing what we call the 'bouncing ball' sing-alongs. The orchestra would do a significant overture, and I would follow the orchestra. Or precede them. They also had newsreels that I'd follow with ten-minute sing-alongs of four to six popular songs of the day. And the stage show would run an hour.

"The owners of the original WOL radio station heard me playing organ and the singalongs, and they invited me up to do a morning radio show from six to nine a.m."

After the war, Brown became a traveling theatrical producer of minstrel and musical shows and played the organ at silent movies in cities such as Richmond and Norfolk before coming to the Washington area.

"I came here as a combination pianist, organist, and disc jockey. After years of hard and devoted work, I have become a combination pianist, organist, and disc jockey."

Fred Fiske

Another Washington AM radio broadcaster was Fred Fiske, who signed off for the last time from his evening talk show in 1986. Area airwaves lost another institution.

Affable, inquisitive, informed, and fair, Fiske was the ringmaster for a long and lively conversational circus when station WAMU FM 88.5. For sixteen years, he hosted thousands of celebrities, politicians, cooks, and Saints, Avril Harriman, Richard Nixon, and Raquel Welch, who valiantly voiced various viewpoints.

Photo : Fiske in his home office. I had taken another picture of Fred with his wife, Ruth, for this *Journal* article. Fred really wanted the *Journal* to feature the double shot of them but the single one ran. He was very disappointed, and Ruth passed away a few months after his article ran. I was always sorry I let him down. Sadly, I have lost the photo.

To one listener, Fiske's show was a town hall where ideas are aired, and resolutions made. It was certainly a free-wheeling, merry-go-round of ideas and attitudes, wide-ranging, provocative, and spirited.

More tolerant and less disturbing than his counterparts in some cities, Fisk always seemed eager to understand the attitudes of his guests and his calling audience—no matter how esoteric or wacky. Still, he was quick to cut off the collar with an abusive axe to grind, and he was a ready referee when combative guests veered toward verbal mayhem.

Fisk could make you feel within minutes you've known him all your life. That openness stems from a life in the public eye, child actor, journalist, soap opera, regular decorated World War II veteran, straight man in the Catskills for Danny Kaye, and top-rated music DJ. "I started in radio in April of 1936 when I was just fifteen." The native New Yorker became a regular on the network weekly Theatre Guild of the Air, appearing with stars like Ronald Coleman and William Holden.

After graduating from Columbia College with speech, drama, and education studies, Fisk enlisted in the Air Force and became a radio gunner on a B24, just in time to fly thirty missions over France and Germany. His Squadron Leader was Colonel Jimmy Stewart. Not long after the war, he answered an ad, which brought him to Washington. He nearly lost that life in a World War II bombing mission after an encounter with 150 Folk Wolf 190 fighter planes over Germany. Only one of the thirty-four aircraft and his group returned to home base. Fisk's plane crash landed in France.

Yet, on occasion, he was not above sparring in a verbal donnybrook or evicting a guest from their studio. "One woman, a Marxist, insisted on giving the names of various bookstores where he could purchase left-wing tracks. And I wasn't interested in providing her the opportunity to do commercials. She kept reading the names of the bookstores from a piece of paper. Finally, I reached over, took the paper, and invited her to leave."

But to his colleagues, Fred Fiske seemed a model of cordiality. "I don't think there's a nicer guy in broadcasting," said WWDC Johnny Holiday on his retirement. "His longevity is due to enormous talent," added Diane Rehm, the then morning talk show host on WAMU. "I've enjoyed working with him."

Fisk lived beyond the gatehouse of a guarded enclave in Bethesda, MD, as he ushered me into his plushy, sunlit condo and settles you into a cushy sofa looking out on a stand of Evergreen Pines. You had to think this guy' led a pretty charmed life, and he was quick to agree.

He explained that he did battle cancer, resisting the advice of a platoon of physicians who counseled the amputation of an afflicted leg. So, faith had been good to Fred Fisk. And that's why he wanted to return the favor by giving every attention then to his ailing wife.

Chapter 46 – Select Radio Signals (FM)

© Marlin Taylor

Marlin Taylor, was born in Abington Township, PA, on 1935. He first arrived in the DC area at Fort Meade's Second Army Recruiting headquarters playing reel to reel tape for radio stations throughout the Mid-Atlantic— mostly on Sunday mornings between like six and eight a.m.

"It was in 1961. I finished my army stint, and with my wife Roberta took an apartment on East West Highway, near 16th Street in Silver Spring. I needed a job and saw some news in *Broadcasting Magazine* about the approval of a permit to build a Class A radio station in Bethesda with the call letters WHFS. A Class A station was limited to 3000 watts. WHFS stood for Washington High Fidelity Station then. The magazine article gave the home address of Bob Carpenter, one of the two principals who won the permit. At the time Bob was an engineer of what was then the Nation Bureau of Standards.

"So, the next Saturday morning I showed up on his front door. Even though I didn't have a lot of experience, but I was twenty-six and seemed like a responsible person. I told him 'I want to work for you,' and he talked with his partner Joe Tynan, and later that day they hired me."

Carpenter, spoke about this encounter: "One Saturday shortly after Broadcasting Magazine announced the grant of our CP, a soldier appeared at my front door, looking for a job. It was Marlin Taylor, then assigned to Ft Meade, MD, but he had nearly completed his enlistment. Marlin became our only full-time employee for most of our ownership. It is impossible to overestimate the jack-of-all-trades effort he put into the station. We had a broad format running from 'HiFi' (including what was known as 'ping pong stereo') music, through light and more serious Classical to Jazz, plus Broadway and full operas on weekends. Marlin was able to pick music for any category."

Marlin says, "Eventually WHFS came to stand for Washington High-Fidelity Stereo. Officially the first stereo station in the DC area. Even though I helped Bob Carpenter put some of the station together, my job was to program. And we didn't go on the air until 4:30 in the afternoon and off at midnight. Eventually, I convinced them expand it noon to midnight. I did all the programming except for jazz. Tom Phillips, who was a drummer but also in commercial real estate, did a two-hour jazz show Monday through Friday at 10 p.m. The station never made much money, but I didn't starve to death.

"Our first sponsor was Campbell Music, one of the hi-fi dealers in Washington. I was not an expert in classical music. What was the address 8218 Wisconsin Avenue in what was then the Bethesda Medical Building. We had some space in the basement. And a White Castle hamburger place was right around the corner. This was a totally low budget home-built radio station.

"Bob and Joe pretty much decided what genres we did. We added Dixieland on Saturday nights, and a Comedy Hour with acts like Stan Freiburg, and an hour of ping-pong stereo that was new at the time. Enoch White was associated with ping-pong music picked up by two different mics—bouncing back and forth from one side speaker to the other.

"Bob Carpenter was a down-to-earth technical type. He was a bachelor. He could walk from his house. He took one pile of junk radio equipment and another pile of new electronic parts and put them all together to make an operating radio station. William 'Bill' Tynan was more on the business side. Bob was the down to earth technical person.

"At Bob's memorial service, I said Bob was a genius which is true. When they were ready to go on the air, there were hardly any radio consoles built for stereo--for two channels--because it was so new to the radio industry. This technology had only been approved in June of 1961. And we went on the air in November. The whole station—stereo wise—was Bob managing to put it all together makeshift."

* * *

Howard Stern

One of my favorite DC radio personalities then was Howard Stern. His first wife, Allison, was my brother-in-law's therapist. He arrived at DC 101 in 1982. I sent him a tape my band made (Steve Carey and Skip Cookman) praising him in song with lyrics like "Howard Stern, You are our hero, Howard Stern, burn DC like Nero..." It was a sophomoric effort, but that didn't stop Howard from using it as his 6 a.m. morning sign-on theme song.

I listened to Howard on DC 101, with Robin Quivers, a University of Maryland alum. At that time, he was empathic, funny, and a loving husband, much like the character he played in his *Private Parts* film. I miss that Howard.

A few words about Robin: She grew up in Baltimore and arrived at the University of Maryland in 1970, the same year I did. I remember seeing her at the Town Hall bar a few times while we were students. My preferred bar was the Varsity Grill, where I briefly worked as the front bartender. I was fired for giving away too many drinks and also for drinking too much myself.

The irony is that the owner then was Leon Zeiger, the same man who bought the Bamboo Garden, a failing Chinese restaurant, in 1953 and turned it into the Casino Royal nightclub where my Mom, Patricia Moore, later worked.

Fun fact about the Casino Royal: In addition to a plethora of stars who played there—Tony Bennett, Sophie Tucker, Johnny Mathis, Dinah Washington, Bobby Darin, Chubby

Checker, Peggy Lee, Frankie Avalon, and Nat King Cole, and more—Aretha Franklin played there very early in her career.

As Zeiger's secretary for nineteen years, Doris Fortune recalled, "Aretha was so nervous she wouldn't sit on the stage. She played piano then, pulled it next to the stage and sat with her back to the audience."

Now, back to Howard: He sent my wife and me a goodbye signed copy of the Journal article that announced his departure and inscribed it, "Yo Steve and Margaret. You guys are the best. Don't ever change," with a "That goes for me, too" word bubble coming from Alison, and signed "Howeird Stern." He sent me a copy of his crazy *Fifty Ways to Rank Your Mother* album, signed by some of his early DC radio crew, Fred Norris and Steve Chaconas.

When I arrived at the University of Maryland in 1970, I could finally get the WHFS radio signal. I soon listened to Cerphe in the evenings. In addition to his soothing, authoritative voice, I became a big fan because he was already known for introducing eclectic, pioneering music by acts like Little Feat, Bonnie Raitt, and Frank Zappa. When I had the idea for this *Capital Acts* book in 1983, he was working at radio station WAVA. I contacted him for the first time to tell him about my project, and he sent me a hand-written letter on WAVA stationery suggesting artists that I should feature in the book. I was very excited to get a hand-written letter from Cerphe. After forty plus years he is still my favorite radio broadcaster.

During the next years, we kept in touch. He had done so much for the listeners I thought he should write his autobiography. Because I had helped both Helen Hayes and Johnny Holiday do theirs, I thought I could help him, too.

When the WHFS movie project was announced by executive producer Jay Schlossberg (with co-producers Dick and Linda Bangham, and Dave Nuttycombe), I ran into Cerphe at a Jeff Beck/Brian Wilson concert. I suggested that now might be the time to do his memoir. He was reluctant and said he "wasn't feeling it." I replied, "You're not going to feel it until you start doing it," and we did just that.

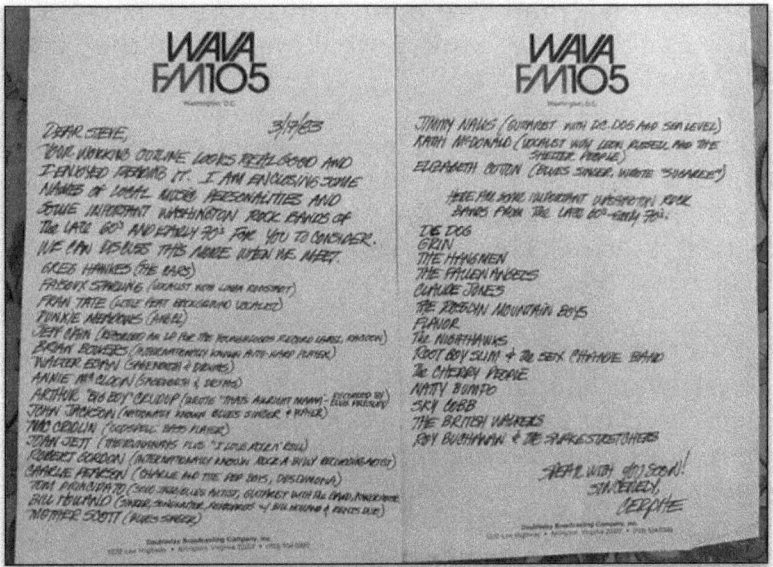

We worked together on the manuscript, with my close friend, **Patty Johnson Cooper**, as our editor, and "Cerphe's Up" was published in 2016. Patty and I met at the University of Maryland as students, later doing a music act as Dakota & Stuff, and then being a couple, and she, at least, was studying. We closely connected when I discovered she knew all the lyrics to "Brown Shoes Don't Make It." Patty also introduced me to

 the future Linda Bangham, who today is co-owner with husband Dick of Rip Bang Pictures. A great artist and friend.

And after "Cerphe's Up" Patty joined me again on "All Roads Lead to The Birchmere" as editor and consultant. This was a very difficult book and my forever gratitude is with my pal, Patty.

The "Cerphe's Up" book's reception was heart-warming, and the reviews were very positive. My favorite review is "Colwell's memoir is pure fun and, for many, a joyful trip down musical memory lane," by *Booklist*, the book review journal of the American Library Association.

After the book's initial reception was over, Buzz McClain published a Cerphe profile for *Northern Virginia* magazine which generously described the man and revisited many of the book's best stories. The following is an excerpt from Buzz's article:

There goes the last DJ
Who plays what he wants to play
And says what he wants to say, hey, hey, hey
And there goes your freedom of choice
There goes the last human voice
And there goes the last DJ
—Tom Petty and the Heartbreakers, "The Last DJ"

Then there was the time George Harrison—the George Harrison—spotted the tantric yoga button on his lapel from across the room and made an effort to get past the usual crush of press and music executives to meet the kindred soul.

"He could see I wasn't asking questions, I was listening, so I was different, and there was this break, and he said, 'Can I get you a cup of tea?' And I'm about to frigging weep."

We are three hours into a visit with Cerphe Colwell, and the stories show no sign of letting up. The names drop like nails on a workshop floor: Bruce Springsteen, Frank Zappa, Bonnie

Raitt, Howard Stern, Jerry Garcia, Stevie Nicks, Van Morrison, Fleetwood Mac, Robert Plant, Rod Stewart, Linda Ronstadt, the Rolling Stones for crying out loud...Is there anyone Colwell hasn't met and befriended?

Cerphe in the studio at WHFS in 1977, had the freedom to debut countless songs that are now considered classic rock. "We spent some time together, and we talked," Colwell says, absurdly calmly, of his encounter with Harrison. "It was lovely."

A photo taken at the event ended up being the cover shot on Colwell's autobiography, Cerphe's Up: A Musical Life with Bruce Springsteen, Little Feat, Frank Zappa, Tom Waits, CSNY, and Many More (Carrel Books), written with local journalist Stephen Moore. Colwell's grin, now that you know what was going through his mind, is priceless.

So, who is this guy? Here's who he is now: For the past years, he and his internet enterprise, Music Planet Radio, have been voted "Loudoun's Favorite Radio Station & DJ" by the readers of the media outlet Loudoun Now. "And that means we beat WTOP-AM, all the FMs, even the country station," he's quick to add.

Colwell, who we will call Cerphe because for the first forty years of listening to him, we had no idea he even had a last name—it was always just "Surf"—has been a fixture of the region's rock 'n' roll airwaves since 1971. Remarkably, in his seventies, he has managed to remain revelatory for listeners across an astonishing spectrum of ages.

His stock-in-trade is "classic rock," but when he started playing the records during his first gig, as a college undergraduate, at Bethesda, Maryland's legendary low-watt, progressive, free-form station WHFS-FM in 1971, it was the first time those iconic songs had ever been played. And now they are "classic."

In other words, the first time Washington heard Springsteen's "Blinded by the Light" in 1973 was, most likely, the first time Cerphe played it on the station's turntable. Now the song is in our cultural DNA, and Cerphe has a framed gold record on the wall in his Leesburg home, sent to him in 1975 by Columbia Records to commemorate Springsteen's milestone achievement of selling more than 500,000 copies of his 1975 album, a little number called *Born to Run*.

The gold record was a reward, in a way, for believing in Springsteen when he was playing Washington's humble Childe Harold venue in 1973; Cerphe brought him to the station to introduce him to listeners. Relationships ensue when Cerphe interviews you.

After nearly seven years, in 1977, Cerphe was fired by the station's owner—most likely for Cerphe's climbing popularity—and went from cultish WHFS to corporate WAVA-FM in Arlington. Suddenly he had 50,000 watts and basically the same mandate—play what you like as long as it's good—and he formed a larger audience. He intensified his on-air persona and became one of the few "must-listens" during FM radio's heyday. It didn't hurt that he worked with other popular jocks, including Howard Stern, a longtime friend.

At WAVA and DC 101, he was the one who teens and young adults listened to on Friday nights; it was as if he was in the car with you, playing those songs just for you. The DJ kept the party rolling, reminding you sotto voce that Friday was "date night No. 1." Squeals ensued.

Cerphe became known, among other things, as "the DJ who wears clogs." The backless wood-and-leather shoes had a day—for men, anyway—in the post-hippie era of the 70s. They were avant-garde and a bit daring in an age when "unisex" was sometimes misunderstood.

He interviewed many musicians at WHFS and beyond. "We were really fans of the music, and we would go out and meet new bands that we liked," he says.

Among those was Lowell George, the leader of the eclectic rock band Little Feat. Cerphe was backstage in August 1977 at Washington's Lisner Auditorium the night the band was to record part of a live album that became *Waiting for Columbus*.

"Lowell [George] just asked me if I would bring the band to the stage," he says, the result of which is on the album: That's Cerphe leading the audience in spelling "F-E-A-T" three times before the song "Fat Man in the Bathtub." These days, the familiar intro is considered part of the song. The record became one of Feat's best-selling albums, peaking at number eighteen on the Billboard rock chart and number thirty-eight on the All-time Top 100 chart.

Buzz's full Cerphe article is available at:
https://northernvirginiamag.com/culture/culture-features/2021/02/05/is-this-the-last-radio-dj/)

Broadcasting since 2009, Cerphe's *Music Planet* radio streams 24/7 at musicplanetradio.com. It's an award-winning radio station with the best music and programming hands down. One of the many wonderful creative shows is **Stilson's Themed Music Hour** on Cerphe's Music Planet Radio.

Motown, Levon Helm, Jon Carrol, Halloween, and LA's Troubadour are a few of Stilson's recent "themes."

Stilson Greene, an artist, opened his graphic design studio in 1980 in Leesburg, Virginia. In addition to multiple graphic awards, he is also the Founder of *Acoustic on the Green* Summer Concert Series, Co-founder of *Jingle Jam Rock n Roll Christmas Charity Concert* for JDRF, *Songs Stories & Gas Money* songwriter music series and organizer of Leesburg's *Cancer Can Rock Benefit* Concert Series.

(Also, thanks, Stilson for designing our *Capital Acts* book cover.)

Adele Abrams

The musical missionary from radio station WHFS (99.1 FM) was how she was described in a *Journal* news profile I wrote in 1987. She had already served the Bethesda radio station a decade plus when my article hit the streets.

She was then the producer/host of Takoma Park Television's *Takoma Tempo* airing on Cable 24 Montgomery County.

"If there's an energy in the music and a spark of originality, I'll give it a chance to be heard and let it rise or fall on its own merit," Abrams told us. *Takoma Tempo* avoided the glittery spandex sexuality of MTV and focused on the music. Live music. The show was taped in the Takoma Park club called Bosco every other Tuesday night. Abrams estimated the show reached 20,000 households. Her volunteer staff and shoestring budget came together in one-and-a-half hours of great spirit. Much of it is guided by Abrams, who projects a kind of knowledgeable, natural, down-to-earth ease.

Today, she is an attorney, safety professional, and trainer who is president of the Law Office of Adele L. Abrams P.C. in Beltsville, MD; Charleston, WV; and Denver, CO. She is a member of the Maryland, DC, and Pennsylvania Bars; the U.S. District Courts of Maryland, DC, and Tennessee; the U.S. Court of Appeals, DC, 3rd and 4th Circuits; and the United States Supreme Court.

But I sure remember first interviewing her in her apartment. She showed me how she taught her small dog, Scooter, to stand on its hind legs, paws outstretched, and walk like an Egyptian, teetering sideways in a dubious tribute to the hit song by The Bangles. She introduced me to the new compact discs with the first Beatles CD.

Her interviews with The Beatnick Flies, folklorists Joe and Kathy Hickerson, and virtually unknown bands like the Psychonauts deserved to be included in a Smithsonian time capsule under vintage 80s neo-psychedelia.

"I'm not the star," insisted Abrams. "The musicians are. The focus is on the music. I try to keep it flowing. Even the 9:30 Club, which I greatly respect, is skewed toward national acts. They are more likely to take an unknown band from Iowa and put them on stage than to book a local group like The Neighbors," said Abrams.

"I'll match the records I get from local groups like the New Keys, Edge City, and B Time to name a few. If just one group out of Washington ends up with a major record deal from exposure on my show, it will all be worthwhile."

Another Favorite DC-Area Concert

"The Cellar Door was my go-to club for live music, along with the Child Herald and Desperados," says Adele. "Joan Armatrading is a most memorable live show at the Cellar Door in February 1977. I was a big Joan fan since she was named best new artist in 1973 by Music Week, and I always played her on my WHFS radio show. Joan is a three-time Grammy Award nominee. In a recording career spanning forty years, she has released a total of eighteen studio albums, as well as several live albums and compilations.

"At this Cellar Door concert, I was surprised to see Joan backed up by members of Fairport Convention, the pioneering band of the English folk rock movement (but unfortunately without Richard Thompson). I was dating John Jennings then, and John played guitar for Bill Holland's Rent's Due band, who opened for Joan that snowy night. I almost didn't go because of the weather conditions.

"Bill and his musicians instantly clicked with Joan and her band backstage in the dressing room. I'd been backstage before because I was a DJ, but this time I was with the band and in their entourage of wives and girlfriends. I got to meet and talk with Joan. We all hung out and instantly liked each other. I know that some of them are still friends today.

"The upshot of this story is that Joan was heading to Philadelphia for her next gig, and she invited all of us to be her guests. We piled into our cars, rode up to Philly, and hung out the next night. It was very collegial—no hard-partying thing—just talking, hearing stories, getting to know each other. I was such a big Fairport Convention fan. I was gob smacked getting to know Joan and talking with everyone I never thought I'd ever meet.

"Later, they ended up on A&M Records and pressed a DJ-only vinyl disk. I begged and pleaded with David Einstein to give me one of the promos. I still have it in my collection. She was awarded an MBE by Queen Elizabeth in 2001 and is still touring—and even writing symphonies—in 2024."

WHFS – *Feast Your Ears* by Marlin Taylor

An October 2023 trip to Frederick, Maryland, for another historic event... a one night only/sneak preview showing of the documentary film, not the actual premiere release, which is still to come. WHFS was a radio station which signed on in November 1961, occupying the last FM frequency available in the Greater Washington, DC, market and is licensed to Bethesda, Maryland—a community which adjoins the District of Columbia border on its northwest side.

Feast Your Ears tells the story of a small, obscure radio station that rose to national acclaim playing artists and recordings being heard nowhere else. While the beginning of the film—where yours truly makes a cameo appearance—covers the origins of the station, the prime focus is on the major transformation that began in early 1968.

© M. Taylor

The showing took place at the beautiful, historic Weinberg Center for the Arts in Frederick. It proved to be a great location—being not that far out from the heart of the nation's capital. This location gave those who attended, mostly faithful listeners of WHFS in those celebrated days forty-plus years ago, a great venue to view the finished film. And nearly 700 showed up to see the ninety-minute production, the brainchild of Jay Schlossberg, who has devoted a good decade of work that led up to this day. His cohort for much of the journey has been Dick Bangham seen here standing in front of the Weinberg.

In promoting the showing, the Weinberg Center described the film this way:

> The legendary and beloved WHFS was more than just a local radio station—it was the voice of a generation. Hear from local, national and international musicians, the HFS deejays, record label veterans, journalists, historians, fans and more as they reflect on a time when the music united a tribe who spoke out via the radio waves about war, equality and a time of great social, cultural and political upheaval.

Marlin's book: Radio: My Love, My Passion.

© **Rip/Bang**

Chapter 47 – Johnny Holliday (Side Two)

Johnny's arrival in the Washington, DC, area would mark a turning point where he sharply honed his performance skills, captivating audiences with his singing and dinner theater performances. He had just left San Francisco radio as that city had become the heart of America's new hippie music movement. Local promoter Bill Graham took over managing the Carousel Ballroom, renaming it the Fillmore West. Neighborhood bands like Sopwith Camel, Blue Cheer, Moby Grape, Juke, Savages, Quicksilver, Messenger Service, and the Warlocks played their mix of pop and blues throughout the city. The Warlocks changed their name to the Grateful Dead and slowly began to build their devout following.

Johnny recalls, "In June of 1967, the first Monterey International Pop Festival took place. Mary Clare and I attended the shows, climbing over bodies sprawled around the Monterey County Fairgrounds. KYA heavily promoted it. National acts like Simon and Garfunkel, Otis Redding, Johnny Rivers, The Byrds, Lou Rawls, Janis Joplin's debut, and Jimi

Hendrix delivered the most spectacular coming-out set. Every performer except Ravi Shankar appeared at the festival for free.

"The concert proceeds were distributed to charities like the UCLA Children's Hospital in the LA Free Clinic. Never before Monterey had over thirty rock bands played together at one event. I certainly didn't realize at the time how important these shows turned out to be. Heck, it was San Francisco. I thought, 'This is the way it was supposed to be.'"

Johnny in Finnegan's Rainbow at the Harlequin Dinner Theater.

Johnny explains, "One tool of the radio trade, is the ability to do impressions. My first impression was Ed Sullivan at a high school assembly. I next mastered easy impressions like Dracula, WC Fields, Cary Grant, and Jimmy "Inka Dinka Doo" Durante. Eventually, my radio career required a serious approach to getting the intonation and words just right as I began building a wider range of character voices. Because I was working in the nation's capital, it made sense to add Reagan, Humphrey, McGovern, Perot and other politicians to the arsenal.

"At one of my first commercial tapings. Renee Funk of Rodel Productions gave me my instructions. 'You'll be doing Richard Nixon for this spot,' Renee said.

"'Who told you I could do Nixon?'

"Larry Lumen, then one of the top voice-over talents in the Washington Baltimore market, pulled me aside and said, 'You can do Nixon. You can do any voices. Besides, they don't have anyone else for this job. At least try.' And so we did.

"An ad campaign for the old Washington Star newspaper, paired my Jimmy Carter with a young Alma Viator doing an Amy Carter impression. Alma Viator later became the public relations Tour de force at the National Theatre. Readers who know Alma will get a big kick out of learning she once did a radio spot as Amy Carter.

"Washington DC's original wax museum used my John F. Kennedy impression for their wax figures's real voice for years.

"Now long gone, I wonder whatever happened to the wax dummies and my Kennedy voice.

"For many years before the Kennedy Center for the Performing Arts opened its doors, Washington, DC, was incorrectly not regarded as much of a performing arts city. I saw my first Broadway show in 1964, *How to Succeed in Business Without Even Trying* at the Shubert Theater. The gorgeous Michelle Lee glowed in the role of Rosemary. I just missed seeing Robert Morse who originated the role, which was a disappointment. Still, I remember being so impressed with the whole show. I sat in the audience thinking 'Hey, I can sing those songs, I can act. I should be doing that. That would be a perfect role for me.'

"When I arrived in Washington I had four productions under my belt: *Finnigan's Rainbow* and *Oklahoma* in Cleveland, and *How to Succeed* in Walnut Creek and Oakland in California. The Longworth Dinner Theater here in DC held auditions for, you guessed it, *How to Succeed*. Only this time it was a paying gig. Not much, mind you, but still a step up in the musical ladder.

"The big question for me was did I want to do this show a third time? Yes, I did. Keith Donaldson directed. Lou Ressiguie, produced and also acted in Longworth shows with his talented wife Barbara. Lou would later tour as Barry Nelson's understudy in the National Company of 42nd Street. Other standouts in the cast were the talented Lonnie Lohfield as Rosemary and Dan Higgs as Bigley.

"On a WGMS radio report, critic David Richards said, 'And then there is a young man named Johnny Holliday who has the face of a chipmunk that has spirited away a week's worth of acorns in his cheek and a smile that reminded me of a harvest moon.'

"Next would come my Harlequin Dinner Theater years. Simply some of the best times in my life. With the initial investment of $7500, Dr. Nicholas Howie, along with Kary Walker and Ken Gentry, founded the Harlequin on East Gude Drive in Rockville, MD. Two productions: *Stop the World* and

Promises. Promises had opened the 400-seat facility before I got a chance to audition for their third show, Stephen Sondheim's *Company*. Since it was Sondheim, the first obstacle I had to overcome was reading the music charts, which I wasn't great at doing.

"My rather nerve-wracking audition was held at American University with Kary at the piano and the good doctor Howie (with his PhD in Theater) sitting in the first row.

"Kary asked me what key I wanted for my song.

"'Uh...whatever key you normally play it in,' was my clever response.

"I soon got the feeling that they knew I might be able to sing Sondheim, but there would be work ahead.

"After I landed the job, Nick asked me what I did for a living. It was at that moment that I thought he was nuts. Here I was, the big morning man on WWDC radio, making serious inroads on WMAL's Harden and Weaver show. I did commercials. I'd been in the newspaper. I was the famous disc jockey from New York. How could he not know who I was? Didn't everybody know Johnny Holliday?

"The answer seemed to be no. Neither Howie nor Walker appeared to have a clue.

"Driving home that night, it dawned on me that I had won the role based on my performance at the audition, and not because of my work on the radio. This gave me a warm satisfaction.

"Company turned out to be a big hit for the Harlequin. The cast included Larry Shue, who had so impressed me when I saw him perform in the previous show, *Promises, Promises*. Shue was a wonderfully talented character actor who drew your attention even when the focus should have been on someone else. Larry and his talented wife, Linda, were a great team. Clearly, Larry was destined for Broadway.

"And so, it was Larry wrote some well received plays. One was *The Foreigner* that opened at NYC's Astor Palace Theater in 1985. Another was *The Nerd* that played Broadway's Helen Hayes Theatre in 1987. Tragically, Larry's life ended when his commuter plane crashed in Virginia's Blue Ridge Mountains in 1985. Ironically, Larry had written about a rough ride in a commuter plane in the second act of his play The Nerd. He was thirty-nine years old.

"With Larry and Linda, Nick Howey put together a resident company that also included Jack Kyrieleison, Michelle Mundell (later Jack's wife,) and Buddy Piccolino, The shows were built around them, and when I say built, that's exactly what they did. They worked on costumes, the sets, and waited on tables. They did it all.

"Buddy Piccolino is a funny performer and a good man, I always enjoyed teaming with him.

The Odd Couple with Buddy Piccolino

Buddy Piccolino: Before Johnny came to rehearsal, many of us wondered if he was going to be a prima donna. But he wasn't. He joined right in with the cast, treated us kindly, gave us lots of publicity on his radio show, and John and I became very close. There were instances in my younger life when I had personal problems and Johnny was always there to lend a shoulder and ear or just a friendly word. Both Johnny and Mary Clare instilled in their family and by example, the importance of giving back to those less fortunate. I have always admired that and have tried to do it in my own life because of them.

He and I once did two shows back-to-back: *The Odd Couple* and *The Music Man*. John had been complaining during our show that he was wasn't getting much time with his wife, Mary Clare. One day after a meal with the cast, he suddenly announced that Mary Clare was pregnant.

I asked, "Who's the father?"

 Another Harlequin player and friend, Jack Kyrieleison co-authored with Ron Holgate a successful play, *Reunion: A Musical Epic In Miniature,* presented at Ford's Theatre. It's about the Civil War and why the North almost lost. Jack received some powerful notices for *Reunion.*

Jack Kyrieleison: I'd been a huge fan of Johnny's morning show at WWDC. I had grown up listening to Ed Walker and Willard Scott's Joy Boys. Staying up till ten and taping entire shows as a kid to try to learn how to write that kind of material. Harden and Weaver were the morning drive kings then. And while acknowledging their mastery of the medium, it must be said that they were just unlistenable as far as I was concerned. Stale, safe, and cliched. But Johnny's morning show was different, edgier, hipper, and a combination of Joy Boys and Bob & Ray, but solo. And played at 45 RPM instead of 33. It could only have been done by someone who'd come from rock'n'roll. But without the meanness or cynicism of an Imus. (My appreciation of him would come later, after I'd been kicked around a little!) Loaded with voice characterizations and quick as a whippet on Benzedrine, Johnny somehow managed to appeal across the board to nine-to-fivers as well as long-haired would-be hippie theatre students like me.

"The Harlequin would be my showcase for the next twenty years. Nick and I once calculated that over 750,000 tickets were sold to the shows I was in. That's a staggering number.

"Critics always were kind hearted to me. For some reason they never slammed me. I don't know how I escaped their wrath. I guess I was always in good shows, surrounded by talented people. In sixty years of doing theater, the highlight came with my Helen Hayes Award nomination for Best Actor in a Musical for Harlequin's *Me and My Gal.* Nominations for Best Actress and Best Musical went to my co-star Liz Donahue

Weber and to the show itself. Stacy Keach and Victor Garber were also nominees that season. Tough competition.

"A significant void in local theater. Especially in the northern area of Montgomery County was created when Harlequin closed its doors in 1991. Nick Howey moved on to launch Troika Entertainment running successful touring companies of such hit shows as *Grand Hotel* and *Cats*. He did well and is happily retired today.

> **Nick Howey**: It had been twenty years for Harlequin, which was a pretty good run. There was a time when dinner theater was hot and we were getting past that time. Johnny never learned to pronounce the name correctly. I've been correcting him constantly. It was "HarleQuin," not "HarleKin." It's become a running gag. I think he did it to spite me.

"With Harlequin gone, there were only a few options left to me if I wanted to continue performing in musicals. The Burn Brae Dinner Theater in Burtonsville, MD, was still in business and had the distinction of being the area's first dinner theater.

"It was John Kinnamon, the driving force behind Burn Brae, who called to see if I'd be interested in doing *42nd Street* again. Sure, why not? I'd be reunited with Trisha Pierce, who had played Dorothy Brock with me at the Harlequin in 1987. Trisha would later pair with Jerry Lewis in Damn Yankees on Broadway. The lure of *42nd Street* attracted some wonderful talent to Burn Bray, including Bill Pierson, Tina Desimone and Mark Minnick.

"My next director was **Toby Orenstein** who had a strong reputation among Washington-Baltimore theater goers at her Toby's Dinner Theater in Columbia, MD. She staged shows in the round with live orchestra and fine cuisine. Toby has won many accolades from recognition for excellence by the Helen Hayes Awards to *Baltimore Magazine's*, 'Best of Baltimore.'

"I visited Toby shortly before vacationing with Mary Clare in Bermuda. I thought Toby might have wanted to discuss 42nd Street for the coming season.

"Instead, she offered me the role of Buddy Plummer in the area premiere of Stephen Sondheim's *Follies*, a show that very few theaters had done. I was unfamiliar with the script and the music, but Toby had both on hand for our chat. I admit I was not that excited about the role for the show, but Toby did one heck of a selling job, promising me it would be one of the most rewarding roles of my life. It turned out she was exactly right. Follies was a real challenge for me, but also a stage experience I'll never forget.

> **Toby Orenstein**: Johnny Holliday is one of the most beautiful people I've ever worked with. He has a humility that many people who has been around the long as he has do not possess. His willingness to stretch (for *Follies*) and work as hard as he did was a joy to watch. I had no idea what it would be like to work with him. He had done a lot of shows and he did University of Maryland and many other things. Sometimes folks like that come with some baggage, but John's baggage was nonexistent.

Johnny continues: "One time Toby called me. And we discussed about me playing the devil in *Damn Yankees* for one of her shows. But at that time, I ended up passing when I agreed to do *The Music Man*, which would be the first show to open the University of Maryland's gorgeous new Clarice Smith Performing Arts Center. The Music Man was sensational and featured a surprise encore every night by the University of Maryland Marching Band. For every performance, it was a stunning effect when the entire band appeared from nowhere at the curtain call, blaring seventy-six trombones."

Opening the Clara Smith Center was very special. The student cast was great: Danielle Pastin, Sarah Hale, Adam Shapiro, Abigail Bortnick, Laura Lichtenberger. Carmen Balthrop (a faculty member of the School of Music) and Drury Bagwell also played key roles. Director: Nick Olcott; and Musical director: Richard Sparks.

"Today my Marian the Librarian, **Danielle Pastin**, is an opera soprano in demand nationwide and abroad. Her wide-ranging repertoire encompasses the classical as well as the contemporary and she is equally at home at the Metropolitan, Nashville, and Pittsburgh opera houses.

"This show would also yield one of my worst reviews—penned by a student critic in *The Diamondback*: The student called my performance 'creepy' and implied I was too old to be playing romantic leads. Maybe he's right, though, but I still had a wonderful time on stage, and the audience seemed to love it."

Just one week before the show opened, two Maryland students, Colleen Marlette, twenty-three, and her sister, Erin Marlett, twenty, of Triadelphia Mill Road in Clarksville, MD, were killed when a freak tornado moved through College Park and lifted their car seventy-five feet into the air barely clearing the high-rise dormitories.

Colleen had been studying environmental policy and looking forward to graduating in January. Aaron was a sophomore sociologist student. They were visiting their father who worked with the Maryland Fire and Rescue Institute on campus. This trailer was adjacent to the theater. The tornado did extensive damage to the College Park campus, but other than broken windows, the new theater was spared.

* * *

In 1978 while his University of Maryland basketball and football play-by-play was going well, Johnny Holliday was also doing short music features for News Channel 4 in 1978 on musicians appearing in town for shows including Perry Como Sha Na Nah, Starland Vocal Band, and many others. He even rode on a motorcycle with soul crooner Isaac Hayes.

Emmylou Harris returned one year after she left Washington, DC, to pursue a recording contract's potential for stardom. She was playing Wolf Trap which was a huge leap from the Red Fox Inn, and Clyde's of Georgetown where she was discovered by Gram Parsons via an introduction by Chris Hillman via Cellar Door regular Bill Danoff's recommendation to Hillman.

In Johnny's segment, he begins by asking Emmylou, "Is it hard to find time to visit family and friends?"

Emmylou: "Yes, it's strange. I'm so busy. I do this music all the time now. Yes, it's neat to come back, but I don't ever have time to even visit with friends or anything. I'm really tied to the road and tied to whatever this success has done for me. All my time and everything is involved in just that. So hopefully what I want to do is have more time on my hands to spend with my daughter and get my household in order, which does not exist at all at this point. That' really what I want to do and of course, I want to continue the music."

Johnny: "Traveling can certainly take its toll. What is your direction of music? What kind of songs do you like to sing?

Emmylou: "I just sing the songs that seem to come to me. You know, that seem right for me, that I feel, and whatever direction that takes me. I don't consciously follow anything." © J. Holliday

The Best Man

"In 2002, LA Theater Works, with executive producer Susan Albert Lowenberg as executive producer, traveled to different cities and put on radio productions like they used to do back in the golden days. Using sound effects like creaking doors opening, cars and planes taking off, and telephones ringing like the old-time radio shows.

"Nick Alcott, who had directed me in The Music Man at the University of Maryland, called me and said they were bringing in actress Marsha Mason and Senator Fred Thompson and others to do a radio presentation of Gore Vidal's *The Best Man*. I think you could play a couple of roles. Nick has been acting, writing, and directing for theatre and opera for more than forty years in DC and throughout the country and was on the faculty of Maryland Opera Studio. His local theatre credits include Arena Stage, Round House Theatre, and others.

"Nick told me, 'Fred Thompson, the senator, is playing Secretary William Russell. Marsha is playing his wife, and Congresswoman Connie Morella's son, Paul, who does a one-man show of *A Christmas Carol* at Ford's Theater every year, will be in the show.'

"I played three roles in this show, including broadcaster Walter Cronkite. At the first 'table read,' we all met for the first time. Marsha Mason couldn't have been nicer. Fred Thompson came in, grabbed my hand, and said, 'Jimmy Holliday?' I said, 'Close. It's Johnny,' and he smiled and said, 'Oh yeah, Johnny. How are you, man?'

"So, we're sitting at this big table for the first read-through. Senator Thompson's got this deep, slow-speaking voice, and we get about three minutes into it. And Nick interrupts and says, 'Fred, let me stop you. We don't want to put the people to sleep. Let's pick this up a bit. Can we have a little more energy?'

"And everybody's like, 'Whoa.' But Thompson says, 'Absolutely. Sure. It's too slow? Yeah, it's a little bit too down. I'll pick it up just a little bit. Okay?'

"He was great, and the audience at the Voice of America theater—about 500 folks—loved it. And I got to be Walter Cronkite on old-time radio."

Chapter 48 – House of Musical Traditions

© S. Moore

David Eisner, the founder of the House of Musical Traditions in Takoma Park, MD, arrived at the University of Maryland from his New Jersey home in 1966. Eisner recalls "Back then when you came to the University of Maryland, you met your student advisor. You go to an orientation. I was an out of state guy coming down on a swimming scholarship. The advisor looked at me and thought, out of state, Jewish, honors, and an athlete so I was accepted into the cool fraternity, Tau Epsilon Phi.

"We would try and get as many of our TEP brothers to be student advisors because we could then get the pick of the crop. We would see who the cool kids were and tell them which fraternities to check out when they started coming to class in September.

"TEP didn't do hazing or any of that sort of thing. We were all tracking towards graduating in four years. Med school. Law school. In my second semester, the position of social chairman came up. I was real interested in music stuff. I hung out in Greenwich Village as a kid. I liked parties. I could serve the fraternity. So, I become the social chairman and I was leading the social chairman life. Having a good time running the parties and hiring the bands.

"The UMD fraternities would have their own 'spring weekend' every year. And what that meant, in our case, was a trip to Virginia Beach and we'd rent most of the rooms in a hotel. And we'd hire a special band like Lawrence (Kidwell) and the Arabians. (Singer/keyboardist) Larry Kidwell and band played for us a lot."

Kidwell lived nearby in Hyattsville Maryland, and they were gigging four nights a week at schools, churches, and teen clubs, arriving in their own van dressed in matching blue tuxedos. They opened for the Turtles at the University of Maryland in 1968.

In 1962, the fourteen-year-old Larry Kidwell and his band Spectrum had their first paying gig at a University of Maryland frat house. "We knew ten songs and we had to play for four hours, so we repeated ourselves quite a bit," says Kidwell, who looking back after just crossing the half-century mark. "We did 'What'd I Say' and 'Tequila' and I probably have forgotten the rest on purpose," he says, laughing. The $10 that each member got had them on top of the world, and Kidwell knew he'd found what he wanted to do with his life.

By 1965, he formed the band Lawrence and the Arabians, and its horn-driven soul music was the toast of the long-vanished "teen club" circuit. That year they recorded their first single, a cover of "Oh Baby Baby" backed by an original, Coincidence and everything was coming up roses for the group of teenagers from Prince George County. For the next three years Kidwell (singing and playing bass and keyboards), Mike Zack (on drums), and their pals balanced concerts and school, becoming one of the most celebrated bands in the area, playing mostly cover versions of soul tunes.

Eric Brace, Musician, Washington Post writer

"Another Larry who was very active in TEP and became our President in my senior year. He was a unique person in many ways, and a very good athlete. He played pretty good fraternity basketball. A baller from Brooklyn. He was so devoted to the fraternity that he almost flunked out. But socially, as kindly as

I can say this, he was a little bit awkward with women. His name was **Larry David**."

Larry in glasses in 1968
© UMD yearbook

"Now we're coming up on the spring weekend and Larry comes to me,

'Uh, Dave. You're the social chairman. You know lots of girls. See if you can find me a date for the Virginia beach trip. I'm going to be at the head table. I don't have a date.'"

Eisner continues, "There was a great bar near the University of Maryland gates called the Varsity Grill. In the back room there was live music, and if it was after 11 p.m. the people who liked to drink would be there.

"Getting Larry David a date for this trip might be considered pimping a little bit, but I'd rather say that I saw this as a personal challenge. So, on a Wednesday night I find this girl. I don't remember her name. It's late at night. I'm pretty sure that she thought that I was inviting her as my date. I get all her information. I go back to Larry and tell him ' I got you a date.'

"On Friday, as we're leaving. She meets Larry. But when we get to the hotel we get into trouble.

"'Where's my room?'" she asks. And we started to explain that she would be sharing the room with Larry. Now she's real sober, real clearheaded. She's like, 'Oh no.' I can't do that. I'm not doing that. I'll sit at the table with him. But no, I'm not doing that."

It turned out all right in the end because many guys had dates there but weren't sleeping with them. David Eisner continued talking "off record" about Larry who has kept up with his fraternity brothers and returns to reunions. The only other secret he would reveal is that Larry's nickname was "Cubes."

* * *

The House of Musical Traditions [HMT] has been in business since 1972 and was voted "Best Place To Buy Musical Instruments" in the *Washington City Paper* reader poll seven times. But it's much more than a music store. It soon became a major community when I lived on Philadelphia Ave with Chris Li, Victoria Lewis, and Frank Simeone the year it opened.

Eisner's father was a dentist in West Orange, NJ, and also first chair violinist in the New Jersey Symphony. By the time David hit College Park he knew his was around musicians.

As a child growing up in West Orange, New Jersey, he was often surrounded by the musician friends of his father, who had a dual career as a dentist in New York City and as a first chair violinist in the New Jersey Symphony. As student advisor to the UMD administrators he also helped produce shows like Sly and the Family Stone, Paul Butterfield Blues Band, Aretha Franklin, and more. And, by his junior year, he was taking elective courses that got him psyched about non-western music.

Dark Horse

Here's another story David shared for this book: "I'm in the store in 1976, the original location on Carroll Avenue. We get a phone call from some Indian musicians that are playing a concert that evening. They tell us they haven't been able to find anybody who can work on their instruments. 'The harmonium is buzzing like mad and we need new strings for the tambura,' they said.

"So, in walks a guy with a couple of Indian musicians and introduces himself to me and my worker, Kevin, as Jim Horn. I had heard the name. Where are you playing tonight? I asked.

"'The Capital Centre,' he said.

"We were able to fix the instruments. Harmoniums are pretty easy to fix. A piece of sawdust or something will work. It is way under one of the reeds, and it will buzz until you blow the freaking piece of sawdust out. They were very happy and asked, 'How much do we owe you?' I charged them thirty bucks and put it in our shoebox. We didn't even have a cash register back then.

"Jim Horn asked, 'Are you coming to the show tonight?'

"'What show?' And he said, 'The Dark Horse tour with George Harrison. Look, you guys have been really nice to us. Here's a couple tickets.'

"'Oh wow,' I said. So I turned to Kevin and asked you want to go to this. And he says, 'Yeah.' When we got to the Cap Center and presented our tickets to the usher, he says, 'You can go wherever you want.'

"'But I want my seat,' and he answered, 'I can't help you with that.'

"What? They weren't tickets. They were *backstage passes*. We go backstage and see our Indian buddies. And people were playing volleyball backstage. Not our Indian buddies but Billy Preston and George Harrison. Yeah.

"They're playing volleyball because a net was already set up. At that time the Washington Bullets played there, and it was their locker area.

"And they were playing hard. Oh, man. And Billy Preston is spiking the ball. And they are all getting into it. Their tour manager is standing close by and I'm thinking if George jams a finger or breaks a wrist because they weren't just going 'Tappy-Tappy.' They were having a blast.

"I go over to the manager standing nearby. I said, 'I don't think this is a very good idea. Somebody could get hurt here.' And the guy looks at me and said, 'Yeah, kid. You go fucking tell them.'

"And that's how I met Bill Graham. Apparently he was down for that tour."

Harrison and band played two shows at the Cap Center (Feb 13 and 14, 1974.) Critics ravaged the tour, and Harrison commented a few years later, "Isn't it a pity that a lot of people missed out on something that went above their heads."

* * *

The **House of Musical Traditions** began in 1972 when Eisner purchased the remaining inventory of a Musical Traditions dulcimer shop in New York City.

David's first storefront in Takoma Park, MD, was at 7040 Carroll Ave until 2008, where they moved to their current location at 7010 Westmoreland Avenue, just a block away.

He started a folk concert series inside the store in the 1980s, which eventually became the Institute of Musical Traditions. In 2017, the store expanded its lessons program, which is now the School of Musical Traditions. Private and group lessons are offered at the school's main location at 7112 Willow Ave, Takoma Park, MD. SMT also offers virtual lessons.

Chapter 49 – Ron Holloway & Horn

© S. Moore

Around 2001, saxophonist Ron Holloway played the Ram's Head Music Club in Annapolis.

"I had this little gig where I performed with one person. Sometimes, Deanna Bogart or Daryl Davis and other musicians I really admired. So, I'm leaving Ram's Head one night, walking toward the parking lot. Some guy asks loudly, 'Hey, what you got in that case?'

"'My saxophone.'

"'Oh, was that you playing tonight? Why don't you come by tomorrow night and play with us?

"I ask, 'Who are you with?'

"He answers, 'Little Feat. I'm their road manager. I'm sure the guys would enjoy you coming by and sitting in.'

"'Okay, I'll be there.'

"Little Feat's guitarist Paul Barrere was a little nervous the next night because the band was recording their show. Dick Bangham was there, and Paul asked him, 'Is this guy with the saxophone all right,' and Dick laughed, 'Yeah.'

"So, I'd never played with Little Feat before, and there was no rehearsal. But I knew their music from the radio. I jammed toward the end of their first set, and one of the songs came out on their next album.

"After I had been sitting in with Little Feat for a few years, (Feat keyboardist) Bill Payne's phone rang, and somebody from the Allman Brothers organization asked if Little Feet could come and open for them the very next night. Fortunately, Little Feet was off. So, I also played with Little Feet at the Nissan Pavilion in Virginia.

"We finished our set. I'm walking off the stage and heading backstage, and Warren Haynes, founding member of the Government Mule band and longtime guitarist with the Allman Brothers band walked by me. He stops and turns around. 'Hey, Ron. How would you like to sit in with the Brothers tonight?'"

Ronald Edward Holloway

Born August 24, 1953, at Georgetown Hospital, the future sax man grew up in the Mayfair Mansions garden-style apartment neighborhood in northeast DC. It was his parents, Marjorie and Winston Holloway, ardent jazz fans who courted while attending Howard University, who encouraged music for young Ron. His father's jazz records influence and fondness for the sax was apparent when Ron began playing music.

Like his father, Ron preferred the jazz horn players—Sonny Rollins, John Coltrane, and Miles Davis primarily—but he also enjoyed playing rock, blues, country, and folk.

"My career started before I played with anybody famous," Holloway explains. "What I began doing in my formative years was trying to get out, play live, and sit in."

Sitting in with as many bands as often as he could—realizing when he must spontaneously blend in, improvise, and contribute to the music, would accelerate his learning is how Ron views it.

"I would sit in with R&B bands, Top 40 bands, blues bands. And eventually, in 1972, I sat in with my first live jazz band at the Luau Inn on 19th Street NW. There, they had a jam session that started at midnight. I also went with my dad to Harold's Rogue and Jar, owned by Dr. Harold Kaufman, a jazz player and psychiatrist.

"Meanwhile, I joined R&B bands like The Sounds of Shea and Mad Dog & the Lowlifers after Montgomery Blair High School in Takoma Park, MD.

"However, I realized I needed to be challenged more. So, I decided to play with some national acts, and I made the effort.

"This worked out very well because in 1974 I met Freddie Hubbard. A couple of years before, he had already won a Grammy with the album *First Light*, which included pianist Herbie Hancock, guitarist George Benson, and bassist Ron Carter, among others. When we met, I brought Freddie a cassette tape I had made playing one of his recordings, and he invited me to sit in with him.

"The next year, Sonny Rollins played at a clinic at Howard University, a specialized music workshop for students and the public, where I joined Rollins onstage to do 'Playin' in the Yard.' We became good friends.

"And in 1978, I went to the Showboat Lounge, which was Charlie Byrd's new jazz club that opening in Silver Spring, MD. Dizzy Gillespie was playing that night. I got there an hour early. Dizzy had a habit of sitting in a dressing room, holding out long tones, and warming up on the trumpet. Sure enough, I followed the sounds to his room, where the door was open. I stood in the door frame holding a little Panasonic tape recorder. I didn't want to interrupt him.

"Finally, when he stopped playing, he looked up and immediately said, 'What you got on the tape?'

"'A cassette of me sitting in with Sonny Rollins,' I answered, and that was the first music of mine he heard.

"And as soon as my solo was over, he whirled around in his seat. We were sitting side by side at this point, and with excitement like a kid, he asked, 'You got your horn?'

"I replied, 'No sir, I didn't want to appear presumptuous.'

"'Presumptuous? Now there's a word,' Dizzy exclaimed. We both cracked up and hit it off together real fast."

Holloway would next show up whenever Dizzy performed in town. One night in June 1989 at Blues Alley, Dizzy surprised Ron by inviting him to a worldwide tour through Europe and the US, landing them on TV shows like Johnny Carson and

Arsenio Hall. Holloway also played on two albums: *Live at Blues Alley* and *The Symphony Sessions*.

From June 1989 until Dizzy passed away on January 6, 1993, Ron was a true member of Dizzy Gillespie's quintet.

This credit help land Ron Holloway in the *Biographical Encyclopedia of Jazz* as a "bear-down-hard-bopper who can blow authentic R&B and croon a ballad with warm, blue feeling."

He has earned forty-two "Wammies, with two as Musician of the Year."

Not Just Jazz

Holloway's penchant for jamming with players soon proved non-denominational as his local prominence evolved. He joined Root Boy Slim's Sex Change Band (as explored in Chapter 39) and shared this surprising story:

"1981 Stevie Ray Vaughn was playing at Desperado's right across the street from the Cellar Door. Stevie had played his first set, and he disappeared. I knew he'd probably gone up to the attic with the club owner, Neil Cohen, because I knew the club well. So, I just made my way up to the attic. Sure enough, there they were, and Neil knew me.

"He said, 'Stevie, I want to introduce you to one of our local great musicians. This is Ron Holloway.'

"*Wow*, I thought and said, 'Man, it was such a pleasure to meet you. I'm a definite fan. I wanted to ask if you ever let a saxophonist sit in with you. Stevie kind of smiled, looked at the club owner, looked back at me, and asked, 'Well, what would we play?'

"And I said, 'Do you know any Hendrix?'

"Stevie laughed and said, 'Yeah, I know a few.'

"But then it came time for him to go back on stage. And I think I said, 'So when do you want me to come up?'

"'I don't know,' Stevie answered. 'Come on up at the beginning of the set.'

"And I said 'okay.'

"With no rehearsal and I didn't know what he was going play—every song was a Hendrix tune. We played 'Fire,' 'The Wind Cries Mary,' 'Crosstown Traffic,' and other famous Jimi tunes. And we traded back and forth, playing separate solos. We had a blast."

Gil Scott-Heron

"Gil is a musician I started hearing on the radio in the 1970s. Cuts like 'Angel Dust,' 'Johannesburg,' and 'Winter in America,' on the black radio stations driving in my car, and occasionally on WHFS because they played everybody. I'd listen to him late at night on Pacifica. After hearing him for years, I thought I've got to meet him because he's really great.

"Dizzy started playing Blues Alley about three times a year when the Showboat around 1981. The waitresses at Blues Alley were encouraging to me and often suggested people for me to sit in with. One was Norman Connors, a jazz drummer popular then who had scored several US hit records with guest vocalists. The most successful of these was *You Are My Starship* with Michael Henderson, Miles Davis's bass player, singing.

"I was off work on Norman's gig night and went and introduced myself. He was very much liked in the DC area. It was packed that night, and it was hard for me to even get up to the stage, but I did. I didn't know what we were going to play, which is not unusual. And it came time for me to solo. Norman gave me a nod, and it went really well. The crowd really enjoyed what I did, and the set ended.

"In the middle of the steps leading from the club up to the dressing room to put my horn away I hear somebody with a baritone voice say, 'Hey, I like how you handled yourself up there.'

"I looked around and immediately burst out laughing because I recognized Gil as soon as I saw him. I said, 'I'm sorry; I don't mean to be laughing, but you caught me by surprise. I never expected you, and didn't even know you were here in the club.'

"Gil and I talked upstairs, and he said, 'I'm starting a new band and want you to play saxophone.' I was one of the few people that he hired directly. This was November of 1981, and our first rehearsal was February 1982. Gil remembered that I was supposed to show up. We had a good rehearsal in a house on 14th Street.

"Most of the band members were from DC. It was Rob Gordon, on electric bass, Ed Brady on guitar. Kenny Powell was our drummer. The horn section was Vernon James, on alto sax and flute, Kenny Sheffield on trumpet and me. We had a three-piece horn section. Glen 'Astro' Turner played keyboards.

"Carl Cornwell would sometimes come and play tenor and soprano sax and flute, but Carl wasn't a regular member. Carl Cornwell had gone to school with Gil, and they were good friends," says Ron.

A 1983 documentary movie called *Back Wax* featured Heron and his Midnight Band. The club scenes were done at the old Wax Museum. Janet Maslin of *The New York Times* reviewed the movie:

"There are musicians whose work can't easily be encapsulated by the documentary film format, and there are others, like Gil Scott-Heron, who make a particularly keen impression this way. *Black Wax*, a seventy-nine-minute portrait of Mr. Scott-Heron made for British television—jadroitly directed by Robert Muggeby—shows him off to excellent advantage.

"The scope of his topical, acerbic songs and poems—among them 'Johannesburg,' 'Angel Dust,' 'Gun' and 'Whitey on the Moon'—is well represented by the excerpts included here, and no single work has a chance to go on too long. The songs are interspersed between scenes of Mr. Scott-Heron wandering through Washington—he has a song about that, too—discussing political ironies as he wanders past national monuments and then ghetto neighborhoods...Besides, Mr. Scott-Heron can make glibness something of a virtue. As he leads into a routine about nostalgia that would do any stand-up comic proud, Mr. Scott-Heron offers a quick and effective series of wisecracks.

"'That's what America wants, the good old days,' he says. 'Remember when we gave ''em hell, when the buck stopped here and you could buy something with it, when the movies were in black and white and so was everything else? Why wait for 1984? Panic now and avoid the rush. So much for the good news.'"

Gil Scott-Heron called himself a "bluesologist," deeply concerned with the origin of the blues. His poem "The Revolution Will Not Be Televised," delivered over a soul-jazz rhythm, was a major influence on hip hop.

Beginning in 1972, Scott-Heron taught creative writing and literature creative writing for several years as a full-time lecturer at Federal City College University, later to be the University of the District of Columbia [UDC] while maintaining his music career.

The influential poet and musician died on May 27, 2011 at the age of sixty-two in New York City. The cause of death was reported to be complications related to heart disease and the previous battle with HIV. He left a lasting impact on hip hop and social commentary through art. His poignant reflections on social issues, race and justice continue to resonate with audiences today.

Ron and Gill from Black Wax

The Ron Holloway Band: Jenny Langer (vocals), Justin Gillen (guitar, Ron Holloway (tenor saxophone), Noah Pierre (bass), Rachel Ann Morgan (vocals) and Barry Sherard (drums)
Photo by Nate Payne.

In the *Biographical Encyclopedia of Jazz*, renowned jazz critic Ira Gitler describes Ron Holloway as "a bear-down-hard-bopper who can blow authentic R&B and croon a ballad with warm, blue feeling."

The cut from Ron's first jamming with Little Feat at Rams Head that made it to release was "Feats Don't Fail Me Now."

Chapter 50 - Dr. Cleve from the Heart

In 2020, Cleve Francis, country music singer-songwriter and cardiologist, celebrated his thirtieth year as a Birchmere music hall headliner.

Growing up poor in Louisiana "Cajun" country, Cleve taught himself guitar at the age of nine, inspired by the music of Sam Cooke, Hank Williams, Nat King Cole, James Brown, Mahalia Jackson, and Elvis Presley. While attending William & Mary University he developed a coffee house following, performing soulful folk music. After graduating in 1973 from the Medical College of Virginia (now Virginia Commonwealth University Medical School)—the first African American to do so—he became a board-certified cardiologist.

Cleve invited me to co-author his autobiography. With *Capital Acts* in progress, I wouldn't have time to do that, but I did agree to help him get a book deal. This is the sample chapter that we wrote and submitted to the CMA. His book, *A Heart's Journey through Music, Medicine, and History* will be published in 2025 by the Country Music Hall of Fame. The following is Cleve telling his Washington DC story about how he made it to Nashville:

On an otherwise ordinary Friday night, 47-year-old Olaf "Pug" Hall was relaxing with his wife, Betty, when he felt nauseous and complained of chest pains. She called 911, and he was next sweating profusely in an ambulance heading to nearby Mount Vernon Hospital, two miles away.

My pager vibrated and the number was the Emergency Room. As on-call cardiologist I straightaway returned the call. The ER physician described Hall's symptoms: I thought a myocardial infarction—"MI" for short—a heart attack for real.

I drove to the hospital in fifteen minutes and read his electrocardiogram. Hall had an acute inferior wall myocardial infarction—the coronary artery supplying blood to the right side and bottom of his heart was clogged. A normal "lub dub" pulse of the heart requires healthy blood flow. Arrhythmias, from the Greek word for "lack of rhythm," could kill him. Another concern was the occluded artery supplying blood to the natural pacemaker of his heart might lead to heart blockage. Then I'd need to immediately implant a temporary pacemaker to keep him alive. My newest patient had heart failure.

None of this was good news for either of us. At minimum it meant an all-nighter for me if I was to save him. These days modern hospitals have advanced critical care units staffed with specialized doctors and nurses. Had he come to the hospital in 2024, they'd send him directly to the cardiac catheterization lab. They'd give him a coronary stent to open the closed artery to prevent muscle damage to his heart.

Unfortunately, this technology was not yet advanced or affordable for widespread use in the late 1980s. It would be only me and his nurse for the next twenty-four hours there to treat him. It was my stubborn mind for his unsteady heart.

We spent the entire night caring for him. As sunlight shown into his room, he was asleep. I was pleased with his progress. Mr. Hall awakened with a "Good morning, Doctor," and told me I looked tired. His eyesight was good. He added, "I hope you get some rest before my brother gets here."

Around mid-morning, the critical care door swung open, and his charismatic 250-pound brother walked in. "Big John" Hall was decked like the Las Vegas Elvis: white pants, white patent leather shoes, white leather belt, blue shirt with wide open collar, silver neck chain, large rings glittering on most fingers of each hand, and wearing dark shades.

Standing at the nurse's station, he announced, "My name is Big John. I'm here to see my baby brother Pug. I want to speak to the doctor who's taking care of him."

I introduced myself and reassured him that Pug was not out of danger but had improved. Pug was in the hospital for a week before being discharged. Olaf "Pug" Hall became my patient and friend. I had no problems with that personal relationship. I visited him at his home, and he was obviously still smoking, although he pretended that he wasn't. But I could see and smell right through him. His brother and I discovered we had music in common. Where we differed was that he was the real deal. "Big John Hall" was a full-time musician with flair.

A former lead singer and the only white member of the Heartbeats, a '50s and '60s R&B/Soul music group. He was still performing in what we called the Chitlin' Circuit. Eddie Jones and the Young Bucks, a local band, backed him up. They played all over the country but mainly in the south.

Big John introduced me to Eddy and his all-Black R&B band from southeast Washington. Southeast was a mainly Black lower economic area of Washington, DC, with a high crime rate. The 1950s history of this poor part of DC reminded me of Jennings during segregation. African Americans faced poverty and discrimination in their everyday lives. They were forced to live in overcrowded and dilapidated housing, attend underfunded schools, and work in low-wage jobs.

Despite the conditions, the Black community of Southeast DC was resilient, tight-knit, and infused with exciting cultural and political energy from schools and churches to social clubs and organizations. The community banded together to fight for their rights, uplift their culture, and create a better future for themselves and their children. Eddie Jones and the Young Bucks were dynamic examples of this vitality.

After listening to my music, John decided that I should consider moving away from playing the guitar into a lead vocalist. He felt that my singing voice was good enough to perform for audiences. He thought this was an art I could learn.

The idea was scary because I always accompanied myself. The acoustic guitar was my security blanket. I could touch and feel the sound, and the timing was all in my control. Now I would be dependent on several other musicians.

John said, "Don't worry. Eddie Jones will teach you how to belt out the tunes without a guitar. Eddie did that for me, but he also helped me search collector's record stores for discs by

Johnny Ace, Jerry Butler, Brook Benton, and Sam Cooke. He believed these artists' melodies would complement my tenor voice—the same ones I grew up listening to and loving.

During the dinner set, John would call me to the stage to sing a couple songs. It was awkward at first. Without my guitar, I had to get used to the timing of the band, when to start, and how to end or extend songs. Gradually I would do more tunes.

During the dinner set John would call me to the stage to sing a couple songs. It was awkward at first. Without my guitar, I had to get used to the timing of the band, when to start, and how to end or extend songs. Gradually I would do more tunes.

After several months, the audience liked my songs so much that I earned the entire diner set. Business picked up. Eddie began calling me to the stage to do ballads during the second show, too. The phone was ringing making sure I was singing.

Next came Big John's invitation to join the band for his show on Coronado Island in San Diego. John was still the real deal, and he let me open with two songs. My duet partner Billy Pierce was not happy with my changes to folk solo. I wanted/needed to try something different. What I did not know was that John had taken a copy of my LP to Miami to the home of Jack Gale, owner of Playback Records. Gale called me in my cardiology office. He said that he liked my voice and was open to recording me. He would find songs that might showcase my voice. He thought that Cleve Francis was ideal for country flavored. © C. Francis.

Chapter 51 – How DC's Early Punk and New Wave Scene Changed the World (Just Kidding)

by Diana Quinn and David Wells

Diana Quinn and David Wells (above), along with Michael Mariotte, co-founded Tru Fax & the Insaniacs, a groundbreaking early punk/new wave band in DC

The early days of punk and new wave saw a tsunami of early stage, not-ready-for-prime-time garage bands in their first efforts to play out. The venues sparked and sparkled with excitement—the exhilaration of seeing and hearing something new—the relief of hearing and making music that wasn't the noodling of mainstream rock bands or the numbing robotics of disco.

> The band White Boy is playing at Shalimar, an Indian restaurant in Arlington, Virginia. The middle-aged lead singer, wearing a green toilet seat cover on his head, is writhing on the floor to the young guitarist's blazingly fast guitar work.

> *Hardcore pioneers Bad Brains are blowing the audience's minds with their acrobatics and speed in a dimly lit, pot-infused yippie townhouse on 18th Street NW.
> *At the Unheard Festival, at d.c. space, a dozen hardcore teenage band members are circling around The Nurses' frontman, Howard Wuelfing, and singing along to The Monkees' "(I'm Not Your) Steppin' Stone."

Our memories of the very early years of DC punk and new wave are sporadic, sometimes hazy, often incomplete. They add up to a blurry snapshot of the surprisingly fast ascent of the DC punk and new wave scene starting in 1979. Those early days influenced many bands to come, including the hardcore punk bands, some of which would become nationally known.

The DC punk and new wave scene in the late 70s and early 80s was one of the first in the US. There was something about the music—its raw, unpolished energy and the way it embraced the outlandish and strange—that enchanted us. Unlike the lumbering status quo rock (now called "classic" rock) and slick disco of the times, the burgeoning punk and new wave scene was an invigorating alternative. The songs were brief and loud. The lyrics were smart, or purposefully dumb. The bands were usually stripped down to drums, bass, one or two guitars, and maybe keyboards. Songs often had no guitar solos and, if there were any, they were short. The scene itself was welcoming, especially for a young band like ours, which had no experience. Everyone knew each other, went to see each other play and often shared the same bill. It was a magical and earth- (and ear-) shattering time, and most people who were part of that scene will never forget it.

The first DC punk band was Overkill, an energetic and raw garage band. They played at the Keg, a dive bar north of Georgetown, in a shabby mini shopping center. Clubgoers could see the nearby strip club's "Clancy's House of Beef" sign from the parking lot. The Razz (later Razz), which also played at the Keg, was too good to be punk, but the flamboyant Michael Reidy and the band's insane brand of power pop were a huge influence on the early bands. The Look was another band which played at the Keg; some of its members later joined other bands, including the Nurses and Urban Verbs.

The Urban Verbs was a band which was too accomplished to be considered punk, but it was integral to the punk scene and very influential on bands which followed. The band rehearsed in the Atlantis Building at 930 F Street NW and put on the first punk show in what would later be called the 9:30 Club. They had ties to the Talking Heads, played at art galleries and museums and, unlike all the other bands, were signed to Warner Brothers and released two albums. The Urban Verbs were very influential in the early punk scene. They got signed, but didn't get national recognition. Most punk bands at the time had little interest in being signed to a major label; they saw how the system worked, and how it didn't benefit the musicians. (For example, Tru Fax slipped label scouts' business cards back under dressing room doors, refusing to talk to them.)

Of course, we saw our heroes come to town to play at places like Louie's Rock City in northern Virginia (The Ramones—although the band wore ripped jeans, fans showing up in similar attire were forced to go to the nearby K-Mart to buy new pants. Back then, new jeans did not already have premade holes or rips!) or the Atlantis at 930 F Street NW. (The Police wore their brand-new, gleaming white Chucks, and their light show was one of those cheesy revolving color wheels with three colors, stuck in front on the stage.) We were happy to see those acts, but we were more interested in seeing other local bands, and in forming our own. The local bands were interesting, unpolished and not yet fully formed. They were exciting!

What were we trying to say? A large part of the punk/new wave movement was a reaction against the music which dominated the industry and the mainstream airwaves. Punk was anti-mainstream and anti-commercial and musically rebelled against many things, not just bloated mainstream rock or robotic disco.

Lyrics often talked about the politics of the day. Tru Fax & the Insaniacs wrote many of what we called "news rock" songs, dealing with topics like nuclear energy or presidential campaigns. We also coined the word "waitron," a genderless robotic server, which was featured in the song "Washingtron," and which is now in the Oxford English Dictionary. Other bands' lyrics varied widely, but one thing they had in common: the lyrics in no way resembled those heard on mainstream radio. For example, Half Japanese's songs were often about monsters.

A partial list of the early bands includes Overkill, The Look, the Slickee Boys, White Boy, The Nurses, The Chumps, Half Japanese, The Penetrators, Thee Katatonix, The Urban Verbs, Tiny Desk Unit, Black Market Baby, The Penetrators, Tru Fax & the Insaniacs, and The Insect Surfers. The bands didn't bother to try to categorize themselves into exactly what kind of music we were playing, we were all part of a new musical thing, and that was what counted.

An early venue for punk bands and a catalyst and incubator for the punk rock movement was the original Madam's Organ (no relation except in name to the current bar owned by Bill Duggan), a rundown townhouse in lower Adam's Morgan (18th Street NW, near Florida Avenue) run by Yippies. Anything was allowed, or, rather, nothing was disallowed. In the dank, dark, and creepy basement, a synthesizer player named Rupert wore an outfit of chain mail and ran psychedelic lightshows. On the first floor, in the boarded-up bay window, bands played on wooden pallets and yes, it was like performing on a creaky, dangerous trampoline. It was almost always completely packed on weekends, but it lasted only about a year.

That was the first place we saw Bad Brains play. They took the hard side of punk and ramped up the speed and the volume, and so did the hard-core kids who followed, like Minor Threat, SOA, Teen Idols, Youth Brigade, Government Issue, and the Untouchables. Out of that scene, Fugazi and SOA's Henry Rollins went on to national recognition. (We're proud to say that we often had some of these bands open for us, and they always got paid.)

The night we saw Bad Brains, the place was jammed, it was smoky, the strong smell of pot was everywhere, and it was loud. When they started playing, the roof might as well have blasted off. They were the fastest band we'd ever seen—much faster than the Ramones. Singer HR was non-stop energy, practically doing somersaults on the bouncy stage, and the musicians were really accomplished. They were also Black, which was very unusual in the DC punk scene. The crowd, mouths gaping, recognized that they'd never seen anything like the Bad Brains. A combination of mismanagement and the band's own personal demons eventually sabotaged their potential success. Later, the group, originally a jazz fusion band, gradually introduced reggae into its punk sound and eventually branched out into other genres.

The scene and the bands owed their sudden popularity and growth to the local independent radio stations, record stores, newspapers, and the fans. Both Georgetown University's WGTB (especially Steve Lorber's Mystic Eyes program) and DJs at independent station WHFS embraced the new sound. *The Unicorn Times* and, later, to a larger extent, the *City Paper*, covered the fresh and scrappy new movement. Punk/new wave record stores Yesterday and Today (Skip Groff), in Rockville, and Record and Tape Exchange (Bill and Melanie Asp), in Arlington, were foci for musicians who weren't only looking for the latest 45s and albums, but also for other players looking to form new bands. Groff and the Asps also ran their own record labels, Limp and WASP, respectively. Dischord Records (Ian MacKaye and Jeff Nelson) formed in 1980 to put out hardcore records, and still releases music by DC-area bands. Clubs like the pioneering d.c. space, the tiny, narrow Psyche Delly in Bethesda, Reeks on the Hill, The Chancery, opened their doors to the punks. The Atlantis and, soon after, in the same space, the original 9:30 Club (Dody deSanto and Jon Bowers) also helped the scene grow, as well as I.M.P. productions (Seth Hurwitz), which paired local punk and new wave bands with touring bands. In Towson, there was the Oddfellows' Club, and, in Baltimore, The Marble Bar made punk rock history. Another important place was Don Zientara's Inner Ear Studios, which offered a relatively inexpensive way for bands to make records.

However, it was those early bands who deserved most of the credit. It was all DIY. You didn't have to know how to play your instrument, but it helped. You didn't have to be a great

singer, but it helped if you could sing in tune. You didn't even have to have your instruments tuned, but it helped to have a tuning fork (automatic tuners had yet to be invented).

Bands found places to play, whether in someone's basement, a park, or an unused storefront. They put up flyers everywhere they could and invited other bands to be on double and triple bills. Some bands only had one set! They designed their own logos, printed their own 45s, and made their own promotional buttons, which often covered their fans' jackets. Some started punk fanzines and gave them out for free.

In the true DIY punk spirit, and the Insaniacs, after months of practicing almost every night, started organizing our own shows in 1979. Our first was in a DC townhouse called the Hard Art Gallery, the organizers of which were two musicians billing themselves as The Bad Seeds. We had sent in the roughest of demo tapes, recorded in our basement, and they invited to play. We were astonished when they commented on our "great hooks," saying, "You guys have actual arrangements." We laughed and laughed.

For our second show, we used an abandoned store near the old Lansburgh department store downtown, not too far from d.c. space, which would become an important DC venue for punk and new wave shows. It was packed. It was also small and hot. We sold cans of cold beer for a dollar out of garbage cans (the same price as admission), and our PA system was two Shure columns, one mic and mic stand, no monitors, and a tuning fork. We used our old 1960s Fender Twins and vintage guitars, and we had to nail David's old drum set into the floor so that Michael wouldn't be able to move it across the "stage" with his powerful drumming. Our bass player, Libby Hatch, played a guitar as big as she was, with an amp that weighed more than she did.

Speaking of Libby, she and Diana were among the early female punk rockers who sang, wrote songs, and played instruments, smashing that dirty glass ceiling for female rockers to come. In the histories of punk in DC, not much is written about those early female players. Perhaps the subject will be a chapter in another book or a book itself.

Those early days were inspirational. It was a small, diverse scene, smart, energetic, sometimes satirical, sometimes tuneless, sometimes tuneful, but always a lot of fun. For us, music was about more than just playing; it was about connecting with our audience through a shared sense of humor, intelligence, and rebellion against the status quo, whether that was top 40s radio, big record companies, or presidential politics.

An addendum:

We owe a lot to the venue owners who gave us chances and stood up for us when we needed it (thanks Dody), to our friends who shared our strange and exhilarating journey, and to our fans, who laughed with us and gave us suggestions for songs (and jokes). This includes our good friend Robbie White, who promoted bands, booked clubs, and who has a radio show called Forbidden Alliance on the independent Takoma Park radio station WWOD-LP. Robbie, who was there from almost the beginning, still carries the torch for those bands and that music.

Thank you
Diana & Dave

Henry Lawrence Garfield, known as **Henry Rollins**, was born Feb 3, 1961, in Washington, DC. An only child of Iris and Paul Garfield, his mother was Irish; his father, Jewish. He grew up in in Glover Park, a neighborhood north of Georgetown.

He attended Bullis, an all-male school in Potomac "preparing graduates for the Naval Academy or West Point." Rollins has said that Bullis gave him a strong work ethic, and it's where he began writing.

After Bullis came one semester at American University, but dropped out in December 1979. He dropped out and began working day jobs, the first as a courier of kidney samples for NIH.

By the time he had worked his way up to being assistant manager at the Georgetown, he had discovered a love for music introduced by Van Halen and Ted Nugent, But in his words he was still looking for something "that really kicked ass," and his friend **Ian Thomas Garner MacKaye,** also born in DC and raised in Glover Park bought an album by the Sex Pistols. Henry thought the singer was "really pissed off" and the guitars were "rude."

A friend gifted Henry Rollins the *Nervous Breakdown* EP by Black Flag, igniting his passion for the band. He began exchanging letters with bassist Chuck Dukowski and later invited the band to stay at his parents' home during their East Coast tour in December 1980.

Henry attended as many concerts as possible, and at an improv show in New York, Black Flag's vocalist, Dez Cadena, invited Henry to sing a song after he had requested it.

Unbeknownst to Henry, the band was looking for a new vocalist as Cadena wanted to switch to guitar. They were impressed by Henry's singing and stage presence, and the next day, after a semi-formal audition, they asked him to become their permanent vocalist.

Rollins quit his job at Häagen-Dazs, sold his car, and moved to Los Angeles. Upon his arrival, he got the Black Flag logo tattooed on his left arm and adopted the stage name **Henry Rollins.**

SM

Chapter 52 – Pat (WPAS) and Mike (WAMA)

Distinguished, fortunate yet sometimes peculiar partnerships have bloomed between the Feds, local DC government, and our vibrant entertainment community over the years.

Today, the Washington DC headquarters of the Motion Picture Association of America is in the Jack Valenti Building, located at 888 16th Street NW, very close to the White House. Both the Smithsonian's National Museum of American History and National Museum of African American History and Culture have extensive collections related to American music, theater, and dance. The Kennedy Center, National Archives, and Library of Congress protect valuable materials related to entertainment. Georgetown and George Washington Universities do the same. There are many others.

And the **National Capital Radio and Television Museum**, located in Bowie, MD, is dedicated to broadcasting history. The land and house where this museum now stands were originally owned by my Great Uncle Alec Harmel. I used to visit him with my grandfather, Richard Harmel on many weekends growing up.

Once the **Harmel Homestead**, and now the National Capital Radio & Television Museum
© S. Moore

The next two DC champions dynamically and selflessly began organizations to promote performing artists. Both worked tirelessly with local and Federal agencies on behalf of artists. We salute them.

Patrick Hayes

When Patrick Hayes died in 1998 at eighty-nine, the *New York Times* wrote, "He was of the last of the American impresarios and virtually the only presenter of musicians, singers, and dancers in Washington before the Kennedy Center for the Performing Arts opened in 1971."

Haye's motto was "Everybody In, Nobody Out." He came from New York to Washington, DC, in 1941 to become the manager of the National Symphony Orchestra. In his forty-year career, Hayes brought to Washington world-renowned classical and opera stars like Marian Anderson, Arturo Toscanini, Van Cliburn, Vladimir Horowitz, Rudolf Serkin, Jascha Heifetz, Leontyne Price, Arthur Rubinstein, and Mstislav Rostropovich. He also booked pop artists, including Louis Armstrong and Judy Garland, and he attracted famous performance companies to the city, such as the Metropolitan Opera, the Dance Theater of Harlem, the Martha Graham Dance Company, the Bolshoi Ballet, and the Alvin Ailey Dance Theater.

But beyond promoting DC's cosmopolitan culture, Hayes enormously helped desegregate the performing arts in Washington. Until the 1950s, the artists who performed in the nation's capital did so in Washington, where segregation was still the order of the day. Hayes brought DC businesspeople together to desegregate the lunch counters and theaters downtown. When he created the **Washington Performing Arts Society (WPAS)** in 1966, he chose the famous baritone Todd Duncan as the board's first chairman. The selection of Duncan, who created the role of Porgy in George Gershwin's *Porgy and Bess* and lived in DC, let the arts community know that African Americans had to be included in their productions. No stranger to racial prejudice in the arts, Patrick Hayes used D.A.R. Constitution Hall for National Symphony concerts when Black opera star Marian Anderson was forced to perform at the Lincoln Memorial instead.

Patrick Hayes, with Todd Duncan © WPAS

Donn Murphy introduced me to Patrick Hayes in 1993. Hayes presented us at a launch party for our book Helen *Hayes: A Bio-Bibliography* at the National Theatre. Many people came to our reception, including my wife, Margaret, and parents.

In 1984, Donn and I interviewed Hayes in Donn's National Theatre office. Hayes's father was Patrick Carney, but he took his mother's name and said he was "born in a trunk."

Hayes explained, "My father was a very fine-looking actor with a bright face, blue eyes, and a big smile; they used to kid him about flirting with the ladies—a typical Irishman. Those were the days of stock companies and touring companies; they worked forty-two weeks a year, had good wages, and took the summer off."

We began our interview with a question to Hayes: What precisely does an impresario do? Hayes replied, "There is no mystery in what show business is, whether it is theater or concerts. You take a contract and do your best in the right place. Remember the three As? The actor or artist, the auditorium where they work, and the audience. You put those three things together, and you got your show. The first two are easy. You can do this on two telephones."

Hayes explained when he got New York calls, "'Is the week of April 18, 1985, open at your theatre?' You say, 'Yes.' They say to pencil it in. At that point, you've got a booking. It's on the book for the artist or company and your theatre. Then, you go to work to build the audience. Subscription plans. Block sales and benefit parties, and it's not as easy as it might seem, but you have lots of time. That's the fundamental heart of American enterprise in the theater." Why is this important?

"I graduated from Harvard University in 1929, just in time for the Depression, and had many jobs, including master of ceremonies in a nightclub.

(l to r) Donn, Patrick, Me, and Mom © Margaret Moore

"I was with the N.B.C. Artists Bureau in a division called Civic Concert Service, setting up music associations in towns and villages that would not otherwise have live entertainment. I'd get a group of members to pay $5.00 a ticket purchase, and for that, during the year, they got three or more concerts by nationally known and the best artists. I served in the Navy during World War II and arrived in Washington, DC, in January 1941 to become the manager of the National Symphony Orchestra. I was 32 and jumped into my work."

When asked what Washington, DC, was like in those days, Hayes responded, "I arrived in January 1941 to become manager of The National Symphony Orchestra. I was fresh from the road, where I had lots of experience in getting ready for my job, which had to do, quite frankly, with audience building.

"Washington was smaller then, more southern than northern, to be equated, I think, with Richmond and Atlanta, not Philadelphia and New York. I found friendliness, openness, gentility, the beauty of the place, and a certain grace of life for all. It was indeed a completely segregated city—black and white—but the potential was there for integration, which we have now accomplished. I think Washington is indeed a beautiful provincial town. I do not regard the word 'provincial' as a naughty word. When I hear people insist that you have to be in New York City, I think, who wants to be in New York City?"

Hayes talked about volunteering for the Navy as an officer during World War II: "When you are away from a certain job or country for three years, in your formative years, things change and you change. Veterans found that out coming back. Many times, it was a serious psychological setback. They were not welcomed to their old job. Someone else had that job. For some, it was less than graceful.

"However, mine was a graceful return, but I found the structure was different, and I had changed. I made my mind up to resign and form my own small corporation called the Hayes Concert Bureau, which functioned from 1947 to 1965. I was what you'd call the local manager dealing with the New York managers and presenting every artist of the time you could imagine in Constitution Hall, and later at Lisner, and then the National Theatre... Call 301-925-7549."

* * *

Mike© Connie Brandt Smith & © WOWD

Mike Schreibman

Born in Washington, DC, in 1944, Mike Schreibman was Class of '62 at Western High School, now the Duke Ellington High School for the Performing Arts. Mike played a pivotal role in shaping DC's burgeoning music scene, especially during the 70s and 80s.

Revered by nearly all who crossed paths, he left a lasting impact on local music from his work—often behind the scenes—in booking and promoting concerts and revitalizing clubs. I met him when I was fifteen at his Emergency Club in Georgetown. It had no liquor license, which was great for younger kids like me. He once hired me to do clean-up and chores for what became a legendary three-day weekend show at Carr's Beach in Annapolis. Carr's was once a vibrant African-American recreation area for families when public beaches were segregated. Mike renamed it Great McGonigle's Seaside Park.

I hung out with Gram Parsons and Emmylou Harris backstage, talking my head off. Today, I can't remember what we said because I worked hardest at drinking the free beer. Mike should have fired me, but that wasn't Mike's style.

Mike booked, served, and helped countless folks in the DC area over the years. He put heroic hours into organizing concerts and connecting artists, giving them a chance to shine when they didn't have a champion. He genuinely cared about helping people.

But despite his historic work, he never found the success you might expect, partly because he was too nice a guy—mild-mannered. He was always lifting others up rather than assertively and ruthlessly doing whatever it took for his own business success.

As great as kindness is, his ultimately made it tough for him to compete in the music marketplace. As this book goes to print, he is retired and living comfortably in a nursing home often visited by his closest friend, Richard Harrington.

* * *

Schreibman's journals and personal papers are now collected in the University of Maryland archives also thanks to Harrington, who warmly praises him in interviews and presentations. One very moving Schreibman tribute by Richard aired in 2021 with essential help from author Mark Opsasnick and hosted by WOWD's *Forbidden Alliance* radio show host, Robbie White.

Since this conversation with Richard Harrington was casual and not originally intended for publication, we've paraphrased his remarks. However, when Mark Opsasnick [MO] plays the taped interview excerpts he did by telephone with Schreibman on May 5, 2009, we present these comments verbatim because Mike agrees they be for publication.

Photo: Richard Harrington at DC Legends show
© S. Moore

Richard Harrington [RH] started the discussion with the address of his Dad's 1408 Wisconsin Avenue Lamp shop where Mike started hosting weekend gatherings in the basement with as many as a hundred people, mostly under eighteen. They'd spill out into the streets. You had to go down this covered alley to reach a patio in the back. The basement is where they'd "hang" and listen to rock and roll records.

(MO: Mike Schreibman): A strange thing happened after the first party. The people I thought I'd never be friends with came back the next day and offered help clean up the place. For whatever reason, people who normally didn't get along or might not have wanted to spend time with one another found some sort of unifying force in that dungeon. I had a dream that one day I would open it up as a nightclub. I worked on improvements, but never did. But the desire was to be involved in the entertainment business started out of that.

What I got from all this is that you can find unknown performers and help shape their careers and make money. What I enjoyed the most was seeing them develop and seeing the reactions they got from the audience. There's nothing like the feeling you get from seeing an artist that you work with, being cheered by the audience and knowing that you had a part in it.

The whole M Street scene started to change in the early sixties. That's when it all started growing. And there were bands and a lot of the bars and new bars were opening up. I had been managing Randy but then I wasn't making enough money. That's when I was determined to get a job either at the Cellar Door or at a new place across the street which was called Smokey's. I started at Smokey's doing lights and sound. Jack Boyle owned Smokey's then. I think maybe it lasted a couple months. And then he decided that he wanted to do this new thing called, uh, a Cinematheque, which showed movies and served drinks during the movie.

That became Groovy's but instead of the "sound and light" guy, I was the projectionist. That lasted about a year. Then I became the roving manager for several of Jack's clubs. So, the night that the manager would be off, I would be in there running the place. I was at Max's, New Max's, Groovy's, and The Crazy Horse.

RH: (Richard Harrington): His next step was the very brief life of the Ambassador Theater. Mike was originally hired to do the concessions. He ended up also doing publicity. And this would be very important. It was July '67—the "Summer of Love"—especially where these psychedelic ballrooms sprang up in San Francisco and other cities...Mike was overworked and underpaid.

(MO: Mike Schreibman): It was just too much of a schedule to try to keep. And my friends owned a club in Harrisburg, PA, called the Gypsy Rover. And another in Ocean City, New Jersey, and I knew the acts that were playing there and was booking some of them. They told me they were going to open a rock theater. They offered me the job of manager. And that was the Ambassador Theater in DC. The new owners of the Ambassador were Joe Mednick, Anthony Finestra, and Court Rogers.

Well, money got really tight really quickly. I didn't get along with one of the partners, and that was the partner whose his family had the most money. Well, I didn't do any of the bookings. I remember sitting in on sessions and making suggestions. I did the publicity. But that wasn't really my job. My job was running the snack bar.

The Ambassador opened on July 28th of 1967 with the Peanut Butter Conspiracy, Mandrake Memorial, and a local band Natty Bumpo. The next booking was an unknown Jimi Hendrix.

A *Washington Post* story by David Montgomery and Jeff Krulik "When Jimi Hendrix came to Washington and Blew It's Mind" published in 2013 describes the shows.

The Jimi Hendrix Experience got paid $1,500 for the week plus rooms at the Shoreham Hotel just up the street. Less than a hundred people showed up on the first night. One hundred people.

The *Are You Experienced* album record was only two weeks old at that point. "Purple Haze" had been released, but airplay wouldn't start until September in DC.

Word of mouth by the last night attracted 800 people, including a very young Nils Lofgren whose band, the Crystal Mesh, would soon open for Ambassador shows Moby Grape and the Hollies.

(MO: Mike Schreibman) I started my own concert promotion company called Capital Concerts. I was working at the Biograph. And I talked four people into being partners on a show. And it was the Country Joe Show. And it did really well. From then on I was in the concert business.

My next show (Ramsey Lewis, Cannonball Adderley Quintet, and Lloyd McNeil Quartet) was not successful. It lost a lot of money, but it was a good lesson. I'm not sure that we really wanted that lesson at the time. And then the Poor People's Concert at Georgetown University.

The main act was Buffy Sainte-Marie with Adlai Stevenson Jr. and Anthony Quinn. They were speakers at the event. And that gave me some entree into GU, where I started booking concerts for the school.

And from doing Georgetown concerts, I started doing concerts at the other colleges in the area, George Washington and Catholic University. I was pretty much the exclusive guy that those three schools used for quite a while. I had also done things at Maryland and American U, but not as much. And then I started spreading out to colleges outside the DC area. And at one time, we were doing a lot of schools up and down the East Coast, and I had some colleges on the West Coast.

RW Robbie White: Our next segment is another important piece of Washington music history, which is the Emergency Club in Georgetown on 2813 M Street. It had once been the Round Table, where many rock bands played. Mike ended up becoming sort of booker and manager when it opened in August of 1969. It only lasted until January 1, 1971. But it [was] owned by people like Daniel Andrew, Peter Delano, Penny Brown, and others. Mike was the only one who had any experience producing shows and managing a club.

RH: (Richard Harrington): The Emergency had its first show, a pre-opening benefit at the end of June, 1969. And then it opened with Love, Cry, Want, followed by Claude Jones, Cosmic Truth, and the Northside Blues Band, and through the end of August, and then September with Claude Jones, Sageworth and Drums, Fat City (Bill and Taffy Danoff) Emmylou Harris, and Catfish Hodge.

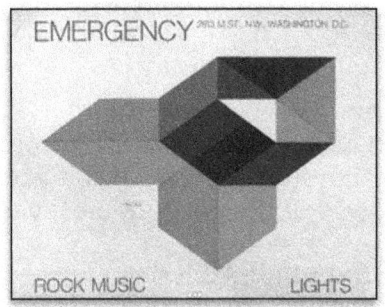

This poster was designed for Mike Schreibman by the artist Paul Reed, who was associated with the Washington Color School.

The *Washington Post* wrote in an editorial when they were going through problems with permits, the need for such a non-alcoholic spot where teenagers can hear live music is desperately needed. This contrasted with the constant opposition by citizen groups, police, and permit people.

John Segraves wrote in his *Evening Star* "After Dark" column when Emergency was just a week old: "It's a far cry from the crummy Ambassador Theater, which a young group took over a couple of years ago and turned into a disco." Segraves did like Claude Jones, "who make for a splendid evening in a setting that no parent would be worried about."

Walter Egan, then Georgetown student who assembled one of the best DC bands at that time, Sageworth and Drums, remembers Mike and the club very well:

> "Mike had been a denizen of the Georgetown campus environs for years, and his ground-floor apartment on 35th Street was a haven for musicians like Sageworth and Drums and many other creatively bent players.
>
> "He had a lamp that could be turned on and off simply by touch, which was very amusing, and he had a reel-to-reel tape recorder on which he allowed Sageworth to record our original

> songs. This was the summer when I gave myself the assignment of writing a new song every day. It was a severe discipline that helped me with my writing chops but didn't produce too many hits.
>
> "Emergency was unique in that it had a wide space inclining in the back of the room from floor to the ceiling, where patrons could lay out or sit up and always have a nice view of the stage. Of course, since it was geared for teens, there was no alcohol served or allowed.
>
> "Mike, as music concert promoter was the personification of the healthy music scene that developed during those years in Georgetown as he tirelessly promoted all of our bands. With his ever-present smile, he was genial and quite a great and generous guy."
>
> **Walter Egan**

Mike's very first concert that he produced on his own about seven months after the Ambassador closed was Country Joe and the Fish with Iron Butterfly at Meriweather Post Pavilion on August, 24th, 1968.

(MO: Mike Schreibman) Yes it was *Capital Concerts*. I was working at the Biograph. And I talked four people into being partners on a show. And it was was the Country Joe Show. And it did really well. From then on I was in the concert business.

RH: Some people didn't appreciate his efforts. Irving Lowens musicologist and then the chief music critic for the *Washington Star*, apparently was not impressed with any butterfly not named Madam. His review was kind of a diatribe on the sound level. He quoted a study on Guinea pigs and how the loud racket destroyed their hearings. He said he couldn't understand the words except for the spelling interchange at the beginning (of Country Joe's song) ...

But for Mike, even though that show was successful, his very next show sort of taught him the perils of concert promotion with his second concert, again, at Constitution Hall. It was Ramsey Lewis, Cannonball Adderley Quintet, and Lloyd McNeil Quartet. And this is what Mike had to say:

MS: And it was not successful. It lost a lot of money, but it was a good lesson. I'm not sure that we really wanted that lesson at the time. And then Poor People's Concert at Georgetown University. The main act was Buffy St. Marie with Adlai Stevenson Jr and Anthony Quinn. They were speakers at the event. And that gave me some entree into GU, where I started booking concerts for the school. And from doing Georgetown concerts, I started doing concerts at the other colleges in the area, George Washington, and Catholic University. I was pretty much the exclusive guy that those three schools used for quite a while. And I had also done things at Maryland and American U, but not as much. And then I started spreading out to colleges outside the DC area. And at one time, we were doing a lot of schools up and down the East Coast, and I actually had some colleges on the West Coast,

RH: It's also worth noting that for both Country, Joe, Iron Butterfly and Ramsey Lewis shows, Mike produced these beginning what was a string of classic posters. This is something that he kind of pioneered by drafting a lot of the area's finest artists, Lou Stovall, Lloyd McNeil, who was a musician and graphic artist, and Richard Jester. Many of them were connected to Lou's Printmaking Studio workshop.

Of course, Lou went on to become one of the best-known DC artists with an international reputation as a master printmaker. He sadly passed away in March 2021. What Mike did with these folks is they did not do the psychedelic West Coast style.

They were often impressionistic. And they were lovely to look at, and it was always clear as to the who, what, where, and when. This that's another area where you can find a lot of these images online. Google them and look in images. So like the pavilion itself, Mike kind of built slowly from 1968 to 1971, he did 15 concerts, half of them at DAR, half of them at Georgetown. But between 1972 and 1975, he did 120 in the same three-year period, including booking colleges around the country, but mostly around here. As for Merriweather, you know, it had opened in '67, partly designed as a summer home for the National Symphony Orchestra, and mostly classical and dance stuff. But its inaugural season was a financial disaster. So by 1968, they started bringing in pop acts like Judy Collins, Simon and Garfunkel Joan Baez. Country acts like Dolly Parton, Conway Twitty, and (others) like Tiny Tim.

Now, Tiny Tim could be theoretically the First Rock concert that he but not because of Tim. "Tiptoe through the Tulips" does not qualify, but because the opening act was, of all people, the Amboy Dukes with Ted Nugent. Again, odd billings abound. There's many of them. But in fact, Merriweather only did three rock concerts that summer, all in the tail end of the season in August, Hendrix, the Soft Machine on August 16th, incidentally, the, the first time he played the "Star Spangled Banner" live in front of an audience country, Country Joe and the Iron Butterfly on the 25th. And the Doors and Earth Opera on August 30th.

And five years later, Merriweather had 50 concerts scheduled-- 25 of them were rock concerts. But then the, the nature of the Beast in 1974, they announced before the season started that rock acts would be banned from the venue altogether. And that would fluctuate off and on through the years. At this time, Mike also was learning how difficult it was to do shows without the the good backing and how difficult it was to get into major halls. And that's when he really had developed the colleges, particularly GU. it was not the greatest of times, but, you know, he built and he learned along the way.

In that era, there was so much trouble at these concerts. There was this "the music should be free" movement. There were counterfeit tickets, but that's often the case. Many venues and colleges would go through periods where they would ban rock acts from performing. It was not uncommon for serious disturbances at the shows. One of those shows was Led Zeppelin and the Who May 29th, 1969, a truly legendary concert. It was the only time those two acts ever shared the same bill and stage. And it was a Lester Grossman/Mike Schreibman presentation...

Mike brought The Who later into McDonough Gymnasium, which he changed the name to McDonough Arena. And they had a $5 ticket, which quickly sold out. Lou Stovall created another classic poster sort of based on Michelangelo's "The Creation."

An **Emergency-Woodwind** Reunion in 1991 is a must-see to get the vibes of the Emergency. It's on YouTube: https://www.youtube.com/watch?v=rTRbKWjVH88

Mike's stories continue in Richard's interview with Robbie at:

https://www.mixcloud.com/robbinewhite/forbidden-alliance-wowd-943-fm-richard-harrington-pays-tribute-to-mike-schreibman/

* * *

The next phases of Mike Schreibman's career include his reopening of the Warner Theater, which revitalized the downtown area near the National Theatre, a revival of the Bayou, which he booked until early 1980, and his management of the Wax Museum in 1984, the biggest nightclub at the time with a thousand seats plus parking attached.

Mike took over the Wax Museum in mid-July, but in November the owners, Colonial Parking, closed it down because they didn't think it was bringing in enough money. Mike had a solid schedule that last month... but it wasn't producing the expected revenues. Harrington says, "This was a very, very tough time for him."

Again, we thank Richard for his contributions to this history and the lists he compiled that honor Mike's legacy.

BAYOU SHOWS UNDER *NEW ERA CONCERTS*
1978
11/5 Mitch Ryder
11/12 Lenny White
11/15 Rory Gallagher
11/22 Captain Beefheart
12/2 Wet Willie, Stillwater
12/6 Kiki Dee, Richie Lecca
12/12 Sea Level, Bob Dubar
1979
1/21 Elvin Bishop, Bill Holland & Rent's Due
1/28 John Mayall w Harvey Mandell, Catfish Hodge Band
1/30 NRBQ, Illusions of Fantasy
1/31 Crystal Haze, Norman Kirk
2/3-4 Face Dancer, King Dazzle
2/11 Only Ones, Chelsea
2/20 Junior Wells, Hubert Sumlin, Jimmy Dawkins, Eddie Shaw; Chris Smither
2/21 New Riders of the Purple Sage, Chris Smither

2/22 Ultravox, Urban Verbs, Original Fetish
2/25-26 James Cotton Blues Band, Allstars
2/27,28 Spirit
3/4-5 Roy Ayers
3/8-9 Dire Straits, Barooga Bandit
93/11 John Cale, Nico
3/13 Grinderswitch, Jimmie Mack
3/14 Peter Tosh, Exuma, The Obeah
3/18 Cheek to Cheek Allstars, Lamont Cranston Band
3/19-20 Roomful of Blues, Lamont Cranston Band
3/25 Boomtown Rats, The Rockets
3/28 B52s, Urban verbs (x)
3/29 Blood, Sweat and Tears
3/30 The Police, Razz
4/1 Face Dancer, Cherry Smash
4/3 Tonio K, King Dazzle
4/4-5 Oregon, Terri Plumeri
4/6 Jonathan Edwards, Artie Traum, Pat Alger
4/8 Southside Allstars with Junior Wells, Hubert Sumlin, Jimmy Dawkins, Eddie
Shaw; Amos Garrett, Geoff Muldaur
4/9 The Nighthawks
4/11 John Lee Hooker, Catfish Hodge
4/18 Roy Buchanan benefit for Dick Heintze
4/19 Black Oak Arkansas
4/21 Amazing Rhythm Aces
4/25 Planet Gong
4/26 Joe Jackson
4/28 Steve Goodman, The Roches
4/29 Root Boy Slim, Albert Collins
4/30, 5/1 Robert Hunter, Father Guido Sarducci
5/2 San Francisco Allstars
5/3 Art Ensemble of Chicago
5/8 Tony Williams
5/9 John Hall, Magnet
5/10 Sun Ra
5/13 Professor Longhair
5/14 Buzzcocks
5/16 Woodstock Mountain Review with Jim Rooney, Bill Keith,   Happy and Artie
Traum, John Herald, Pat Alger
5/22 Nantucket, Tin Huey

5/23 Sly Dunbar and Robbie Shakespeare
5/24 Nektar, Nikki Buzz
5/27 Sam & Dave
5/29 Passport, Rich Shydner
6/3-4 Tom Robinson, The A's
6/5 James Cotton, Billy Price
6/10 Seawind, Lee Ritenour and Friendship
6/11 Moby Grape
6/12 999, The Know w Gary valentine
6/14 Jay Ferguson, Jerry Doucette
6/19-20 Kingfish, Chris Rush
6/24 The Damned
7/3 Razz, Slickee Boys
7/9 Henry Paul Band, DC Dog
7/10 Flying Burrito Brothers
7/19 Rachel Sweet and Fingerprintz
7/22 Steve Hackett
7/25 Squeeze
7/26 Asleep at the Wheel
7/27 Tim Curry, Laughing Dogs
7/29 Magazine
7/30 Herman Brood and His Wild Romance
8/1-2 Nighthawks
8/7 Buddy Rich
8/8 Rick Danko and Paul Butterfield Band
8/12 Pousette Dart Band
8/13 NRBQ, Payday
8/14 Nitty Gritty Dirt Band, FCC
8/15 Suzi Quatro, Greg Sutton
8/16 Sam & Dave, Booby and the Nightstars
8/19 Jack DeJohnette's Directions w John Abercrombie
8/22-23 David Bromberg, Michael Katakis
8/24 John Cougar, Primadonna
8/26 Taj Mahal
8/28 Jan & Dean, Papa Doo Run Run
8/30 The Records, DC Dog
8/31, 9/1-2 DC Dog
9/2 Alan Price, DC Dog
9/12 Rick Danko, Paul Butterfield Band
9/13 Albert King, Allstars
9/19 Jack DeJohnette's Directions with John Abercrombie
9/20 Urban Verbs, 4 Out of 5 Doctors

Capital Acts: Washington DC Performing Arts

9/23 Stephane Grappelli
9/24 Eddie and the Hot Rods, Johnny Thunders
  and Wayne Kramer's Gang War
9/25 Mary Wells, Flamingos
9/26 Oregon
9/27 Face Dancer
9/30 Screamin' Jay Hawkins, Fabulous Thunderbirds
10/3 The Members, Tina Peel
10/7 The Shirts
10/8 Asleep at the Wheel
10/9 Tribute to Mingus w Jimmy Knepper, Randy Brecker,
  John Handy
10/10 The Yachts
10/14 Danny and the Fat Boys Reunion
10/17-18 Hall & Oates, The States
10/21 Karla Bonoff, Jack Tempchin
10/22 Commander Cody, Chris Rush
10/24-25 Esther Satterfield & Eddie Henderson
10/28 Davis Werner
10/30 City Boy
10/31 Halloween with Razz, Roy Loney
11/4 Yellow Magic orchestra
11/5 Steve Forbert
11/6 Jonathan Edwards
11/7 Bobby "Blue" Bland, Billy Price (x)
11/8 Maria Muldaur
11/11 Tony Williams, L. Shankar
11/12 B.B. King, Sunnyland Slim (x)
11/15 Sinceros, Motels
11/20 David Bromberg
11/27 Wreckless Eric, Live Wire
11/28 D.C. Star
11/29 David Johansen, Razz
12/2 Pat Metheny
14/4 Horslips, The Hags
12/5 Ian Gomm, The Beat
12/6-8 Prima Donna
12/9 Catfish Hodge Band, Cryin' Out Loud
12/12 .38 Special, The Blend
12/16 *Unicorn Times Benefit* w. Allstars, Silver Spring,
  Prima Donna
12/31 Nighthawks

1/28/1980 Memphis Blues Caravan with Furry Lewis, Ma Rainey, Sam Chatman,
   Memphis Piano Rad, King Biscuit Boys (cancelled, club sold)

1960s
Rooftop Singers (first concert) Philly
Country Joe and the Fish, Iron Butterfly Aug 24, 1968 at *Merriweather Post Pavilion* 1968
Ramsey Lewis, Cannonball Adderley Quintet, Lloyd McNeil Quintet Oct 31, 1968 at Constitution Hall

Led Zeppelin and The Who, *Merriweather Post Pavilion* May 1969
The Who, Love Cry Want at *McDonough Arena Georgetown University* November 1969

Procol Harum, Guess Who June 20 1969 at DAR
Arlo Guthrie, Mountain, Tractor Oct 10 1969 at *McDonough*
1970
Manfred Mann's Chapter Three, Crank May 5 *GWU Student Center*
Chuck Berry and Bo Diddley, May 11 1970 at *Lisner Auditorium*
1971
Paul Butterfield's better Days, Bonnie Raitt, Little Feat *GU*
Grin, Crank Jan 30 at *Gaston Hall, GU*
Wet Willie Sept 27 1971 *Gaston Hall GU* 7:30 and 10
Sea Train July 30 1971 *T.C. Williams HS*, Alexandria
Steve Goodman, Emmylou Harris Nov 30 *McMahon Hall, CU*
Jr Walker, Stairsteps, Continental Four, Carolyn Carl Sept 1 1971 *Carr's Beach*
1972
Steve Miller. Merry Clayton, Crank feb 6 GU
Mary Travers, Jackson Browne Oct 15, 1972 CU Gym
Bonnie Raitt, Arthur Big Boy Cruddup Oct 13 1972 *U of Md Baltimore*
Poco , Sageworth, Tractor Oct 9 *McDonough, GU*
Fanny Feb 4 1972 *The Commons, , Roanoke VA*
Ike & Tina Turner Oct 15 1972 *GU McDonough Arena*
Mary Travers, Jackson Browne Oct 15 *Catholic U*
New Riders of the Purple Sage, Livingston Taylor,

Capital Acts: Washington DC Performing Arts

John Pousette-Dart Dec 9 1972 *McDonough GU*
Dave Mason, Taj Mahal, Sky Cobb March 19 1972 *Catholic University Gymnasium*
1973
Byrds, Brewer and Shipley Feb 9 1973 *McDonough GU*
Guess Who, Northwind Feb 24 1973 *McDonough GU*
Beck Bogart and Appice, Wet Willie March 31 *McDonough GU*
Bill Withers, the Spinners April 4 *Catholic U*
Paul Butterfield's Better Days, Little Feat, Bonnie Raitt April 7 *McDonough GU*
Mahavishnu Orchestra, Cris Williamson April 10 *DAR*
Stephen Stills and Manassas April 15 *Roanoke Coliseum*
Shawn Phillips April 16 at *Lisner*
Leo Kottke April 26 *Trinity theater*
Good God May 5 *Wheeling College*
Commander Cody May 9 *Trinity Theater*
Kris Kristofferson and Rita Coolidge May 19 *Roanoke College*
Frank Zappa May 19 *McGonigle's Park*
Kris Kristofferson and Rita Coolidge May 19 Roanoke College
Babe, Crank, Grits, Liz Meyer, Sky Cobb, Wells Fargo, Reekers May 27 at *McGonigle's*
Bo Diddley, XX May 28 at *McGonigle's Park*
Hollies, Hooktoof June 2 at *McGonigle's Park*
Weekend of Good Time Music June 15, 16, 17 at Great *McGonigle's* Seaside Park with former Byrds and Burritos; Clarence White, Gram Parsons, Emmylou Harris, Gene Parsons, Rick Roberts, Byron Berline, Chris Etheridge, Ken Wirtz, Roger Dash, Allen Munde; also 15---Tracy Nelson and Mother Earth, Eric Weisberg, New Grass Revival; 16--Tracy Nelson, Charles River Valley Boys, Chris Smither, Townes Van Zandt, Norman Blake, New England Bluegrass Boys, Russ Kirkpartrick, NRBQ; 17---Tracy Nelson,
Jonathan Edwards, NRBQ, Norman Blake, Orphan, Liz Meyer, Brian Bowers
Little Feat, Liz Meyer and Friends Sept 21 *Lisner*
Redbone Oct 1 *Washington Monument Grounds*
Richie Havens, David Bromberg Oct 13 *GU*
Dave Mason Oct 14 Catholic U
Bonnie Raitt, Arthur Big Boy Cruddup Sept 23 *Catholic U*
Roy Buchanan Nov 2 GU

Redbone Oct 1 *Washington Monument Grounds*
Dave Mason Nov 2 *Catholic U*
Chick Corea, Good God Nov 16 *GU*
Steve Goodman, Emmylou Harris Nov 30 *Catholic U*
Livingston Taylor, Reeve Little Dec 1
    Montgomery College, Rockville
Roy Buchanan Dec 2 *Lisner*
New York Dolls, Babe Dec 14 *Lisner*
1974
Bonnie Raitt, Arthur Cruddup Jan 20 GU
Chuck Mangione, Sonny Terry and Brownie Mcghee
    Jan 25, *GU*
Grin and Dubonettes Jan 26 *Gaston Hall GU*
Two Generations of Brubeck, David buskin Feb 1, 2 *GU*
Chris Rush Feb 2 *Northwestern U*
Duke Ellington and his Orchestra Feb 10 *Gaston Hall*
Jackson Browne, Linda Ronstadt Feb 27, March 5 *GU*
Bruce Springsteen, Orleans March 3 *Gaston Hall*
Phil Ochs March 6 *Northwestern U*
Robert Klein March 19 *Rhode Island College*
Three Dog Night March 22 *McDonough*
Arthur Hurley & Gottlieb March 23 *AU Coffeehouse*
Orleans, Face Dancer March 29 *CU McMahon Hall*
Billy Cobham, Donal Leace April 6 *Gaston*
Lydian Chamber Players April 13 *Gaston*
Roberta Flack April 20
Billy Cobham April 22 *Colby College*
Chambers Brothers March 22 *GU*
Johnny Rivers April 21 *GWU*
Mountain, Spooky Tooth, Sharks, April 22 *GU*
Leon Russell May 19 *RFK Stadium*
Billy Cobham April 22 *Colby College*
Ry Cooder, Rev, Pearlie Brown April 26 *Gaston*
Bonnie Raitt May 10 *Bates College*
Larry Coryell and 11th house May 24 *Utah U*
Grin June 8 *Kennedy Center Concert Hall*
Little Feat June 30 *Lisner*
Souther, Hillman Furay July 14 *GWU*
Incredible String Band July 30 *Lisner*
Commander Cody Aug 2 *Lewiston Armory*

Capital Acts: Washington DC Performing Arts

Climax Blues Band Aug 11 *Lisner*
Bonnie Raitt Aug 17 *DAR*
Livingston Taylor Sept 1 *Lisner*
James Montgomery Sept 7 *Lisner*
NRBQ Sept 13 *Bates College*
Sha Na Na Sept 13 *McDonough*
Jonathan Edwards Sept 20 *Lisner*
Hot Tuna Oct 2 *Colby College*
Rare Earth Oct 11 *Lisner*
National Dance Company of Mexico Oct 13 *Lisner*
Bonnie Raitt Oct 22 *DAR*
Chick Corea, Taj Mahal Oct 24 *Temple U*
Taj Mahal Oct 25 *GU*
Kansas Oct 26 *Montgomery College*
Dave Mason Nov 2 *GU*
Canned Heat Nov 2 *Broward College*
Brewer & Shipley Nov 8 GU, 9 *Ambler Theater*
Weather Report Nov 9 *Northwestern U*
jerry Jeff Walker Nov 15 *St. Joseph's College*
Nitty Gritty Dirt Band Nov 15 *Northwestern*
Harry Chapin Nov 22 *GU*
Raspberries Dec 7 *Bates College*
National Lampoon Dec 7 *GU*
Todd Rundgren Dec 10 *DAR*
        1975
Alvin Lee and Company Jan 19 *GWU*
Billy Cobham jan 24 *Bates College*
Cactus Jan 28 *Fairfax Theater*
Blood Sweat and tears Feb 1 *Bowdin College*
Melissa Manchester, Robert Klein Jan 31 *GU*
Labelle Feb 15 *Northwestern*
Wendy Waldman Feb 23 *Colby College*
Clancy Brothers March 15 *GWU*
Alex Harvey March 15 *GWU*
Billy Cobham Feb 23 *Catholic*
Hall & Oates, March 7 *Roanoke College*
Flying Burritos March 14 *Montgomery College Rockville*
Martin Mull March 20 *Colby College*
Chuck Berry , Bo Diddley March 23 *GU*
Chuck Mangione April 4 *GU*

Martin Mull April 4 *Montgomery College*
Supertramp April 13 *GU*
Bonnie Raitt April 19 *GU*
Little Feat April 21-23 *Lisner*
Bonnie Raitt April 26 *Case Western*
Bonnie Raitt May 7 *Auditorium Theater*
Emmylou Harris May 24 *Lisner*
Golden Earing June 5 *GW*
Monkees Sept 19 1975 at Constitution Hall *(cancelled)*

POST 1975
Karla Bonoff at *Lisner* 8/4/79 7:30 and 10:30
Little Feat May 9-11 1977 *Warner Theater*
The Records Aug 30 1979 Bayou
Joe Jackson, Original Fetish Sept 8 1979 *Ritchie Coliseum*
Dire Straits Sept 17 1979 *Smith Center GWU*
   1980
Jan and Dean Feb 3 1980 *Lisner*
Joe Jackson, the Inmates Feb ˋ4 1980 *Ontario Theater*
Urban Verbs, Natural Bridge April ˋ4, 1980 *Lisner*
Warren Zevon, Dirk Hamilton April 21 1980
Lisner 7:30 +10:30
The Jam, The Beat March 27 1980 *Ontario Theater*
Jerry Jeff Walker at Ontario 7:30 and 10:30
   (moved to Eskimo Nells)
Rachel Sweet May 12 *Gaston Hall*
Pure Prairie League June 14 *Harrington Fairgrounds*
John Kay and Steppenwolf June 22 *Ontario* 7:30 and 10:30
Karla Bonoff Feb 4 *Lisner*
Joan Armatrading July 28 *Kennedy Center Concert Hall*
Bonnie Raitt Aug 23 Private concert, *Lorton*
Stephane Grappelli Oct 5 *Lisner*
Joan Armatrading Oct 8 *DAR*
Crystal Gayle, David Saye Nov 10 *Kennedy Center*
Chicken Legs, Nighthawks Nov 17 *Warner*
Steve Forbert Nov 20 *Lisner*
Rocky Horror Show Nov 23-30 *Warner*
Rockpile Nov 30 *Warner Theater*
            1981
Mickey Gilley Jan 22 *Kennedy Center Concert Hall*

Capital Acts: Washington DC Performing Arts

Rodney Dangerfield Jan 26 *Constitution Hall*
Chuck Mangione March 28 *Kenndy Center Concert Hall*
George Jones May 30 *Fairfax High*
Toots and the Maytals July 24 *Warner Theater*
Yellowman, Unconquered People, Black Sheep Nov 17 *Howard Theater*
Jerry Jeff Walker Nov 19 *Warner Theater*
Joe Jackson Dec 3 *Warner Theater*
1982
Bonnie Raitt, John Hall April 28 *Towson State*
Waylon Jennings, Hank Williams Jr and the Bama Band, Jessi Colter, the Cricket, Sonny Curtis, Rosslyn Mountain Boys June 13 moved to June 27, Laurel Race Course
1983
Tony Bennett June 14 *Kennedy Center Concert Hall*
Beach Boys March 23 *Cole Field House U of MD*
Keith Jarrett June 16 *Kennedy Center Concert Hall*
1984
Fairport Convention, July 24-25
Chick Corea and Gary Burton Feb 10 *Lisner*
Herman's Hermits, Billy J Kramer and the Dakotas, Gerry and the Pacemakers, The Troggs, Badfinger Aug2, *Washington Hilton Ballroom*
Southside johnny and the Jukes, Skip Castro Band Dec 31 *Warner Theater* 8 and 11
Smash and DC Star Oct 27 *Pavilion at the Old Post Office*
Skip Castro Band Dec 31 *Washington Plaza Hotel Ballroom(*

THE EMERGENCY CLUB
1969
Nov 10-15 Fallen Angels
Nov 17-22 Stillroven, Gregg Kihn
Nov 24-29 Stillroven
Nov 28-29 Catfish
Dec 1-6 Fat City, Sageworth & Drums
8-13 Elisabeth
10-13 Grin
16-20 Northside Blues Band, Ox Petals
22-27 Claude Jones
29-Jan 3 Claude Jones

1970
January 9-10 Catfish, Stillroven
12-15 Grin
16-17 Cold Blood w Lydia Pense
19-24 Buffalongo, Brian Bowers
26-31 American Dream, Stillroven
February 2-7 Edison Electric Band, Sageworth and Drums
8 Benefit Stillroven, Sageworth and Drums, Claude Jones, Dearborn
9-14 Brian Bowers
9-12 Pookah
16-21 Elisabeth, Fat City
22 Stillroven
18 Renaissance23-28 Pilt
23-25 Cold Blood
26-28 American Dream
March 1 American Dream, Felix the Cat
2 Blues Project, Crank OR 2-4 Frost??
3-7 American Dream, Crank
9-14 Stillroven, Crank
16-24 Bead Game, Fat City
18 Renaissance
22 benefit Second Eagle, Heavy Load, Stillroven, Bead Game, Brother Fox and the Tarbabies. Fat City
26-28 Pilt, American Dream
28 Crank, Sea East Utopian Mission
29 Bob Seger
30 Roxy, Howdy Doody
April 1-4 Roxy
4 Living Stage
5 Brass Lamp, Nicky C and the Chateaux, Jackie Smith, Sageworth
6-11 Buffalongo
12 This Is Us, Clayton Unger, Jerome Tolbert, Monolith
13 Redbone
20-25 Claude Jones
25 Living Stage
27-29 SRC
30 Insect Trust
MAY 1-2 Insect Trust

Capital Acts: Washington DC Performing Arts

4-6 Manfred Mann
7-9 Hamilton Face
10-12 Blodwyn Pig
14 Insect Trust
18 NRBQ
26-28 Amboy Dukes
31 Fairport Convention
June 1-4 Fairport Convention
11 The Kinks
12-14 Insect Trust
19-21 It's a Beautiful Day
July 16-19 Country Funk
21-26 Claude Jones
31—Aug 1 Grin
1971
Sept 24-26 Crank
Oct 1-3 Fat City, Sky Cobb
8 Tree Beard, Naked Dog
9-10 Boomerang, Itchy brother
14 Tonk, Wild Rice
15-16 Blues Project, Dave Griggs
22-24 Sageworth, Emmylou Harris
29-30 J.B. Hutto and the Hawks, Dave Griggs
31 Rory Gallagher, Dave Griggs
Nov 5-6 Claude Jones, Emmylou Harris
12-14 Exuma, Itchy Brother
16-17 Freddie King, Dave Griggs
18-19 Crank, Michael
20 Tiswin, Michael
21-23 Atomic Rooster, Len Jaffee, Kamakasi
24-25 Dion
26-28 Wet Willie
Dec 3-5 Peter Yarrow, Lazarus, Lamb
7-11 Shanti
9-11 Eric Andersen
12-13 Atomic Rooster
14-18 Rockin' Foo
19-20 Sky Cobb
21-25 Shanti
27-31 Claude Jones

31 Crank, Grin, Claude Jones, Grits, Sky Cobb, Itchy Brother
March 5-7 Edison Electric, Crank
March 9-14 Buddy Guy
March 16-24 Quill
Nov 11 Goose Creek Symphony
Feb 18 Elizabeth, Fat city
Feb 16-21 Cold Blood
Feb 23-25 American Dream

Fortunately, Mike Schreibman's phone would ring after the Wax Museum closed and it wasn't just another call. It proved to be the promise of a new beginning

Chapter 53 – Clubs, Committees, and Cool

In 1984, **Michael Jaworek**, the long-time promoter for the Birchmere was then working as a booking agent for Sam L'Hommedieu, owner of the Warner Theater.

"I first met Mike Schreibman doing shows at the Bayou. I can only talk about my own interactions, which were solid and honorable. I had come to work. in 1978 at the University of Maryland. We had an outdoor show on campus with Bob "Catfish" Hodge who Mike was managing.

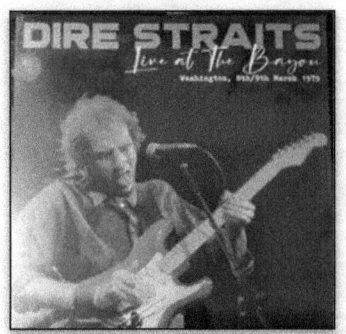

The student in charge, Steve Grossman, introduced me and we chatted. Mike was pleasant, friendly, and more quiet than noisy.

"And then I knew him from shows at the Bayou, like Dire Straits who he brought in on their first run in the U.S. And he did Little Feat and Bonnie Raitt who stayed with Mike as the Cellar Door took more and more shows in the market. I began realizing that although we have some amazing talent and history here in Washington it wasn't getting the national attention in the marketplace, like Philly, Chicago, the Bay Area, Boston and, of course New York City. I thought this was wrong.

I called Mike and the late Tom Carrico who was managing Mary Chapin Carpenter and asked them what they thought of the idea of doing a Washington, DC, Awards show. They liked it and we got the nod of around twenty other DC music folks to meet at the Wax Museum to discuss. It was almost like a diplomatic meeting where you have people from various countries. Some of the (leaders in the music business then) were very interested in promoting the local music scene but they didn't seem to be emotionally invested. It was all about the money.

But many of the meeting attendees were very community minded. Now I was only thinking narrowly about an awards show. I wasn't thinking about an association that would provide assessment or focus in any other ways. I can claim that the Wammie awards was my idea, but beyond that, in terms of a greater organization, or I should say an organization, period, that was indeed, Mike Schreibman's idea.

After the initial meeting, the number of people who were involved with WAMA dropped to a smaller group. There was Charles Stephenson and John Simpson.

We never saw the people from Cellar Door again. In many respects, it was me, Tom, and Mike. It was interesting how successful that first WAMA event was. Emmylou Harris and Joan Jett showed up. But after that it was never quite as important and or well attended, even though we did the Kennedy Center.

Mike Jaworek with Marshall Crenshaw, and Birchmere founder/owner Gary Oelze in 2022. © S. Moore

* * *

The first WAMA awards program took place at Lisner Auditorium in September one year later in 1985, where over forty music awards were distributed among more than 200 nominees. This inaugural event highlighted the rich and diverse musical talent in the Washington area and set the stage for what would become a cornerstone of the local music scene. WAMA's mission was clear from its inception: to serve as a nonprofit, tax-exempt organization comprised of music industry professionals dedicated to elevating the profile of the region's music community. Its primary goals included promoting Washington-area music and achieving national recognition for the region as a vital center for both live and recorded music. Through its efforts, WAMA aimed not only to celebrate local talent but also to foster a supportive environment for musicians and industry professionals alike.

Mike Schreibman became WAMA's devoted, beloved, and resilient leader for three decades.

* * *

Born in Newark, New Jersey, Jaworek started promotion as a University of Illinois student in 1972. He and three friends formed Blues Power to produce concerts.

"The first show we did was Hound Dog Taylor and the House Rockers. We needed to make $500 for their show in the Student Union and ended up making $1,500. *Gee, this is easy*, we thought. Boy, was I wrong," Michael says.

He went on to produce many Chicago blues acts, and after graduation, became a concert promotion advisor for the Universities of Tennessee and Maryland. In 1985 he joined Chesapeake Concerts, a spin-off of Cellar Door concerts which eventually became Live Nation.

"At Chesapeake, it became apparent we needed a local club to book shows and around 1988 I cold-called Gary Oelze at the Birchmere and told him I thought I could increase and help diversify his business and also help ourselves as well. So, I worked with Chesapeake to help produce shows at the Birchmere, Ram's Head, Painters Mill, and other clubs."

In addition to diversifying the club's acts, Jaworek introduced a method of moving acts that outgrew the Birchmere to larger Washington area venues.

"Gary also wasn't doing any shows outside the Birchmere except ones that included the Seldom Scene. Gary wasn't in the business to book the acts to greater glory in larger venues when their popularity outgrew the Birchmere."

"I said to Gary, 'You can book this as a concert club like the Cellar Door, which was long gone by then, where you could do a variety of genres of performers that fit the geography,' as I put it, 'of the room and the general thrust of a seated concert club.' This meant it didn't suit metal or hip hop, but whether it was R&B, blues, comedy, jazz or whatever, we could successfully present it."

* * *

However, on December 29, 2017 the news wasn't good. The **Washington Area Music Association** called it quits after thirty-three years. The official announcement was: "WAMA has had an incredible thirty-three-year-run, mainly because of Mike Schreibman and founding members Tom Carrico, John Simson, Michael Jaworek, and Charles Stephenson. The countless hours donated by volunteers, including the inimitable Loralyn Coles, gave WAMA its wings to produce the Wammies, the Crosstown Jams, concerts, workshops and other events over the years."

© S. Moore

The organization, based in Washington, DC, offered professional development services, networking opportunities, and elements such as assistance in obtaining barcodes for recordings and production of live events. It organized the Washington Area Music Awards and released and promoted recordings from various member artists. Shelley Brown

Richard Harrington, our most respected and influential music writer, wrote about her in 2003: "Five years ago, when Shelley Brown joined the Washington Area Music Association board, she discovered their published **WAMA Timeline**, which celebrates the region's musical heritage. Brown, vice president of programming at Strathmore Hall Arts Center in Rockville, had been working in music for ten years, she recalls, yet "there were so many interesting things on the Timeline I felt nobody knew—things I didn't know. So, I started working to get it published, to get underwriting for the Timeline as a poster or travel brochure, and to promote the music and the people who represent this area's incredibly fertile environment."

Today Brown is the Managing Director of the Dumbarton Arts & Education Association. She's been there full-time since 2016, overseeing programs that include the concert chamber music, jazz series, and extraordinary early childhood arts-integrated literacy and pre-math programs for DC students.

In 2024 she's also Adjunct Faculty with American University teaching graduate level Entertainment Marketing. She has provided talent buying, programming advice, production budgeting, and project management for DC area events, producing concerts, festivals, conferences, private functions, and non-profit events.

Many DC area musicians are immensely grateful for her seventeen years as vice president of artistic directing and programming for the Strathmore Hall Foundation. Shelley continued her story for *Capital Acts*:

"I was constantly involved with music in my teen years. I had a family who patronized music a lot. We went to see the symphony and ballet. I took a ton of lessons. I wasn't an excellent musician, but I could play piano. I now play a mandolin. Music was a very acceptable way to spend time. It was a fantastic resource to go do, so my family were music enablers.

"But when I got to Washington in 1988 after graduation, I couldn't believe the richness and the depth of the talent and the amazing array of people who lived here. And I felt like, 'God, if this was in Denver, this would be a big deal.' I started evaluating things using that lens. I was just constantly like, 'Whoa, everybody's going to want to know about this, and we should tell them about it.' I had this feeling of having new eyes that the DC residents didn't realize were the riches here. Yeah."

She began working in the press office at the Kennedy Center. She'd tell them, "Look, I know you're looking for national acts, but there is all this (local) talent here, and we've got to give them a stage and a whole building for the performing arts." Her interest in the history of the area's music led to her becoming the festival manager for their open-house arts festival, grand foyer series, and holiday celebrations, which would later become the Millennium Stage.

"I was there for almost ten years. We grew the programs and were very successful at getting funders and developing the initiatives in a way that would be sustainable," she says.

The soft-spoken, modest Shelley is proud of her success and the fact that the Millennium Stage presentations continue in 2024.

"For local performers, it continues as an important stage. I mean, it's a work program. Yet the scale of free performances every day at six o'clock sounds simple, but the operations behind booking 364 free concerts yearly. Sometimes, we were kind of burdened by our own success.

"Once, we did a big event with Marcus Johnson. 5,000 people arrived in the grand foyer, but we hadn't hired enough ushers. Sometimes, in those early days when the media would get hold of something early and it was hard for us to know exactly what would happen."

Today, the Kennedy Center promotes its program: "With a free performance every day since March 1, 1997, Millennium Stage has allowed millions of people in DC and around the world the chance to view a live performance, regardless of their background or any perceived limitations."

Ron Newmyer on Bandhouse Gigs
© S. Moore

"My thoughts in 2004 were that I loved playing music, but I still wasn't a musician where I received the kind of satisfaction that I would like to get. I'd been in some really good bands. I've toured behind Nils Lofgren across Europe and Japan. I've played with Max Weinberg, Ringo, Springsteen and more. But even behind all that, I knew I wasn't the greatest bass player.

My brother, Louie, is a way better player, and there's a whole bunch more talented than me. But I wouldn't let that stop me from enjoying playing music.

"And in 2004, I get a phone call from Mike Schreibman from the Washington Area Music Association, and he says 'WAMA's doing a thing with Strathmore for the *Timeline* series of concerts honoring influential DC musicians, like Marvin Gaye, Duke Ellington, Patsy Cline, Danny Gatton, etc. and we would like you to organize something for Nils Lofgren.' Mike knew I was close with Nils and the family. I had been over to their house even before Nils started playing guitar.

"I said, 'Wow, when will this be held?' He said August 25, and it would be outside. The theater was being built then, and it was just the Mansion there.

"'What will the tribute be like?' I asked him.

"'Just get a band together and play some of his songs.'"

Mike knew that I had been on the road with Nils in 1989, 90, 91, 95, and then again in 2004 and that I had this history with Nils.

"'Are you expecting Nils to come and perform with us?'"

"Mike said, 'No, but it would be great if Nils wanted to.'

"Ron next called Nils's brother, Tom, and Grin drummer Bob Berberich and asked them to be involved. 'Yes, it sounds like fun,' they responded. 'Maybe I'll call Nils,' I told them. 'Good luck,' they replied.

"Bob Gordon, Grin's bass player, had died, so I would fill in on playing, and I called Nils and asked him to consider coming and joining in.

"'So, I would be playing at my own tribute?' Nils asked. 'Wouldn't that be weird?'

"I answered, 'Well, if we played some Grin songs, I don't think anybody would think anything other than THIS IS GREAT!' He agreed to attend.

"This organizing of Nils's tribute began early in 2004, which allowed Ron to observe how other WAMA tributes were being developed.

"I observed how Bill Kirchen's show was planned. They had great singers like Ruthie Logsdon, Dede Wylan, and Bill's wife Louise singing different styled songs. And I began to see how I might organize this tribute for Nils. I next had the idea of calling Tommy Keane, one of the biggest Nil's fans in the world.

"I got Tommy on the phone and told him about Nill's tribute, and he immediately said, 'I'm there.' Someone told me Skunk Baxter was in town, so I got his number, and my drummer Chuck Sullivan started working with me and helping. I put the show together, and it turned into this big thing.

"I also learned that Nils had been asked numerous times to do a Grin reunion. He told me they had been offered pretty good money to do it and hadn't done it in thirty-five years. And it was a free show on the lawn at Strathmore. Five thousand people showed up. It was within walking distance of where we grew up, right down the road from Walter Johnson High School.

"The first half of the show was tributes from all these other artists singing Nils songs from different periods of his career. The show's second half was a ninety-minute Grin set where we went deep into the catalog. People were just ecstatic. And I had put this thing together.

"It was the first time in my life that I felt like here is something I can do better than anybody I know. The Strathmore was thrilled, and we got publicity with a nice article in the *Montgomery Journal* and others. Montgomery County Executive Doug Duncan declared it 'Nils Lofgren Day.' For me, it was life changing."

The 2024 Bandhouse Gigs 20th Anniversary "Tribute to DC Legends" concert was a triumphant celebration of DC area music. Richard Harrington wrote the lovely, eloquent program, and the show was wonderful, and nostalgic, bringing back so many great memories.

Bandhouse Gigs 20th Anniversary Concert

© Rip/Bang

My Professional Music

Cool early musical memories for Steve Moore includes me moving from my southeast home where my grandparents had raised me to my mother's new apartment in Suitland, MD, in

1966. She married my stepfather, Milton Krause, who had been a seventeen-year-old Navy minesweeper on D-Day.

I was thirteen years old—completely lost to the Beatles and learning guitar—when I met Guy Taylor, an older "professional" guitarist living in Silver Park apartments and playing with The Leftovers band. Guy became our pied piper helping to organize my new friends, Steve Carey (bass) and Skip Cookman (lead guitar), and me on rhythm guitar into my first band, The Fine Coogies.

In a very generous move to win my young heart, my new stepfather took me to Giant Music and bought me my first pro guitar, a white Gibson non-reverse Firebird. It cost $200, which was real money back then, and I cherish it today.

Steve M. in 1968, and Guy Taylor in 1971

Other musicians Guy and I both knew from the neighborhood and played with include Rob Windsor (drums), Joe Rosenfield (bass), and Mark Nelson (guitar). I did a bikers' gig with Rob in a DC dive that I'll never forget. I was fourteen, drinking beer, having fun, and I got paid!!!!!

The Leftovers featured singer-guitarist Rick Neary, bassist Mike Lyons, saxophonist Denny Solinski, and drummers John Kincaid and Mike Marucci. They rebranded themselves as The Phantoms, and performed at various venues, including Suitland high school, Marlow Heights Community Center, and the District Heights Municipal Building.

They recorded a song titled "Lesa,"—written by Guy—and the band played the 1023 Restaurant in Southeast DC. The band dissolved in 1968, after which Guy adopted the stage name Toby and became one of the New Telstars. During the early 1970s, he

spent time in New York City playing with a soft rock band called The Road Apples. Today, Guy resides in California, where he is cherished by all his friends.

Mark Nelson, me, and Guy Taylor in 2014 © M. Moore

I continued to play professionally throughout my life with fiddler **Hilton Sclawy.** My last band from 2008 until Covid was **The Razors**, that included my son **Charlie Moore** (drums), **Jonathan Gadsden** (vocal), **Ron Cihlar** (bass), and **David Rodler** (lead guitar).

Early Razors Band ad—and me with son, Charlie Moore

© S. Moore

Blues Alley poster

Chapter 54 - Stephen Wade Banjo Luminary

I first heard about Stephen Wade when my mother showed me her signed program from his one-person performance, *Banjo Dancing* at the Arena Stage. Next, she and my stepfather, Milt, shocked me by proclaiming *Banjo Dancing* the best show they'd ever seen.

Well, that couldn't be possible, I thought, because Mom waitressed in music clubs in the fifties and saw many of the greats like Sinatra, Ella Fitzgerald, Johnny Ray, and Duke Ellington. She partied down Route 301 on the weekends for years, where country music icons like Johnny Cash and Willie Nelson entertained. I inherited her signed Stagebill programs from the National Theatre shows starring Yul Brynner, Katharine Hepburn, and others. She took me to my first musical (at the Carter Barron Amphitheater), where John Raitt (Bonnie's dad) and Jan Clayton (Lassie's first Mom) did *Carousel*.

So...who was Stephen Wade? And how could one banjo player who sings, tells stories about musicians, and does a little clogging impress my musically sophisticated and deeply discerning mother?

Let's get some opinions:

"An impassioned banjoist, a nimbly authoritative clog dancer, a soulful singer of folk music and an enthralling tall tale raconteur ... a wondrous artist, this Stephen Wade."
– **TIME MAGAZINE.**

"A man of rare ability; a one-of-a-kind all-American original."
– **WALL STREET JOURNAL**

"Wade is a phenomenon, a curly-haired, gentle voiced enthusiast in a crumpled suit ... nor is he sentimental: just in love with his old banjo and all those sad, sardonic, stories he can tell to it."
– **THE TIMES (LONDON)**

"He's a kind of people's court jester, an archivist who puts us at ease with our folk heritage, making us feel at home with the tales and melodies he's collected as if they were our personal heirlooms. He is, in a way, a walking, talking banjo himself."
– **SAN FRANCISCO EXAMINER**

"Mr. Wade is a one-man-band, folklore society, history museum, and beguiling tale spinner...the sweetest way I know to access an earlier America of steam trains, riverboats, street-corner salesmen, backwoods and a vast, awe-inspiring wilderness. Without hokey folksiness, Mr. Wade can fuse his stories with his music to produce a thrilling theatrical entertainment."
– **DALLAS MORNING NEWS**

May 15, 2024, was the forty-fifth anniversary of the first performance of *Banjo Dancing*, his one-person medley of music, American culture, and folk humor. It began in Chicago, where Wade was born in 1953. He had started playing blues guitar at age eleven but switched to the five-string banjo in his teens after hearing Earl Scruggs on the radio. In 1972, Wade began to play locally, eventually including a benefit at Second City when a friend, Ray Nordstrand, President of Chicago's WFMT radio station and publisher of *Chicago Magazine*, suggested that Stephen put together a one-person show. Ray was calling on Hal Holbrook's celebrated *Mark Twain Tonight* at the time.

This idea sparked Wade's creative journey to create the show. He debuted it in 1979 at the artistic, prestigious Body Politic theater, where David Mamet's first Chicago production, *The Duck Variations*, had opened in 1972. This *Banjo Dancing* was called "enchanting" when it opened. The reception was whole-hearted.

DC Beginnings

"My brother had a Federal job in Washington, and I followed him here when I turned eighteen in 1971.

"During that time, I worked at a record warehouse for a distributor located in an unincorporated district of Fairfax County. There was no subway then, so it took three buses to get there and back. I'd get up around five every morning to get to work on time. Apart from filling orders intended for local retail chains, I was mostly tasked with shipping defective eight-track tapes back to Ampex, taking the plastic wrapping off LP records, repackaging them with new sleeves, and then affixing a new price sticker. The repetition of these tasks became near-automatic gestures.

"I already knew that DC was a bluegrass town, and that the Library of Congress's Archive of American Folk Song had been established in 1928. In 1942, the Archive started issuing albums, and I would listen to those albums back home at the Chicago Public Library."

In DC, Wade further blossomed by studying this music history at the Library of Congress itself, seeing the Seldom Scene in their second appearance at the Red Fox, witnessing Roy Buchanan at the Crossroads, and being involved in the Folklife Festivals, later serving for twenty years on the board of the National Council for Traditional Arts, and more.

He brought *Banjo Dancing* to the Arena Stage in 1981. His opening was all set for a three-week run in the Old Vat Room. When this hit show closed ten years later, an estimated 334,000 folks had loved it.

* * *

Wade's well-informed perspective is brilliantly infused and preserved in his records and books, demonstrating his comprehensive understanding of the banjo's evolution and significance within the larger American culture.

However, his writing and related work on the air and recordings in this realm are not limited to the banjo. In his 2012 book *The Beautiful Music All Around Us: Field Recordings and the American Experience*, there is only one banjo piece figuring among the thirteen performances he chooses to describe, analyze, and reveal, captured on Library of Congress field recordings made in locations ranging from Southern Appalachia to the Mississippi Delta and the Great Plains.

As *Banjo Dancing* is a Washington joy, we also choose this *Bluegrass Unlimited* review by author and musician Richard D. Smith of Wade's *A Storyteller's Story* album. Published in May 2020, this critique, too, expresses our community's appreciation of someone who truly became a Washington institution:

A STORYTELLER'S STORY: SOURCES OF *BANJO DANCING*
Patuxent Music CD-333

Four decades ago, *Banjo Dancing*—a one-person show conceived, created, and performed by musician and writer Stephen Wade—premiered in a small theater in Chicago. The original show was subtitled *The 48th Annual Squitters Mountain Song, Dance, Folklore Convention & Banjo Contest*

And How I Lost, which gives you a delightful sense of its mix of music, jokes, and storytelling. With this modest but almost monumental landmark, Wade had helped revive the venerable tradition of banjo players being all-around entertainers. Folk music fans and theater critics alike were enthralled. Its reception in Washington, DC, says it all. Wade was invited to perform at The White House and then began a three-week booking at a DC venue. The run extended into ten years (yes, ten years).

To celebrate *Banjo Dancing*'s 40th anniversary, Wade has released *A Storyteller's Story: Sources Of Banjo Dancing* which will surely appeal to fans of American roots music and the folklorists who trace its roots. It's a true treasure trove, right from "Banjo Serenade," the masterfully written and truly captivating stage-setter. Among its many other gems: an authentic fiddle & banjo rendition of "Leather Britches," featuring New Lost City Ramblers founding member Tom Paley; Wade appearing with country music pioneer Doc Hopkins on a *Voice Of America* overseas radio broadcast; and banjo legend Hobart Smith talking about music and then performing "Cumberland Gap."

The stylistic range here is impressive. The listener is treated to old-time music, stone-lonesome blues, and even strutting jug band sounds. And, of course, there are great dollops of Wade's priceless humor and storytelling on the recitation "The Far-Famed Fairy Tale Of Fenella" and the final track "Chicago," in which Wade streams affectionate one-liners that praise of his beloved city.

Making this collection even more valuable is its impeccably researched booklet. Its forty-two pages contain the history and context of each selection, plus further introductions to the marvelous folks who created or preserved all this powerful and timeless music. Throughout, the eclectic virtuosity and unending joy of Stephen Wade's playing and voice ties it all together, never failing to entertain while enlightening. You can practically see his joyful and unpretentious grin. Special praise must go to Wade and his production contributors for assembling tracks that were sometimes recorded decades and hundreds of miles apart yet blended here into a smoothly flowing and virtually seamless whole. Highly recommended. (Patuxent Music, P.O. Box 572, Rockville, MD 20808, www.pxrec.com.) Richard D. Smith

Stephen shared a few of his favorite career mementos during our discussion for *Capital Acts*. Thank you. © S Moore

Encore - Keeping the Beat for Local Music
Perspective by John Kelly. 8/22/2017

It was the 1960s, and the Washington Evening Star's nightlife columnist **John Segraves** happened to be working at the precise instant that the typical newspaper music critic was morphing from someone like him—short hair, white shirt, jacket and tie—to someone more like Animal from the Muppets.

Of one musician's psychedelic DC performance in 1968, he wrote: "I do hope if he comes by our town again he lowers the decibels a few hundred degrees so one can appraise his voice. His guitar emits so much blatant noise that it too becomes indistinguishable."

The artist was **Jimi Hendrix**.

"Dad hated rock-and-roll, and he never came around to liking it," said John's son, **Mark Segraves**. "But, that said, I remember for my thirteenth or fourteenth birthday, he bought me the Beatles *White Album* and a radio and tuned it to WHFS."

John Segraves, Mark's late father, in the 1960s and 1970s, wrote a music and nightlife column in the *Washington Evening Star* called "After Dark." (Family Photo)

And so the younger Segraves became steeped in both music and journalism. His mother, **Frances**, worked at newspapers in Frederick, MD, and Baltimore, and his father was a veteran scribe who went from Senators beat writer at the *Star* to assistant national editor, while also penning a twice-weekly music column called "After Dark."

Mark is a reporter at Channel 4-WRC and an enthusiastic music lover. It's something he learned at his father's knee.

"He would take me to shows: **Peggy Lee**, **Sammy Davis Jr.**, **Roberta Flack** at Mr. Henry's," Mark said. "I remember all of that vividly. After the show he'd have to go to the *Washington*

Star in Southeast and write his column. I would run around the *Star* building at midnight or 1 a.m. while he was banging out copy on a typewriter. It was just great memories for me."

The elder Segraves loved jazz and the *Great American Songbook*. If he missed the boat in some ways—did anyone else want Hendrix to turn it down so they could hear his singing? —he was prescient in others. Of a 1969 performance by **Janis Joplin** at Merriweather Post Pavilion, he wrote: "Can the voice within this cute little girl from Port Arthur, Texas, continue to take the strain and still work by the time she's thirty? We'll know in four more years."

Sadly, we knew sooner than that.

John died after a heart attack in 1978. He was forty-eight. Mark was seventeen.

"One of my great regrets is that he never got to see me as a journalist," said Mark, fifty-seven, who has also worked at WJLA and WTOP.

One thing Mark never did when he was a boy was read his father's "After Dark" columns. But he's reading them now, in the scrapbooks John left and online via the DC Public Library's website. And he's teamed up with local drummer **Tom Bowes** to organize concerts that will raise money for local musicians in need. The effort is called the After Dark Fund, after John Segraves's column.

Tom and Mark were involved in earlier fundraising events, including concerts for Hank Dietle's the Rockville, MD, roadhouse damaged by fire in February; for **Carrie Hancock**, widow of local roots rocker **Billy Hancock**; and for Vinyl Acres, a musician-owned record store in Frederick that suffered a flood in May.

"We've got to look out for these people," Mark said. "It's just heartbreaking when you see a post on Facebook about someone who got cancer and needs help or got his guitar stolen or whatever it is."

The first After Dark show was September 2 at Pearl Street Warehouse in Southwest Washington. It was a <u>rockabilly vs. soul battle of the bands</u> featuring the Rock-A-Sonics and the **Ray Apollo Allen** Band, with **Sam Paladino** and **Curtis Pope**. Tickets were $15. Visit <u>facebook.com/AfterDarkFund</u>.

I run into Mark all the time at shows around town. He told me he plans his excursions carefully, plotting out ahead of time which venues to hit and in which order.

"Now it's kind of a challenge to me," he said with a laugh. "If I don't get to at least two places a night, I'm kind of a loser."

A final note.

I found a nice quote in a John Segraves story from 1970. It's in an interview with drummer Buddy Rich, who was closing a six-day stint at the Cellar Door with his big band: "People like to label everything," Rich said. "It's either pop or it's rock or it's folk-rock. Labels schmabels. Music is academic—it's either good or it's bad. The category doesn't matter."

© Brooke Lowe

The Airport 77s fly out of Washington, DC.

No, they're not airline pilots, but they do want to take you somewhere special: to that magical place where tight harmonies, chunky guitars and a relentless beat can make the world right, if only for three minutes at a time. Guitarist **Andy Sullivan** toured internationally with beloved Minneapolis country-punk outfit Steeplejack in the 1990s before moving to Washington.

Drummer **John Kelly** kept the beat in the 1980s DC power trio The Item. After two critically acclaimed albums with founding bass player **Chuck Dolan**, The Airport 77s invited Cal Everett into the cockpit. Fans may remember Cal from **4 Out of 5 Doctors**, who released two records on CBS.

Appendix 1:
Thank you Gary Oelze

As I reflect on these stories and experiences gathered over the past forty years I am filled with immense gratitude for the people in these pages that have shaped my understanding of performing arts and life itself.

Among those who have left a profound impact on me is Gary Oelze. Though Gary was a quiet person by nature, his influence reverberated through the lives of a thousand musicians and music loving audiences, alike.

Working alongside Gary to help him give voice to his Birchmere memoirs was not just a collaborative effort; it was a journey of inspiration.

© Connie Brandt Smith

His life was a melody of dedication, passion, humility, and humor resonating deeply within the hearts of everyone he encountered, as well as Gary's unwavering support for the artists. This blend spoke volumes about his character and underscored the beauty of a life dedicated to uplifting others.

Gary, Susan, and Wilkes II. © S. Moore

We are happy to share these photographs by **Connie Brandt Smith** and myself both as a celebration of Gary's life and as an expression of heartfelt thanks. His spirit lives on.   Steve

20th anniversary cake.

W/ John Jennings © C. B. Smith

With Kentucky Colonel proclamation. © S. Moore

With Guy Clark © C. B. Smith

With Steve Earle

Mike Auldridge, Gary, Jerry Jeff Walker and Tony Rice © C. B. Smith

W/ Arlo

W/ Dawn Williams

W/ Kevin Bacon.

W/ K.C. Alexandria and Sugar Bear

W/ Ron Tomlison

W/ Buzz MCclain

Al Gore, Kim Ritchie, Bill and Gary © White House

Teresa O'Brien, and Gary © S. Moore

W/John Hartford.

W/ Ricky Skaggs

W/ Billy Wolf

W/ our book shirt

Gary at 16.

W/ Ray Benson

W/ Vince Gill &Tony Rice.

Susan at Gary's Celebration of Life

Appendix 2:
Bookshelf of Inspiration

The following are recommended books that informed Capital Acts and also ones that beautifully capture detailed stories beyond our pages.

Fast Forward Play and Rewind
Michael Oberman

"The best thing about the book is the interviews. Whenever possible, Oberman sat down with these people, and the resulting quotes are illuminating of the performers and the times. Consider the range of musicians featured in the book. There are both the period big names—David Bowie (encountered on his very first visit to the U.S,), the Beatles (via his brother), The Rolling Stones, The Doors, Led Zeppelin, Joni Mitchell, The Byrds, Jefferson Airplane, Janis Joplin, Rod Stewart—and, delightfully, a host of half-forgotten performers. Remember Emitt Rhodes, the Bonzo Dog Band, Starland Vocal Band (local DC favorites), Ian Matthews, Country Joe and the Fish, Quicksilver Messenger Service, the Sir Douglas Quintet, Lee Michaels, Brinsley Schwartz and a whole lot more." **New York Journal of Books**

"Oberman's compilation is as charming an artifact as its title suggests....An appealing slice of pop music history for fans and researchers of the era."
Library Journal

Photo: Michael, his brother Ron, and David Bowie © M. Oberman

493

Capital Rock and *Rock The Potomac*

Mark Opsasnick

Capital Rock is a comprehensive cultural history of Washington, DC, area rock and roll focusing on the early era of rock music in the nation's capital (1951-1976).

In *Rock the Potomac*, Mark Opsasnick provides a comprehensive history of popular music in the Washington, DC, area from Colonial times to the end of the Vietnam War in 1975, with a strong emphasis on the emergence of rock and roll and its early development in the nation's capital.

Thanks Mark.

Authors Bios

(L to R) Stephen Lorenz, Stephen Moore,
Johnny Holliday and Charles David Young

Johnny Holliday

As a top-rated DJ in the golden era of Top 40 radio, Johnny Holliday had number one ratings on Cleveland, New York City, San Francisco, and Washington, DC, stations. His dally sports reports reached audiences from coast to coast on the ABC radio network. Also, he covered eight years of Olympic Games for ABC.

He was the announcer for NBC's *Hullabaloo* and *Roger Miller* TV shows. His voice was featured on ABC's *This Week* with David Brinkley and later Sam Donaldson and Cokie Roberts. His ubiquitous radio and TV commercials were evergreen favorites. Among many other sponsors, he was Nissan's national spokesperson.

In the field of musical theater, Johnny has taken on leading roles in productions like *Oklahoma*; *Bye Bye Birdie*; *42nd Street, Follies*; *How to Succeed in Business Without Even Trying*; *Finnegan's Rainbow*; *Same Time, Next Year*; *The Music Man* and others. *For Me and My Girl* earned him a Helen Hayes Award nomination.

Additionally, he's hosted and provided play-by-play commentary for Navy and George Washington University sports. He is currently in his forty-sixth year as the voice of the University of Maryland's basketball and football Terrapin teams.

Thank you, Johnny. Go Terps!

Charles David Young

Thanks to Steve Moore for reviving my voice as a music and entertainment writer after I'd spent decades dispensing dull sales reports for New York-based publishers. When Steve invited me to be a contributor to his collaborative effort with Gary Oelze on their book about the beloved and historic Birchmere music venue, I realized how much I'd missed writing about music.

My first published piece of music writing was at George Mason University after I caught a concert by Liz Meyer and Friends, featuring Danny Gatton on Telecaster and occasional banjo. It was Americana before Americana had a name. I went on to write more about Danny Gatton, Nils Lofgren, Emmylou Harris, Bill Holland, Root Boy Slim, and others for four years writing monthly pieces for *Unicorn Times*, the DC entertainment monthly. I wrote under the byline of Charles D. Young, so as not to be confused with Charles M. Young of *Rolling Stone*.

My published pieces in *Stereo Review*, *TV Guide*, and *Entertainment Weekly* all were in the form of letters, but the subject of one of those letters was Mark Russell, the great DC-based political satirist profiled in these pages. I also contributed CD booklet notes for the Bill Holland and Rent's Due anthology titled *Way Overdue*. After Steve lined me up for this project, I became a regular contributor to the monthly music magazine, *Americana Rhythm*. Thanks again, Steve!

Stephen Lorenz

I am a writer, educator, and cultural historian teaching social studies and music for Montgomery County Public Schools. I grew up in Alexandria and graduated from T.C.

Williams High School in 1986, where I edited the school paper and co-captained the varsity crew team. After rowing for Rutgers, I ended up with a BA in English from Washington College.

My first jobs immersed me in DC's vibrant cultural scene, working at Video Vault in Georgetown and Olsson's Books and Records in Dupont Circle, where a perk was free shows at the 9:30 Club. Later I was office manager for the Art Therapy program at GWU, but long inspired by Stephen Wade's *Banjo Dancing*, I took advantage of tuition benefits to earn my doctorate in American Studies, focusing on vernacular music.

Along the way, I married my supportive spouse, Myra McGovern, and we have three wonderful children who've grown up listening to DC's finest music.

For over two decades, I have recorded music from around the globe for the Smithsonian Folklife Festival held on the National Mall and helped produce the Lead Belly boxed set for Folkways Records. Recent editing projects include *See That My Grave Is Kept Clean*, a biography of Blind Lemon Jefferson, and *Capital Bluegrass* by Kip Lornell.

I enjoy exploring the "art of protest" and focusing on Washington, DC's unique history. I currently live in a historic mid-century modern neighborhood in Kensington with my lovely wife, children, and many pets, where I serve as the neighborhood archivist.

Stephen Moore

Born on January 3, 1953, at Providence Hospital, this only child grew up in Southeast DC, where many friendly neighbors near Fairfax Village knew my name (and screwups). I loved the attention—and my city.

My day job for forty-four years was at Georgetown University supporting research technology. By night, and sometimes by day while pretending to work at GU, I became a professional musician and writer.

Work on *Capital Acts* began in 1983 when I had a dream. Like an unexpected plot twist, or rather, discovering an aspirational, passionate goal that woke me up at 3 a.m., I began contacting native Washingtonian entertainers to request interviews for a book, already named in my dream as *Capital Acts*. I was totally inexperienced and had never published anything before. As you'll see in these pages, many folks surprisingly enjoyed sharing their stories with me. I believed they sensed that I genuinely needed help.

I deeply appreciate my late wife, Margaret, son Charlie, daughter Suzie, and granddaughter, Kona Sage, for giving me family love and emotional support during this very prolonged, and passionate paper chase.

And to everyone who helped make this book possible, I am eternally thankful. That's right, even beyond my lifetime. You can then call me Grateful Dead. Imagine how beautiful the music will be on the flip side.

And thank you Georgetown University!

Acknowledgments

To all who lent their voices, talents and stories we thank you for making this history sound less like a lecture and more like a jam session. This book tries to navigate some of the rich history of performing arts in our vibrant region.

Let's dive into the roster of those who made it possible—Johnny Holliday, Charlie Young, Steve Lorenz. And I thank the following:

Carroll James and "Young" Dave Brown who jump started the project back in 1983.

To Donn B. Murphy, my friend and mentor, and his partner Jon Carrow who both welcomed me to their world of National Theatre friends in 1984: Richard Coe, Patrick Hayes, Jim MacArthur, Hal Diamond, and Helen Hayes, who with Donn helped me write lady Helen's bio-bibliography.

To my first editor, Buzz McClain, for friendship and leadership. Buzz helped me immeasurably become a journalist. Thanks for the Foreword.

And again, to Johnny Holliday whose biography, *From Rock to Jock*, forged our friendship.

To Dick and Linda Bangham, Adele Abrams, Robbie White, Bob Berberich, Daryl Davis, and Steve Houk, for getting the early *Capital Acts* book interviews into high gear and open doors.

To Cerphe and Susan Colwell for the opportunity of *Cerphe's Up*, our forty years of friendship, and helpful suggestions early in the project. And to Patty Johnson Cooper for continued support and true friendship.

Thank you Mark Opsasnick, Michael Oberman, Daryl Davis, Pete and Maura Kennedy, Dave Nuttycombe, Michael Jaworek, Diana Quinn, David Wells, Ron Holloway, Al Petteway, David Eisner, Ron Newmyer, Cleve Francis, Walter Egan, Cathy Ponton King, Arch Campbell, Bill Starks, Ken Ludwig, Ken Avis, Kathy Ponton King, Patty Reese, Jay Schlossberg, Marlin Taylor, Robert Embrey, Mark Segraves, Jon Steinman, Teresa O'Brien, Dave Statter, Susan Gordon, Linwood Taylor, David Chappell, Ken Roseman, Andrew Ratliff, Toby Taylor, Neal Augenstein, and John Kelly for generous info and support.

Our thanks to the late Gary Oelze for pioneering our *All Roads Lead to the Birchmere* history, and to my Birchmere family, Susan Oelze, Stuart Wodlinger, Dawn Williams, Ben Finkelstein, Bud Gardiner, K.C. Alexandria, John Meadows, Bud Gardener, and David Beebe who helped inform, prepare, and condition us for this project.

Our thanks to my co-author G.T. Keplinger for support and *John Duffey's Bluegrass Life* contributions.

To our friends at the National Theatre Archives and Columbia Historical Society for generous help.

To Margaret, Suzanna, Kona, Oscar, Charlie, and Aire.

For the **After Dark Fund**, Afterdarkfund@gmail.com, the non-profit aimed at helping musicians who fall on hard times as well as promoting local music. A portion of our book proceeds will go to the After Dark Fund. Thanks Mark Segraves,

To ABC-CLIO, LLC for reprint rights for our "Lady Helen Hayes" chapter from our book, *Helen Hayes: A Bio-Bibliography.*

To Brian Belanger at the National Capital Radio & Television Museum in Bowie, Maryland. A great treasure and it's located in my Great Uncle's house.

To Richard Harrington for his example, info, and vision; Adam Myers for teaching me computational skills, and my former family at Georgetown University for professional training, my day job, and now retirement.

And to all our contributors with love: Mark Russell, Ed Walker, Willard Scott, Billy Eckstine, Mike Schreibman, Brian Mathieson, Abaad Behrens, Mark Noone, Marshall Keith, Patty Ferry, Pete Ragusa, Jan Zukowski, Dave Elliott, Felix Grant, Rick Harmel, Patricia Krause, Mark Russell, Shirley Feld, Miller Dixon, Rick Frank, Shelley Brown, Del Ankers, Nelson Funk, Jim and Jane Henson, Ed Walker, Willard Scott, Father Gilbert Hartke, Ardoth Hassler, Richard Taylor, Mark Noone, Chuck and Alan Levin, Paul Reed Smith, Weasel, Sarah Bonner (and Hank Dietle's) Jayne Blanchard, Joan Jett, Sharon Johnson, Robert Embrey, Chris Adams, and Charlene Woolery.

Index

A

Abrams, Adele, 247, 355, 397
Adams, James, 5
Adams, John Quincy, 7
Adele, 120
Adleman, Ben, 214
AFI Silver Theatre, 310
After Dark Fund, iii, 486, 500
Al Cohen's Magic Shop, 306
Alan, Bruce, 83
Albert, Marsha, 58, 62
Aldridge, Ira, 24
Alexa, Emery, 217
Alexandria, K.C., 180, 491, 500
Ali, Muhammad, 150
All Souls Church, 205
Allison, J.B., 321
Allman, Duane, 248
Allman, Greg, 248, 365
Alvin Ailey Dance Theater, 442
Americana Rhythm, 496
Ammons, Gene, 141
Anderson, Garland, 42
Anderson, Marian, 148, 237, 442
Andrew, Daniel, 449
Ankers, Del, 47
Arch, Alcantara,, 253
Archive of American Folk Song, 481
Armat, Thomas, 44
Armstrong, Louis, 42, 96, 118, 171, 184, 335, 442
Arnold, Eddie, 237
Asp, Bill and Melanie Asp, 437
Astin, John, 127
Atkins, Chet, 237
Augenstein, Neil, 82, 230
Avis, Ken, 200, 205

B

B.o.B, 287
Bach, Johann Sebastian, 3
Bailey, Hachaliah, 53
Bailey, James Anthony, 53
Bailey's Crossroads, 10, 235
Baldridge, Tish, 105
Baldwin, James, 101
Balthrop, Carmen, 411
Bands
  Abstracts, The, 154
  Adams Apples., 223
  Allman Brothers, 247, 248, 249, 422
  Army Big Band, 226
  Artful Dodger, 61, 228, 243
  Assassins, The, 380
  Backyard Band, 344
  Bad Brains, 434, 436, 437
  Bad Seeds, The, 438
  Beatnick Flies, 398
  Big Yankee Dollar, 258
  Black Flag, 440
  Blue Grass Champs, 368, 369
  British Walkers, 350
  Canned Heat, 296, 319
  Capital City All-Stars, 156
  Cherry People, 223
  Chumps, The, 436
  Claude Jones, 245, 450
  Crackerjacks, The, 55
  Crossroads, 218
  D. Ceats, 214
  Darrell and the Day Rails, 277
  Edge City, 399
  Fabulous Hubcaps, 223
  Folklorists, 398
  Government Issue, 436
  Grateful Dead, 249

Grin, 207, 211, 212, 213, 215, 243, 473, 474
Half Japanese, 436
Hangmen, The, 207, 210, 212, 216, 227
Hot Tuna, 317
Insect Surfers, 436
James Gang, 212
Jarboe and the Nighthawks, 225
Jimmy Smith Trio, 379
Joe and Kathy Hickerson, 398
Johnny Bombay and the Reactions, 228
Johnny and the Headhunters, 278
Jr. Cline and the Recliners, 222
Junk Yard Band, 344
Lawrence and the Arabians, 227, 416
Legendary Blues Band, 278
Little Feat, 365, 421
Look, The, 436
Love, Cry, Want, 450
LSG, 274
Marquees, The, 283
Mars Everywhere, 310
Method Actor, 334
Minor Threat, 436
Neighbors, The, 399
Neons, 250
New Keys, 399
New Telstars, 476
Night Owls, 223
Nobody's Children., 223
Nurses, The, 436
Overkill, 434, 436
Ozarks, The, 368
Patriots, The, 316
Peter, Paul, Almond, and Joy, 351
Police, The, 435
Psychonauts, 398
Rainbow Mountain Boys, The, 374
Ramones, The, 437

Rare Essence, 338
Ray Apollo Allen Band, 486
Razz, 217, 218, 228, 229, 230, 243, 434
Reekers, The, 209, 210
Reese and the O.M.G, 344
Rent's Due, 348, 399, 496
Ric Powell Trio, 178
Road Ducks, The, 278
Rock-A-Sonics, 486
Rootettes, 350
Rosslyn Mountain Boys, 70, 207, 212
Runaways, The, 263
Sageworth and Drums, 450
Sex Change Band, 160, 347, 350, 424
Sly and the Family Stone, 418
Smash Band, 228
SOA, 436
Soul Searchers, 343
Starland Vocal Band, 87, 162, 258, 271, 336, 347, 411
Steel Mill, 211
Teen Idols, 436
The Assassins, The, 380
Tiny Desk Unit, 436
TL and the Barons, 377
Triumphs, The, 317
Tru Fax & the Insaniacs, 433, 435, 436
Tuff Darts, 313
Turtles, The, 416
U2, 222, 287
Under Cues. The, 316
Urban Funk, 382
Urban Verbs, 435, 436
Van Dykes, 378
White Boy, 433
Wild Cards, The, 278
Young Bucks, 431
Youth Brigade, 436
Bangham, Dick, 159, 347, 348, 350, 421
Bangham, Linda, 348, 393, 394
Banjo Dancing, 479, 480, 481, 482, 483, 497

Barrere, Paul, 377
Basho, Robbie, 296
Battle of Chosin, 34
Bautista Jr, David, 135
Baxter, Jeffrey "Skunk", 274
Bayou concerts, 454
Beach Boys, 149, 150, 328
Beatles, The, 56, 57, 58, 59, 60, 62, 63, 64, 69, 71, 89, 170, 171, 173, 207, 209, 210, 246, 247, 287, 350, 359, 476
Beatty, Warren, 15, 101
Becker, Walter, 351
Beethoven, Ludvig, 3, 31
Behnke Nurseries, 341
Behrens, Abaad, 218, 228, 243
Benkert, George Felix, 32
Berberich, Bob, 70, 207, 214, 215, 243, 473
Berberich's Shoes, 208
Bernthal, Jonathan, 135
Berry, Chuck, 42, 172, 208, 245, 278, 279, 281, 288, 321, 323
Betts, Keter, 183, 201, 203, 206
Big Band Society, 82
Biograph Theatre, 160
Biondo, Chris, 339
Birchmere, v
Birney, David, 128
Bishop, Anna, 7
Black, Lewis, 164
Blaine, Hal, 155
Blake, Eubie, 115, 116
Blakey, Gene, 141
Blanchard, Jayne, 262
Blatty, William, 102
Bligh, Laura, 333
Bliss Electrical School, 44
Bogart, Deanna, 353, 421
Bolshoi Ballet, 442
Bonaparte, Napoleon, 3
Bonner, Sarah, 227
Bonta, Peter, 70
Booklist
   Cerphe's Up review, 394
Books

A Heart's Journey through Music, Medicine and History, 429
Atlantic Records
   The House That I Built, 175
Capital Bluegrass, 497
Cerphe's Up, 271
DC Go-Go 10 Years Backstage, 345
DC Jazz, 120
Helen Hayes: A Bio-bibliography, 195
How Bluegrass Ruined My Life, 292
John Duffey's Bluegrass Life, 371, 373
Joy of Living,The, 49, 78
Klan-Destined
   A Black Man's Odyssey in the Klu Klux Clan, 43
Lizard King Was Here, The, 157
Music is My Mistress, 115, 120
Nothing's Sacred, 164
Orange Brick in Warm Sun, 157
Papa John, 155
See That My Grave Is Kept Clean, 497
The Beautiful Music All Around Us: Field Recordings and the American Experience,, 482
The Folksong Revival, 182
The Joy of Living, 79
Tone, Twang, and Taste
   A Guitar Memoir, 70
Washington DC Jazz, 144
Boone, Pat, 384
Booth, Edwin, 8, 22, 125
Booth, John Wilkes, 4, 17, 18, 19, 22
Borska (harpist), 7
Bossa Nova, 93, 97, 202, 203
Bowers, Jon, 437
Bowes, Tom, 486

Boyds, Maryland, 267
Boyer, Greg, 345
Boyle, Jack, 268, 447
Brace, Eric, 416
Brack, Dennis, 57
Bradley, Owen, 240
Brady, Ed, 426
Brennan, Eileen, 102
Brice, Fanny, 37
Briggs, David, 212
Broadcasting Magazine, 389
Bromberg, David, 356
Brooke Manor Country Club, 109
Brooks, Josh, 210, 351
Brown, Art, 385
Brown, Bonnie Blair, 128
Brown, Chuck, 335, 337, 339, 340, 343, 345
Brown, Dave, 57
Brown, James, 245, 378
Brown, Marvin, 179
Brown, Ruth, 276
Brown, Shelley, 470
Brownlees bar, 94
Buchanan, Roy, 210, 215, 229, 481
Buchwald, Art, 87
Buckley III, Timothy Charles, 274
Buddy Holly Howard contract, 56
Bullock, Sandra, 133
Burke, Billie, 126
Burn Brae Dinner Theater, 409
Busbise, Wayne, 110
Busby, Buzz, 110
Bush, George W., 348
Bussard, Joe, 293, 294
Butler, Jerry, 343
Butler-Truesdale, Sandra, 144
Byrd, Charlie, 58, 139, 182, 199, 203, 379, 423
Byrd, Joe, 203

C

Cahill, Bobby, 247
Calhoun, John C., 7
Calloway, Cab, 42, 139, 200
Calvert, Leonard, 2
Camp David, 135
Campbell Music, 390
Campbell, Arch, 359
Cantor, Eddie, 37, 110
Capitol Ballet Company, 151
Capitol Heights, 343
Capitol Records, 64
Carey, Steve, 391
Carmichael, Stokely, 298
Carney, Patrick, 443
Carpenter, Bob, 389, 390
Carpenter, Mary Chapin, 257, 258
Carrico, Tom, 258, 260, 261, 467
Carroll Arms Hotel bar, 85
Carroll, Jon, 70, 271, 336
Carroll, Marvin, 235
Carroll, Pat, 159, 160, 161, 162
Carter Barron Acts, 58
Carter, Amy, 135
Carter, Jimmy, 57, 58, 135, 224, 246, 254, 281, 367, 404, 423
Carusi, Giatano, 7
Casady, Jack, 250, 317
Cash, Rosanne, 258
Cass, Peggy, 154
Cassidy, Annette, 341
Cassidy, Eva, vi, 333, 335, 337, 340
Catholic U's alumni, 25
Cavalier, Felix, 379
Celeste, Celine, 15
Cephas, John, 295
Cerone, Jimmy, 379
Cerphe, 281, 364, 385, 392, 393, 394, 395, 396, 397
Cerra, Stephen, 98
Cerri, Dick, 145, 298, 299
Chappell, David, viii, 365
Chappelle, Dave, 120, 122, 135, 181
Charles, Ray, 209
Chicago Magazine, 480
Chuck, Brown Way, 345
Churchill, Winston, 14

Cihlar, Ron, 477
civil rights, 148, 150
Civil Rights, 15, 41, 43, 121, 295
Civil War, 8, 9
Clapton, Eric, 245, 279, 280
Clark, Anthony "Swamp Dog", 316
Clark, Roy, 237, 239, 369, 384
Cliff, Mary, 145, 146
Cline, Patsy, 237, 238, 240, 369, 384, 473
Clinton, Bill, 70, 252
Clubs
   1023 Restaurant, 476
   219 Jazz Club, 338
   601 Club, 177
   9
      30 Club, 70, 118, 217, 220, 398, 435, 437, 497
   Atlantis, 435, 437
   Bayou, 160, 163, 164, 222, 249, 263, 278, 313, 335, 336, 347, 380
   Bethesda Blues and Jazz, 357
   Billy's, 179
   Birchmere, 69, 86, 146, 157, 180, 201, 212, 253, 254, 258, 260, 261, 274, 317, 325, 335, 371, 429, 467, 469, 500
   Birdlland, 60
   Blues Alley, 334, 336, 337, 423, 425
   Bosco, 398
   Byrd's Nest, 379
   Cafe A Go-Go, 210
   Captain Guy's, 88
   Casino Royal, 391
   Cat's Eye Pub, 366
   Cellar Door, 58, 145, 155, 183, 211, 252, 268, 269, 271, 278, 315, 337, 347, 399, 412, 424, 447, 467, 468, 469, 487
   Chancery, The, 437
   Childe Harold, 230, 322, 325, 352, 396
   Childe Herald, 356
   Club Hillbilly, 368
   Clyde's of Georgetown, 412
   Crazy Horse, 448
   d.c. space, 434, 438
   De Lisa, 141
   Desperados, 278, 399
   Dixie Pig bar, 319
   Dubliner, 358
   Emergency, 270, 271, 445, 449, 450, 451, 453
   Famous bar, 239
   Fatty's, 337
   Fleetwood's, 338
   Food for Thought, 259
   Gallagher's Pub, 259
   Gentry bar, 316
   Gentry Bar, 316
   Groovy's, 448
   Hank Dietle's, 207, 486
   Harold's Rogue and Jar, 422
   Hillbilly Heaven, 326
   Keg, 229, 434, 435
   Kramer Books and Afterwords, 259
   Louie's Rock City, 435
   Madam Organ's, 288
   Madam's Organ (original), 436
   Marble Bar, 437
   Mick Fleetwood's, 334
   Mr. Henry's, 177, 485
   Murray Casino, 118
   Oddfellows' Club, 437
   Peppermint Lounge, 223
   Poodle Dog Cafe, 115
   Psyche Delly, 230
   Psychedelly, 437
   Ram's Head, 421, 469
   Red Fox Inn, 412
   Reeks on the Hill, 437
   Saba, 316
   Saba Club, 316
   Shadows, 181
   Shamrock, 319
   Showboat, 181, 182, 201, 202, 423, 425
   Spread Eagle Tavern, 5

Stardust Inn, 277
The Button, 210
The Famous, 368
The Flame, 201
The Frog, 223
The Keg, 217, 230, 313
Tivoli Club, 176
Varsity Grill, 218, 266, 391, 417
Wax Museum, vii, 161, 278, 357, 405, 426
Coakley, Margaret, 355
Coalition Anti-Nuclear Rally, 152
Cochran, Eddie, 313
Coe, Richard, 16, 196
Cogan, Sheila, 298
Cohan, George, 39
Cohen, Ellen Naomi, 153
Coleman, Danny, 358
Coles, Loralyn, 470
Collins, Albert, 224, 288, 316, 357
Collins, Judy, 252, 259
Columbia Theater Players, 189
Colwell, Cerphe, 230
Colwell, Susan, 499
Connell, Dudley, 370
Connors, Norman, 425
Conover, Willis, 97, 98
Cook, John Harwell, 119
Cookman, Calvin "Skip", 391
Coolidge, Calvin, 109, 111
Coolidge, Elizabeth Sprague, 24
Cooper, Patty Johnson, 393
Copeland, Aaron, 72
Copeland, Johnny, 316
Corcoran Art Museum, 13
Corcoran, William Wilson, 13
Cornwell, Carl, 426
Count Gore de Vol, 309
Country Music Association, 233
Country Music Foundatio, 236
Country Music Hall of Fame, 369
Craig, Bill, 228
Crandall, Henry, 28
Creative Cauldron, 69, 206
Creighton, Richard, 250

Crosstown Jams, 470
Cullen, Gilbert, 356
Cummings, Whitney, 135

D

Dahl, Bill, 299
Daly, George, 211
Dances
    Charleston, 116
    Foxtrot, 116
Danoff, Bill, 258, 270, 347, 412
Danoff, Taffy, 86, 87, 110, 267, 450
David, Larry, 417
Davis Jr, Sammy, 485
Davis, Daryl, 42, 245, 321, 421
Davis, Jr., Sammy, 43
Davis, Miles, 141, 142, 178, 422, 425
Dawson, Bob, 211, 286
DC Stadium, 65, 89, 225, 247
De Paul, Gene, 273
Dean, Jimmy, 214, 235, 236, 237, 238, 239, 240
Delano, Peter, 449
Denver, John, 183, 268, 269
Deppenschmidt, Buddy, 203
Derringer, Rick, 315
deSanto, Dody, 437
Diamond, Neil, 223
Dickerson's Quarry, 318
Diddley, Bo, 55, 185, 224, 282, 283, 285, 287, 288, 357
Dodd, Jimmy, 275
Donaldson, Keith, 405
Dorham, Kenny, 141
Dorsey Brothers, 226
Douglas-Home, Sir Alec, 57
Douglass, Frederick, 119
Downbeat Magazine, 178
Dr. Demento, 162, 296
Draper, Guy, 179
Drennon, Eddie, 286
Duffey, John, 69, 368, 371, 373, 374, 375

Duggan, Bill, 436
Duke Ellington School Alumni, 120
Duke Ellington's Washington PBS Documentary, 119
Duke's Serenaders, 116
Dumbarton Arts & Education, 471
Duncan, Todd, 15, 442, 443
Dylan, Bob, 67, 145, 148, 156, 173, 181, 182, 281, 369
Dyszel, Dick, 309

E

Early recording studios, 285
Eckstine Bebop Orchestra, 142
Eckstine, Billy, 281
Ed Sullivan, 60, 63
Edison, Thomas, 383
Edwards, Archie, 295
Egan, Jack, 95
Egan, Walter, 450, 451
Einstein, Damian, 350
Einstein, David, 400
Eisner, Michael, 275
Ellington, Duke, 42, 115, 140, 204
Elliott, Dave, 325
Ellsworth, Sterling, 373
Embrey, Robert, 499
Emergency-Woodwind Reunion, 453
Emerson, Bill, 368
Epstein, Brian, 59
Ertegun, Ahmet, 175, 183, 184
Esputa, John, 31

F

Fagan, Donald, 210
Fagen, Donald, 351
Fahey, John, vi, 291, 319
Fairfax Village, 497
Feld Brothers, 53, 54, 55, 246
Feld, Irvin, 54, 55, 56, 57

Ferro, Sammy, 88
Ferry, Patty, 220
Films
  "The Singing Fool, 41, 44
  A Clockwork Orange, 292
  A Farewell to Arms, 192
  A Plantation Act,, 40
  Accidental Courtesy, 280
  Airport, 187
  Attack of the 50 Foot Woman, 128
  Back Wax, 426
  Black Orpheus, 202
  Black Wax, 426
  Bonnie and Clyde, 15
  Cabaret, 262
  Cloning Around, 160
  Curse of the Atomic Greasers, 160, 163
  Heavy Metal Parking Lot, 230
  Insurance Salesmen from Saturn, 161
  Invasion of the Paramecium Men, 160
  Last Bus to Bladensburg, 163
  Led Zeppelin Played Here, 230
  Light of Day, 263
  Manhandled, 112
  Obscurity, 163
  Play Misty for Me, 177
  Private Parts, 391
  Razz (The Documentary), 230
  Rumble: The Indians Who Rocked the World, 312
  Stars and Stripes Forever, 34
  The Bayou: DC's Killer Joint, 160
  The Departed, 229
  The Exorcist, 102
  The Jazz Singer, 37, 38, 40, 41
  The Muppets Take Manhattan, 47
  The Red Shoes, 16
  The Sin of Madelon Claudet, 187
  The Wizard of Oz, 41
  Trapeeze, 358

When Chuck Met Eva, 339
WHFS
  Feast Your Ears, 400
Fine Coogies, 476
Finestra, Anthony, 28, 448
First Shakespeare plays, 6
Fiske, Fred, 58, 386
Flack, Laron, 175
Flack, Roberta, 145, 150, 175, 178, 183
Flaherty, Edmund, 125
Flatt & Scruggs, 372
Folger Shakespeare Library, 24
Folger, Henry Clay, 23
Folklife Festivals, 481
Folklore Society, 146, 298
Fonville, Benny, 200
Forbidden Alliance, 439
Ford, Gerald, 111
Ford, John Thompson, 21
Ford's Theatre orchestra, 32
Forrest, Edwin, 8
Fort Stevens, 9
Foster, Fred, 214
Francis, Cleve, 429, 432
Franklin, Aretha, 365, 392, 418
Franks, David, 352
Frederick, Maryland, 58
Freedom Rides, 297
Funk, Nelson, 500
Funk, Renee, 404

G

Gabbard, Krin, 43
Gabriel, Betty, 136
Gadsden, Jonathan, 477
Gale, Jack, 432
Gargoyle fanzine, 182
Garland, Judy, 442
Garvey, Marcus, 118
Gasteyer, Ana, 134
Gatton, Danny, vi, 2, 70, 229, 279, 281, 314, 321, 322, 323, 324, 325, 339, 379, 381, 473
Gay, Connie B., 233, 236

Gaye, Marvin, 172, 285, 286, 377, 473
Gentry, Ken, 405
Georgetown Hospital ER, 268
Georgetown University Yearbook, 255
Gershwin, George, 15, 16, 40, 42, 359, 442
Getz, Stan, 203
Giant Rangers club, 302
Giant Records store, 207
Gifford, Kathy Lee, 132
Gill Jr., Johnny, 274
Gillen, Justin, 428
Gillespie, Dizzy, 60, 141, 423, 424
Ginsburg, Uncle Dave", 307
Glen Burnie record store, 27
Godfrey, Arthur, 78, 82, 238, 383, 384
Golkin, Peter, 236
Gorbulew, Mark, 210
Gordon, Bob, 215
Gordon, Dexter, 141
Gordon, L. Susanne, 251
Gordon, Rob, 426
Gordon, Robert, 313
Gordon, Roger, 76, 77
Gordy, Barry, 285
Gormly, Bill, 306
Graham, Bill, 419
Graham, Billy, 57
Grand Medley Entertainment, 6
Grandpa Jones,, 237
Grant, Felix, 93, 94, 97, 201
Grant, Henry, 116, 119
Grasso, Cherie, 347, 350
Graves, Denyce, 181
Gray, Tom, 371
Gray, Wardell, 141
Greene, Stilson, 397
Greer, Sonny, 116
Gregory, Dick, 150
Griffith Stadium, 56
Grimes, Keith, 333, 334
Groff, Skip, 437
Guernsey, Tom, 210

Guy, Buddy, 357, 365

H

Hagman, Catherine, 335
Hall, Big John, 431
Hall, Jr, Chick, 250
Hall, Regina Lee, 136
Hamburger, Andy, 365
Hamby, Larry, 260
Hancock, Billy, 486
Hancock, Carrie, 486
Hansen, Randy, 316
Hanson, Barrett Eugene, 296
Hard Art Gallery, 438
Hardwick, Otto, 116
Harlequin Dinner Theater, 168, 405, 408
Harmel, Alec, 441
Harmel, Richard, 441
Harmel, Rick, 250
Harrington, Dave, 145
Harrington, Richard, 60, 146, 163, 171, 283, 321, 338, 339, 350, 446, 447, 448, 450, 470, 474
Harris, Bill, 204, 276
Harris, Emmylou, 71, 145, 183, 259, 325, 412, 446, 450, 468
Harris, Tony "Reese", 344
Harrison, Beth, 220
Harrison, George, 56, 288, 394, 419
Hart, Beth, 365
Harter, John, 302
Hartke, Fr. Gilbert, 16, 25, 101, 194
Harvey's restaurant, 10
Hatch, Libby, 438
Hathaway, Donny, 177, 178, 179
Hathaway, Lalah, 180
Hawn, Goldie, 129
Hayes Concert Bureau, 445
Hayes, Alison, 127
Hayes, Cheryl, 56

Hayes, Helen, 16, 17, 56, 127, 183, 189, 192, 194
Hayes, Patrick, 442, 443
Heinecke, Rich, 219
Heintze, Dick, 250
Helm, Levon, 243
Henderson, Michael, 425
Hendricks, Jim, 153
Hendrix, Jimi, 210, 243, 286, 312, 315, 321, 323, 404, 448, 486
Henson, Jane, 47
Herrmann, Edward, 129
Hester, Carolyn, 181
Hiatt, John, 243, 259, 357, 377
High Schools
    Anacostia High School., 250
    Armstrong High School, 116, 276
    Bethesda-Chevy Chase, 372
    Bladensburg, 226
    Blair High School, 129
    Bullis School, 440
    Cardoza, 284
    Duke Ellington School, 181
    Gar-Field High School, 325
    George Washington, 154
    Gonzaga, 130, 153, 217
    Good Council, 160
    Hoffman-Boston, 176
    Landon School, 184
    Linton Hall, 155
    McKinley, 206
    Northwestern, 48, 293
    Northwood High, 130
    Our Lady of Good Council, 160
    Sidwell Friends School, 135
    Springbrook, 363
    St. James (boarding) school, 348
    Suitland, 222, 476
    T.C. Williams High School, 497
    Walt Whitman, 313
    Walter Johnson, 213, 474
    Wheaton High School, 261
    Wooten High School, 277
Hill, Buck, 143

Hines, Earl 'Fatha', 141, 143
Hines, Geoffrey, 334
Hoffman, Sam Jack, 71
Holland, Bill, 258, 348, 399
Holliday, Johnny, 52, 63, 84, 93, 97, 115, 167, 169, 170, 173, 411
Holloway, Ron, 162, 347, 421, 424, 428
Holly, Buddy, 380
Holmes, Wendall, 9
Hoover, J. Edgar, 57
Hopkins, Doc, 483
Horn, Shirley, 143
Hoskins
   Tom "Fang", 297
Hospitals
   Chestnut Lodge Psychoanalytic, 103
   Mount Vernon Hospital, 429
   Sibley Memorial, 82
Houk, Steve, 252, 377, 499
House of Musical Traditions, 419
Houston, Alex (with Elmer), 235
Hovington, Frank, 292
Howe, Julia Ward, 10
Howey, Nicholas, 407
Howey, Nick, 409
Howling Wolf, 279
Hubbard, L. Ron, 51
Hudgins, Ruth, 81
Hughes, Gov. Harry, 109
Hull, Martha, 214, 217
Human Kindness Day, 150
Hurt, Mississippi John, 298
Hurt, William, 131
Hurwitz, Seth, 219, 437

I

I.M.P. productions, 437
Ickes, Harold, 149
Inaugural Balls, 7
Indians
   Algonquin, 1
   Nacotchtank, 1
Sacs, 14
Sioux, 14
Irwin, Scotty, 235

J

Jackson Five's Victory Tour, 65
Jackson, John, 145
Jackson, Mahalia, 148
Jackson, Maurice, 120, 144
Jackson, Polk,, 7
Jackson, Samuel, 130
Jamaica, 97
James, Betty, 63
James, Skip, 291, 293, 294, 295
James, Vernon, 426
Jaworek, Michael, 146, 180, 363, 467, 469, 470
Jazz Samba, 203, 205
Jefferson Jr., Joe, 8
Jefferson, Joe, 8
Jefferson, Joseph, 8
Jefferson, Thomas, 2, 6
Jenkins, Charles Francis, 44
Jennings, John, 258, 260, 261, 399
Jerome Robbins Ballet, 105
Jett, Joan, 261, 262, 468, 500
JFK assassination, 59
Joe Lee's Record Paradise, 349
Johansen, David, vii
Johnnie, Miki, 347
Johns, Brooke, 109, 127
Johnson, George, 110
Johnson, Jimmy, 223
Johnson, Kevin "Pooch", 344
Johnson, Lyndon, 57
Johnson, Marcus, 472
Johnson, Olive "Johnny", 59
Johnson, Sharon, 265
Jolson, Al, 110
Jones, Davey, 61
Jones, Eddie, 431
Jones, Herbie, 235
Jonnie, Micki Lee, 350
Joplin, Janis, 486

Journal Newspaper, vi
Joy Boys, 408

K

Kane, Kim, 217, 218, 219, 221
Kao, Archie, 136
Kaptain Kidshow, 310
Kaufman, Harold, 422
Kaufman, Sam Jack, 275
Kaukonen, Jorma, 317
Kaye, Danny, 387
Keane, Tommy, 474
Keene, Tommy, vii, 218, 219
Keith, Marshall, 217, 218, 220
Kelly, John, 111, 146, 228, 285, 286, 349, 487, 499
Kelly, Winston, 347
Kennedy, Jacqueline, 103
Kennedy, John F., 21, 60, 88, 104, 148, 164
Kennedy, Maura, 69, 70
Kennedy, Pete, 69, 70, 71, 254, 260
Kennedy, Robert F., 23
Kentucky Club Orchestra, 117
Keplinger, G.T., 371, 374
Kernan, James L., 9
Kidwell, Larry, 227, 416
Kindler, Hans, 244
King, Cathy Ponton, 243, 288, 358
King, Erik, 133
King, Rev. Martin Luther, 148, 164, 179, 329
Kinnamon, John, 409
Kirchen, Louise, 473
Klick, Mary, 235
Koehler, Ted, 273
Koehler's film music, 273
Kornheiser, Tony, 169
Krauss, Sara, 335
Krieger, Robby, 157
Kristofferson, Kris, 214, 260
Krulik, Jeff, 230, 448
Kyrieleison, Jack, 407, 408

L

Lahr, Burt, 37
Lambros, Pete, 182, 200, 201
Lancaster, Ernie, 347
Langer, Jenny, 428
Langerman, Keith, 288
Langley Punks, 159
Lankford, John Anderson, 117
Large Venues
   (DAR) Constitution Hall, 236
   Baltimore Civic Center, 62, 65, 246, 264
   Capital Centre, 236, 245
   Clarice Smith Performing Arts Center, 410
   Constitution Hall, 235, 244, 368
   DAR Constitution Hall, 67, 148, 178
   DC Coliseum, 62, 65
   Fredericksburg Arena, 311
   Glen Echo amusement park, 313
   Great McGonigle's Seaside Park, 446
   Lisner Auditorium, 347, 396
   Merriweather Post Pavilion, 249
   Painter's Mill, 248
   Painters Mill, 469
   Palladium, 358
   Red Cross Auditorium, 298
   RFK stadium, 65
   Shady Grove Music Fair, 244
   Strathmore, 146, 282, 470, 471, 473, 474
   Washington Coliseum, 61
   Wolf Trap, 243, 296, 338, 412
LaRosa, Julius, 385
Leace, Donal, 145, 151, 181, 182, 183
Lead Belly, 271, 272
Learned, Michael, 128
Led Zeppelin, 230, 279, 280, 315
Ledbetter, Huddie, 271
Lee, Joe, 349, 350, 351

Lee, Peggy, 485
Lee, Sondra, 263
Leesburg, Virginia, 385
Lennon, John, 287
Lepson, Tommy, 353, 365
Levin, Allen, 329
Levin, Chuck, 327
Levin, Marge, 328
Levin, Robert, 329
Lew Dockstader's Minstrels, 39
Lewis, Shari, 384
Lewis, Victoria, 418
Li, Chris, 418
Library of Congress, v, 272, 302
Life Magazine, 57
Lincoln Memorial, 149
Lincoln, Abraham, 5, 9, 18
Link Wray Fan Group Poster, 320
Linley, Tony, 58
Little Richard, 208, 209, 278, 288
Live Aid, 224
Live Aid,, 224
Living on Music, 252, 253
Lofgren, Nils, 211, 215, 449, 472, 473, 474, 496
Logsdon, Ruthie, 370, 473
Lomax, Alan, 57, 175, 272
Long, Sen. Russell, 89
Long, Steve, 382
Longworth Dinner Theater, 405
Lorber, Steve, 437
Lornell, Kip, 497
Lou, Barbara, 405
Louis C.K, 134
Louis-Dreyfus, Julia, 133
Love, Mike, 149
Lowe, Brooke, 487
Lowe's Capital Theater,, 385
Lowenberg, Susan Albert, 412
Ludwig, Ken, 245, 359, 363
Lumen, Larry, 404
Lyon, John, 97
Lyons, Mike, 476

M

MacArthur, Charles, 191
MacColl, Ewan, 177
Mackahan, Rufus, 127
MacKaye, Ian, 440
Mackenzie, Foster, 353, 382
Mackenzie, Scott, 154
MacLaine, Shirley, 15
MacLaughlan, D. L., 64
Magruder, Robbie, 70
Malachi, John, 141, 142, 278
Mamas and the Papas, 155
Mansfield, Officer Dick, 308
Manzarek, Ray, 157
March of Dimes, 194
March on Washington, 147
Mariotte, Michael, 433
Marlett, Erin, 411
Marlette, Colleen, 411
Martha Graham Dance Company, 442
Maryland Fire and Rescue Institute, 411
Maryland Opera Studio, 412
Maryland State Teacher's College, 98
Mask & Bauble Society, 102
Mask and Bauble Society, 105
Mason, Marsha, 412, 413
Mathieson, Brian, 153
Matt Kane's Irish bar, 358
Matthews, Wade, 380
May Day, 149
Mayfield, Curtis, 179
McCartney, Paul, 56, 59, 65
McClain, Buzz, v, 48, 69, 394
MCclain, Buzz, 491
McComiskey, Billy, 358
McCoy, Jim, 239
McCullough, John, 19
McCune, Mac, 210
McDaniel Jr, James, 132
McGovern, George, 155
McGovern, Myra, 497
McMahon, Ed, 25
Meacham, Roy, 49

Meadows, Punky, 223
Mednick, Joe, 28, 448
Metropolitan Opera, 19, 442
Meyer, Liz, 321, 325, 326, 496
Miley, Bubber, 118
Millennium Stage, 472
Miller, Kim, 379
Minnie Pearl, 237
Mitchell, Happy, 15
Mitchell, Joni, 152
Monk, Debra, 130
Monroe, Bill, 372
Monterey Pop Festival, 319
Monty Python's Flying Circus, 32
Moon, Keith, 210, 243
Moore, Charlie, 250, 477
Moore, Harv, 223
Moore, Margaret, 149, 341, 498
Morgan, Rachel Ann, 428
Morocco, the Thinking Horse, 5
Morrison, Jim, 154, 157, 245
Morrison, Russell, 57
Moulton, Flora, 295
Mount Zion Church, 343
Movie Theaters
    Grand Movie Palace, 26
Mr. Henry's audience, 176
Mudd, Roger, 22, 244
Mudd, Samuel, 23
Muggeby, Robert, 426
Mugwumps, The, 155
Mundell, Michelle, 407
Munito, the Talking Dog, 5
Muppet headquarters, 47
Muppets, v, 47, 49
Murphy, Donn, vi, 81, 105, 187, 192, 193, 443
Murphy, Donn B., 499
Muscular Dystrophy, 307
Music, USA
    Radio Shows, 97
Musicals
    42nd Street, 405
    Alcoholics Unanimous, 161
    Bombo, 37
    Carousel, 58
    Crazy for You, 361

Crazy for You, 245
Finnigan's Rainbow, 405
Follies, 409
Hair, 102
Hello, Dolly, 200
La Belle Pare'e, 39
The Music Man, 154, 407, 410, 412
Vera Violetta, 39
West Side Story, 20, 179, 312

N

NAACP, 54, 131, 134, 136, 148
Nanton, Joe "Tricky" Sam, 118
National Endowment for the Arts, 345
National Guard Armory, 208, 238
National Intelligencer Newspapers, 14
National Symphony Orchestra, 244, 442, 444
National Theatre performers, 17
National Theatre segregation, 15
National Theatre Tryouts, 20
Native Cast -DC actors, 125
Navarro, Fats, 141
Neary, Rick, 476
Nelson, Annette, 14
Nelson, Mark, 476
New Era Follies, 281
New York Dolls, vii
Newmyer, Louie, 246
Newmyer, Ron, 365
Newspaper
    Amsterdam News, 41
    City Paper, 418
    Unicorn Times, 217, 218, 313, 348, 437, 496
    Washington Post, 16, 56, 60, 64, 111, 146, 160, 161, 163, 171, 180, 196, 202, 228, 285, 296, 306, 321, 322, 338, 339, 349, 351, 359, 384, 448, 450
    Washington Times, 368

Newspapers
  Alexandria Gazette, 5
  Baltimore Jewish Times, 154
  Diamondback, The, 411
  Evening Star, 7, 57, 77, 96, 246, 450, 485
  National Intelligencer, 5
  New York Times, 64, 109, 162, 426, 442
  Washington Afro-American, 57
  Washington Post, 416
  Washington Star, 160, 404
Nighthawks, The, 55, 217, 223, 224, 225, 248, 249, 348, 380
Nightingale Serenaders, 22
Nixon, Richard, 111
Noone, Mark, 218
Nordstrand, Ray, 480
Norman, Phillip, 59
Norton, Edward, 135
Nuttycombe, 159, 161, 162, 163, 393

O

O'Brien, Teresa, 491
O'Leary, Bill, 160, 354
Oberman, Michael, 245, 493
Oberman, Ron, 493
Oelze, Gary, 73, 258, 260, 261, 489
Okun, Milt, 269
Olcott, Nick, 411
Olivier, Laurence, 15, 17
Olsson's Books and Records, 335, 497
Opsasnick, Mark, 157, 446
Orbison, Roy, 214
Orenstein, Toby, 135, 409, 410

P

P Street Beach, 211
Paar, Jack, 58
Paley, Tom, 483
Parker, Bobby, 287, 288
Parker, Charlie, 141
Parsons, Gram, 412, 446
Paschall, Valerie, 66
Pastin, Danielle, 411
Patti, Adalina, 7
Patton, Charley, 296, 297
Patuxent Music, 484
Paul, Les, 55, 321, 322, 323, 325, 330, 343
Payne, Bill, 422
Payne, John Howard, 8
Pearl Harbor, 43
Pennington, Ann, 112
Perkins, Pinetop, viii, 245, 277, 278
Perry, Doc, 116
Petrosky, Sonny, 365
Petteway, Al, 58, 254
Phalen, Jim, 159, 160, 162
Phillips, John, 154
Phillips, Michelle, 155
Phillips, Tom, 390
Piccolino, Buddy, 407
Pie, Chip, 345
Pierre, Noah, 428
Pinchbeck, William, 5
Pino, Carmello, 110
Pitts, David, 183
Plays
  "Barefoot in the Park.", 15
  "The Foreigner", 406
  Aladdin and the Wonderful Lamp, 18
  Amadeus, 359
  Amen Corner, 101
  Children of the Ghetto, 39
  Clari or The Maid of Milan, 8
  Davy Crockett, 14
  Day After the Wedding, 6
  How to Rule a Husband, 6
  Jack the Giant Killer, 189
  Ken Ludwig's Plays, 361
  Man of the World, 13
  Mary Hamilton, 9
  Mary of Scotland, 193
  Midsummer Night's Dream, 189

On the Hiring Line., 191
Our American Cousin, 19
Our Boarding House, 14
Reunion, a Musical Epic In Miniature, 408
Richmond As It Is, 21
School for Reform, 6
School for Scandal, 6
She Stoops to Conquer, 8
Tam Lin, 9
The Best Man, 412
The Elephant Man, 102
The House of Blue Leaves, 102
The Magic Flute, 105
The Marquise, 126
The Mountain Nymph, 14
The Prince Chap., 190
The Prodigal Husband, 191
The Razzle, 245
The Secret, 4
The Spoiled Child, 8
The Wives' First Lesson, 6
Venice Preserved, 4
Victoria Regina, 188
Polensky, Dan, 218
Pop, Iggy, 313
Powell, Kenny, 426
Prasada-Rao, Tom, 334
President's Marine Band, 6
Presley, Elvis, 60, 236
Preston, Billy, 419
Previti, John, 324
Pride, Charlie, 237
Principato, Tom, 325, 348, 378
Puleo, Johnny, 358

Q

Quantico Marine Base, 241
Queen Elizabeth, 400
Quesada, Virginia, 356
Quinn, Diana, 433, 439
Quivers, Robin, 391

R

Radio Programs
　Music Americana, 299
Radio Shows
　All Things Considered, 62
　Dr. Demento Show, 161
　Duke Ellington Hour, 98
　Farm and Home Hour, 234
　Folk Music of America, 145
　Music Americana, 145
　Traditions, 146
　Voice of America, 98
　WGMS, 405
Radio Stations
　AFN (Armed Forces Radio Network, 306
　BBC Radio 2, 340
　DC 101, 57, 163, 391, 396
　WAMU, 77, 82, 386, 388
　WARL, 234, 292, 368
　WASH, 373
　WAVA, 145, 298, 364, 392, 396
　WAVA-FM, 145, 396
　WBAL, 58
　WERA 96.7, 147
　WFMT-FM, 480
　WGTB, 221, 351, 437
　WHFS, 159, 171, 247, 248, 249, 251, 350, 351, 389, 390, 392, 393, 395, 396, 397, 400, 401, 485
　WINX, 95, 209
　WINZ 940, 170
　WJSV, 368
　WLMD (Laurel), 356
　WMAL, 58, 81, 93, 95, 96, 167, 168, 201, 214, 240, 384, 406
　WMUC, 248, 355
　WOOK-AM, 208, 209
　WOWD, 217, 350, 445, 446
　WPGC, 79, 80, 223
　WPIK, 80
　WRGW, 298
　WTBO, 98

WUST 1120, 118
WWDC, 58, 59, 63, 64, 84, 93, 95, 171, 373, 374, 387
WWOD-LP, 439
Rado, James, 102
Ragni, Gerome, 102
Ragusa, Pete, 228
Rainbow Mountain Boys, 373
Raitt, John, 58
Ramones, The, 435
Randolph, A. Philip, 147
Ranger Hal Shaw, vi
Ray, Johnny, 208, 479
Raye, Don, 273
Reagan, Ronald, 111
Record Albums
  "Leace on Life", 183
  "Live It Up", vii
  88 Elmira St, 381
  A Storyteller's Story: Sources Of Banjo Dancing, 483
  Anthology of American Folk Music, 297
  Bent Out Of Shape, 288
  Blue Grass Champs: Live from the Don Owens Show, 369
  Bo Diddley is a Gunslinger, 283
  Direct Current: Washington Comes Alive!, 347
  Eva By Heart, 339
  Fingerprints, 253
  Glorious Results of a Misspent Youth, 265
  Guitar Gangster, 319
  Here I Am, 336
  Hometown Girl, 257, 258, 261
  Joe's Garage, 319
  Live at Blues Alley, 335, 424
  Reincarnation, 270
  Robert Gordon with Link Wray, 314
  Sentimentally Yours, 241
  Shine Me Up, 288
  Shotgun, 226
  Some Girls, 26
  Songbird, 339
  State of the Heart, 261
  Sunflowers, 149
  Teen Comedy Party, 162
  The Legend of Blind Joe Death, 291
  The Other Side, 337
  The Symphony Sessions, 424
  The Transfiguration of Blind Boy Death, 292
  Their Satanic Majesty's Request, 220
  Thrilller, 206
  Untouchable, 339
  What's Going On, 284, 285
  White Album, 485
Record and Tape Exchange, 437
Record Labels
  Adelphi Records, 349
  Atlantic Records, 276
  Black Top records,, 288
  Blix Street Records, 339
  Cadence Records, 312
  Capitol Records, 59, 63, 154, 156
  Casablanca Records, 265
  Chess Records, 281, 283
  Chrysalis, 296
  Columbia Records, 40, 371, 396
  Decca Records, 57
  Dischord Records, 437
  Folkways Records, 497
  Fonotone label, 294
  Jubilee Records, 185
  Limp, 437
  Monument, 214
  Monument Records, 207
  Okeh, 297, 367
  Polygram, 381
  Quality Records, 185
  Quartet, 55
  Rhino Records, 296
  Ripsaw Records, 214
  Super Disc, 55
  Takoma Records, 296
  V-Tone Records, 288
  Warner Brothers, 352, 435

WASP, 437
Recording Studio
  Big Mo, 323
Recording Studios
  Bias, 211, 258
  Capitol Transcriptions, 372
  Criteria (Miami), 351
  Edgewood Studios, 156, 288
  Inner Ear Studios, 437
  LOC Folksong Archive studio, 299
Redmond, Mary Ann, 336
Reed, Paul, 450
Reese, Patty, 253, 283, 344, 363, 365, 378, 499
Reeves, Al, 38
Reichenbach Jr, Bill, 206
Reichenbach, Bill, 139, 206
Reidy, Mike, 228
Reinagle, Alexander, 3
Reinagle, Nelly, 3
Ressigue, Lou, 405
Reviewers
  Danton, Charles, 190
  Joe Sasfy, 313
  Mark McStea, 314
  Mark Spivak, 296
  Maslin, Janet, 426
Reynolds, Lee, 305
Rhodes, Jan, 250
Rhue, Madlyn, 128
Ricks, Ursula, 366
Right, Adolf, 278
Rinzler, Ralph, 300
Rip Bang Pictures, 348
Rivera, Chita, 20, 128
Robert Gordon albums, 314
Roberts, Roy, 275
Robeson, Jim, 70
Robinson, Max, 305
Rock & Roll Hall of Fame, 272, 287
Rock & Roll Hall of Famers, 57
Rodel Studios, 49, 51
Rodler, David, 477
Rogers, Anthony, 28, 448
Rolling Stones Warner Show, 27

Rollins, Henry, 436, 440
Rollins, Sonny, 422, 423
Romero, Joey, 222
Ronald McDonald, 79
Roosevelt, Eleanor, 148
Root Boy Slim, 330, 356
Rose, Tim, 153
Rosenfield, Joe, 476
Rosenthal, Gene, 294, 298, 349
Rounds, Chris, 217
Ruger, Tommy, 353
Rumble, Blair A., 120
Rupert, synth player, 436
Russell, Kathe "Special K, 350
Russell, Mark, 85
Rutledge, E. R., 129
Ryan, Buck, 235

S

Saint Elizabeth's Hospital, 353
San Francisco Venues, 403
Sanders, Bill, 84
Sansing, John, 61
Santana, Carlos, 331
Sarandon, Susan, 25
Scanlan, Bill, 163
Schif, Richard, 132
Schlossberg, Jay, 249, 393, 401, 499
Schools
  Duke Ellington School for the Performing Arts, 120
Schrader, Paul, 263
Schreibman, Mike, 29, 270, 281, 445, 447, 448, 449, 450, 451, 466, 468, 469, 470, 473
Schultz, Lois, 364
Schwarz, Joseph, 149
Scimonelli, Frank, 227
Scimonelli, Paul, 324
Scott, Willard, 49
Scott, Willard, 78
Scott-Heron, Gil, 425, 426, 427
Scruggs, Earl, 480
Seeger, Mike, 181

Segraves, Frances, 485
Segraves, John, 450, 485
Segraves, Mark, 485
Seldom Scene, 69, 260, 371, 375, 469, 481
Shah of Iran, 106
Shapiro, Adam, 411
Shaver, Jack, 207
Shaw, Ranger Hal, 304
Shaw, Rosemary, 305
Sheffield, Kenny, 426
Sherard, Barry, 428
Shoreham Hotel, 88, 238, 448
Simeone, Frank, 418
Simon, Jeff, 224
Simone, Nina, 150, 183
Simson, John, 470
Slack, Bobby, 373
Slickee Boys, 214, 217, 218, 219, 222, 436
Slickee Boys, The, vii
Slotnikoff, Joel, 295
Smith, Arthur, 55
Smith, Captain John, 1
Smith, Connie Brandt, 73, 445, 489
Smith, Hobart, 483
Smith, Jimmy, 252
Smith, Kate, 202
Smith, Paul Reed, 330, 331, 347, 353, 500
Smith, Richard D., 484
Smith, Steuart, 377
Smith, Steuart, 353
Snowden, Elder, 117
Solinski, Denny, 476
Sondheim, Stephen, 406, 409
Songs
    "Hey Little School Girl.", 185
    "The Liberty Song, 147
    "Angel Dust", 425
    "April Showers", 40
    "Avalon", 40
    "Bo Diddley Is a Lover", 285
    "Boogie Till You Puke", 347
    "Boogie Woogie Bugle Boy", 273

"California, Here I Come", 40
"Creeque Alley.", 154
"Fat Man in the Bathtub.", 397
"Fever", 335
"Fields of Gold", 339
"Forbidden Alliance", 217
"Harlem Nocturne", 326
"Heartbreak Hotel", 313
"Hey, Bo Diddley", 283
"I Got News For You", 380
"I Told Santa Claus I Want You", 223
"If I Were a Song", 213
"Irene Goodnight", 272
"John Brown's Body, 147
"Love Potion No. 9", 276
"Ole Man River", 16
"On the Road Again", 319
"Ragging the Baby to Sleep", 40
"Rumble", 313
"Sh'boom", 49
"Sonny Boy", 40
"Stormy Monday", 338
"Strawberry Fields Forever.", 220
"Stuck in the Chimney", 223
"Subterranean Homesick Blues", 281
"Summertime Blues", 313
"Swannee", 40
"Take Me Home, Country Roads.", 270
"The Single Petal of a Rose.", 204
"The Spaniard That Blighted My Life", 40
"There's a Man in China.", 270
"Too Much Monkey Business.", 281
"Tzena, Tzena, Tzena, 145
"Walking After Midnight", 239
"Washingtron", 436
"What a Wonderful World.", 336
"Where is the Love?", 179
"Whole Lotta Love", 280

"Yankee Doodle Dandy, 147
"You Need Love", 280
"You're Automized.", 222
Tenderly", 97
Songs, 357
Songs:, 149, 227, 271, 273, 311, 314, 347
Sousa Junior High, 274
Sousa, John Philip, 19, 31, 188
Sparks, Richard, 411
Spiller, Jo, 176
Spottswood, Dick, 293, 294
Spottswood, Louisa, 299
Springsteen, Bruce, 212, 251, 287, 314, 328, 394, 395
St. Andrew's Episcopal Church, 379
Stallone, Sylvester, 132
Stambaugh, Susan, 62
Starks, Bill, viii, 244
Starling, Walt, 232
Stein, Ben, 129
Steinman, Jon, viii
Stephenson, Charles, 470
Stern, Alison, 391
Stern, Daniel, 131
Stern, Howard, 391
Sternhagen, Frances, 128
Stewart, Billy, 185
Stewart, Jimmy, 387
Stewart, Mike, 299
Sting, 339
Stone, Sly, 172
Stoneman Family, 367
Stoneman, Ernest "Pop", 367
Stookey, Paul, 269
Stopak, Charlie, 80
Swann, David, 373
Swanson, Gloria, 112
Sweatman, Wilbur, 117
Sykes, Wanda, 134

T

Talmud Torah Congregation, 38
Tarkington, Booth, 191

Tau Epsilon Phi, 415
Taylor, Linwood, viii, 281, 315, 316
Taylor, Marlin, 389, 400
Taylor, Richard, 26, 230
Taylor, Rip, 128
Taylor-Young, Leigh, 129
T-Bone Walker, 279, 280
Temple, Lafayette Parker "Pick, 301
Temple, Parker, 302
Temple, Pick, vi
Thackery, Jimmy, 224, 380
Tharpe, Sister Rosetta, 56
The Humbler DVD, 356
The Journeymen, 182
Theaters
  Aldridge Theater, 24
  Ambassador, 448, 450
  Arena Stage, 101, 128, 130, 202, 245, 306, 412, 479, 481
  B. F .Keith's, 110
  Biograph, 163
  Canterbury Hall, 8
  Carusi's Theater, 9
  Chestnut Theater, 4
  Coolidge Auditorium, 24
  Earl Theater, 26
  Ed Sullivan Theater, 384
  Eisenhower Theater, 360
  Ford's Athenium, 22
  Grover's National Theater, 18
  Grover's Theater, 13
  Holiday Street Theater, 22
  Howard, 56, 118, 139, 140, 200, 209, 345
  Kennedy Center, 72, 82, 103, 112, 151, 178, 259, 260, 405, 441, 442, 471, 472
  Kernan's Lyceum, 9
  Knickerbocker, 28
  Lisner Auditorium, 25
  MacDonaugh Arena, 281
  Mecca Temple, 15
  National Theatre, 13, 14, 15, 16, 17, 19, 101, 103, 126,

187, 188, 191, 199, 359, 404, 443
New American, 7
New American Theater, 8
Palladium, 204
Shubert Theatre, 101
The Washington Theater, 5
Warner Theater, 25, 28, 467
Washington Theater Comique, 9
Washington Theatre, 7
Washington Theatre Comique, 32
Weinberg Center, 401
Theaters:, 10
Theatre Guild of the Air,, 387
Theatres
    Howard, 115, 117, 140, 200, 283, 313
    Lincoln Colonnade, 117
    Odd Fellows Hall, 117
Thompson, Fred, 412, 413
Thong Club, 294
Toad Hall, 211
Toby's Dinner Theater, 409
Tombs, 252
Tommy Dorsey Band, 95
Tork, Peter, 129
Torpedo Factory, 154
Torres, Ben Fong, 169
Trouble Funk, 344
True Reformers Hall, 116
Turner, Dale, 235
Turner, Glen "Astro", 426
TV Shows
    "Wing Ding", 328
    'Pick Temple Giant Ranch, 301
    "Countdown Carnival", 306
    "Creature Feature", 310
    "Milt Grant's Record Hop", 306
    "Saturday Night Live.", 171
    "Stars of Tomorrow ", 302
    "The Big Question", 369
    "Town and Country Time", 235
    Ed Sullivan, 246, 288, 358
    Good Morning America, 62
    MTV's Basement Tapes, 222
    Steve Allen Tonight Show, 52
    Sunday Morning, 355
    The Honeymooners.", 162
    Wonderama, 151
TV Shows:, 50, 156, 398, 495
TV Stations
    WJLA, 486
    WRC, 50
    WRC Channel 4, 485
    WTOP, 302, 304, 486
TV theme songs, 221
Tyler, George C., 191
Tynan, Joe, 389
Tynan, William "Bill", 391

U

Uline Timeline, 66
Unicorn coffeehouse, 294
Universites
    Brown, 259
Universities, 238
    American, 79, 129, 154, 156, 237, 293, 295, 297, 306, 406, 440, 471
    Amherst College, 23
    Catholic, 145, 194
    Catholic Univeristy, 449
    Catholic University, 16, 25, 101, 130
    District of Columbia (UDC), 427
    George Mason University, 325, 496
    George Washington University, 25, 51, 86, 156, 183, 298, 347, 441, 449
    Georgetown, 101, 102, 103, 164, 422, 434, 437, 440, 441
    Georgetown University, 449, 497
    Hampden-Sydney College, 156
    Harvard, 359
    Howard, 120, 142
    Howard Law School, 119

Howard University, 139, 176, 178, 180, 284, 286, 343, 422
Mary Washington College, 133
Maryland, 165, 310, 364, 378, 415, 416, 417
North Carolina, 304
Oberlin Conservatory, 119
Prince George's Community College, 227
St. John's College, 184
St. Mary's College, 330
Tennessee, 130, 245, 398, 469
University of Illinois, 469
University of Virginia, 156
Virginia Commonwealth Medical School, 429
Virginia Commonwealth University, 336
Washington and Lee University, 238
Wheeling Jesuit University, 267
Yale, 348
University
   Georgetown, 275
   Howard University, 101, 134, 179, 183, 225, 278, 423
   Maryland, 247
US Marine Band, 31

V

Van Buren, Martin, 14
Van Ness, John P., 5
Van Zandt, Steven, 312
Vass, Sara, 210
Vaughn, Sara, 141
Vaughn, Stevie Ray, 424
Veronneau, Lynn, 205
Vestine, Henry, 319
Viator, Alma, 404
Video Vault, 497
Vietnam War, 102
Vincent, Gene, 313
Vinyl Acres record store, 214
Virginia Beach, 416
Von Brandt, Andy, 217
Von Sydow, Max, 103

W

Wade, Stephen, 479, 480, 482, 483
Wald, Gayle, 57
Walker, Ed, 20, 75, 79, 81, 82, 83, 97, 408
Walker, Joe Louis, 316
Wall, Russell, 49
WAMA Timeline, 470
Wammies, 146, 260, 338, 364, 378, 424, 470
Wanktones, The, vii
Ward, Thomas, 13
Warner Brothers, 26
Warren, Beatty, 17
Warren, Dr. Joseph, 147
Warren, William, 7
Washington Area Music Association, 260, 470, 473
Washington Color School, 450
Washington Music Center, 327
Washington Performing Arts Society (WPAS), 442
Washington Theatre, 6
Washington, George, 2, 3, 53, 155
Washington, Martha, 3
Washingtonian Magazine, 61, 62
Washingtonian Magazine', 181
Watergate, 89
Waters, Ethel, 42
Waters, John, 20
Waters, Muddy, 245, 279, 280, 294, 315
Watts, Richard L., 60
Weasel, 230
Weaver, Jackson, 84, 304
Weavers, The, 145
Webb, Clifton, 34
WEBCO records, 109
WEBCO studio, 110

Weber, Andrew Lloyd, 360
Webster, Daniel, 17
Weider, Doug, 245
Weissman, Dick, 154
Wells, David, 433
Wells, Gertie, 116
Wells, Kitty, 237
Wenner, Mark, 224
Wenner, Mark, 230
Whetsol, Arthur, 116
WHFS
    Radio Stations, 210, 399, 400, 425
WHFS Pipeline newsletter, 248
White House, 6, 13, 31, 98, 104, 105, 109, 115, 126, 127, 135, 148, 150, 188, 189, 193, 195, 281, 286, 297, 328, 353, 441, 483
White, Bukka, 291
White, Enoch, 390
White, Josh, 148
White, Robbie, 217, 439, 446, 449
White, Walter, 148
Whitley, Keith, 73
Whitley, Pat, 84
Wiggins, Phil, 295
Wignell, Thomas, 4
Wiley, Denise, 137
Wilkins Coffee, 51
Williams, Hank, 372
Williams, Reginia N., 144
Wilson Line, 235
Wilson, Jo, 58
Windsor, Billy, 323
Windsor, Rob, 476
Wisdom, Robert, 131
Wisor, Jeff, 321
Wogan, Terry, 340

Wolcott, Oliver, 2
Wolf, Billy, 492
Wolf, Steve, 281
Wolfe, Charles, 369
Wonder, Stevie, 150, 151, 243, 286, 328
Wood, W.B., 7
Wray Jr, Fred, 311
Wray, Link, 314
Wright, Todd, 336
Wylan, Dede, 473
Wysong, Lori, 275

Y

Yarborough, Glenn, 252
Yesterday and Today record store, 437
Yippies, 436
Yoelson, Asa, 38
Young, Bob, 159, 160, 162
Young, Neil, 161, 211, 212, 215
Young, Paul D., 34
Young, Trummy, 143
Yune, Rick, 136

Z

Zabel, Larry, 160
Zack, Mike, 227, 416
Zangwill, Israel, 39
Zappa, Frank, 220, 319, 339, 392, 394, 395
Zeiger, Leon, 391
Ziegfeld Follies, 20, 109
Zientara, Don, 437
Zukowski, Jan, 222, 223, 224

www.ingramcontent.com/pod-product-compliance
Lightning Source LLC
LaVergne TN
LVHW040013151224
799056LV00001B/1